Prophets of Past Time

Prophets of Past Time

Seven British Autobiographers, 1880–1914

Carl Dawson

THE JOHNS HOPKINS UNIVERSITY PRESS
BALTIMORE AND LONDON

© 1988 The Johns Hopkins University Press
All rights reserved
Printed in the United States of America

The Johns Hopkins University Press, 701 West 40th Street,
Baltimore, Maryland 21211
The Johns Hopkins Press Ltd., London

The paper used in this publication meets the minimum requirements of American National Standard for Information Sciences—Permanence of Paper for Printed Library Materials, ANSI Z39.48-1984.

Library of Congress Cataloging-in-Publication Data
Dawson, Carl.
  Prophets of past time : seven British autobiographers, 1880–1914 / Carl Dawson.
    p.   cm.
  Bibliography: p.
  Includes index.
  ISBN 0-8018-3587-9 (alk. paper)
  1. English prose literature—19th century—History and criticism. 2. Autobiography. 3. English prose literature—20th century—History and criticism.
4. Authors. English—19th century—Biography—History and criticism.
5. Authors, English—20th century—Biography—History and criticism. I. Title.
PR788.A9D38   1988
828'808'9—dc19   87-30025
                                                            CIP

For Carl Woodring
and in memory of Gary Lindberg

They are as a creation in my heart;
I look into past time as prophets look
Into futurity.
   William Wordsworth, verse fragment

Contents

	Preface	xi
	Acknowledgments	xix
1	Of Memory and Imagination	1
2	Transforming the Past: The Autobiographies of W. H. White and Father George Tyrrell	25
3	Strange Metamorphoses: Samuel Butler's "Unconscious Memory" and *The Way of All Flesh*	70
4	The Consciousness of Self: Edmund Gosse's *Father and Son*	98
5	Contemplations of Time: George Moore's *Memoirs of My Dead Life*	125
6	The End of an Epoch, the Closing of a Door: Ford Madox Ford's *Ancient Lights*	149
7	Fragments of a Great Confession: W. B. Yeats's *Reveries over Childhood and Youth*	177
8	Recollecting Selves: The Province of Memory	205
	Notes	217
	Index	249

Preface

> "How wonderful, how very wonderful the operations of time, and the changes of the human mind!" And following the latter train of thought, [Fanny] soon afterwards added: "If any one faculty of our nature may be called more *wonderful* than the rest, I do think it is memory. There seems something more speakingly incomprehensible in the powers and failures, the inequalities of memory than in any other of our intelligences. . . . —We are to be sure a miracle every way—but our powers of recollecting and of forgetting, do seem peculiarly past finding out."
>
> Jane Austen, Mansfield Park

When I began writing this book, now several years ago, I sat looking out from the porch of a Maine cottage. There came to mind not just the substance of the book, but its effect, a sense of what my reading had meant to me—how long the time, how precarious the understanding. The first words I wrote were these:

> As I look back in coming months and years at this moment, I shall remember the lake, blue in its southern reaches, yellow gray to the north, where the clouds are still thick. Somewhere behind the trees my son fishes for bass or pickerel, slipping across the water in his canoe. A cool breeze whines occasionally around the house, pushing the trees gently, as if the already brittle leaves would otherwise break and fall. I shall remember this as a kind of event, a moment that, even as I write, slips into the unreality of the past. And what exactly will I remember? Will the memory have anything to do with the clumsy words I have found to record the moment? And what, after all, is the moment, the instant, that I seek to record? And how and why will it matter?

In thinking about that summer morning, I am reminded once more of the passing of time, of recapitulation and loss, of the whole process of learning and forgetting that has preoccupied me and led, over the last few years, to the writing of this book. Although what follows is not, strictly speaking, personal, it grows out of strong personal interests that have shaped the writing as they became clearer to me. Given the range of the topics I touch on, I can only offer a provisional and exploratory essay, a small attempt at understanding. I have neither written with nor arrived at an overriding thesis. I have looked as well as I can at seven loosely contemporary writers, all of whom seem obsessed by thoughts of their past lives, all of whom speculate about the workings of memory.

Human memory has been a subject for wonder as well as disagreement throughout centuries of Western thought. For philosophers as different as Plato and Bergson, Aristotle and Heidegger, Locke and Husserl, the power to recollect has involved matters of cognition, self-definition, *being*.[1] Whether associated with history or (as in Plato) divorced from external things, memory has defined people at their most fully human and raised insoluble questions as to the nature of that humanity. What was "a gift of the gods" to the Pythagoreans became, for Saint Augustine, a way toward God, a process through and beyond ourselves.

> Great is the power of memory! An awesome thing, my God, deep and boundless and manifold in being! And this thing is the mind, and this am I myself: what then am I, O my God? What is my nature? A life varied and manifold and mightily surpassing measurement. Behold! in the fields and caves and caverns of my memory, innumerable and innumerably filled with all varieties of innumerable things, whether through images, as with all bodies, or by their presence, as with the arts, or by means of certain notions and notations, as with the passions of the mind—for these memory retains even when the mind does not experience them, although whatever is in the memory is also in the soul. . . . So great is the power of memory, so great is the power of life, even in a man's mortal life![2]

Augustine admits to being "lost in wonder" when he considers the problems of memory. Others have been lost since. The philosopher David Hume—disturbed he admits by his own ruminations—settled on memory as the one faculty to give human beings a sense of continuity or identity, albeit without Augustine's assurance of a vast memory (God's) to which we can aspire or in which we live.[3] Generations of writers after Hume worried about his worries, about his reluctant elevation of memory and his implicit emphasis on individual judgment, on self and continuity, on the relative virtues of memory and imagination.

My original idea for this book was a series of essays on retrospective writers from Wordsworth to Yeats or Virginia Woolf. Because Wordsworth was so important to later English writers, it seemed appropriate to focus on his works first, then attempt to follow the development of other works of remembering across the century. Since, from opposing assumptions, Blake and Coleridge objected to Wordsworth's reverence for memory, associating memory with dessicated philosophy or corrupted art, there was an opportunity to define what seemed to be the extremes of debate for a century to come. The advantage to such a book would have been its range and its continuity, for though it would have left much out, it would have given a sense of forward movement with a kind of backward looking. It would also have allowed some attention to eighteenth-century philosophic trends which Wordsworth both drew upon and rejected.

The book I have written still addresses large topics, but it has more manageable limits. It focuses on the last two decades of the nineteenth century and on the first decade (actually the years before the war) of the twentieth century. In a broad sense, its emphasis is on writers who worked in the new climate of the *fin de siècle,* who wrote with a self-consciousness that was as historical as it was personal. Autobiographical literature in these years is both distinctive and prolific. A writer like Wordsworth matters enormously to late nineteenth-century autobiographical writers, but as William Hale White makes clear, Wordsworth's inheritance presents problems for those who wrote in another era, who understood themselves and have to be understood in terms of the intellectual climate of their age. I am aware, however, of the problems inherent in such a remark. What is "intellectual climate," for example? Does it mean "culture"? And can that overworked nineteenth-century term still carry meaning? The anthropologist Clifford Geertz has approached "culture" much as Arthur Lovejoy approached "romanticism," deploring our use of the word in loose and unwarrantedly encompassing ways.[4] Two persuasive but wholly distinct works bearing on my topic will illustrate some of the underlying issues.

In *The Culture of Time and Space,* Stephen Kern discusses the effect of science and technology on the "culture" of the United States and Europe from about 1880 to 1918. He argues the multidimensional impact of the telephone, the moving picture, the Special Theory of Relativity, the developments of cubism (with its application to military camouflage) upon people's mental and psychological states.[5] Kern knows the pitfalls of false causality, but his associative arguments imply a great deal of cause and effect (which might in some of his instances seem reversible), while his title insists on the importance of "culture," a word he never begins to define. Kern's emphasis is, with only a few backward glances, on the conditions of the time.

James Olney's *Rhizome and the Flower: The Perennial Philosophy,*

Yeats and Jung is quite another sort of book, but on overlapping topics. Olney's thesis is that Jung and Yeats both independently illustrate the resurgence of "the perennial philosophy," the matter of Heraclitus, Pythagorus, and other pre-Socratics, as fulfilled in Plato.[6] Although emphasizing what Jung might have called the "synchronicity" of common interests emerging at the same historic moment, Olney discusses his subjects almost as if they could have lived at any time, independent certainly of Einstein or J. J. Thompson, Edison or Bell. Whatever its historical distortions, Olney's study is as valid as Kern's. Supposing, as Coleridge suggested, that all people are either Platonist or Aristotelian (and the argument was common in the nineteenth century), perhaps scholarly books are, too. Kern argues cause and effect, fact and association; Olney argues eternal and recurrent truths.

My own approach emphasizes both continuity and context: continuity of autobiographical obsessions, as represented by earlier models (Augustine, Wordsworth, Rousseau, Gibbon, Goethe); and context, which can mean either the place of the specific work I discuss in terms of the author's other works or the author's connection with ideas of the time. It seems useful to remember that all people are historically grounded, that we do not escape our social and intellectual circumstances, let alone, in Marxist terms, the material determinants of our lives. If, in the words of the German historian-philosopher Wilhelm Dilthey, "autobiography is the highest and most instructive form in which understanding of life confronts us," that is because we are all, fundamentally, "historical being(s)."[7] Yet the course or history of a life, as James Olney elsewhere argues, is not always the same as the perceived spirit of a life, which is elastic and extensive. Autobiography combines an assertion of "self" or "selves" with *bios* or story.[8] Yeats equates his own memory with the "great memory"; George Moore can project himself into ancient Greece and another life; Samuel Butler thinks of himself as inheriting memory from primal slime. Reading and imagination take us beyond the apparent boundaries of history. How, for example, do we deal with the modernity of a writer like Yeats, who read the fragments of Heraclitus but was scarcely intimate with their modern analogues in Einstein? We might say that he was no less of his age but that Dilthey was right: an individual life is not a composite of the time but rather "the only complete, self-contained and clearly defined happening" in time.[9]

Without pretending to definitive answers about the nature of autobiography or about the distinctions between autobiography and other forms of fictional discourse, my aim here is to explore what I see as a fundamentally "modern" phenomenon, the continued breakdown of generic boundaries, in which the workings of memory and speculations about memory played an important role. If we remember that Ruskin was writing *Praeterita* in the 1880s, that Proust, who idolized Ruskin, was already at work on *The Remembrance of Things Past* early in the first decade of the twentieth century, that Gosse's *Father and Son* and early drafts of Joyce's *Portrait of the Artist* were nearly contemporary, that Conrad and W. H. Hudson, Havelock Ellis and Ford Madox Ford, were all contemporaries, we can appreciate the range and concentration of autobiographical writings in the years around the turn of the century.

Quite apart from the autobiographical writings in these years, a great deal of speculation was going on about the nature of memory: about the reasons for and the ways that people remember and recollect. The psychologists William James, Wilhelm Wundt, James Sully, Richard Semon, and Theodule Ribot developed radically new ideas about the workings of memory; no less, philosophers argued the centrality of memory for epistemological inquiry—in England F. H. Bradley; in France Henri Bergson; in Germany Edmund Husserl. These were productive years for new theories and powerful new voices. Semon may not have been known much beyond Munich, nor Husserl beyond Göttingen, but Semon's description of "engrams" anticipated later psychological theories, and Husserl's *Phenomenology of Internal Time-Consciousness* marked the real beginnings of phenomenology and of its obsession with questions of time.[10]

Other inquiries led in radically different directions. The field of psychology itself soon split into competing strands, one of the foremost of which was psychoanalysis. Perhaps only Havelock Ellis in England came close to the assumptions of Sigmund Freud, but psychoanalysis was, throughout Europe, a symptom of the kind of self-scrutiny or self-obsession manifest in Proust and Thomas Mann, Arthur Symons and George Moore. While not a central topic of this study (I do touch on *The Psychopathology of Every-Day Life* in the conclusion), Freud offers insight into notions of "the great memory" or racial, national, unconscious, collective memory, and in this context alone he seems to incorporate not just a generation of French and German (or Viennese) psychology but also a few generations of European thought.

Freud also suggests an apparent bias in my study, which focuses almost entirely on the autobiographical writings of men. We know from Alice Miller's and Jeffrey Masson's critiques how Freud's analyses either distorted women's testimony or misleadingly emphasized the psychology of men.[11] Studies of autobiography have tended to define the genre or make assumptions about its qualities on the basis of similar emphases. Obviously, autobiography is not exclusively a male genre, and I do not mean to suggest that the seven writers I study are either most deserving of attention or most reflective of their times. Writers such as Elizabeth Sewell, Mathilda Betham-Edwards, Annie Besant, and above all the early Virginia Woolf, would have offered alternative and appropriate subjects. For another study I have thought of comparing autobiographies by men and women (British and American) around World War I, concentrating on their responses to public events, to *history,* and asking generally about the ways they perceive or create their written lives. But as Estelle Jelinek and others have argued, women autobiographers present special problems and deserve a kind of attention I cannot give here.[12]

Because of the intimate links between the writers I do discuss, I would have liked to include more autobiographers who touch on common matters. I might have focused on Augustus J. C. Hare, perhaps, or Herbert Spencer; or even more likely, W. H. Hudson, because of his pastoral re-creations; or J. B. Crozier, because he construed his life in terms of large, evolutionary models; or Robert Louis Stevenson, because of his struggles to write an autobiography at a time of doubt and uncertainty.[13] Stevenson's solitary confrontation with himself as he sat, lonely and isolated, in San Francisco, sums up the kind of situation faced by most of the men I write about; it deals with the issues and the personal problems with which they are preoccupied. I came to realize that these writers shared important emotional and professional qualities, and that I felt most comfortable or most interested in talking about them as a group. Actually *cluster* is a better word than *group.* Some of these men knew each other and each other's works, but the connections between them are not those of a "school" and rarely those of friends. They reflect in fact an arbitrary, although useful and representative selection. For they look back with overlapping hopes and doubts, on their lives and in their written lives.

Two final notes. Since I have already spoken loosely and variously about *memory,* a working clarification may help. Without trying to define the term, I want to suggest how it is used in this book. The object of memory, according to Aristotle, is the past, the retrieval of which requires images.[14] Images are not necessary for Plato, whose concept of memory extends well beyond the associations of a given individual. On this as on so many issues, these two thinkers pretty well define the contexts in which memory has been understood. Aristotle notwithstanding, memory may involve remembering how to *do* something (hammer a nail, play an instrument) or remembering *to* do something or that we *can* do something; it involves our ability to speak in codes and other languages, the words and declensions of which we remember without, much of the time, realizing that we do remember. At any rate, it is the recollection of "the past" that concerns me here. The question is, which or whose past? My answer is wholly descriptive. I am interested in any ways that writers look back, whether to a personal, a historic, or an "unconscious" or "collective" past. For my purposes it does not matter whether the remembering is willed or involuntary, only that it is said or thought to be "remembering" (or even "recollecting"). Nor does it matter that remembering may be a function of present consciousness, the past a projection of determining tenses or present needs. If writers think of themselves as exploring the past or recreating their lives from memory, it makes little sense to say that autobiography does *not* "represent recollections or memories of the past."[15] It makes more sense to ask what autobiography does with those memories and what relation exists between present consciousness and an obtrusive or absorbing sense of pastness.

In emphasizing memory, I comment on diverse theories and on the relationship between theoretical thinking and the workings of literary texts. I should make clear that mnemonic theories are merely a way of approaching a larger issue. I am really talking about Mnemosyne, mother of the muses, who not only is restored to prominence in the late nineteenth century but indeed becomes *the* muse for large numbers of writers, who incorporate history and lyric, comedy and tragedy, perhaps even epic, in works that reimagine selves while redefining the boundaries of their art. Such writers may want, like Augustine, to move beyond "the powers of memory," to achieve a disciplined and emotionally satisfying discourse; but they write of and about a remembered self.

Acknowledgments

I have incurred many debts in the writing of this book. Particularly, I would like to thank my friends Seamus Deane, of University College, Dublin, and Michael V. DePorte, Charles Simic, Vasant Shahane, David Watters, Patsy Schweickart, Jack Richardson, and David Leary, colleagues at the University of New Hampshire. I am also grateful to Janice McGroary, Susan Goodman, and above all, Chris Fauske, who have either tracked things down for me or offered generous criticisms of the text itself. Tory Poulin and the office staff in our department have been as always kind and patient; I thank them. My thanks, too, to the National Endowment for the Humanities for a fellowship at an early stage of the book; to the Central University Research Fund; and to deans Raymond Erickson and Stuart Palmer of the University of New Hampshire. Finally, I would like to thank Arthur Balderacchi, Celeste DiMambro and, especially, Hanne Dawson for her patience throughout. I dedicate this book to Carl Woodring, friend and unmatched teacher, and to Gary Lindberg, my former colleague.

I trust that my indebtedness to scholars in the field will be apparent from notes and other references. So much has been published on so many of the topics I have written about that I have often felt more beleaguered than helped by recent work, some of which I have had to defer to a more leisurely time. Since I began the book, for example, James Olney has published his edition, *Autobiography,* as well as *The Rhizome and the Flower;* A. O. J. Cockshut has published *The Art of Autobiography in Nineteenth- and Twentieth-Century England;* Philip Davis has published *Memory and Writing from Wordsworth to Lawrence;* Avrom Fleishman has published *Figures of Autobiography: The Language of Self-Writing in Victorian and Modern England;* Linda Peterson has published *Victorian Autobiography: The Tradition of Self-Interpretation;* Brian Finney has published *The Inner I: British Literary Autobiography of the Twentieth Century.* . . . These are just a few of the important items in the field of autobiography alone. I have tried whenever possible to account for or at least acknowledge work that parallels my own, but it has not been entirely possible since several of the following chapters have been substantially finished for two or three years. Where there may be overlap, the differences I hope are clear. In any case, although this is not exclusively a study of autobiography, it draws heavily on what is now a generation of studies about autobiography. I am especially indebted to the works of James Olney, Roy Pascal, Karl J. Weintraub, Avrom Fleishman, William C. Spengemann, Francis Hart, Patricia Meyer Spacks, John R. Reed, and to the anthology, *Approaches to Victorian Autobiography,* edited by George P. Landow.

Prophets of Past Time

1 Of Memory and Imagination

> *The exaggerated pastness of our narrative is due to its taking place before the epoch when a certain crisis shattered its way through life and consciousness and left a deep chasm behind. It takes place—or, rather deliberately to avoid the present tense, it took place and had taken place—in the long ago, in the old days, the days of the world before the Great War.*
>
> Thomas Mann, The Magic Mountain

This is a book about men in crisis, about middle-aged men looking back on their lives from across that "deep chasm," not of war, but of time. Some, like William Butler Yeats and Ford Madox Ford, lived well beyond the Great War, writing into the 1930s; some, like Samuel Butler and George Tyrrell, were dead before the war began. Only Ford Madox Ford marched—like Mann's Hans Castorp—into the mud and suffering of the Somme, and only Ford made the war a central topic of later books. Yet, as Ford himself suggested in *The Good Soldier* (1915), war had been on people's minds for years prior to mobilization or the August battles of 1914. Hence, although William Butler Yeats's *Reveries over Childhood and Youth* appeared in 1915 without a hint of Armaggedon, Yeats, no less than Ford or George Moore or William Hale White, was apprehensive about what lay ahead. All these men came to maturity with the sense of the end of an era, with a heightened consciousness of change, and with war at least one likely agent of things to come.

Mann's novel is a look back on prewar days with the ironies of postwar knowledge. The books I deal with here look back with comparable ironies on a dead or disappearing Victorian past, for which the turn of the century is both a personal and a public milestone. If the end of a century, as Frank Kermode has shown, generates intense self-consciousness and self-reflection, the end of the nineteenth century was especially upsetting.[1] Thomas Hardy's "The Darkling Thrush," written on December 31, 1900, symbolizes the depths of feeling shared by many people who had witnessed enormous change and who looked ahead with apprehension or attenuated hope. George Tyrrell dated one section of his autobiography to indicate both the beginning of a new century and his own birthday in troubled middle age; he assessed himself in relation to disquieting social, aesthetic, and above all religious upheavals of his time.

Tyrrell's Catholic "modernism" is very different from William Hale White's or Edmund Gosse's modified Dissent, and it is certainly different from Yeats's explorations after myth and nation. But Tyrrell exemplifies a common feeling. William Hale White often speaks of things "modern," of the changed order of the world in which he lives, of the "close of the nineteenth century."[2] For these writers, a key word is *history*, and they regard themselves as historians: Gosse and White of Dissenting childhoods, Ford of the last years of the Pre-Raphaelites, Samuel Butler of oppressive Victorian institutions, Moore of the symbolist and naturalist movements in art, Yeats of a "tragic generation." "I have," says Yeats, "an historian's rights."[3]

Some years ago Karl Weintraub argued the nineteenth-century association between autobiographical works and historical perspectives. The spate of autobiographical writing from the late years of the eighteenth century coincided, he suggested, with the new historicism, the tendency to see and understand the world in historical terms, as though, in Ortega's phrase, people have no identity, only a history.[4] By the end of the nineteenth century, the passion for history had scarcely abated, but much had happened to shift the relationship between historical inquiry and autobiographical modes. Wilhelm Dilthey (1833–1911) could insist that autobiography was the primary historical document, while saying that introspection (which he dismissed as self-indulgence) had no place or importance in autobiography.[5] If autobiography was to be a part of historical ordering, it had, presumably, to move away from private ends.

Dilthey's sense of a natural historical progression has become for modern writers what Nicola Chiaromonte identifies as the "paradox of history": an inevitable narcissism or obsession with self and self-history, based on the failure of collective values, which developed through the nineteenth century and culminated in the disillusion surrounding the Great War.[6] Chiaromonte looks at works of literature and politics from *The Charterhouse of Parma* to Martin du Gard's *Summer, 1914*, essentially describing the relationship between individual lives, or the understanding of individual lives, and the nature of historical change. Tacitly, he speaks of the problems faced by autobiographical writers, whose sense of separateness (he begins with Stendhal) is a common nineteenth-century phenomenon, but for whom, increasingly, personal history becomes divorced from public history, public meaning from private meaning.

Paul Fussell has explored the implications of the Great War for autobiographical writers, and, like Chiaromonte, he sees the war as having changed everything with its enormity, its previously unimaginable horror. But since Fussell begins with Hardy as a harbinger of later wartime and postwar attitudes, he too implies that major changes had already taken place.[7] Doubtless the feeling of *fin de siècle* is different in kind from the sorrows and anguish of war, the unfathomable loss and chaos that Flanders meant for the Western world. When, nevertheless, Ford Madox Ford describes the Boer War as having ushered in a new world, he speaks with a finality akin to that of Siegfried Sassoon or Robert Graves or Vera Brittain, who look back on World War I as a personal as well as a national or an international turning point. However little anyone might have anticipated the advent of a "Great War" (the German High Command excepted), the sense of potential apocalypse is an important part of turn-of-the-century thinking.

I have spoken of this book as a study of "men in crisis," and, as the foregoing would suggest, by the phrase I mean two related qualities: a crisis of midlife, of the sort described for our own time by psychologists like Daniel Levinson,[8] and a crisis of history, which — real, imagined, or anticipated — touches very different sorts of writers. Even Freud, writing in Vienna and about apparently separate issues, approximates the English and Irish writers I discuss, equating his own professional dilemmas with the problems of other Jewish professionals and with a relatively somber outlook on politics and change.[9]

The sense of personal and public crisis in an autobiographer like Yeats is to a great extent a function of his times, a response to large historical developments, which stimulates retrospection and sets him apart from earlier or later writers of autobiographical works. Yeats agrees with Goethe that the specific era makes an enormous difference to collective or individual lives, and for Gosse or White, Moore or Ford, the awareness of great change and the desire to characterize a lost age become a major impetus to writing. "I am," wrote Havelock Ellis in *My Life,* "a child of my own time."[10] There is no question, for example, that Tyrrell's absorption in current ideas, which undercuts for him the authority of the Roman Catholic church and forces his awareness of new ideologies, means that he assesses his life in a self-conscious and historically grounded way. Unlike Cardinal Newman, whom he so much reveres, he himself has read Newman from a later vantage point and knows that, for him at least, Newman's conclusions need painful adjustment. He has read social thinkers from Europe, corresponded with his friend Baron von Hügel, reflected on the discrepancies between the needs of the poor and the rulings of the church at this particular moment in history. Ford Madox Ford is equally specific. When he speaks of "changes," he cares most about the climate for literature, but he dwells on the sprawl of London, the lighting of the Underground, the quality of newspapers, the value of restaurants, the status of the theater, the amount of smoke, the effect of the telephone—anything that seems to him a sign of what has happened over a quarter century of remarkable transformation. The London of his today is as different from the London of his yesterday as he is from his boyhood self, that tiny waif who seems always to have worn a blue pinafore.[11]

What holds for Ford and Tyrrell holds in parallel ways for Samuel Butler or Edmund Gosse, George Moore or W. B. Yeats. But arguing that autobiographical writings reflect their times risks an obvious truism and does not suggest, beyond the specific references to late nineteenth- or early twentieth-century events, what makes these books distinctive. It might be more useful to be able to define how differences in historical understanding affect the vision of and access to one's own past, or how different assumptions about self direct thoughts about retrospection and recall. Throughout the following chapters I address issues of this sort, but with a clearer sense of shared attitudes or responses than of ways that assumptions about a historical past guide autobiographical narrative. There are indeed fascinating parallels, common interests, shared effects (in the way of influence or foreshadowing later literature), and there is great similarity, often enough, between works that are ostensibly fiction or announced as autobiography.

On the other hand, I do not think it possible to establish the kind of categories for autobiography that Hayden White, for example, posits for the writing of history or Northrop Frye for the writing of fiction.[12] If White essentially argues a historiographical analogue for Chiaromonte's view of the declining faith in history as progressive, so that irony, for Nietzsche, say, becomes a means of dealing with paradoxical visions and metonymy its accompanying trope, White's distinctions seem too exclusive for the study of autobiography. They would have the status of William Spengemann's categories of autobiography, which culminate in "the poetic," something loose enough to include great variety, but probably too loose to bear usefully on a given text.[13]

Hayden White does, however, offer a guide to thinking about autobiography as historical writing. If, for example, certain writers emphasize metaphor and others synecdoche or metonymy, we might begin to explore how language can reflect personal, aesthetic, or social problems or what literary tropes have to do with implied attitudes about past lives or present perspectives on those lives. This was Roman Jakobson's assumption when he divided metaphoric from metonymic ways of thinking and extended his categories to explain "romantic" as opposed to "realistic" literary modes.[14] However overlapping (and suspect) such categories are, they at least invite us to ask about the shared perceptions in different works, the ways that writers approach that gulf of time, which is and has been for autobiographers the critical test both of invention and of order. Unfortunately, although the writers I discuss break down into two general groups, it seems unsatisfactory to categorize Moore, White, and Butler, for example, as metonymic or ironic writers, and Yeats, Tyrrell, and Ford as metaphoric writers. Style matters enormously; style *is* the man, as Butler and others proclaim, and with particular importance for writers of autobiography. But categorical divisions of tropes afford only limited insight into autobiographical shaping or generic qualities.

Figural or rhetorical considerations are of course essential in considering any text, the more so when, as with Ford or Moore, authors themselves insist on their importance. Moore, for example, speculates in *Memoirs of My Dead Life* (1906) about the historical and personal vision allowed by tenses, suggesting that French tenses compel a different response to the past than English, say, or German. Moore recognizes the power of verb forms, which are not simply temporal indicators but means of understanding related to a whole cultural and linguistic patterning. Moore's speculations bear directly on his own writing, and they bear on the writings of other contemporaries as well. Since, as Moore suggests, tenses are also a function of imagining, they allow a variety of re-creations or approaches to historical materials, and they may put in doubt the historical authenticity of past events. In Moore's own writing, chronology is no longer an underlying assumption of his retrospection, but a choice to be made. Despite the assertions of critics like Burton Pike, who have argued the fundamentally chronological impetus of autobiographical writing,[15] Moore — and Yeats and Ford, among others — suggest that autobiography is a kind of a supreme fiction, focusing on the self but using the self for a whole range of tense projections. If, as the pioneering psychologist Theodule Ribot suggested, "nothing that has been can cease to be," it is also true, as Edmund Gosse put it, that "nothing abides in one tense projection,"[16] in part to be sure because time passes, but also because the recuperative and conservative powers of memory vie with both the discontinuities of shifting perspective and the needs of the imagining mind.

Moore and Gosse indicate how widespread such speculation had become. Saussure's famous distinction between "synchronic" and "diachronic" was, for example, not at all an uncommon way of thinking about historical analysis, and the practice of autobiographical writers such as Moore or Gosse clearly implies the staying of time for a kind of synchronic meditation, all effected by the temporal integration of words.[17] Moore at least appreciates memory, not just as a repository of past information, but as a kind of incorporative consciousness, articulated through and by tenses for potentially limitless ends. Once again, however, instead of definitive approaches to particular authors, we have informing complexes of ideas, hints about shared concerns, angles of vision rather than clear answers.

Putting aside for the moment the question as to whether the writers I discuss are best described as "autobiographers," they all approach their autobiographical works as professional writers, convinced that their reflections on past lives will be different in kind from the autobiographies of scientists, say, or other individuals unused to translating thoughts into writing or to contending with the burden of past literary authority. Apart from the sometimes disheartening awareness of their experiences becoming "literature" as they write, they are drawn to the creative and mnemonic processes of recollection, to a whole complex of meanings prompted by the consciousness of remembered selves. All, as I suggest, seem to be involved in what might be called a spiritual searching, for which the workings of memory are at once unavoidable and problematic.

Spiritual crisis for Edmund Gosse has implications for the estimate he makes of himself as a writer, and Gosse is typical of the other writers I take up because of his recurrent questions about writing, about the translation of private matter into public discourse. Butler, who desires a kind of inherited "grace," begs his reader to dismiss him because he *is* a writer, and though Butler's point is that the writer draws on conscious rather than unconscious, or "true," memory, his quandary as to the value of writing, added to his sense of the mistranslation of personal thoughts in writing, points to concerns he shares with other authors. Tyrrell follows Augustine and earlier religious autobiographers in worrying about the relationship of spiritual health to the exercise of authorship, and, with past failures impinging on present reflections, he is obsessed with his written confession as a means of judging his life. Tyrrell's countryman, Yeats, writes *Reveries* as a kind of private, journal-like document (indistinguishable at times from his journals), which yet makes public selected reminiscences of the man for both public and private ends: the imagining of an acceptable Ireland and the defining of himself as poet.

For writers concerned with spiritual development, a sense of loss coincides with a desire for some happier state, which may mean a version of a recollected or an imagined Edenic time. Often, as in Gosse and Tyrrell, Yeats and White, it involves both. For many of these writers, as for Marcel Proust, the only "true paradises are the paradises we have lost."[18] At the same time, most look back to selective moments of happiness and insist, like Gosse and Ford, on the loneliness, if not the misery, of childhood. It is the looking back which is central here, the encounter with a lost self and a vanishing world, and the autobiographical impulse shared by these writers links them clearly and inseparably with the preoccupations of their contemporaries.

The sorting out and recounting of personal memories had become crucial to writers in altogether different spheres of work. Darwin, for example, worried seriously about his scientific gifts so long as he failed the test set by his father: the necessity for a scientific genius to have an acute memory for his childhood past.[19] Darwin's *Autobiography,* a stolid act of reminiscence, in a sense testifies that detailed memory does not matter, while written in a form which implies that it does.

How important considerations of memory were for scientists can be seen in William James's repeated quotations from Wordsworth, especially Wordsworth's retrospective passages in *The Excursion*,[20] and in Francis Galton's various studies — apart from fingerprints, a tangible trace of the past — on the recollective powers in different kinds of thinkers. Galton, who was Darwin's cousin, insisted on the importance of childhood memories but said that scientific thinkers tended to have less vivid memories than writers or artists, a conclusion at which Darwin apparently also arrived.[21] The point is that so many thinkers in divergent fields insisted on the centrality of memory in any discussion about the nature of time or human identity. Memory, for writers as unlike as George Lewes and Friedrich Nietzsche, constitutes the defining kernel of humanity, in that animals lack the power to conceive of a past, to know of their history.[22]

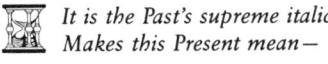
It is the Past's supreme italic
Makes this Present mean —

Emily Dickinson

To introduce the writers who are the focus of this book, it will help to move back one or two generations and comment on a forgotten writer from the mid-nineteenth century. Charles Bland Radcliffe published his *Proteus; or, The Unity of Nature* in 1850. At least technically contemporary with Wordsworth's *Prelude,* Radcliffe's book is a spirited, polemical discussion of memory as the primary mental faculty, and

8 *Prophets of Past Time*

Radcliffe's association of memory with nature, or, rather, his use of recollection as a key to natural phenomena, reveals the passion of a true believer. In part because of his strong feelings, he illustrates the stature of memory in his era.

We might look first at Radcliffe's enthusiastic citing of Coleridge, who says that all people are either natively Platonists or Aristotelians. In Radcliffe's view, Plato represents the ultimate rebuttal of Aristotelian—and associationist—views of the soul. At a time when Plato was coming into English universities as an important subject for study, Radcliffe used him as a kind of prophet, the symbol of antimaterialism. "In a word, the difference between Plato and Aristotle is substantially that which exists and ever will exist, between the so-called spiritualists and the so-called materialists."[23]

Preoccupying Radcliffe are the problems inherited from English empiricism, which he sees as correspondent to the mechanical character of an entire civilization. As Roy Park has shown, the attack on the empiricists took two quite separate directions. The rejection of mechanics—in Carlyle and others—was for writers like Hazlitt not the primary issue, which centered instead on abstraction. Empirical thought was abstract, dangerous, hostile to the imagination.[24] Whatever the precise grounds of the attacks on empiricism, they expressed hostility to an Aristotelian inheritance, so that the areas of mechanics and abstract thought could be, for Radcliffe, overlapping or intertwined.

Radcliffe's appeal to Plato is eclectic and unspecific but at the same time so extreme as to be prophetic—prophetic certainly of Walter Pater's reading of Plato, but equally of the explorations of mind we associate with Freud or Jung, Husserl or Cassirer, of a later generation. The essential matter is a fusion of self-knowing, cognition, and a symbolic understanding of the natural world. Cognition, or what Radcliffe emphasizes as *re-cognition,* is knowledge rediscovered, relearned, drawn from a common storehouse of memory, from what Yeats would speak about as "the Great Memory." Plato's accounts of recollection, his emphasis on the previously known, offer for Radcliffe the challenge to empirical theories of knowledge and a key to paradoxes like those in Coleridge's distinction between imagination and fancy. Radcliffe accepts the organic metaphors of Coleridge but tacitly prefers the Wordsworthian model, the unifying experience that depends above all on the interpenetration of present consciousness by a vital past. Memory is the enabling process, reducing the gulf between matter and spirit, man and nature, man and himself.[25]

In associating English empiricism with a vacant materialism and an abstracting and polarizing mental activity, at once barren and misleading, Radcliffe addresses the subject-object separation at the heart of scientific thinking since the Renaissance (albeit Radcliffe no less than his opponents claims Francis Bacon as a forerunner). Like Blake and Coleridge before him—and so many modern thinkers after—he rejects a process of thinking that calls for detachment on the part of the observer and a method of knowing that leaves subordinate and limited the role of the observer.

By appealing to Plato and to the myth in the *Odyssey* of Meneleus, Eidothea, and Proteus, Radcliffe draws on an earlier generation of writers—Shelley and Keats, Schiller and Schelling—who urged a new kind of understanding, a merger of observer and observed; he also directly anticipates the "protean" concerns in Joyce's *Ulysses*. Radcliffe seeks a unifying epistemology, but also a kind of faith; he wants a hermeneutics, an art of understanding that involves both a way of living and a way of reading. The past, like a literary text, requires sympathetic interpretation. Appreciating the meanings of the encounter between Meneleus and Proteus will show, says Radcliffe, that Eidothea guides Meneleus to the secret of Proteus, who "may . . . serve for the authentic symbol of nature."[26] Such an act of sympathetic reading is at once a gesture against the mechanistic science of English empiricism and an appeal to a nature that for Radcliffe weds unparalleled beauty and our only sure way to meaning. The key to any cognitive act is memory, the powers of which drive Radcliffe to repeated hyperbole. "In speculating upon the phenomenon of memory," he says, "I cannot prevent my thoughts from soaring to a region where the limitations of time and space are unknown, where, without loss of identity in either, body and spirit are substantially one."[27]

From the way Radcliffe addresses memory, it would seem to have been a thing abhorred by English materialists, as if Radcliffe and others of his persuasion had rediscovered a faculty lost since the days of Plato. In fact Hobbes, Locke, and David Hartley, or interpreters of English empiricism in Scotland—Hume, Reid, and Dugald Stewart, for example—while they may distrust imagination, do not in any way dismiss the importance of memory. "Among the various powers of the understanding," wrote Stewart toward the end of the eighteenth century, "there is none which has been so attentively examined by philosophers, or concerning which so many important facts and observations have been collected, as the faculty of Memory."[28]

Radcliffe would have it that, because of the efficacies of memory, there can be no fundamental difference between memory and imagination; ironically, and from opposing premises, Hobbes and his followers had said what appears to be the same thing. Here is Radcliffe:

The history of the memory is substantially the history of the imagination also, any difference being no greater than that which is produced in one and the same song by altering the key and words.[29]

And here, two hundred years earlier, is Hobbes:

This decaying sense, when wee would express the thing in itself, (I mean fancy itselfe), wee call Imagination. . . . But when we would express the decay, and signifie that the Sense is fading, old, and past, it is called Memory. So that Imagination and Memory, are but one thing, which for divers considerations hath divers names.[30]

Whatever the merits of Hobbes's nominal distinctions, the equation of memory and imagination relates him not only with Radcliffe but with the entire later tradition of English associationist thought. James Mill, in the early nineteenth century, would also equate memory and imagination, and his arguments were essentially those inherited from Hobbes. Crucial to such arguments is the assumption that personal meaning and personal identity are inextricable from the functions of memory. David Hume, who shares Hobbes's low estimate of imagination, calls memory "superior" in force and "vivacity" and states what most English philosophers would have agreed upon: "A memory alone acquaints us with the continuance and extent of this succession of perceptions, and it is to be consider'd . . . as the source of personal identity. Had we no memory, we never shou'd have any notion of causation, nor consequently of that chain of cause and events, which constitute our self or person."[31]

If memory for Hume provides our only sense of self or identity, it may raise questions that undercut Hume's rationalism or at the least call for clarification. This was Kant's view when he recognized that any philosophy would have to deal with Hume's devastating conclusions, would have to reconstitute, organize, and make sense of heterogeneous experience. And it was something that occurred to Hume himself. Hume in a sense responded to his own theorizing with as much dismay as Coleridge exhibited when responding to David Hartley, or Wordsworth to William Godwin. He wrote, to conclude Book I of *A Treatise of Human Nature:* "I am at first affrighted and confounded with that forlorn solitude, in which I am placed in my philosophy, and fancy myself some strange uncouth monster, who not being able to mingle and unite in society, has been expell'd all human commerce, and left utterly abandon'd and disconsolate."[32] Here in anticipation of Mary Shelley is the Frankenstein innovator, creator of his own hell who finds himself trapped within it. Oddly enough, the man whom someone like

Radcliffe would consider to be the enemy, the pre-eminent rationalist, is also an undesired ally, a witness to the strains contingent on materialist philosophy and a spokesman for the powers of memory.

Radcliffe's interests in memory offer a commentary on the mainstream of English mnemonic theories, from Hobbes to James Ward, or other late-nineteenth-century psychologists. He points to a number of central concerns, which might be summarized as follows.

1. Radcliffe associates memory with human identity, like Hume, but he also associates it with human creativity. Without mentioning autobiography or autobiographical works such as Wordsworth's, he offers a tacit apology for life histories, which he sees as both idiosyncratic and representative. Radcliffe's claims for the imaginative powers of memory set him apart from so many Victorian writers, who distinguish between "creative" and "meditative" works (Dante, Shakespeare, and Goethe, standing against Wordsworth and Keats) and who look with dismay on what John Stuart Mill called "morbid self-consciousness."[33] Radcliffe seems to recognize the importance of the meditative poets and the irony of critical principles that exclude an essential if unwanted introspection in the literature of the age. By the end of the nineteenth century poets and writers of fiction came to acknowledge the relationship between personal reminiscence and creative forces.

2. Creativity for Radcliffe weds two apparently disparate areas: one's past self and the physical world. Hence, although Coleridge, for example, disparages memory (much, though not all, of the time),[34] he and his generation become central as the advocates of "unity," unity all the more difficult in a world apprehended as mechanical and heterogenous. A later nineteenth-century writer like Bernard Bosanquet typically asserts the importance of German philosophers (Schelling, Kant, Hegel) in his discussions of personal identity, which Bosanquet, like Radcliffe before him and Yeats after, associates with "unity in multeity."[35]

3. The emphasis on creative thinking binds memory with a hermeneutic approach to the physical world, since a "reading" of literary texts and a reading of the natural world seem equatable. (Darwin testified to an appreciation of Wordsworth and other poets during the years he came to marvel at the wonders of nature.) The seeds of such assumptions are diverse but are manifest in Wordsworth's discussion of "Books," for example, wherein the poet's reading stretches into matters of dreams and physical nature, which are inseparable from the poet's inheritance from literary texts. Wordsworth himself turned to the Bible for poetic authority, and the Bible was the first and most important text for hermeneutical exegesis. Radcliffe in this sense is using

a "pagan" source for a similar spiritual end, but the language of most nineteenth-century English autobiographers (even of the pagans such as George Moore) echoes the King James Version.

4. Radcliffe indicates the lasting importance of Plato for mnemonic theorists. This is true of later philosophers, like F. W. Colegrove, who construe Plato through Schelling and other intermediaries. Schelling, according to Colegrove, "represents the individual ego as retaining faint mementos of the path upon which it arose, but forgetting the path itself. Schelling makes it the duty of philosophers to reconstruct the forgotten part in order that the Ego may be able to recall its history."[36] The desire for a kind of reconstructive transcendence was also true of the amateurs like F. W. H. Myers, who wanted to assert the continuity of life after death but who had little faith in formal religion.[37] Myers, who was a poet and critic, drew even-handedly from Wordsworth and Plato to illustrate the powers of memory, which are for him, as for Radcliffe, almost magical.

5. Radcliffe's equation of space and time anticipates later theories of the relativity of time, or of time and space, in Einstein's "Special Theory of Relativity" (1905) and offers a tacit apology for Wordsworth's notion of the "spots of time." Apart from the restorative or renovative powers of the spots of time, Wordsworth's conception of remembered moments obviously looks forward (through De Quincey) to George Moore's "echo-augury" and to Joyce's better-known "epiphanies," which suggest that for Joyce as for Wordsworth, the remembered or privileged moments enjoy a power and meaning intimately tied to the matter-of-fact. When the psychologist James Sully speaks about the private nature of memories, as opposed to the public nature of history, he recognizes the mysterious quality of remembered moments; and like William James, he posits a "stream of consciousness" that brings back such moments to present cognition.[38] I will return to this and to the related view of history in the thought of Nietzsche.

6. A symbolic view of nature and memory reflects the preoccupations of John Ruskin ("The Lamp of Memory" is almost contemporary with Radcliffe's book) and looks forward to symbolic and aesthetic theories in Pater and Pater's progeny, especially perhaps Arthur Symons. As Symons himself recognized, much of what he associated with the symbolist movement in France was available in Pater and in such little-known writers as Radcliffe, who thought in terms of "mystery," symbolic visions, and "eternal memory."[39]

7. Radcliffe's hyperbole equates memory with a sort of spiritual plenitude. Although Kierkegaard's theory of memory (more or less contemporary with Radcliffe's) inverts "Greek" or Platonic remembering,

so that we should remember forward, seeking a higher "repetition," Kierkegaard argues like Radcliffe for a spiritual alternative to mechanical thought.[40] That alternative is a richness and fullness of spiritual life, predicated on a theory of memory, inverted or wishful as the theory might be.

Although none of the writers I discuss mentions Radcliffe, much of what he asserts and many of his values are implicit in the autobiographical literature of coming generations, with one major difference. Whereas Radcliffe sings a paean to memory and finds its associations consistently pleasing, autobiographers such as Moore or White look for his Edenic world without finding it and hope where he asserts. It will help to explore some reasons.

Anyone who approaches, without preconceived ideas . . . the classical problem of the relations of body and soul, will soon see this problem as centering on the study of memory.
Henri Bergson, Matter and Memory

Bergson's comment from *Matter and Memory* indicates how prophetic Charles Radcliffe's speculations had been. What Bergson sees as the key to unresolved paradoxes may be more rigorous and extensive than Radcliffe's explorations, yet Bergson follows Radcliffe in thinking of memory as the primary faculty or process for the elucidation of human thinking and the explanation of what is fundamental in human lives. Materialism remains the enemy, and creativity becomes even more the ideal, opposed to determined and mechanistic notions of mind. In fact, creative forces for Bergson and his contemporaries are indistinguishable from theories of remembering. Bergson will attest how memory continued to intrigue philosophers, how it became—in Dugald Stewart's terms from the century before—more than ever "attentively examined." The late nineteenth century saw the proliferation of theories of memory, not only among philosophers like Bergson but also among psychologists, historians, anthropologists, and a host of amateurs like Samuel Butler who could be both eclectic and forward-looking.

I will turn to a few mnemonic theorists in later chapters, especially in the chapter on Butler. Here I want to address ideas of late-nineteenth-century thinkers that appear to bear most on autobiography and "the autobiographical consciousness"[41] and that are major preoccupations for the writers I discuss. For convenience, we might isolate these complexes of ideas as "memory and present consciousness," "memory and the unconscious," "memory as collective remembering," "memory and anxiety" (or crisis), and "memory and forgetting." Obviously I can do no more here than sketch what are vast tracts of speculation and concern.

Memory and Present Consciousness

One of the recurrent themes in psychological discussions of the last decades of the nineteenth century is the matter of consciousness, which is tied intimately to theories of personal memory and psychic energy. On evolutionary models, a host of writers speaks of *ontogeny* following *phylogeny* (both terms from the 1870s), the individual enacting the history of the species, personal history a miniature of evolutionary development. Such models involve a challenge to consciousness, as Samuel Butler indicates, or a diminishing of its importance. When Bergson spoke about "duration," he had in mind a flow of time marred by intellectual separation into subject and object or even into past and present, though he used the terms. Seeing memory as purposive or "creative," Bergson thought that to interfere with its intuitive force was to introduce mechanical alternatives, which marred health and future thinking.

Particularly, Bergson objected to what he thought of as the "spatializing" of time in the consciousness by the isolation of past moments, a process of "geometrical" thinking, which ran counter both to the "single intuition" of past moments and its corollary in creative living.[42] Despite the widespread popularity of Bergson's theories, they go to some extent against the understanding of time and memory that we see, for example, in Wordsworth, whose spots of time imply a clear desire not only to stay time, or time in memory, but also to associate past moments with fixed places. Wordsworth's understanding is no less defensible than Bergson's, as recent theorists such as E. H. Gombrich and Rudolf Arnheim suggest. According to Arnheim, "Memory works not only to preserve . . . the fleeting moments as a sequence but must also convert that sequence into simultaneity, time into space."[43] Self-understanding may well be predicated on the disruption of temporal flow but not, Bergson would argue, without cost. He might have accused Wordsworth of circularity and inconclusiveness, of a backward-looking that he, like Kierkegaard before him, wanted firmly to reject.

Implicit in the two approaches to the past is a basic disagreement as to the workings and purposes of memory. Proust, for example, drew on Bergson in the sense that he used an analogous notion about the duration of consciousness, but Proust also turned to Ruskin (and indirectly to Wordsworth), who accepted a necessary spatializing of past moments, especially when he praised the recollective powers of a painter like Turner.[44] In any autobiography, there is probably an implicit contradiction between the desire for a whole, continuous life, and the recognition of a fragmented past, which may yet be pulled together by synecdochic or emblematic moments—privileged moments that we identify as spots of time, epiphanies, or what Virginia Woolf calls "moments of being."[45]

But how in fact do we arrive at these views of memory? On what assumptions are they based? To construe the workings of memory there needs to be a recognition of the importance of a present "now," with all its implications for the sentient mind. Hume's radical view of the self, held together with tenuous fragility by memory, implies a perpetually new consciousness without limit or guidance. The potential nightmare of this had already occurred to Locke and Swift, who realized that sanity and insanity were perilously close, since dreams and other "abnormal" states produced memories and invited belief no less than the "real" thing.[46] Our present thoughts are inherently susceptible to error and are, in any case, of short duration.

In the late nineteenth century *consciousness* became a heavily worked term for philosophers as well as psychologists. And consciousness seemed to be subject to even more doubts than Hume's critique allowed. The philosopher F. H. Bradley speaks, for example, of "the qualitative point," that brief moment of awareness and discrimination which enables our perception and, because moments almost instantaneously disappear, necessitates our assessment of the past. In an essay for *Mind* (1887), Bradley wrote a fascinating article, "Why Do We Remember Forwards and not Backwards?" Treating some of the issues he dealt with at length in *Appearance and Reality,* Bradley basically addresses the relationship of present consciousness to past events. He works in two almost contradictory ways. In the first place, he uses (like most writers of autobiography) fairly conventional metaphors about the "flow" of time. From a Heraclitean sense of the river into which we cannot step twice, Bradley goes on to a string of metaphors about boats and directions, so that "when we steam against the sea from our native shore, if we thought of ourselves we should go forward against the waves. But as our hearts are left behind, we follow each wave that sweeps backwards and seems to lengthen the interval."[47]

For Bradley, "the qualitative point" is a means of understanding, or placing, which emerges from a sense of time or direction, but it is also a source of value and discrimination. It differs from the more mechanical "point of consciousness" of James Mill and approximates Walter Pater's "significant and animated instant," the *moment* of perception essential for full awareness and creative life, and Friedrich Nietzsche's "single point," which involves analogous paradox.[48]

Bradley's sense of the present moment bridges two divergent but conflicting views of time in his age: the psychological time of the individual's consciousness and the macrocosmic time of the new sciences. He speaks about "the enormous degredation of the present," a statement implying a whole range of speculation about time and history as well as individual consciousness.[49] In terms of macrocosmic time, Bradley may have in mind the countless millions of years predicated for evolutionary theory, with its corollary implication of a dwarfed individual, and the potentially disquieting notions of time in entropic views, which posited a negative development of waste and loss. A degraded present may suggest a personal duration or a present consciousness affected by the awareness of vast tracts of time. I do not mean to overstate. Hume had certainly anticipated problems of present consciousness and its interaction with memory; nor were thoughts about the brevity of ideas or feelings new to the late nineteenth century. What we do find in writers such as Samuel Butler or Edmund Gosse is specific reference to the ideas of scientists or metaphors that draw upon them. Yet even here the situation is less than simple. When Gosse tells of his father's struggle with theories of evolution, he uses metaphors similar to Bradley's or Dilthey's—metaphors of rivers and streams. He speaks of rivers converging, of polluted streams overpowering pure waters, of will and determinism in the flow of time. So in a sense Gosse is drawing on ancient metaphor while investing it with modern ideas: wrestling with the ideas of Darwin, or reporting the struggle his father underwent, and speaking of the struggle as, in itself, an illustration of evolutionary principles.

On a smaller scale, Bradley's sense of "the qualitative point" suggests an altogether different direction in contemporary psychological theory. The notion of a "stream of consciousness" in William James and James Sully (or in James Ward, who spoke of a "continuum")[50] involves a far less dwarfing view of the self, whose present is certainly fleeting but whose self-awareness somehow empowers. Sully wrote:

> The consciousness of personal identity is said to be bound up with memory. That is to say, I am conscious of a continuous permanent self under all the surface-play of the stream of consciousness, just as I can, by an act of recollection, bring together any two portions of this stream of experience, and so recognize the unbroken continuity of the whole.[51]

Sully and other contemporary psychologists find in the stream of consciousness a fusion of remembered past and lived present, and the fusion involves the defining condition of our identity. What is central, then, is the possibility of a continuous *whole,* a way for the individual to "bring together" the apparently disparate elements of a remembered life. Obviously, as Joyce and Woolf and other later novelists make clear, Sully's assumptions carry over into fiction. They are also directly pertinent for contemporary autobiographers, who speculate in similar ways and who are just as insistent on the importance of remembering. Like Bradley they speak about the fragility of consciousness and the need for orientation; like Sully they either assume a "whole" or try desperately to find one, the act of writing a promising means to that end.

Memory and the Unconscious

All too many studies of psychoanalysis have repeated the point that Freud discovered the "unconscious" or was the first real student of sub- or unconscious processes.[52] Perhaps in a special analytical sense the claim is justified. Yet Freud himself dismissed Eduard von Hartmann, for example, who not only explored the unconscious but also wrote a book in the 1870s called *The Unconscious.* His contemporary, Ewald Hering, defined memory as an unconscious process, as did Samuel Butler, who translated some of Hering. But even apart from Carlyle, to read Coleridge or Schopenhauer or any number of early nineteenth-century writers is to see how far back the roots of the idea as a modern concept actually extend. For his own clinical and metaphysical purposes, Freud assimilated as well as redefined decades of speculative work.

Assumptions about unconscious mnemonic processes underlie a great deal of late-nineteenth-century thinking about personal recollection and identity. I spend some time on this topic when discussing Samuel Butler, but a few points can be made here. For Butler, the remembering self is really a composite of selves, of ancestors and parents, who may be unrecognizable to the remembering individual but who empower him or her to live and act. Present consciousness is to Butler a grudged necessity, a fly in the ointment of unconscious workings, as well as an inescapable given for the writer of fictional autobiography. Butler's is, typically, an extreme position, although his ideas on heredity and other "remembering" parallel those of Herbert Spencer, Thomas Laycock, and other contemporaries. His are, in a way, Hume's ideas turned upside down, with memory still the sole source of personal identity, but now an *im*personal power.

Though the unconscious in a writer like George Tyrrell is of a very different sort, it is just as compelling. Without dismissing conscious processes, Tyrrell assumes like Butler that much of himself is unknowable, perhaps the greater and better part, and he accepts an analogous inheritance of evolutionary or hereditary strains. To William Butler Yeats, the unconscious is another form of collective remembering, closely related to Jungian ideas of a collective unconscious and with Plato and Shelley as clear authorities. If, for Tyrrell, unconscious powers have to do with the spiritual condition of men and women searching for an unknowable God, unconscious powers for Yeats have to do with what Freud called "archaic" or "racial" memory, the *spiritus mundi* a vast and indeterminate repository.

The *spiritus mundi* is for Yeats what God as the ultimate memory is for Augustine, and for overlapping reasons. When Miguel de Unamuno wrote, in *The Tragic Sense of Life,* that "we live in memory and by memory, and our spiritual life is at bottom simply the effort of our memory to persist," he addressed this issue; memory serves the individual as "tradition" serves "a people."[53] It promises continuity, community, identity with a capital *I*. Unamuno's statements bear not only on an entire generation of poets such as Yeats and T. S. Eliot, whose pronouncements on tradition seem to blend Bradley and Unamuno, but also on innumerable autobiographers, who look within their own lives for a larger identity.

The hope for a collective past may be offset by the realization that as we remember we are most ourselves because most intrinsically alone. "Solitude," writes Nicolas Berdyaev, in *The Beginning and the End,* "is a late product of advanced society." And solitude and memory are closely connected.[54] When the Russian psychologist Luria describes his patient Sherebensky, he speaks of a man who could not forget and who was, as a consequence, trapped in the solipsistic world of his own remembering.[55] To recognize a communal past or a shared inheritance has little to do with the feeling of aloneness in the act of recalling, and while Sherebensky suffered from a prodigious capacity to remember, his plight bears on that of autobiographers who also look back with a kind of lonely compulsion. "Perhaps," says George Moore, "life is essentially a lonely thing, and the married and unmarried differ only in this, that we are lonely when we are by ourselves, and they are lonely when they are together."[56] To Edmund Gosse, the only clear memories are those originating in lonely times, or at least times of solitary perception, and what is true of the remembered is equally true of the remembering moments. For "it is only solitude that dissolves the thick cloak of shame that isolates us from one another; only in solitude do we find ourselves."[57]

Memory and Anxiety

I have touched on this topic in speaking not only of solitary lives but also of that fragile self constructed by so many thinkers after Hume and defined so eloquently in Bradley's notion of "the qualitative point." An association of memory and anxiety makes sense for a number of reasons, among them even etymology. The Greek roots for memory and for anxiety are evidently related.[58] This perhaps accidental connection at least reminds us of the difficulties for autobiographical writers who look back in search of a past self or a more certain belief and who find, like George Tyrrell, only more troubling thoughts about who and what they are. Jean-Paul Sartre's *Les Mots,* his self-accusing autobiography, does not comment on the word *memory,* but for Sartre as for his hero Roquentin (in *La Nausée*), construction of the past leads to anxious doubting more than to a Proustian recovery of a lost paradise. And perhaps this is the reason for the inner drama of so many autobiographies that move readers deeply: they hover between that search for meaning in the past, however elusive, and the recognition of the author's inconsequentiality, be it personal, professional, social, or spiritual.

Sartre's own "loathing" of his childhood self is not an uncommon feeling among autobiographers.[59] George Tyrrell came to despair of the direction of his life, and William Hale White implied that his life had taken a false and irreversible course. Such realizations have to do with professional success as well as spiritual satisfaction, have to do, that is, with the issue raised by Roy Pascal in his pioneering work on autobiography. "All good autobiographies," says Pascal, who has both high and arbitrary standards for "good," "are the story of a calling."[60] As I have suggested, the autobiographers who are the subject of this book are writers, men with a genuine calling, whose self-assessments grow out of and pertain to their other works. George Moore knows that his looking back is different in kind from that of an autobiographer who is not a professional writer because he can manipulate the past, appreciating both the protean and the capricious nature of his recollecting. But the power to imagine is also the power to ask disturbing questions or explore unpleasant avenues, and hence Moore's final chapter of *Memoirs of My Dead Life* speculates in a self-punishing way about the burden of a writer's life. Even Yeats, who seems to have no doubts about his poetic powers, reminisces at the end of *Reveries* with unhappiness and disillusion. Looking back on one's life involves the recognition of work not done or of unfulfilled talents. Ford Madox Ford contends with the awareness that he is not the "genius" he was intended by his elders to be, that instead of a literary "giant" he has become merely a writer. Not being a genius and knowing one is not a genius is, as Lionel Trilling suggests, a special anxiety of modern writers, those ironic descendents, thanks to Diderot, of "Rameau's nephew."[61]

Anxiety is, to be sure, a vague word, and a word used with a variety of meanings, especially in postexistentialist times. With the exception of White and Yeats, it is not a word that occurs with frequency to the authors I look at here. *Tragedy,* however, is. Moore and Gosse and Tyrrell all attest that life is tragedy. I shall return to this later, but it is well to mention that Yeats's comment—"We begin to live when we have conceived life as tragedy"—applies to many of the autobiographers of his time.[62] Whether they see life in general or their own particular lives as tragic, they use the word with some urgency, as if recollection has engendered an unexpected awareness. In this regard, Unamuno's *Tragic Sense of Life* seems a fitting emblem of the thinking of the times for, like Unamuno, these writers associate recollection and its attenuated hope with the admission of their lives as tragic and their spiritual condition as arid.

Memory and Forgetting

Another strong spokesman for the view of life as tragic (or both tragic and comic) was Friedrich Nietzsche, whose first important work, after all, was *The Birth of Tragedy from the Spirit of Music* (1872). Nietzsche speaks just as pointedly about another aspect of autobiography although he does not, any more than Bradley or Bergson, address autobiography directly. In "The Use and Abuse of History" (1874), Nietzsche equates the tragic condition of life with the issue of remembering, which he treats in a typically paradoxical way. Following Schopenhauer in making memory the primary human quality, Nietzsche says: "He [mankind] may ask the beast—'Why do you look at me and not speak to me of your happiness?' The beast wants to answer—'Because I always forget what I wished to say'; but he forgets this answer, too, and is silent; and man is left to wonder."[63]

Alas, says Nietzsche, memory is both our distinguishable quality and our curse. To understand the real conditions of life, to live fully in the present and to anticipate the future with courage, we need not just the capacity for remembering but the power of forgetting. "One who cannot leave himself behind on the threshold of the moment and forget the past, who cannot stand on a single point, like a goddess of victory, . . . will never know what happiness is." He will also never appreciate the tragic vision, which requires the strength to break up the past, bringing it "to the bar of judgment" in order to "condemn" it.[64]

Nietzsche is speaking of history, especially the faith in history—and the tendency to "Ironic" history—of his German contemporaries, rather than of autobiography, although he does censure the kind of modern hagiography urged by Carlyle. His version of "Critical" history, however, emphasizes the subjective and personal, so that "the art of forgetting" includes a personal as well as a cultural past. "This is the parable for each one of us: he must organize the chaos in himself by 'thinking himself back' to his true needs. He will want all his honesty, all the sturdiness and sincerity in his character."[65]

When he stresses the destructive weight of memory and the need for the creative alternative of the imagination, Nietzsche recalls Blake's dismissal of the "daughters of memory," who also subvert a creative self. In this sense, what Nietzsche argues in *The Use and Abuse of History* sums up a great deal in the English debate about the merits and the powers of memory as we have seen them embodied in Charles Radcliffe and his philosophical enemies. Nietzsche argues like Radcliffe for a new individualist and, at the same time, collective culture, but he does so while rejecting the very authorities a man like Radcliffe invokes. Even more than Kierkegaard, he distances himself from Plato and Plato's emphasis on a limiting, or predetermined, memory, since this is injurious to subjective freedom and creative choice. Like the theories of von Hartmann, Plato's ideas inhibit and stultify, contributing to mankind's natural and regrettable tendency to seek answers in a past. "The deeper the roots of man's nature," Nietzsche says with typical paradox, "the more will he take the past into himself."[66] He will not be subject to the tyranny of another.

Nietzsche's questioning of memory, which is, again, an onslaught on the historical discourse in his time, bears on the understanding of "self" apart from broad historical categories and perhaps helps in the assessment of autobiographical narratives that look back on past lives for sustenance or rely on the workings of memory as a means to narrative understanding. The works I am concerned with in this book all seem to be on the borderline between what we would be likely to call "autobiography" on the one hand and "fiction" on the other. In a sense, the development of early modern fiction, in Joyce, say, or Lawrence, or Ford Madox Ford, might be thought of as fiction that illustrates Nietzsche's admonitions, that involves "the use" of the past, or self-history, along with the suppression of the past in the way of imaginative selecting and forgetting.

The relation of memory and forgetting can be looked at in another way, which will help to pull a few of my points together. To think of writers like Radcliffe, who extol memory and praise its creative powers, or philosophers like Nietzsche, who see its tyrannical and uncreative potential, is to recognize vast tracts of difference and disagreement. It is one thing to say that memory is an essential quality in early modern literature, that it helps in the understanding of autobiographical works or clarifies the relationship of those works to a larger literary or social or philosophical life. It is another to define the hows and whys. In fact, the functions of memory are staggeringly diverse, even within individual works — and certainly between them. At the risk of gross simplification, I want to suggest a kind of heuristic division, two complementary traditions, both of which are represented in the authors I discuss, both implicit in the previous pages.

Can we say that on the one hand there is the tradition of Wordsworth, with his spots of time, his immersion in time which leads to an escape from time, the past moments visionary and prophetic, "types and symbols [however mundane] of eternity?" And that on the other hand there is the comparatively unacknowledged but nonetheless insistent tradition of Rousseau, for whom memories are confessions, life implicitly both sinful and deterministic? Rousseau's account, "in all the truth of nature," announces his life as unique and displays it as a burden. Wordsworth's example in *The Prelude* may be inescapably personal, but it assumes both transcendence and power. What is the relationship between the two? Even granting, as Phyllis Grosskurth has argued, that Rousseau was conspicuous throughout the nineteenth century in the failure of British writers to invoke him, Rousseau still mattered. Apart from Hazlitt early in the century, J. A. Symonds took Rousseau as a model, as Grosskurth makes clear, but so did Havelock Ellis and John Ruskin, who thought of himself as an English Rousseau.[67] Pater certainly honored Rousseau, and Edmund Gosse praised Rousseau as an unappreciated writer, with the *Confessions* his finest work, implying that English writers had learned much from Rousseau's example, the more so if they wanted to realize an adult world. When Ford Madox Ford, in *Ancient Lights,* says that the influence of Rousseau is on the wane, he implies his own and other writers' awareness, if not indebtedness, to the *Confessions*. George Moore admits that he could not have written his *Confessions of a Young Man* if he had read Rousseau, but it is hardly likely, with his vaunted knowledge of French literature, that he had not encountered Rousseau's book or had lived conveniently ignorant of its influence.[68]

That recurrent nineteenth-century distinction between "meditative" and "creative," or "imaginative," usually places Wordsworth among the highest ranks of meditative authors; at the same time, the desire for creative genius, for a Shakespeare or Dante, has little to do with the capacities or interests of the contemporary writers themselves, who were obsessed by contemplations of self and time. No doubt Tennyson and other mid-Victorian writers were suspicious of personal indulgence and desirous of a higher order of poetry, but *In Memoriam* demonstrates an incessant self-absorption. Since, as Arnold repeatedly argued, contemplation or meditation seemed unavoidable for such writers, and since meditation is inseparable from mnemonic processes, it is as if their choice lay between Wordsworth and Rousseau, between two sorts of meditative writing.

Nietzsche's theory of "forgetting" looked to an independence from the past while positing a new creativity. Another way of thinking about "forgetting" is to see it as Wordsworth's method, too, in which the privileged moments debase another order of remembering for what are largely spiritual ends. But the alternative used by Rousseau, the full recounting, may be spiritual in an overlapping way. I shall, as suggested, be speaking in the chapters that follow about two general groups of writers: William Hale White, George Tyrrell, Samuel Butler, and Edmund Gosse, on the one hand; George Moore (*Confessions* excepted), Ford Madox Ford, and William Butler Yeats, on the other. For the former, sin (in large sense of a blameworthy or an unfulfilled past) seems almost equivalent to a historical self; for the latter, moments of exaltation lead to a kind of grace, or redemption from the self. Tyrrell does not finish his autobiography, perhaps because he cannot find the way of the saint or the visionary, because he feels himself bound by a past he cannot redeem. Even Samuel Butler, with a conviction of "subordinate" selves, fails to square his personal life with his proposed myth of unconscious "grace," and Butler, too, leaves his autobiographical work unfinished.

Although a distinction between the two general kinds of narrative makes a certain sense (it may suggest the difference, for example, between *Stephen Hero* and *Portrait of the Artist*), it has its drawbacks. Rousseau's influence or authority is, to begin with, rarely independent of Wordsworth's. Ruskin, Symonds, Gosse, and Moore are all intimately familiar with Wordsworth, who sets standards of awareness and insight—his "public voice," as Herbert Lindenberger describes it—approximating the historical self, emphasizing personal origins and development along with social interaction.[69] What we have in the autobiographical works I discuss is, then, more than a choice between competing literary authority. Yeats and Ford are obviously "autobiographical," and not alone in books labeled as autobiography, whereas Tyrell and Gosse know epiphanic and redeeming moments, whatever their final doubts.

Perhaps for each of these writers, the equation holds between sinning and self, epiphany and grace. In giving privileged status to certain moments, an author is not describing the formation of self so much as the escape or liberation from it. And this is what makes Butler and Tyrrell, Gosse and Yeats, Moore and Ford, *modern*. To liberate the self from that which the self creates, or that which obsesses the self, to realign the idea of truth (as epiphany) to that of untruth (fiction, self, sin) may be both to emphasize memory and, in the end, to reject it, to go beyond memory, as Augustine said, but for different ends. It is in the realignment that the anxieties of modern autobiography about the reliability of memory, the status of language, the possibility of general truth would seem to be expressed. These at least are issues I explore in the following pages, beginning with the religious autobiographies of two unacquainted but closely related men.

2 Transforming the Past: The Autobiographies of W. H. White and Father George Tyrrell

> *Great religious natures like Augustine and Pascal are the eternal models for insight drawn from personal experience.*
> Wilhelm Dilthey, Meaning in History

When Wilhelm Dilthey probed the meanings of history and the relationship of historical understanding to individual lives, he addressed some of the fundamental questions of his age. Convinced that autobiography is "the highest and most instructive form in which the understanding of a life confronts us," and also that "individuals are as much the logical subject of history as communities and contexts," Dilthey nevertheless disliked what he called "introspective methods of self-knowledge," which deny systems and meaning, connections and relations. Playing with his recurrent, if hackneyed, metaphor of the river of life, he speaks of leaving an individual life to contemplate—as a historian—the infinite sea of humanity, with the sea suggesting both a vast scale and an atemporal vantage point of philosophical awareness. Because humanity understands itself "only in history, never through introspection,"[1] a higher order of historical understanding denies to self-history the virtues of introspection that would seem to be its essence. Dilthey's ambivalence reflects the preoccupations of his era with two apparently conflicting assumptions: the importance and unavoidability of the individual consciousness on the one hand, and the dwarfing perspective of great movements and countless eons on the other.

Dilthey's comment on Pascal and Augustine complicates his arguments even more, for "eternal insight" implies a vision from within the autobiographical or confessional process, so that personal experience in spiritual autobiography would seem to reach a higher order of awareness without the historical distancing which Dilthey finds desirable. For Dilthey, as for so many later students of autobiographical works, Augustine is the "eternal model," obviously not because the *Confessions* is an informative document detailing the life of the Bishop of Hippo, but because Augustine's insights grow out of and move beyond a factual account, becoming a paradigm of spiritual development. Augustine's written life certainly offers what Dilthey claims in the way of insight, and the insight in spiritual autobiographies may transcend that in other kinds of works. But from where, except from introspection, does the insight emerge? And how does the confessor's personal vision illustrate the arguments about historical understanding? If, as Dilthey argues, historical understanding is the highest understanding and if autobiography is the basic language of historical expression, then spiritual autobiography emerges as a peculiar anomaly: historical and ahistorical, self-confessing and self-effacing, "personal" and "eternal" within one ambivalent mode.

Contemporaries of Dilthey and painfully sensitive to the paradoxical nature of religious self-histories, both William Hale White ("Mark Rutherford") and Father George Tyrrell are self-consciously aware of late-nineteenth-century social and intellectual developments and quick to see their situations as at once representative and idiosyncratic. White was an apostate dissenter; Tyrrell a Catholic convert, Jesuit priest, then excommunicate. If Tyrrell, in his own words, was a *"fin de siècle* Jesuit,"[2] White was a *fin de siècle* puritan. In fact neither is easily labeled. Their autobiographies, reflecting the times and addressing issues beyond the times, serve to introduce other autobiographers who construe life as a pilgrimage, or define their own lives in terms of spiritual loss and gain. Whether or not either was "a great spiritual nature like Augustine or Pascal," they were profoundly religious men, obsessed by matters of faith yet hesitant about the kinds of books they were writing. Tyrrell looks back to Augustine (and John Henry Newman), and White's model, though not Pascal, is another radical Christian: John Bunyan, in whose chapel he learned to worship and whose faith he came to reject.

WILLIAM HALE WHITE

> *My character is so little myself that all my life it has thwarted me.*
> William Butler Yeats, Explorations

> *How much of what I say is an echo; how little is myself. Sometimes it seems as if my real self were nothing.*
> William Hale White, More Pages from a Journal

When he had a chance to meet George Tyrrell, William Hale White declined. He admitted to respecting Tyrrell and said that at least one of his books closely approximated his own ideas.[3] An articulate and pious Jesuit priest made him, however, uncomfortable, as if Tyrrell might influence him unduly or upset his hard-won but fragile convictions. This begging off is typical of White, who guarded his privacy as well as his ideas.[4] Feeling—as Tyrrell also felt—that he was too easily stifled by others, too rarely able to assert his own view, he considered himself a victim of his times, sensitive to new ideological as well as historical conditions. In *Mark Rutherford's Autobiography* he speaks of Christ as a poor, solitary thinker, confronted by two enormous and overpowering organizations, "the Jewish hierarchy and the Roman state." Struggling with antagonistic forces and his own compulsions, Christ lived in "absolute loneliness."[5] White may not have associated himself directly with Christ, but he assessed his life and the lives of others like him in terms of lonely confrontation.

Beyond insisting on what both men assumed to be the "tragic" nature of life—in which so much good can be imagined and so much evil exists—White and Tyrrell considered their personal lives to be wasted as well as isolated. Subject to melancholy, to nervous illness, and in their own estimate to ill-temper, they advocated a kind of stoical behavior, convinced of the necessity for rigorous ethical standards in the face of a hostile and inexplicable world. "The more perfection a thing possesses," says White, "the more it acts and the less it suffers."[6] Unfortunately, the action of both men takes the problematic form of writing, which can intensify suffering and which in any case they regarded with ambivalence. They saw their writing as needful expression of ideas rather than as professional work, distancing themselves from the world of letters, although White worked as a journalist and Tyrrell wrote compulsively for a variety of publishers and periodicals.

Despite their profound distrust of dogma and religious authority, White and Tyrrell craved what they rejected and emphasized with reluctance the unavoidability of private judgment in matters of faith. Whereas Tyrrell engaged such issues in public debate, arguing positions, questioning his church, White chose to avoid controversy, which he deplored, confiding little in others, keeping his writing and his authorship secret. No less than Tyrrell, he worked in a public arena, whether reporting the activities of the House of Commons for newspapers or serving through a long career in the Admiralty. But this was from economic necessity. He sought whenever possible a reclusive and anonymous life.

The autobiographies of these two men reflect diverse circumstances as well as characters. Tyrrell wrote his unfinished work in the midst of his career, between books, and as a temporary escape from a life of controversy. He died in his mid-forties. White began the writing of books with *Mark Rutherford's Autobiography* (1881) and *Mark Ruth-*

erford's Deliverance (1885) when he was already in his fifties.

Since White insisted on writing as "Mark Rutherford," the term *autobiographies* may be inaccurate, except to describe *The Early Life of Mark Rutherford* (1913), written when he was an older man, and offered as a corrective and supplement to the early volumes. It is characteristic of White that he would write about his boyhood and youth under his original pseudonym, which continued in theory to hide his identity and which was of a piece with the earlier books. In fact, White wrote all of his fiction and most of his essays as "by the author of *Mark Rutherford,*" and the identification between author and pseudonym is close. White pointed out, with a revealing passive sentence, that "there is much added [to the Rutherford stories] which is entirely fictitious," and in the sense of historical facts this is true.[7] We know from Wilfred Stone's and Catherine Maclean's studies how much White's life paralleled Rutherford's: the Bedford, Dissenting, puritan, and lower-middle class background; the training for the ministry; working in London for a publisher (where White met George Eliot); drudgery in an office, albeit White survived his.[8]

Above all, Mark Rutherford's story emphasizes the spiritual course of White's life. Unlike Rutherford, who becomes for a time a Dissenting minister—Independent, then Unitarian—White never entered the ministry. He was, however, dismissed from a seminary while being trained. (There are parallels with Samuel Butler, who also imagined life as a clergyman, exploring through "fiction" what might have been.) Minister or no, White remained obsessed throughout his life with religious issues, and the young man whose principles forced his expulsion from the seminary carried his spiritual struggles with him no less than his imaginary autobiographer. Rutherford's gradual discomfort with the tenets of Nonconformity, his growing impatience with Calvinist and other dogmas, reflect directly the situation of his author, who similarly remained under the influence of Puritanism and was never satisfied with the alternatives he found.[9] Although William Hale White lived on for many years beyond those accorded to Mark Rutherford, his autobiographical study touches his own life through most of its pages. Rutherford's death is at once a peculiar assertion that this is not a book from the hand of a living person (but safely *ex morte*) and a simple termination of story by a writer who came to despair of creating plot.

White recognized well enough his tendency to speak autobiographically, to "tell" his life "under a semi-transparent disguise."[10] His dilemma approximates that of Edmund Gosse or Samuel Butler, for he worried about a necessary fictionalizing in any narrative and wanted desperately to come to the truth of things while introducing fictional conventions. His books occupy a gray area of literature, though a familiar one. Like Gosse's and Butler's, they look forward to a later generation of books, which also use a writer's experience for stories that blur generic boundaries. They also look backward. If we were to think of parallels with, say, Goethe's *Wilhelm Meister,* to whose progeny Mark Rutherford probably belongs, we could see how closely identified White seems to be with his pseudoself, how little of Goethe's distance or humor he effects.[11] In tone—and what White would call his "seriousness"—his books are closer to *The Sorrows of Young Werther,* with which they share the tendency to reflect a mood of the times: a sort of late-nineteenth-century *Sturm und Drang.* Werther and Rutherford both live, to use White's term, in an age of "disintegration,"[12] but whereas Werther exists as a symbolic projection of the young Goethe, Mark Rutherford relives, with minor variations, the life of his author.

The mere question of facticity seems at once central and irrelevant to the issue of autobiography: central because readers seem to want some assurance that autobiographies essentially reflect the course of a life; irrelevant because they so often do not. Rousseau's *Confessions* may well be the finest French novel of the eighteenth century, as it has been called, but it will probably remain *autobiography* for most readers, despite Rousseau's inveterate capacity to tamper with "events" or to create a more acceptable self-history.[13] Any autobiographer rewrites or re-creates his or her life to fit present needs, let alone present incapacities. A *life* itself is a construct of autobiography, an imposition of order and meaning on those inchoate or at least disparate recollections that provide the matter of autobiographical discourse. We can persuade ourselves that we know the intent of an author, or that a "pact" is established to allow the proper construction of facts and fictions, truth and design, but this remains self-flattery.[14] Jane Eyre protests that she is not writing an autobiography, but so too does Edmund Gosse in *Father and Son.* Autobiography tests the limits of conventions and trust, as Rousseau and Casanova, Gosse and William Hale White may suggest. All autobiography, as Gérard Genette has written of Proust, involves a kind of whirligig of intent and effect, the reader caught in a revolving emotional and intellectual door.[15] White's displacements and self-projections turn with particular urgency, bred of conflicting values and self-contradictory notions about the merits of writing.

In a review of Walt Whitman (himself a clever creator of public selves), White wrote that "fiction" was somehow a false escape, an illicit choice for a writer. "Least of all," he said, "must we stop short and hide ourselves in fiction; but if afflicted by doubt must go forward."[16]

This is understandable from White, who failed to recognize fictional qualities in other writers and usually "hides" behind the pseudonym of Rutherford. Always, he wants to press forward, with his Bunyan-like resolution, to some measure of truth, with life projected as spiritual journey or pilgrimage. Given the antithetical needs of personal truth and self-displacements, White's "autobiographies" illustrate the necessary indeterminacy of autobiographical texts, which offer at once an assertion of self and an avoidance of self, progression and stasis. Whether we call the Rutherford stories autobiographies is, perhaps, less important than whether they work autobiographically: what they say, that is, about the process of recollection, and how they create a historical or continuous self.

To read *The Autobiography of Mark Rutherford* is to recognize those late-nineteenth-century qualities which Walter Pater projected back on Coleridge: "that inexhaustible discontent, languor, and homesickness, that endless regret, the chords of which ring all through our modern literature."[17] White was very much aware of his age and of his relationship to his age, yet he also recognized that his "modern" ideas were the result of wide reading in an earlier literature. His "passionate and merciless honesty" in depicting his feelings has been compared to that of Tennyson, whom he admired greatly, and to that of John Henry Newman.[18] In a sense his closest parallel is with Cardinal Newman's brother, Francis Newman, another early contemporary who had pursued "truth" to an uncomfortable degree, whose aspirations and self-doubts anticipated his own, and who wrestled, in his autobiographical writings, with the issues of self that preoccupied White.

Surprisingly, White did not appreciate Francis Newman. Much like Matthew Arnold, he said that Newman was a carrier of negative messages, and he was suspicious of writers who indulged "personality," or who engaged in "the uselessness of publishing doubts."[19] Francis Newman himself had similar misgivings. *The Soul* (1849) and *Phases of Faith* (1850) record the thoughts and intellectual life of a man who arrives with great reluctance at his present situation and who publishes only because he feels he has to: no less than White he says he is driven by the needs of truth and veracity. And his confession or articulation of "doubts" foreshadows much of White's own. He too underwent a kind of negative conversion, on the model perhaps of Carlyle's implied in *Sartor Resartus* and with the same sort of inner turmoil and doubt. White's association of himself with Carlyle—"the voice which in our century came from the deepest depths"—extends beyond the advocate of work and duty to the skeptical critic of mindless belief.[20] A fellow apprentice like Francis Newman may be too similar to allow his sympathy. For unlike Carlyle, who at least pretends to certitudes, Newman acknowledges the necessity of self-consciousness or introspective revelation which is at once inescapable and apparently at odds with a more universal truth. This is, again, the dilemma implicit in Wilhelm Dilthey's speculations about autobiography and history, personal vision and philosophy. For White it is a constant topic as well as an insoluble problem.

White's "confessional imagination" runs against his or Rutherford's conviction that he "never can really speak [himself]" (89), as well as the related sense of the limited importance of his own life. Rutherford says, "But mine is the tale of commonplace life, perplexed by many problems I have never solved; disturbed by many difficulties I have never surmounted; and blotted by ignoble concessions which are a constant regret" (1). With its motif of regret, this is the modest, "serious" tone of the *Autobiography*, which undercuts its speaker-author while tacitly announcing his importance. If he does not matter, that is, if he is to be defined by a string of negatives, why bother at all to recount his story? If doubts should only be expressed by great thinkers and those who refuse to compromise, what can be gained from the ruminations of a self-styled "failure"?

White's hesitancy about confessing personal doubts or recounting his own meager life can be seen in the fictional barriers he creates to separate self from self. He published his autobiographical studies in the name of "Mark Rutherford," who is to White what Ernest Pontifex is to Samuel Butler, and like Butler, White introduces yet another, distancing voice for his presentation. Instead of an Overton, who tells the story, however, he resorts to a conventional "editor," responsible for a dead man's writings. Reuben Shapcott, a kind of thick-headed and epicurean skeptic, considers "one fourth of life . . . intelligible, the other three quarters . . . unintelligible" (viii), and his conclusion from perusing his "friend's" story is that we should ask as few questions as possible while enjoying life to the fullest. Proposing what neither Rutherford nor White as a young man seemed able to achieve, Shapcott offers an escape from gnawing, unanswerable questions beyond the capacity of a Mark Rutherford to avoid.

For narrative purposes, a relatively dispassionate editor can serve to defend Rutherford against charges of egotism and selfishness, which are for White (Epicurean remarks notwithstanding) the worst of qualities, but which seem inevitable in autobiographical works. Shapcott can tell the reader that Rutherford was both a generous man and a true friend; he may also free the ostensible author from the necessity of self-praise and self-indulgence, while providing direct commentary on the document itself. No doubt White subscribed to some of Shapcott's philosophy. Mark Rutherford speaks with sorrow, for example, about people like himself who waste their lives on projects and thoughts beyond their capacity while ignoring the beauty and affection of the world around them. At the same time, Shapcott's comments complicate further White's relationship with his autobiographical work. The problem is not just the issue of expressing doubts or the hesitancy of a failed man to write his autobiography, but also White's suspicion that any such project defeats some intrinsic pleasure of life for an always dubious end. In the whirligig of personal scrutiny and generic turning, White tacitly questions not just Shapcott's announced values but also those implicit in the narrative itself.

Beyond this, Shapcott's intervention is so obviously self-protective (obscuring as well as deflecting) and, in White's terms, so obviously "fictional" that it detracts from the confessional quality of the work, which is another, competing virtue for White himself. As someone who was to praise *Grace Abounding* as much as *Pilgrim's Progress,* White admired confessional literature for its potential truth and "sincerity." One tribute to Carlyle, for example, speaks of a man "so thoroughly truthful that we may be sure he would never assume a self not his own."[21] He does not mention the fictional guises of *Sartor Resartus* and the ways—analogous to his own—that Carlyle found to express himself by assuming selves. Nor does he begin to explain why, given such convictions, he would write an autobiography at a kind of third remove. Much, however, is implied. For writers like White, conscious of their own limitations while absolute in their spiritual ambitions, autobiographies as well as novels imply a compromise with a projected if not historically realized truth. Yet to the extent that separation of self from self, one's *now* from one's past, establishes personal narrative as fiction, it also allows the creation of symbolic and more revealing truth, truth predicated on the recollecting "I" but useful for kindred readers.

A man writes either for his neighbors or for God. I decided to write for God with a view to saving my neighbors.

Jean-Paul Sartre, Words

Atheist as he was, Sartre says that he decided to write for God, the choice being limited and his neighbors, however construed, more in need of help than worthy as an audience. Sartre brushes aside the other possibility for writers: writing for oneself, which he implies is self-deluding or somehow onanistic, like his own early attempts at fiction in which the young Jean-Paul figures as intrepid hero. No doubt William Hale White would have looked askance at some of Sartre's paradoxes, designed as they were to shock his "neighbors" and to see the worst in himself. Sartre speaks, nevertheless, to the kinds of problems facing White, whose own *mal de siècle* informs his books and who sees the dilemma of the lonely writer as central to any understanding of alienated men and women. "To escape the desolation of created things," says Sartre, "I prepared myself for the middle-class solitude for which there is no cure: that of the creator. This change of tack must not be taken as a genuine revolt: you rebel against a tyrant, and I had only benefactors."[22]

Middle-class solitude, the revolt against benevolent adversaries, the life of the "creator": all this describes William Hale White's growth to carefully nurtured but evidently delicate independence, and White looks back, if not with Sartre's "loathing," certainly with ambivalence on a needed and rejected past. He knows that his writing comes at the expense of ease and friendship; it requires a state of lonely self-absorption, at once choice and compulsion; its job is salvation more than art, but its effects are dubious, given the intrinsically personal nature of the matters White describes.[23] Although White's own achieved freedom is vastly different from that of Sartre, he defines it in terms of analogous middle-class values and beliefs, one feature of which is ambivalence about the world of books. Only through writing can "salvation" be attained, yet for White no less than for Rutherford, writing remains the activity most likely to elicit self-deception and self-importance.

Like Sartre, White describes his lower-middle-class background, appreciating his present independence in terms of childhood circumstances. In his autobiographies as well as his novels, he is conscious of class distinctions and differences: the twin worlds, for example, in *Mark Rutherford's Autobiography*, of Dissent and Anglicanism, which divide what is actually the Bedford of his childhood and which define the limits or possibilities for all who live there. Oddly enough, while Sartre, who comes to reject his family almost completely, dwells on his mother and grandfather (his father having died), White has relatively little to say about his immediate family in the Mark Rutherford stories. Only in *The Early Life of Mark Rutherford* does he begin to explore the character of his father, an independent and courageous bookseller, against whom, in a sense, White chooses not to have Rutherford rebel. The struggle comes against Dissent as a social force and against the church or churches which seem to White as they would for Tyrrell to reduce the power and the meaning of religion to something mean and dull, like the shopkeepers and tradesmen whom Rutherford encounters.

Rutherford's history of his early life works by exclusion or a kind of synecdoche, representative parts suggesting a larger, undescribed whole.

In contrast to a writer such as Tyrrell or Gosse, whose metaphors, like those of many autobiographers, crowd one another, jostling for attention and reaching for clarification, White uses only a few conventional metaphors to portray his life. He clearly distrusts figurative language, which invites all the problematic uncertainties of "fiction" and all the unraveling of a delicate ego. When he accounts for his childhood, it is as though he omits not just his family but also a great part of himself. Indeed, his entire story of childhood as such takes only a dozen pages. The absence of parents and the reluctance to seek out (as so many autobiographers do) earliest memories or those vivid re-creations that Freud was to call screen-memories, gives the Rutherford autobiographies at least two distinctive qualities. In the first place, Rutherford comes across as a kind of orphan, another David Copperfield or Jane Eyre, but with an important difference. Whereas those writers stress the events of childhood, Rutherford dwells on its effect. Except for a few flashes of intimate memory, he is content with summary and example, as if using his childhood to illustrate rules or ideas, writing "biographically," as Susanne Langer has called it, instead of with the vivid "flashback" recollections in which other autobiographers so often delight.[24]

What seems—in the second place—even more peculiar from this admirer of Wordsworth, this lover of the physical countryside, this man in crisis, is his sketchy treatment of announcedly formative stages of Rutherford's life. Rutherford even says that "nothing particular happened to me till I was about fourteen" (9), at which point he describes like Gosse's his formal "conversion," an empty ritual, a nonevent that signals the beginning of his adult life. Rutherford's true conversion, along with the meanings that he finds for his uneventful life, grows directly out of Wordsworth. His reading of *Lyrical Ballads* "conveyed to me no new doctrine [he says typically], and yet the change it wrought in me could only be compared with that which is said to have been wrought on Paul himself" (18). Despite the grand language, Wordsworth's effect is scarcely dramatic. Rutherford speaks of pastoral escapes and introduces consciously Wordsworthian touches, yet his descriptions remain muted or derivative: "Those were the days," he says of his childhood, "when through the whole long summer's morning I wanted no companion but myself, provided only I was in the country, and when books were read with tears in the eyes" (19–20).

The following account suggests the tentative nature of his description, which often retreats before it advances; it might be compared with Browning's description of the Dissenting chapel in *Christmas-Eve and Easter-Day* or with Butler's anecdote of Theobald Pontifex visiting a dying woman:

The atmosphere of the chapel on hot nights was most foul, and this added to my discomfort. Oftentimes in winter, when no doors or windows were open, I have seen the glass panes streaming with wet inside, and women carried out fainting. On rare occasions I was allowed to go with my father when he went into the villages to preach. As a deacon he was also a lay-preacher, and I had the ride in the gig out and home and tea at a farmhouse.

(8)

From this circumspect, self-interrupted description, Rutherford goes on to weigh the "advantages" and "drawbacks" of his upbringing, as if totally separated from the life he describes. He mentions "passion," but expresses none of the passion of a Dickens or Brontë for the childhood years. Instead of Gosse's vivid account of his conversion, Rutherford slips from passive constructions to a string of peculiar negatives:

But conversion, as it was understood by me and as it is now understood, is altogether unmeaning. I knew that I had to be "a child of God," and after a time professed myself to be one, but I cannot call to mind that I was anything else than I always had been.

(10)

Rutherford's evocation of his past is intimately connected with his response to Wordsworth, who represents for him the ultimate spokesman for a seductive vision of nature and a kind of philosophical dead end. Like his author, Rutherford wishes that Wordsworth could provide consolation and answers; he would welcome the sort of outlook advocated by Charles Radcliffe, which weds literature and natural beauty and allows a private escape from present ugliness. But this is not at all what he achieves. His process of conversion moves *through* Wordsworth into a kind of stoical uncertainty. As the passage about the long summer morning suggests, Wordsworth affords Rutherford a brief passionate acceptance of the "God of the Hills." In contrast to a dessicated Calvinism, Wordsworth speaks for love, beauty, meaning. Rutherford's nostalgia for the few joys of childhood is, at the same time, also nostalgia for Wordsworth's faith in nature, the church without structure or dogma but replete with affirmation and joy. He pointedly ignores Wordsworth's own dark struggles or Wordsworth's need for recurrent "renovation" of his faith. In any case, while ignoring parallels with Wordsworth's spiritual dilemmas, Rutherford comes reluctantly to question the efficacy of his vision.

When I was living in the country, the pure sky and the landscape formed a large part of my existence, so large that much of myself depended on it, and I wondered how men could be worth anything if they could never see the face of nature. For this belief my early training on the *Lyrical Ballads* is answerable.

(149)

The word *training* links Wordsworth with other potentially damaging influences of childhood and with illusions, however pleasant or seductive, that he can no longer accept. Wordsworth's influence goes beyond himself to other writers of his age, and its larger effect is pernicious:

> I cannot help saying, with all my love for the literature of my own day, that it has an evil side to it which none can know except the millions of sensitive persons who are condemned to exist in great towns. It might be imagined from much of this literature that true humanity and a belief in God are the offspring of the hills or the ocean; and by implication, if not expressly, the vast multitudes who hardly ever see the hills or the ocean must be without a religion.
>
> (149)

Whereas a writer like Edmund Gosse learns what he asserts as lasting lessons from Wordsworth (after his mother's death and when he and his father leave London for Devon), White realizes that his early substitution of Wordsworthian thinking for the tenets of puritanism will also not suffice. With reluctance and astuteness, he explores implications of the word *nature* and questions Wordsworth's assumptions about the general benefits of country life, even when viewed in retrospect. Although the word *multitude* expresses some of White's apprehension about masses of people, and although his own belief in God was anything but simple, his attack on the Wordsworthian legacy implies an alternative belief, a composite perhaps of the remnants of his original faith together with a sense of potential joy from Wordsworth, all made meaningful by convictions of duty, sincerity, and veracity. Whatever the components of his new belief, Rutherford comes to learn that the realities of a place like London cast doubt on a philosophy of consolation, and that, while consolation is the issue, it proves unavailable through the evocation of pastoral recollections.

The scrutiny of Wordsworth in terms of late-nineteenth-century realities—industry, technology, poverty, human dereliction—says as much about the narrative Rutherford writes as about his overall attitude toward life, for the failure of a benevolent nature has to do with his implicit doubts about the renovating qualities of retrospective writing, however much he may be forced into the world of his own past.[25] Since "the position of mortal man seemed to me infinitely tragic" (76), little will be gained from remembering attenuated past joys or investing them with meanings travestied by present difficulties. His narrative recalls, nevertheless, how inescapable for White and for others like him Wordsworth's model had become. At one of his low points as a clergyman, he suffers all the uncertainty of Wordsworth's own brief, moral truancy, and he endures, like John Stuart Mill and others who were able to live through their crises with the help of Wordsworth's ministrations. Like Gosse, his moment of illumination comes in Devon:

> I went . . . to Ilfracombe. I had been there about a week, when on one memorable morning, on the top of one of those Devonshire hills, I became aware of a kind of flush in the brain and a momentary relief such as I had not known since that November night.
>
> (37)

Unfortunately, "it was not permanent, and perhaps the gloom was never more profound, nor the agony more intense, than it was for long after my Ilfracombe visit" (37). In spite of the despondency and pain, Rutherford's few pleasures are Wordsworthian pleasures. When he speaks of rare childhood joys, they are tied almost exclusively to the countryside and solitary rambles, as opposed to the social prison of Sundays with their regimen of endless sermons and cold food. Like Gosse, he measures himself in terms of his childhood world (similarly dividing his week into Sundays and all the other days). Unlike Gosse, he emphasizes his detachment, not from adult self—this would be equally true of Gosse—but from childhood, a stage of his life he reaches back to as from a great distance.

The treatment of childhood events shows in what sense White was "writing for his neighbors," those of the nineteenth century and those of today. Mark Rutherford describes pathetically how he has always wanted a friend to whom he could unburden himself: "The real truth is, that nobody more than myself could desire self-revelation" (23), but he has never found people in whom he could confide and has always thought of himself as socially inept and conversationally awkward. Despite his reported doubts about publishing it, Rutherford's autobiography is an open confession to readers who might be compassionate, at once a reaching out and an alternative for friends and sympathetic listeners. To justify what might seem like "notes" from underground, solipsistic or egocentric, Rutherford emphasizes the public nature of his work. Here too anticipating Gosse, he speaks of his autobiography as a history: "In the first place, it has some little historic value, for I feel increasingly that the race to which I belonged is fast passing away . . ." (2). He then thinks of it as a more directly useful and therapeutic document. Precisely because he has lacked his own confidants, Rutherford says that he knows about loneliness in others and that the mere statement of woes can be beneficial. "So it is not impossible that some few [like Milton's and Wordsworth's 'few'] may, by my example, be freed from that sense of solitude which they find so depressing" (2).

According to this argument, although the confessor may be speaking indirectly or covertly, by creating fictional allegories, he nevertheless finds consolation in the implicit help he offers to others. But a sign of Rutherford's uncertainty is that he does not stop with implicit help. When he preaches as a clergyman to bored parishioners he speaks about the suffering of Christ and the democratic underpinnings of Christianity, expressing himself, he says, as fully as he knows how. In fact, he admits to "pouring" himself out to his listeners, carried away by his own passion and conviction while correspondingly insensitive to his audience. Although he does not in his sermons presume to tell people how to live their lives, knowing full well what is wrong with his own, he is somewhat less careful with the readers of his autobiography. He comments on child-raising, for example, and says, "Before leaving this subject I may observe that parents greatly err by not telling their children a good many things which they ought to know" (9). He has already praised discipline, advised diversion for developing boys, and generally indulged in a page of platitudes. Still, Basil Willey is largely right to say that White is not a didactic writer, close as he sometimes comes.[26] The early admonitions on child-rearing and (what may be at odds with those views) living fully diminish in the later sections, and White refers to *The Imitation of Christ* in an epigraph to *Deliverance*: "I teach without noise of words, . . . without the assault of arguments" (143). What he seems to prefer is a paradoxical silence, which means an act of writing that denies the rhetoric and the implicit authority of its own medium.

Rutherford appreciates how inappropriate pat advice is from a man of his temperament. No less than for Tyrrell and Samuel Butler, *contradiction* is the word that keeps recurring to him, and his contradictions tell of a mind unable to be absolute. This is a man who thinks of himself as subject to the tyranny of outside forces, who sees the idea of others "preying" on him. As it is in conversation, so it is in the protean state of his own mind. The more he speaks of his own mind, of his doubts and vacillations, the less he is tempted to give advice, or at least the less he does give advice of the sort that comes so easily in the early part of the *Autobiography*. Another reason for this becomes obvious in Mark Rutherford's account. If as he says he writes for people who share his feelings, confessing for those who have also been unable to confess, his sense of people, the "multitudes," is divided like his sense of himself.

Sympathetic as he is to others that he meets—poor or socially outcast, comparable or different in points of view—his vision of his fellow human "neighbors" is, finally, ambivalent. Mark Rutherford speaks about his effort to imagine a God presiding over an indiscriminate eternity, which he views as a frightening kind of memory. He says, "[My] greatest difficulty was the inability to believe that the Almighty intended to preserve all the mass of human beings, all the countless millions of barbaric half-bestial forms which, since the appearance of man, had wandered upon the earth, savage or civilised." "Best," he says, "would be a happy forgetfulness" of failures (76), his own perhaps included. He wants to remember neither multitudes of historical deaths nor the possibility of his own, but of course this creates for him peculiar problems. Apart from writing "as if from the dead" (through the deceased Rutherford and Rutherford's dispassionate editor), he deals reluctantly with most of his life, excepting the religious or spiritual problems which he sees as its center. It is almost as though he denies his audience in the attempt to reach it just as he denies his "life" in the attempt to present it.

As if to combine the privileged view of Calvinism with echoes of Tennyson, he goes on: "Is it like Nature's way to be so careful about individuals, and is it to be supposed that, having produced, millions of years ago, a creature scarcely nobler than the animals he tore with his fingers, she should take pains to maintain him in existence for evermore?" (76). In this passage he has characteristically shifted his emphasis from the Almighty to Nature, for a nature red in tooth and claw consorts ill with a forgiving and saving God, the more so for a writer who, like Tolstoi, wants to think of God as love. In any case, Mark Rutherford, or his author, is as unresolved about his audience as he is about his religion and himself. His books are an exploration of his own spiritual condition in the act of looking back, an attempt at what he repeatedly calls "perspective," rather than a recapitulation of his past.

> *Man, then, is a synthesis of psyche and body, but he is also a synthesis of the temporal and the eternal. That this has often been stated I do not object to at all, for it is not my wish to discover something new, but rather it is my joy and dearest occupation to ponder over that which is quite simple.*
> Søren Kierkegaard, The Concept of Anxiety

Not without his usual irony, Kierkegaard begins with these words a disquisition on time and eternity that makes the despised Hegel or even Kant seem "simple" by contrast. I do not want to pursue the intricacies of Kierkegaard's arguments but to borrow his comments for another perspective on *Mark Rutherford's Autobiography* and *Deliverance,* works that with neither joy nor laughter propose to talk about basic truths, their resonances assumed in the hearts of sympathetic readers.

When William Hale White admitted that he could not help being serious,[27] he meant in part that important issues concerned him, but also that he could only come to terms with life from a particular temperamental angle. The irony implied in Kierkegaard's understanding of the writing process might have escaped him, as the literal reading of Carlyle suggests. There is not, in fact, much conscious irony in *Mark Rutherford's Autobiography,* although there are touches of verbal irony and satire. Mr. Snale, the draper, who attacks Mark Rutherford and moves with the qualities associated with his name, serves a satiric purpose. He illustrates all the worldly and hypocritical qualities of a modern Mr. Badman, as his sniveling letter to the local paper suggests: "Sir, I will say nothing . . . about a minister of the gospel assisting to bind burdens—that is to say, rates and taxation—upon the shoulders of men grievous to be borne. Surely, sir, a minister of the Lamb of God, who was shed for the remission of sins, should be *against* burdens" (44). Elsewhere White is almost sardonic, as in his few, angry words to characterize Mrs. Snale: she is "a woman . . . cruel, not with the ferocity of the tiger, but with the dull insensibility of a cart-wheel, which will roll over a man's neck as easily as over a flint" (30).

White delighted in Dickens's portraits, and there are times when he draws analogous portraits of his own.[28] Even so, he rarely laughs. The Snales are a reminder of things temporal and irritating to someone whose values and thoughts are elsewhere, who sees, like Kierkegaard, an absolute gulf between the tedious compromise of lived time and the imagined reality of eternity. But while Kierkegaard speaks about insoluble spiritual and intellectual conundrums, he acknowledges, actually relishes, the ironies of his writing as well as the bewilderment of his readers. Truths are not simple, nor are the words we find to address them. His own highly charged personae are there less to simplify than to complicate, to show the entangled problems of either/or, aesthetics and ethics. Kierkegaard confronts the issues with energy and laughter, with a "seriousness" that White, perhaps, would not have understood. In the passage from *The Concept of Anxiety,* he speaks appropriately of "joy," and his joy emerges from the anxious confrontation with ideas rather than with their avoidance.

Joy is a key word in descriptions of religious experience, as, for example, C. S. Lewis's *Surprised by Joy* would suggest.[29] Lewis understands those epiphanic moments of joy as acts of retrospection that allow a forward living; they are what George Moore in a largely nonreligious frame of mind called "echo-auguries." It is astonishing in White's books how infrequently Rutherford's life is associated with *joy*. *Gloom* is common, and *darkness*. Life is lived on the edge of an *abyss*. But joys are rare at best, while deep joy seems never to have come to White's life. This perhaps helps to explain the narrative progress of the *Autobiography* and its increasing emphasis through *Deliverance* on "digression." Unlike those of a writer like Lewis, who can deal with his life in terms of religious stages, White's books seem tied to a past that neither changes nor comes into meaningful focus. George Tyrrell will cut off phases of his past lives and speak of "finality." Kierkegaard looks forward to a newly enriched future, the past transformed. White seems more like the victim of his past described by Nietzsche, someone unable to "forget" or think toward a future, someone, as White himself would say, unable to put things in "perspective," except in terms of *waiting* and *endurance*. The result is a peculiar dialogue with his reader, the matter of which is the haunting residue of his own remembered experience. Although White's story of Mark Rutherford deals in its way with questions of time and eternity—as with personae—it makes of Mark Rutherford a victim and a sufferer; it is a story of Job for modern times, or a *Pilgrim's Progress* in which a wounded Christian never makes his way.

White longed to have it otherwise. Indeed if he could not attain the religious joy of a writer like Kierkegaard, he wanted at least the clear vision and the moral severity of Spinoza. His ambivalent views about confessional literature and rigorous belief emerge in his response to both Spinoza and Bunyan, though he refers only to Bunyan in *The Autobiography of Mark Rutherford*. White respects Bunyan as a spiritual predecessor, but his admiration for Spinoza is equally strong and oddly based. Despite Rutherford's distrust of system and codification, White admires in Spinoza a truth that is impersonal if not mathematical, hostile even more than himself to imagination or figurative language. Long before writing the Rutherford stories, he translated and wrote a commentary on what he called Spinoza's *Ethic*, the singular form indicative of his concerns. Spinoza, as one of the world's great thinkers, lived by his convictions and refused to compromise. For all White's ambivalence, he craves a Spinoza-like system: a system that clarifies and sanctions behavior, if need be at odds with the world around, a system that is explicable, rigorous, and infinitely larger than oneself. This man who kept lists of maxims and "dogmata"—appropriate he says for any occasion and a sure guide to none—admired in Spinoza what was lacking in himself: not just systematic thought, but also the logical and personal power to create "a religion of humanity."[30]

White was also to write a book about Bunyan, whom he respected for very different but overlapping reasons. Worlds apart as they are, Spinoza and Bunyan share for White an absolute commitment to truth, which even in Spinoza reflects an unattached and isolated vision. "There is no theological dogma so important," White says, "as the duty of veracity."[31] Bunyan was driven by rock-hard belief; Spinoza spoke fearlessly and unbendingly about what he deduced to be the truth. It is in the context of such powerful voices that White tries to find his own, aware not only of the discrepancy between the authority of those he admires and his relative insignificance, but also of the fact that he lives in similarly dispiriting times.

Part of White's admiration for Bunyan has to do with his implicit sense of Bunyan as a modern hero. He speaks of *Grace Abounding* as "a terrible story of the mental struggle of a man of genius of a peculiarly nervous and almost hypochondriacal temperament [in short, like White himself]; whose sufferings, although they are intertwisted with Puritanism, have roots which lie deep in our common nature."[32] White may be the first of those many English writers who, as Paul Fussell has shown, turned to Bunyan for a story of spiritual development while seeing their own lives as broken and discontinuous. Fussell describes later writers—Siegfried Sassoon is a case in point—who cope with the experiences of the Great War by allegorizing its horrors in relation to *Pilgrim's Progress* and *Grace Abounding*.[33]

One of Rutherford's allusions to Bunyan suggests how close he was in some ways, how far in others, from Bunyan's spirit. After disheartening episodes in two chapels, Rutherford ends his career as a clergyman and—like George Lewes's Ranthorpe, Thackeray's Pendennis, and so many other would-be authors—comes to London. Unable to see his way, Rutherford thinks of a temporary career as a teacher and secures a job as assistant master in a third-rate public school. He stays, however, only a matter of hours. Then, overwhelmed by his recovered freedom, his realization that he is not going to be another Mr. Mell, Rutherford describes his escape from the school, couching his language in metaphors of "arrest," "pursuit," "shrouds," and "fever," as though he has come through some long sickness or travail, the relief out of all proportion to the actual events or their capacity to hurt him. For this apparently minor and actually negative deliverance, "I literally cried tears of joy—the first and last of my life" (115). His honesty requires him to say that "my trouble was but a bubble blown of air," and he wonders, characteristically, "whether I have done any good by dwelling upon it" (115). He has as a matter of fact described a waking nightmare, in which the events and the emotions may be at odds but the feelings of fear, suffering, and claustrophobia are intense. Through much of his narrative, times of enclosure are times also of emotional power, whether in the chapel of his boyhood, the home of Ellen, his betrothed, when (as if to parody Kierkegaard) he escapes their engagement, or the office where he finally dies. As he looks out from the suburban school at the streets of London, the gloomy city becomes the place of deepest darkness, and it is in imagining those vast, fog-covered "regions" that he feels his most overwhelming panic. By contrast, the fields near his boyhood town and, toward the end of his life, the seashore, represent an escape, always expressed (like the Ilfracombe episode) in terms of light, space, and freedom from responsibility.

Although Rutherford ends his chapter of escape by wondering how he could have dwelled on anything so trivial, he begins the following chapter with the topic very much in mind. Within a few lines he is thinking of Mary, the woman he loves at the time, and of Bunyan, who helps him define his feelings, just as he has helped him shape the episode that has just occurred.

> When I had been lying alone and awake at night, I had thought of all the endless miles of hill and valley that lay outside my window, separating me from the one house in which I could be at peace.
>
> (116–17)

His language is suggestive. He inverts his usual pastoral oppositions in associating Mary with enclosure and the landscape with alienation and separation. Yet *peace* is still what he seeks, from the women he loves or from his religion. Peace means freedom from pain and suffering, avoidance rather than engagement. When thinking of "the endless miles," he is reminded—that is, consciously reminded—of Bunyan's Christian, at the same time recognizing in himself something of a fellow traveler:

> With the morning light, however, would come cooler thoughts, and a dull sense of impossibility. This, I know, was not pure love for her; it was a selfish passion for relief. But then I have never known what is meant by perfectly pure love. When Christian was in the Valley of the Shadow of Death, and, being brought to the mouth of hell, was forced to put up his sword, and could do no more than cry, *O Lord, I beseech Thee, deliver my soul,* he heard a voice going before him and saying,

> *Though I walk through the Valley of the Shadow of Death, I will fear none ill, for Thou art with me.* And by and by the day broke.
>
> (117)

Christian can sing of a "world of wonders," whereas Mark Rutherford can only upbraid himself for inadequate strength, love, and vision, or recollect past sufferings. Day breaks for him as it breaks for Tennyson in *In Memoriam*, without hope and without change. Rutherford even speaks of his allusion to Bunyan as yet another "digression," an index of his feelings but not of his spiritual or emotional progress.

To consider Rutherford's progress in relation to Bunyan is to understand an essential quality of the two books, for which *progress* is inappropriate and *stasis* or *recurrence* more to the point. Basil Willey has asked why the title of the second volume should have been *Deliverance*, inasmuch as Rutherford finds himself in the same fundamental dilemma even at the close of the second volume. "Deliverance from what? He was already emancipated from Bedford and its creed before the end of the *Autobiography*, and the second part is not warmed by any sense of final liberation from the ills that dogged him to the end: loneliness, self-distrust, nervous obsessions, speculative doubts, unsatisfied love." Willey interprets the deliverance as Rutherford's acceptance of White's own religion, a composite he says of Wordsworth and Spinoza, brought about by Rutherford's "returning upon himself, negating his own former negations." Then, too, his deliverance is a recognition of the social mission of Christianity, evidenced by Rutherford's work in the slums. Finally, deliverance comes in the form of conjugal love, since Rutherford marries his early love, Ellen (and Willey associates this with White's much later marriage to Dorothy V. Horace Smith, however strained the connection).[34] The difficulty with Willey's argument is clear from his own description of Rutherford's nondeliverance from his besetting conditions. Add to this that Wordsworth's God of the Hills seems to him inadequate, that unlike his author Rutherford seems not to be able to draw on Spinoza, whose ideas he neither mentions nor even approximates, and that he makes clear the inadequacy of his slum work, for which he is no more fitted than Ernest Pontifex in *his* comparable venture, and we are left with the realization that his deliverance is problematic at best. Perhaps his only real deliverance is death: his final escape from the insoluble burdens which he carries no less through the second volume than through the first.

Mark Rutherford's life has been compared with the pattern of negation, indifference, rediscovery, and dedication to be found in *Sartor Resartus,* a book with which he was very familiar. "It was," after all, "the *Heroes and Hero-Worship* and the *Sartor Resartus* which drew [Mark Rutherford] away from the meeting-house."[35] But again, to argue a shape or a progress where none exists is scarcely to flatter White, who knew full well his limitations as a storyteller and who was honest enough to accept that he had not found answers for Rutherford any more than he had found them, with certainty at least, for himself. Irresolution and lack of closure are the necessary if discomforting certainties in his displaced and indirect autobiographies. From Carlyle as from Bunyan he takes a welcome fervor and intensity, a *seriousness* of purpose, a hope for some sort of salvation. The result is less a pattern of conversion than a narrative meditation on his life; he tells of recurrence rather than renewal, self-immersion rather than what White says insistently he wants: the suppression or management of an unsatisfactory self.

This is to simplify. White was well aware of the complexity of "selves," and he was also alert to the problem of what he called "tampering with the self" (42), which he understands in terms of public responsibilities with their attendant risks of hypocrisy. Yet the management of self is a central concern in these books, Rutherford's death testifying to failure more than success. Rutherford dies, in fact, like his friend Edward Gibbon Mardon, of what is finally a loss of energy or joy rather than a disease, "atrophy," as he says of Mardon, the effect of "tragic" self-knowledge unaccompanied by self-fulfillment.

Adequately rendered, the Pilgrim's Progress of the soul through life should be as fascinating, even as noble a record, as Bunyan's, and still more instructive.

Havelock Ellis, My Life

To complete Mark Rutherford's stories, Reuben Shapcott adds an appendix of three short pieces by Rutherford, none of which, he says, found a publisher during Rutherford's lifetime. In a sense, the appendixes are an excuse for White to include some additional writing or maybe even a way of filling up his volume. The "Notes on the Book of Job"—part essay, part sermon, part exegesis—serve, however, an intrinsic purpose and tell rather more about the preceding book than about the book of Job. Here again White seems to imply the synecdochic quality of Rutherford's life, which is of a piece with all works of doubt and suffering, Job's not excepted.[36] With a predictable kind of intimacy, Rutherford follows the Job narrative step by step, as if the author sits in the room with Job, observing his responses while also shouldering his troubles. At the same time, the shift to Job implies just the perspective that White (like Dilthey) wants from autobiographical accounts but is unable to achieve with a more intimate persona.

Job is, says White, a *modern* book, for it deals with issues "resultlessly [sic] asked by us all" (282). It works experientially to show the difficulties of faith in the midst of suffering, the burden of guilt without a crime, with Job the intelligent, unbending analyst of his own condition, which remains of course an enigma. Isolated by his losses, dispossessed in the most elemental of ways, Job is for White the archetypal representative of a man needing signs from God that life is more than the punitive, inexplicable, and tragic process that it seems to be. He moves from Job's sufferings to mention a young woman he has known, someone of remarkable qualities who has, with her infant child, recently died. Can one protest? Is it possible to understand? How does suffering fit with a sense of the plenitude of nature or the hopes and aspirations of people? Beyond this, of course, how does one speak one's own suffering, even in the most intimate of documents, the autobiography? It is as though White needs another sort of format, a deflected, apparently impersonal medium to deal with what he could not fully come to terms with in the Rutherford autobiographies themselves. The commentary on the Book of Job involves further issues. I shall return to Kierkegaard's comment that Abraham and other passionate religious figures could not write their own stories. This is pertinent for White no less than for George Tyrrell. As he re-creates, or re-tells and observes Job's sufferings, White makes clear at least two of his own preoccupations: his distrust of argument, and his sense, like Tyrrell's, that suffering beggars our language. The "orthodoxy" of received interpretations ill serves Job, whose language is unmediated if unavoidably repetitious.

Throughout *Mark Rutherford's Autobiography* and *Deliverance* White has introduced discussions that test Rutherford's convictions or force his painful estimate of his spiritual condition. Edward Gibbon Mardon, the atheist, challenges Rutherford's belief, forces him to see that nonbelievers can live ethically defensible lives, just as they can die with dignity and without hope. In the House of Commons, Rutherford witnesses another form of debate: usually fruitless, senseless, and uninformed. Whether engaged in defining his own views or witnessing the discussions of others, he expresses his dislike of polemical exchanges, including the conflicts inherent in ordinary conversation. Feeling helpless in debate, he is convinced of its inutility. As he follows Job's arguments with Bildad or Eliphaz, his sympathy is naturally with Job—albeit he respects Job's friends for being friends—in part because Job is impatient with mere exchanges of words, in part because Job remains, finally, inarticulate about matters that will not bend to fit ordinary discourse.

When Mark Rutherford says, "I can never really speak myself" (89), he means that he gets bested in an argument, but more importantly he hints at a larger question of language and the expression of self. Language, he suggests, involves compromise, accommodation, whereas "Job is the type of those great thinkers who cannot compromise; who cannot say *but yet;* who faithfully follow their intellect to its very last results, and admit all its conclusions" (284). We can see here a further reason for White's thinking Job to be "terribly modern" (282), with *terribly* holding its original power. Rejecting like Christ the "platitudes of the theologians" (284), Job is not content with easy solace or simplified explanations, and he is as a consequence alone in his suffering. Since he understands Job to be a thinker, White appreciates his independence in relation to "modern" problems of faith and dogma, but not without contradictions of some of his other statements. If "the example of Job protects us from the charge of blasphemy in not suppressing our doubts" (282), how are we to accept the dismissal of someone like Francis Newman because he expresses *his* doubts? We have to assume opposing qualities in White's temperament. He shares with John Henry Newman and Matthew Arnold a reluctance to trouble the incapable many with the problems of the enlightened few, although for White the reasons have to do with his background in Dissent, which left him with a conviction of *"distinction, difference,* a higher and a lower" (85), elect and nonelect. If he thinks of himself as among the elect, his fear of excessive "egotism" (57) diminishes his sense of worth, which he measures in terms of the abysses and crumbling foundations, darkness or failing light. This involves, in Paul De Man's terms, "defacement" of an acute order, the continuous creation of an unstable text "that undoes the model as soon as it is established."[37] Projecting through Rutherford and other personifications of his dilemmas, White imagines analogous suffering and isolation, his own buried self unavailable for the kind of self-knowledge he seeks.

White seems to know the value of his tortured, fictional projection and to be proud of attained "calm" or "endurance" (206). With its sense of "passion spent," "calm" is what White admires in his character Miss Arbour, who tells Rutherford the story of her life from a distance of years, with her suffering in perspective. And perhaps the artifice of a Reuben Shapcott or a Mark Rutherford (or Mark Rutherford's death) affords White the emotional distance he needs from his life in order to be able to tell it. Evidently wanting to understand his life-struggles in the paradigmatic terms of a Christ or a Job, to see himself as a representative sufferer, though with a distinctive sense of life's tragedy, White tacitly announces his right to speak, to offer his unresolved and unresolvable self-history as a helpful model. While he cannot approximate "joy" or speak about passionate "love" and "enthusiasm," he can, like Tyrrell, report the privations of a negative way to truth.

THE AUTOBIOGRAPHY OF FATHER GEORGE TYRRELL

> *The secret of the fascination of the historical past is due to the transfiguring action of memory. Memory does not restore the past as it was, it transforms the past, transforms it into something which is eternal.*
> Nicolas Berdyaev, The Beginning and the End

As we have seen with William Hale White, there are special problems for the spiritual autobiographer, who may, like Berdyaev, feel that memory can transform the past, but who worries about responding adequately to the future or living with full, ethical responsibility in the present. This was Kierkegaard's fear, in *Repetition,* for example, or in *The Concept of Anxiety,* where he essentially ridiculed a division of time into past, present, and future while dismissing personal history and, under various pseudonyms, writing it to prove his point. The true believer cannot so aestheticize or distance himself from his work. Abraham could not write his own history. It is only by an act of transfiguring, or transcending, the past that one avoids indulgent nostalgia, or the bondage of the uncommitted soul.

George Tyrrell's reluctant autobiography engages such issues. Apprehensive about the self-indulgence he thinks necessary for the recollecting of his life, Tyrrell like White is aware of the risks inherent in the telling. In the first place, he has an ineradicable distrust of language, speaking in *The Soul's Orbit* (1904) of "the utter inadequacy of even the most delicate wording."[38] With Kierkegaard, he seems to think that the telling of self histories involves an aestheticizing, an escaping from moral and religious engagement, which he associates with present moments of authentic and timeless revelation, each Christian intuiting the epiphanic experiences of Christ—who, presumably, could not write his autobiography either.

Whenever he speaks of personal reflection, or memory and recollection, Tyrrell implies its necessity and its pitfalls. He sees personal writing as a form of confession, but he distrusts both himself and the process. Even religious confession is, he says, subject to dissembling. "For it is not the sin, but the verbal description of the sin, upon which the confessor passes judgment; and the relation of the latter to the former is, at the very best, . . . much like the relation of a rough etching to the palpitating life of a natural landscape."[39] Tyrrell seems to have little faith in an understanding God; nor, despite his increasing "dissent" from church doctrines, does he, like the Dissenters, admit the possibility of a direct address to God. With chronic ambivalence, Tyrrell can speak of a kind of eternal recurrence, of a historic and personal past working as Berdyaev suggests; yet for Tyrrell the recovery of his own past serves less to reveal its internal qualities than to demonstrate the crooked and unpredictable ways required toward insight and faith.

Tyrrell began his life story "to make a review of what the Curé d'Ars calls *ma pauvre vie.*"[40] He would not, he says, have begun at all without the urging of his friend Maude Petre, who, some years after Tyrrell's early death, published the unfinished autobiography along with a supplementary, biographical account of Tyrrell's life from 1884 to his death, in 1909. The circumstances of his writing may recall those of Carl Jung, whose autobiography originated at the suggestion and with the help of Aniela Jaffé. The more Jung explored his own earlier life, the more meaningful and compelling the project became, so that Jung himself finally assumed the writing of *Memories, Dreams, Reflections.* Although Tyrrell approached his autobiography with fewer reservations than Jung, he apparently wrote with increasing aversion, ultimately giving to Maude Petre both the unfinished manuscript and the right to do with it as she saw fit.[41] Jung grew to appreciate his life and could see his boyhood in relation to the powerful psychic forces and collective memories which occupied his professional speculations; Tyrrell faced a more disquieting recognition. Whether he no longer found the leisure for what he thought a self-indulgent project, or whether he lost interest in his life (in a double sense of the word), he was appalled at the discrepancy between his earlier self, with its innocence and love, and the Jesuit priest who now looked back. Aware of himself as "an unconscious disciple of Nietzsche" (93), Tyrrell deplored what he accepted, stunned by his "tragic" vision, by his need to revise his past, and by a playing of "roles" that implied an invented or inauthentic self. No wonder he reconstructed his memories with growing unease.

As life grows more complex every year one lives, each new experience being the resultant of one's whole past and present conditions, it becomes less and less capable of sure analysis and of any sort of simplification. It were easier almost to find a unifying law for the whole of physical nature than for the chaotic world of one's own soul.
George Tyrrell, Autobiography (149)

Tyrrell's is a remarkable autobiography. He wrote most of it around his fortieth birthday, dating one section, "February 6, 1901" (149), to indicate his own stage of life and the turning of the century.[42] What he wanted from the candid "analysis" or retrospect was some glimmer, if not of a unifying law, at least of purpose and meaning. He confided in this way to Maude Petre:

> I began the story of my paltry life a few days ago, but was interrupted by other work. As soon as there is enough to make it worthwhile, I will send it. But I am writing so principally for my own sake, in order to piece together this battered personality of mine into some flattering semblance of unity and coherence, that much detail will be absolutely unintelligible to you, and what, to me, is a bond of countless memories, and a fountain of tears or laughter, to you will be as lifeless as an unknown lock of hair.[43]

Few statements could say more about Tyrrell and the autobiography he was beginning, except that little in his story is "lifeless" and that it is unlikely readers would dismiss his memories without the tears and the laughter. As perhaps he recognized, a disclaimer intended to warn his reader serves also to entice. Tyrrell insists that he is writing "purely for my own sake" (1), with no thought of publication; yet, as his letter suggests, he is conscious of an audience for whom events may be unintelligible or to whom he may be making illegitimate demands for sympathy and approval, and he will settle for nothing but the most deflating and punishing of confessions.

While Tyrrell is not always so ruthless in asserting the insignificance of his life, he typically refers to it as "paltry," "crooked," or "uninteresting." In his own mind almost preternaturally distant from himself, he says that "nobody could approach himself more impartially, or with greater detachment, or even dislike, than I do" (2). The dislike is obvious, the detachment less so. Despite the gulf of years, Tyrrell still speaks with passion about events and about people; and though self love comes hard for that broken or "battered personality," love for family and friends does not. Nor, oddly enough, does the laughter. Consistently deploring a lack of humor, Tyrrell thinks of "earnestness" as a nasty quality. He can quote the famous "Oh God, if there is a God, save my soul, if I have a soul," and then add that he has never been sanguine about his own salvation. He comments on "'the world'—a term which, in the mind of a Jesuit novice, embraces the somewhat mysterious and profane fraction of the universe which lies outside the college of the Society" (200). "Facts," he says at another time, "are stranger than Cardinals."[44] His humor is rarely "detached" or distant, or apparently consoling; it seems instead to maintain the ironies of his life as Tyrrell recalls them and to insist on their full emotional force, then and now.

Tyrrell was born into an evangelical, Anglican family in Dublin. His father, an impecunious but evidently gifted journalist, died before George was born, leaving the family in difficult circumstances. "Adrift" is the word Tyrrell uses to describe the family's makeshift and usually inadequate attempts at lodging and subsistence. (The story, with one residence like Leopold Bloom's on Eccles Street, suggests the life of a Stephen Dedalus who chose to become a Jesuit priest.) Sensing like Samuel Butler that we are in incomprehensible ways our ancestors, Tyrrell speculates about his dead father, whose very handwriting seems identical to his own, and who becomes across the years so important to the son he never knew. Tyrrell emphasizes his father's quick temper and his integrity, qualities he sees within himself. His older brother, Willie, also shared certain of his father's traits. Surviving a nursery accident, Willie lived his short life tormented by physical handicaps and intense pain. Gifted with extraordinary intellectual abilities, he distinguished himself at school and at Trinity and began, before his death, to make an academic reputation. Tyrrell contrasts himself with Willie, whose almost cynical atheism challenges his younger brother and whose death is another milestone in Tyrrell's growing up.

> Some would say that Willie's death was for me providential, so much did I fear and yield to his keen, ruthless, iconoclastic logic, and feel my mental inferiority. For myself I am too much oppressed with the complexity of good and evil ever to dare to determine what is and what is not providential. If Providence had been disposed to upset the established order of things in favour of my valuable soul, I cannot understand why the intervention was not earlier and more effectual, as judged by common sense.
>
> (116)

As if looking with Willie's own "satirical eyes" on the effect of his brother's death, Tyrrell refuses either to discount the loss or to exploit it.

In addition to Willie, Tyrrell's family included his mother and a sister, Louy (Louisa), apparently a quiet and emotionally dependent girl, who idolized her brother; he feels her absence when she enters a convent and associates her with the other family losses, the most painful of which is his mother's death. The *Autobiography* begins with thoughts about the father Tyrrell never met and continues with the remembered heartache of his mother's love. In treating his mother's death and his sister's retreat into a convent, Tyrrell comes to a realization probably unanticipated at the beginning of his autobiography and no doubt disconcerting to himself as a Catholic priest. He discovers how much his family and his love for his family matter, and how little—good friend though he was to many people—his latter relationships and emotions mean to him. In spite of organizing his life as a development toward the church and his profession, he insists on a counterdirection, mourning his loss and deprivation. He speaks with pride about his "God-given natural affections, . . . which even Jesuit asceticism can never wholly uproot" (278), and the characteristic organic metaphor makes clear both the strength of his emotions and the repulsion he felt for his chosen profession.

At the time he wrote his *Autobiography,* Tyrrell was already involved in the struggle with his order that would lead, eventually, to dismissal and denial of the sacraments. As he recalls his slow process toward conversion, his infatuation with ritual, his recognition one day in London of his sympathy with Catholic worshippers, he always distinguishes between the church and the Jesuits, even hinting at one point that he chose the Jesuits because he thought them, of all the orders, the one lax enough to admit George Tyrrell (139). For Tyrrell as for White and Edmund Gosse, there came no dramatic conversion, nothing like the sudden and absolute experience of Augustine, changed utterly in that garden in Milan.

How much Tyrrell's unhappinesss informed his remembering would be hard to say. Wilfrid Ward argued that Tyrrell grossly overstated his early sins or personal failings, and no doubt his ironical commentary on his conversion or his disaffection with the Jesuits intensified with the years.[45] But some reluctance or distrust came early. He mentions several times his temptation not to continue as a novice, his sense of waste or repugnance. Clearly yearning for the authority of the church—perhaps even joining the church because it provided authority—he developed a distrust of and distaste for arbitrary power that made accommodation with the church almost impossible. The signs were there from the beginning; the real problems came later. After ordination, he performed several kinds of responsibilities, apparently with success and satisfaction. He worked among the Catholic poor in St. Helens, Lancashire, taught in a seminary, and wrote for Jesuit papers. Assigned to the Jesuit establishment in Farm Street, he emerged as an articulate spokesman, defending his order as well as his chosen faith, and was soon recognized to be an influential writer. Then by the mid-1890s, he began to take a more independent and, to his superiors, more troubling course. Friendships with men like Baron von Hügel, who introduced him to the thinking of Loisy and other radical Catholics, led Tyrrell to further questioning, if not at first about the Catholic church as such, certainly its present direction and its respective orders, his own above all. Increasingly he spoke about the importance of *experimental* and *internal* approaches to faith, expressing dissatisfaction with dogma, formalism, Papal authority, and, as he put it (in 1899 lectures to Oxford undergraduates), with "external religion."[46]

By the turn of the century he tended to emphasize two problematic, and essentially "modern," ideas: the immanence of God in everyday life; and what he, like his contemporary Miguel de Unamuno, calls "the tragic sense of life." Tyrrell speaks about tragedy a number of times in the *Autobiography,* and he seems to have in mind a complex of assumptions, including the inevitable disappointment of life, the lack of fulfillment, the conspiring of circumstances, and the limited solace provided by organized religion. Shortly before beginning his autobiography, he wrote, "In fine Christianity is in the hands of Christians like the *Imitatio Christi* in the hands of a child—it has no meaning for him now, but he may grow to its meaning when he has tried life and found it a failure."[47]

Not uncharacteristically, he is inconsistent about his sense of tragedy, which is sometimes a universal condition and sometimes his own. He says that "a certain stoical indifference as to the future . . . is not fatalism but faith,"[48] and also that there "is no such thing as chance" (121). Elsewhere he says that "our fate is determined by straws," with the course of history altered by a fleck of dust in a man's eye (94). The tragic condition seems at one time to be a matter of fate or luck, at another time to be the state of mind of any religious person who seeks in vain for signs of God. And here a further problem arises. If it is the individual soul that apprehends God, and if God's signs are few in a world that would seem, says Tyrrell, to be of the Devil's making, what does this imply about the confessional process? "It is," Tyrrell says (in *Nova et Vetera*), "the lingering memory of . . . [Christ] that sets the soul aglow with passionate love." Unfortunately, such spiritual memory, which is both personal and cultural, is offset by "the false joy of pride and self-satisfaction arising from continual self-remembrance and self-contemplation—the 'fool's paradise,' in which we dream our dreams."[49] Like Wilhelm Dilthey and William Hale White, he can argue for the necessity of confessional writing while doubting its efficacy.

No less than his countryman George Moore, Tyrrell appreciated Walter Pater's *Marius the Epicurean,* which he found "strangely fascinating," because it appeared to contrast so utterly with his own kind of thinking. With an almost willful ignoring of Pater's interior vision, he said that Pater "gives one that 'far off' and 'from outside' view of life which is so healthy and needful a tonic for those like myself, who are apt to take their part in the drama a little too seriously, and miss the divine humour of it all."[50] Tyrrell does not mention Pater's "The Child in the House" (1878) with its third-person but otherwise "inside" view of childhood and with its suppressed pain about the process of growing up. But "the child" or Marius or those other more or less doomed young men who appealed to Pater speak to Tyrrell's own assessed condition. Occasionally Tyrrell will try a "from outside" view, but the tendency of his writing was, no less than Pater's, in another direction, which he at once distrusts and advocates. "There is less apology needed," he writes to introduce *Oil and Wine* (in 1900), "than might perhaps appear at first sight for offering to the public a book which is hardly more than a record of private musings."[51] His justification is that, while private musings may introduce nothing new, they can express the "passion" and the love essential for religious intuition. Life may be designed to disappoint, yet only through a sort of dark night of the soul can lasting insight emerge. Invoking one of his favorite analogues, Tyrrell speaks of Dante's *silva oscura,* through which we must descend "to the very depths of Hell, before we can again behold the stars."[52]

Dante represents for Tyrrell the ultimate spokesman for "Mid Life." And few people have been more obsessed—or repulsed—by their own middle age than Tyrrell himself. *Nova and Vetera* (1897), *External Religion* (1899), and *Oil and Wine* (withdrawn but ready for publication in 1900) all focus on moments of personal and religious crisis, which Tyrrell explores from his own idiosyncratic perspective. It is as though he sees, like White or Francis Newman, that "each self is unique," while at the same time he reduces all lives to a kind of predictable and sad paradigm: "In the history of each one," he writes in *The Soul's Orbit,* "is the same oft-repeated tale, of early hope and confidence, shattered by sad experience, recovered in lowliness and faith."[53] Even then the remaining faith seems to bring little personal or professional satisfaction. Letters of the time, like the *Autobiography* itself, show that Tyrrell appreciated the implications of his books, the likelihood that they would lead to his separation, if not dismissal, from the order, and that they expressed a point of view at odds with the entire direction of the church. In these works Tyrrell explores a range of theological issues, including "development," the immanence of the divine spirit, the functions of language in religious thought, the status of church authority, and the role of "private judgment" and "inward experience."

Tyrrell's importance as a Catholic thinker has been recognized in recent years, and he has been described, along with Newman, as one of two distinguished English Catholic theologians.[54] No less than Cardinal Newman, Tyrrell can be understood as a profoundly personal thinker, someone who construes religious matters in terms of his own life or situation. Tyrrell might have said, with Cardinal Newman, as with Francis Newman: "It is not at all pleasant for me to be egotistical; nor to be criticized for being so."[55] But as he himself was well aware, Tyrrell differed from John Henry Newman in fundamental ways. He was not a systematic or consistent thinker, and he approached religion with a deep-seated distrust of theology. His writings insist on the ways by which theological and authoritarian thinking obtrude in religious experience, hurting individuals and rendering the church itself unfit for its essential tasks. Although he never seems to address the paradox of his own attraction to and revulsion from authority, which is at the heart of his dilemma, Tyrrell was a prolific writer about theological matters, rather few of which he left untouched. He should be appreciated, in Nicholas Sagovsky's phrase, as a "theological journalist,"[56] whose books are heterogeneous collections of essays and diverse pieces, often reflective of contemporary events, drawn together for republication. At his best, he writes aphoristic, exploratory work, tied closely to his own agonized searching and addressed, openly and fearlessly, to a diversity of listeners.

Tyrrell accepted his tendency not only to change his ideas in response to new readings and experiences, which he knew to be healthy, but also to write in heat and anger, so that he often forgot what he had said earlier and slipped into inconsistency and contradiction. In this he resembles Samuel Butler, who also argues the paradoxical nature of language and definition, assuming that "contradiction belongs to thoughts, not to things" (202) and that unity and meaning escape mere intellection. Because of his crushing spiritual struggles, however, Tyrrell's inconsistency involves more fundamental problems than Butler's. Without citing Pascal, his parallel sense of human contradiction, of man as the opposite of himself, comes close to Pascal, whom Lucien Goldmann calls "the first modern man."[57] Pascal would not perhaps have thought of himself as "modern"; George Tyrrell did.

In the name of truth, Tyrrell spoke for reform of his order and wholesale change in church policy, along with an implied and unattainable standard of behavior for himself. His championing of "modernist" principles—specifically the opening of the church to larger groups of people, its acceptance of greater social responsibilities, its acknowledgment of scientific and other intellectual findings—led him to increasingly perilous relationships with superiors who admired him and wanted nothing more than his continued work as church apologist.

The church delayed publication of *Oil and Wine*, a kind of essayistic equivalent of the *Autobiography*, even though Tyrrell intended to issue it anonymously (a practice he came to use without scruple whenever he felt it imperative to express his ideas). There were even greater difficulties with the later writings. Before the final rift with his order, Tyrrell had relentlessly challenged antagonists, caught, as the title to one book suggests, "between Scylla and Charybdis," between the rock of the church and his own unbending will to speak.[58] Whether he "burned himself out" in a decade of frenetic and polemical writing,[59] he certainly described his horror of all religious strife while conceding its necessity: "Controversy is in some sense the indispensable condition of our progress in the apprehension of truth."[60]

Tyrrell's fatalism (or as he would say, his faith) seemed to court an open condemnation, which finally came. Nor did Tyrrell relent after being dismissed by his order. When the *Pascendi* (1907) of Pius x singled him out with other modernists, Tyrrell did the inexcusable. Writing for more than Catholic readers in letters to the *Times* and the *Giornale d'Italia*, he openly criticized the Pope, as if demanding what he had both dreaded and willed. Rome more or less excommunicated him, denying him the sacraments. He died soon after of Bright's disease, unforgiven and unrepentent.[61]

Relatively little of Tyrrell's polemical activities enter into his autobiography. Since the narrative time of the book ends before his ordination, it does not come to terms with the man's troubled professional career, however much it implies the issues and principles that drove him into isolation. But as a ledger of loss and gain (Tyrrell uses Cardinal Newman's terms frequently), the story of his early years and his movement toward conversion is a clear accounting. It makes obvious, for example, that Tyrrell faces the telling of his professional life with reluctance. Indeed, that such a prolific writer would leave his autobiography unfinished suggests that he found it disheartening to deal with the later years, recognizing how disparate and shattered his life had become. In this acceptance, it becomes clear how different Tyrrell's sense of his life was from William Hale White's. White would do almost anything to escape confrontations, even to the extent of avoiding a potential adversary like Tyrrell. And though White's resolution of religious and personal matters seems no more convincing than Tyrrell's, his displaced or indirect autobiography at least announces order and resolution. Tyrrell's book, written to piece together "this battered personality," could not be finished. It remains a poignant and fragmentary attempt to set things in order before Tyrrell turned once again to the life he had come to hate and could not avoid: the life of controversy, dissension, and uncertainty.

> To seize each "now" and make the very best of it, is, in some sense, the secret of a successful life; for past and future are imaginary, whereas the "now" is real. Yet on closer inspection this "now" dwindles into a metaphysical abstraction, a mere point between past and future—between our memories and our expectation; and what we really live on is retrospect and prospect.
>
> Tyrrell, Oil and Wine

Like the philosopher F. H. Bradley, Tyrrell contemplated the meanings of a "dwindling" or what Bradley called a "degraded" present consciousness, a "qualitative point" without which there can be neither meaning nor direction to our lives.[62] This is the import of Tyrrell's beginning passage of the *Autobiography,* with its uncharacteristic optimism and lightheartedness: "It seems to me that our experience is given to us to be the food of our character and spiritual life; but, in point of fact, we spend our whole life in storing up food, and never have the leisure to lie down quietly, with the cows in the field, and ruminate, bit by bit, what we have swallowed so hastily" (1). However much pastoral undertones recur throughout the book, this is the last time Tyrrell speaks about leisure, almost the last time he mentions food, which he seems to have disliked, and perhaps the last time he implies the possibility of "a successful life." Drawn with both pleasure and dismay to his past, this Jesuit priest has surprisingly little to say about things to come: "retrospect," in his own words, overwhelms "prospect."

Memory had, for Tyrrell, legitimate if sometimes dubious claims. I have mentioned the attack on "continual self-remembrance" in *External Religion* (1899), with the admonition to remember the model and the sufferings of Christ, the risks, that is, of self-indulgent rumination. In *Oil and Wine,* Tyrrell recognizes a more sophisticated function of memory and testifies repeatedly to the need for "a satisfactory retrospect," for an interlocking "mosaic of memory," which like a number of his contemporaries he associates with "unity of the race."[63] By the time Sigmund Freud published *Interpretation of Dreams* (1899), Tyrrell was speculating about the importance of a "subconscious" self, evidently convinced like Samuel Butler that important matters are always "entrusted . . . to subconscious thought" (187). He was to call the subconscious the "not present," or the past and future of ourselves, well aware of the dubious stature of present consciousness and the murky difficulties of separating present from past, present from future, or subconscious from conscious self.

Tyrrell's preoccupation with an elusive and at times hated self is, then, intimately connected with his sense of the complexities of time and memory. Throughout the *Autobiography* he explores the one in relation to the other, asking about the present self looking back, the nature of the self observed, the ties between a historical past and memory, and the selecting and judging necessitated by the perspective of the immediate present. His distinction between the "then-self" and the "now-self" (41), as he calls them, draws attention to the changes in people and the complications of remembering, but it also implies the continuity of the "then-self" in ways available only to subconscious remembering. "For with the soul . . . there is a continual circulation between earlier and later, past and present, each portion of experience flowing into and modifying all the rest; so that every memory . . . is modified by the changing self of each moment." Because memory is so intangible and because the evocation of memories is subject to competing pressures, "we cannot remember the same thing twice in the same way" (41). Tyrrell recognizes that "the view one takes of one's present self" makes the act of writing an autobiography inherently "questionable" (42); and he is forced, here and elsewhere, to ask about his recollection, to wonder about kinds of recollection, from earliest memories to the substance of knowledge. He both distrusts the functions of memory and bemoans his own inadequate remembering.

Like radically different autobiographical writers—Rousseau, for example, or Restif de la Bretonne—Tyrrell seems to take pride in saying the worst of himself, as though, as I have suggested, confession requires the minutest revelation of fault, or as though confession in a literary form approximates the confessing of sins.[64] Doubtless, too, there is something self-protective in telling himself and his friends to expect little of him. Yet he knows that even his minimal self-regard, his hopes for himself at the present moment, push toward formal and unifying arrangement, the more so because he wants to make sense of his life and accepts his autobiography as a means to that end. Throughout his book he speaks about things "whole," things in "context" missing in his life and perhaps only discoverable through his written life. If he can "pull the whole thread [of his story] out of my mouth," he says, using the legendary figure, things may be made "whole."[65] The thread, alas, may not be reliable. "Nothing," he says, "would be easier and pleasanter than to run on, *currente calamo,* with the story of one's life, as it surges up in imagination, bit by bit; and, with a few additions and suppressions, it might make an agreeable work of fiction; but fiction it would be none the less, whereas truth alone is in quest at present" (42). At odds are the possibly fictionalized versions of selected and edited memories and a hypothetical ideal of ruthless truth-telling, itself inseparable from selecting and editing. Tyrrell seems to acknowledge the irony but not the necessity of irony in the very act of writing. He does acknowledge the changing nature of recollections, from the first little streams to the later "rolling flood" (42).

Tyrrell hates nothing more than show or pretense, which he attacks in a variety of forms throughout his narrative, and the love of which, ironically, had helped to nudge him in the direction of the Catholic church. "Self deception" or inadvertent pretense is the besetting difficulty in autobiographical writing. But how to decide between episodes of one's life? How to know what is self-inflating? How to choose the revealing and the convincing words? This dilemma, this struggle between irreconcilable poles of rhetoric and "truth-telling," emerges in two contradictory kinds of comments. In one passage, Tyrrell praises Dickens as the master portrayer of "genteel" families, wishing for his skill (73). But such skill is of course that of the fiction writer, whose work Tyrrell finds at odds with his own task. Indeed, "the very style . . . of this analysis which I make of myself may perhaps tend to falsify things, by reflecting my present mind" (106). Tyrrell is saying more than that it "is difficult for a man of forty to think of himself as a child of seven or eight, except in the light of later years" (41), albeit this is at the heart of the difficulty. He is facing the kinds of issues that troubled both Rousseau, for whom most kinds of literature but novels especially were a betrayal of individuality, and Augustine, his begrudged but unavoidable authority.

Much as he disliked "the jargon of Augustinian theology" (121), Tyrrell admired Augustine the confessor. "Like the youthful Augustine," he says at one point, "I was ashamed of my scruples" (93–94). He seems to understand his life as a kind of bad reflection, or "reflex," as he would say, of Augustine, who, in spite of being a dogmatic church father, wrote the basic text on matters of self and time. When (in a letter of 1900) he cites Augustine on time, he implies some of the paradoxes of memory in their relation to the enigma of language: "It is Augustine's view about time; Don't ask me what it is and I know; ask me, and I don't know."[66] Augustine looms large in Tyrrell's autobiography, as an enabling model and as a tyrannical authority.

In the tenth book of the *Confessions,* Augustine looks back not only on his own life but on the account he has written about his life, now complete. At first he seems elated. He knows that without memory he would not be what he is, would not be able to pay tribute to God for the shape of his life, would not have the capacity for understanding or confession. Memory may be self-deceiving, arbitrary, even boastful, but it is what distinguishes us from animals and propels us toward God. Augustine begins to play, however, with disturbing questions. If, as he insists, memory is not merely an instrument that we use but also a capacity both unpredictable and overwhelming, then memory becomes almost Godlike.

> Great is the power of memory, exceeding great is it, O God, an inner chamber, vast and unbounded! Who has penetrated to its very bottom? Yet it is a power of my mind and it belongs to my nature, and thus I do not comprehend all that I am. Is the mind, therefore, too limited to possess itself? . . . . Great wonder arises within me at this. Amazement seizes me. Men go forth to marvel at the mountain heights, at huge waves in the sea, at the broad expanse of flowing rivers, . . . but themselves they pass by.[67]

The apparent directionlessness of remembering, implicitly contradicted by a forward, narrative process, can be circular as well as linear, tangential as well as purposive. Augustine is fascinated by the power of memory to return and recapture (Ralph Harper has shown how his metaphors closely parallel those of Proust),[68] and his heavy quotation from the Bible suggests a constant recalling of known and resonant contexts. Since Augustine speaks often about returning to his mother's faith, the implication is of opposing directions, a forward inevitability complemented but possibly undercut by the need to go back. The depths of memory and its potential to move in different directions, often unpredictably, raise the possibility of rival narratives, drawn as they may be from the same limitless store of experience, with the hint that his story may finally be arbitrary or even fictional.

Augustine's sense of memory, like his sense of time, seems to shift with the process of exploration. In the passage cited by Tyrrell, he says of memory what he says of time: that he knows what it is until he tries to say what it is. "I name memory, and I recognize what I name. Where do I recognize it unless in memory itself?"[69] Since memory can only be known as an image of itself, our whole sense of a personal past and thus our sense of identity may be illusory. By the end of the chapter Augustine's pursuit of paradox has led to contradictions, for though memory at first distinguishes us from beasts, Augustine comes to acknowledge that beasts too have memory; and hence memory can only serve as one more additional step in the complex, often retrograde, journey toward God. To the extent that Augustine's perplexities can be resolved by his appeal to the incorporative memory of God—passing "beyond this power of nature"[70]—complete remembering implies the sort of timelessness posited in Kierkegaard's theory of repetition, along with its implied strictures on confessional or autobiographical narrative.

Tyrrell's own questions about memory would seem to grow out of, just as they echo, Augustine's; the applications of the questions are, however, quite different, not only because Tyrrell's thinking reflects philosophical speculation of his own era, but more importantly because he finds for himself so little of the confidence underlying Augustine's work. He can never assume the authoritative tone of Augustine, who knows the paradigmatic quality of his thinking and his life much as he may understand life as trial and hardship.

The contrast with Augustine suggests how remote Tyrrell felt himself to be from authoritarian church fathers, how near to some of his contemporaries. As with White, his quoting from Tennyson's *In Memoriam* illustrates complicated feelings: " . . . an infant crying in the night / And with no language but a cry."[71] Apart from emphasizing the vulnerable child, Tyrrell associates his life with the failure of language, which remains, for all crucial purposes, inadequate. This means that his own language is mixed, its resonances incorporating, with the Biblical echoes of an Augustine, some of the crabbed and exploratory styles of his early contemporaries. Tennyson seems especially to have appealed to him. When Tyrrell published his *Versions and Perversions* (a book of translated poems with some original verses of his own), he chose especially poems of Heine emphasizing grief, loss, anguish, and the inability to find appropriate words. Included among these works is his own imitation of stanzas from *In Memoriam:*

Enough, enough, one glimmering spark
  From worlds beyond this world of Night,
  Forgive, O Sun and source of light,
A foolish child that feared the dark.[72]

In the *Autobiography* itself, Tyrrell relies on such metaphors, while projecting himself as a kind of innocent, or fallen innocent. He looks back on himself as a boy—much as Ford Madox Ford was to do—as someone *very* small, very helpless. The loss of innocence is a challenge to discover what his life has meant, to make sense of it one more time. There are, nonetheless, underlying anomalies, and these raise once again the connection with Augustine. Although repeatedly reminding himself and his readers that we do not live for ourselves alone, Tyrrell almost seems to pride himself on the singularity of his feelings. When he echoes David Copperfield's perception, "What trifles to record!", he asserts once more that the trifles are for him alone: "They interest me, and it is for myself I write, though the very act of writing or speaking calls up an imaginary reader, who will say: What intolerable egotism!"[73] He is, again, continually aware of the imaginary reader, but the reader overhears a kind of soliloquy, whereas Augustine's reader listens to what amounts to Augustine's humble but self-assured dialogue with God. A full reckoning of sin and salvation may, as Augustine suggests, seem redundant in the eyes of God and still serve as a useful document for fellow human beings, those at least who can be relied upon to read it for other than salacious curiosity. In this way the confessor's remembered journey toward God becomes an index to readers who might, perhaps, take a moral shortcut toward grace. For Tyrrell's imagined audience there is an altogether different role. Dismayed at people "loving me for what I was not,"[74] he appeals to the reader to judge, to criticize, with perhaps a tacit appeal for sympathy. Nowhere does he disdain his reader or assume a superior moral position. This is not Tyrrell the polemicist speaking with derision or pronouncing with a Chesterton-like glibness, but rather a man reaching for his audience through painful self-scrutiny.

By contrast we might think of another Anglo-Irishman who wrote "confessions" with Augustine's model in mind. George Moore presents the trivial or "banal" details from his experience to enjoy the reminiscence or to explore the memories for their own sake, as if—to use Tyrrell's metaphor—"ruminating" on his past in moments of leisure. For Moore, the piecing together is as incidental as the self-judging. He speaks about loss and change and appreciates, like Augustine, the extraordinary powers of memory as a sign of humanity. Only in the concluding chapter of *Memoirs of My Dead Life* he is overwhelmed by the emotions recollected and generated in his telling, as if taken by surprise. Even at the end, however, Moore's story remains aggressively provisional, the fictive materials gladly admitted, whereas Tyrrell clearly wants a final, composite account of his life thus far.

Final is, in fact, the word that might occur to any of his readers, for the author will never want to subject himself again to such analysis; nor does he seem to think there will be a chance. With the quality of a final testament, his book is reminiscent of confessions by seventeenth-century Quakers and other Dissenters, who offer their written lives ostensibly for the benefit of their children and coming generations.[75] At the same time, much of the poignancy of Tyrrell's book comes from the end of family and continuity, all of which he implies in "a good-bye forever" to his boyhood (138).

With his appreciation of paradox, Tyrrell can speak, like Augustine, of the circularity of memory and the fusion of "earlier and later, past and present," and at the same time think of his life as so many definite phases of change or progression. In the next—and last—section, I want to look at two opposing views in the *Autobiography*, both essentially retrospective: one has to do with the sense of finality, or endings, the other with life and growth.

> *Organic growth, whether of plant or animal but more especially in the case of higher animals, is characterized by a sort of backward process, as though what is last should be first; and what first, last. There is throughout an anticipation of, and preparing for, what is to come; and much that is at the time unmeaning and aimless finds its justification fully but only in the finished work.*
> Tyrrell, Oil and Wine

Prodigal of metaphors as he was, Tyrrell perhaps resorts to that of growth more than to any other, even including journeys and seeing. He thinks of growth in a variety of ways, as though "organic growth" subsumes his other metaphors or gives them meaning. Hence "progress" in the realm of science and ideals, the development of individual lives, even of "the whole race," spiritual development, the intellectual movement of cultures: all appear to him as part of a "dynamic view" of change and growth.[76] In the *Autobiography*, Tyrrell does not emphasize what he elsewhere holds up as essential for the church to consider: the scientific world of evolution and entropy, of immeasurable time and space, which force new questions about humanity and its beliefs. But the reference to organic growth in the contemporary *Oil and Wine* makes clear Tyrrell's understanding of growth and development as related to scientific discoveries, and he implies, like Samuel Butler, the continuity of memory in that backward process which links us with other creatures as well as with our earlier selves. Only in retrospective vision can the signs be seen or the meanings understood.

Apart from evolution and that whole dark backward and abysm of time, the retrogressive process for Tyrrell involves the recovery of a childlike self. Sounding much like Proust, who feels similarly about a paradise lost, Tyrrell says, "The rest of our life goes in trying to reconstruct . . . and to recover slowly the forfeited simplicity, purity and candour with which Nature first clothed us" (39). Again, this process of recovery entails a more than personal end, for the "power of sympathy—of becoming a little child" (16)—is at once the secret of education and the fundamental crux of religion. "What we need is one greater, wiser and stronger than ourselves, who can also become little and enter into us and then expand and raise and strengthen us; else what does the Incarnation mean?" (16). The present church does not have the capacity, institutionally, to become as a child; nor do most individuals. No doubt aware that he was echoing Augustine, Tyrrell speaks of his mother as a person with such a gift, and he emphasizes the need of himself and others to return to their mothers, becoming "not children, but as children" (39).

When Tyrrell says that the Jesuit system is "a hindrance to spiritual growth" (40), he is saying the worst about his order. For spiritual growth matters above all, but growth seems predicated on the power to look back, whereas the Jesuits seem to have lost all important sense of time. The problem cuts, for Tyrrell, in at least two ways. His own spiritual growth, recorded with such scrupulous doubts in the *Autobiography*, has been irreparably hurt. But other Catholic souls, and people who should become Catholics, have been hurt as well. The Jesuits in defending dogma and conservative authority underplay personal revelation, which is the necessary condition for spiritual understanding. "Since the true spiritual self . . . is the image and likeness of God, to find God . . . is morally the same thing as to find and be united with our true self."[77] The question remains, of course, as to what that self should be.

In considering his own lack of spiritual growth or unity, Tyrrell often thinks of John Henry Newman, who seems to him so admirable, so opposite to himself in his faith and confidence. Tyrrell was not pleased with Newman "the Cardinal," because he was rarely pleased with cardinals at all, and because he thought that Newman the man had become lost in the church figure.[78] The historical Christ, as he keeps repeating, bore little relation to Roman cardinals. Newman the thinker was equally suspect. Despite his interest in Newman's speculations and his sense that the "Essay on Development" offered the best commentary on the historical church, Tyrrell came to the realization that the accretion of dogma interfered with revelation. The mystery of God was essential, theological commentaries divisive or unimportant.

Newman himself remained for him a challenge and a model. At one point — and with typical precision — he says that he has been reading the *Apologia* for the seventh time,[79] appreciating in Newman's autobiography how "the whole mind moves," how spiritual and intellectual growth could be one and coherent. Unfortunately, he sees, too, how successful Newman had been in his intellectual and spiritual development, how Newman has managed, as he has not, to make "truth . . . one and simple." He can speak of "Poor Newman" and wonder "what his inmost thoughts were,"[80] but his usual attitude is quite different. In fact, he epitomizes his life as "the story of Newman *à rebours*."

> In that pure soul the presence of God in the voice of conscience was from the first—I think rather exceptionally—as self-evident as the fact of his own existence; although the outward evidence of the world's condition seemed to him to make for atheism, and to stand as a cumulative difficulty against this luminous interior intuition.
>
> (111)

> Newman's Catholicism was the outcome of his theism, practical and speculative; that was the firm basis on which it stood. He passed from light to fuller light. . . . I, in my dark and crooked way, almost began with Catholicism, and was forced back, in spite of myself, to theism, practical and speculative, in the effort to find a basis for a system.
>
> (112)

It is in contrast to Newman that he speaks of the "anarchy" of his thoughts or "the skein of my tangled life" (111), the implication always being the lack of order or direction, the unattainable conviction of coherent growth. If the entire universe is for Tyrrell a "great tree," a metaphor of growth and stature should obtain, even for lives the most "paltry" or troubling. When thinking of Newman, Tyrrell is reminded of Newman's "luminous" and consistent state of belief, but also of the organic whole of his life. He may sense that "poor Newman" is something different from the public man, and he may be able to reject some of Newman's thinking. Still he sees in the *Apologia* all that he finds missing in his own life, whether the written or the experienced.

Tyrrell's sense of his comparative failure influences the shape of his narrative, which has distinctive features at odds with his themes of recurrence (or with the timelessness of a subconscious self). If recurrence and unity represent one kind of growth, division and separation represent another. After commenting on the power of memory to expand and contract time, to dwarf what had seemed to be years into periods of only a few months, he speculates about the extent and the quality of his childhood. Then he says:

> And so here I draw a black line to mourn my departed innocence, and separate it from the period when I began to tamper with and spoil the self that God had given me. . . . This line is not to be taken absolutely, as hard and fast; but as representing a period of twilight, or, rather, the first undoubted beginnings of twilight.

(38–39)

However intended, the line demands "to be taken absolutely," as demarcation or separation, a sign of things irretrievably lost. Although Tyrrell seems to write with unabated innocence, or at least with an unnerving directness and lucidity, he himself thinks of his childhood, once accounted for, as a period dead in his life and disposed of in his narrative. In a letter to Maude Petre, he says that he has been able to re-create his childhood with a sense of his own and of other children's innocence, but that he must, having dealt with this "clean period of life," begin to come to terms with less attractive later stages.[81] Gone with the act of writing are the dead father, the family love, and—for all its "fear" and "terrors"—"that golden haze of happiness, which is so generally attributed to the whole period of childhood" (12), and which he admits to having enjoyed in brief installments.

Once he had introduced his dividing line, Tyrrell evidently recognized its usefulness. He was to draw two more before putting his autobiography aside. The other lines also speak to a finality and loss, no longer of innocence, but still of family. When he evokes "my last day at home" (and his last in Ireland), Tyrrell writes: "Those two [his mother and sister] . . . whom I forsook—for what? in the name of all that is sane and reasonable? For a craze, an idea, a fanaticism? or for a love of and zeal for the truth, the Kingdom of God, the good of mankind?" (141). All he seems sure of at this point is that he has cut himself off from his own past, "crooked, selfish, untruthful" as it might have been (142).

Tyrrell's third line, toward the end of his book, reiterates the feelings concentrated around the second, but reflects a different situation. Whereas the second line marks his leaving family and Ireland, the third marks the death of his mother, the separation from his sister, and his final commitment to the Jesuit order, which seems to him in retrospect a betrayal of family and self. He regrets, "with bitterness, how I abandoned the life of affection for the service of so barren a mistress as truth, and let the substance of life escape me in the pursuit of shadows. And here, once more, I draw a line" (229). The identification of his losses comes in his writing with the force of actual separation and loneliness, and in this sense Tyrrell does emphasize the recurrence or circular quality of the memories he records; at the same time the lines represent his own wrenching gesture, the autobiography cutting off the past it evokes. As he proceeds, Tyrrell frequently uses the words "strange" and "strangely," calling attention to his own, almost surprised sense of alienation, which compounds the lost love of family and friends and the disappointed expectations in the religion he has chosen, or at least in the order to which he has dedicated his life. The choice is *strange;* he is a *stranger.* It is as if he sees himself as modern literary character. His "chameleon gift" notwithstanding, he finds he cannot adjust to the life which his autobiography has begun to define any more than the autobiography can "make reparation for the past" (192).

When Maude Petre introduced Tyrrell's autobiography to readers in 1912 — and effectively destroyed whatever was left of Tyrrell's reputation among Catholics — she insisted that Tyrrell's book came closer to Augustine's than to Newman's model, for "it was not . . . written for self-justification in the eyes of the world, but for self-accusation in the eyes of himself and another."[82] Yet in a sense Tyrrell does write a kind of apology, and certainly he writes with Newman and Newman's English audience in mind. He also knows that Augustine's confession was not just for God's ears and was more than a long, self-accusatory accounting. It is true that he could later take pleasure in thinking of God rather than his contemporaries judging his life and work, but he had written for another audience, even in his autobiography. As a polemicist who admitted to self-contradictions and as a priest who distrusted even himself and his chosen order, Tyrrell writes something approaching both apology and confession. He wants to show how the most unlikely and unworthy can find faith, and also to reassure himself that his life has some semblance of purpose and meaning. The incomplete story of his life can hardly have satisfied him. From a later perspective, however, he could look beyond the disappointment and the loss and write with a resigned or stoical pride:

> It seems to me . . . that I have not altogether run in vain, or wasted my life, if I have done no more than win to my present clearness of moral conviction through many tribulations . . . , even though I end, weary and exhausted, at certain commonplace principles which are the public heritage of my age and country. Yet it seems to me that I possess them and feel them in a way that they never can who have had them for nothing.[83]

"Nothing" is another of Tyrrell's favorite words, and *nothing* seems for this saddened man the more common judgment on his achievement, which in the passage above he characterizes by negatives. "Life," he says in the *Autobiography* itself, is an "essay . . . one shot at the mark, for which no preliminary practice is allowed, and no second chance" (150). If, as Berdyaev suggests, memory can transfigure, or transform, making the past into something eternal, memory may also be intransigent or even punitive. Tyrrell's attempt in his unfinished autobiography was to find some transforming power in a past that seemed at first preferable to his present life, but what he discovered was enormous disillusion along with a bewildering sense of fatalism and tragedy.

Tyrrell's sense of personal extremity suggests a comparison with Gerard Manley Hopkins, whose own difficulties with his chosen calling, his profound unhappiness and self-doubt made his life in the Society of Jesus so overwhelmingly burdensome. To some extent like Tyrrell, Hopkins found it difficult to square his writing with the values of his superiors, who quite naturally found it strange, and this man who felt "the fell of night," no less than Tyrrell, wrote for an audience unavailable in his lifetime. Another Anglican who sought the security of the church and the discipline of the Jesuits, Hopkins, like Tyrrell, never found his vocation in his calling, never felt, that is, the satisfaction which originally drove him—with help from Newman—to his difficult conversion. If Hopkins, as John Robinson says, found no still center with which he might protect himself, the same might be said of Tyrrell, who said it of himself.[84] There could be for neither man a time of peace or "rumination," a satisfaction with responsive superiors or with appreciated writing: no "still center" or "still point," but rather a frightening spinning of the wheel. Tyrrell and Hopkins both stare at the possibility of a world without hope, even, at times, without God, and both understand the ways in which their own plight touches on the condition of their time. No less than Tyrrell, Hopkins seems to lead the life of his spiritual mentor *à rebours.*

These two exacting and determined men also reach out to readers in a comparably intense, personal way. They are self-consciously "ahead of their times," the one with his radical verse, the other with his radical ideas. Both are "modern," accepting the pain of their modernity, though both chose a church and a calling that seemed essentially conservative. In certain respects, however, Hopkins and Tyrrell are very different kinds of men (just as they are entirely different kinds of writers). Hopkins never admitted, for example, that joining the order had been a mistake. Tyrrell was far less circumspect. Hopkins' private, unpolemical manner suggests William Hale White's more than it does Tyrrell's aggressive, sometimes bantam-like posture, and though both Tyrrell and Hopkins could be easily hurt, they responded in contradictory ways to the ills of the world.

Perhaps for all his spiritual longing, Tyrrell is closer to a writer like Samuel Butler than he is to Hopkins. Certainly his language of chance and fate suggests that of Butler, another man who chose not to publish his autobiographical study and left matters in the hands of literary executors.[85] Contrasting as Tyrrell and Butler may seem, both were isolated and lonely men, hungry for love and incapable of accepting it. Both wrote an odd collection of books, not surprising in view of their distrust of language and their shared conviction that deeper realities reside in the unconscious rather than conscious mind. Their books tend to be contentious, to reflect immediate controversies, to hammer at authority as though it bore themselves some direct ill will. Like Tyrrell, Butler was a greedy reader, a repository for new ideas, and his pronouncements were often the effect of his uncertainties rather than the expression of lasting convictions. Butler prided himself on his knowledge of modern science, in which he looked for the kinds of answers that Tyrrell felt science had made so difficult. And both men were obsessed by paradox, which offered an escape from unresolvable if also unavoidable spiritual dilemmas. Except that he would have substituted "unconscious" for "conscious," Butler might have said with Tyrrell (and White and Yeats, for that matter), "There is a timeless, spaceless self in [people] that revolts against the limits of his organic, individual self, and cannot rest but in a conscious relation to the Universal and Eternal. The world of clear knowledge is not enough for us."[86]

3 Strange Metamorphoses: Samuel Butler's "Unconscious Memory" and *The Way of All Flesh*

> *It drives one almost to despair of English literature when one sees so extraordinary a study of English life as Butler's posthumous* Way of All Flesh *making so little impression that when, some years later, I produce plays in which Butler's extraordinary fresh, free and future-piercing suggestions have an obvious share, I am met with nothing but vague cacklings about Ibsen and Nietzsche.*
> George Bernard Shaw, preface to Major Barbara

Extraordinary seems the right word for Samuel Butler as well as for *The Way of All Flesh*. Whether Butler had the powers Shaw credited him with, rivaling Voltaire with his "abnormally strong" and independent mind, he was unarguably original. Few writers would have persisted as he did, publishing to silence or contempt, challenging the powerful and entrenched, living in a kind of intellectual isolation. It is largely as a "great" thinker that Shaw praises Butler, and in the preface to *Back to Methuselah* he credits Butler with most of the anti-Darwinian and "creative" evolutionary principles that he himself so strongly urged. Shaw makes it clear to his English readers that while they would accept new ideas from Scandinavians or Germans, above all from Irishmen, they would not accept them from Samuel Butler. The loss, he says, is theirs. Although too radical or too much ahead of his time, Butler offered in fiction what Shaw was to offer in drama. *The Way of All Flesh* remains "one of the great books of the world."[1]

It is easy to see what Shaw admired in Butler: the iconoclast, the plain-dealer, the thinker impatient, if not mischievous, with authority. Who else would include Dickens's novels among the "literary garbage of the day" or speak of Darwin with something like ridicule?

> In Mr. Darwin's case it is hardly possible to exaggerate the waste of time, money, and trouble that has been caused by his not having been content to appear as descending with modification like other people from those who went before him.[2]

How drastically Butler rejected conventions, especially literary conventions, or to what extent he escaped from the intellectual prisons he described are still open questions. But there is no doubt that he was daring or that he did shock. Without the discipline of a Thomas Hardy, he was perhaps less than Hardy able to live by his social or literary ideals. While praising social adaptation and "grace," he remained an irritable and baffled outsider.

I want to say that Butler, for all his anti-Victorianism, is the "arch Victorian" that Malcolm Muggeridge saw in him;[3] but that Butler is also a "modern" writer in a radical sense, far more modern than E. M. Forster and Virginia Woolf, for example, recognized him to be. In her half-facetious comment that human nature (hence modern literature) changed in December of 1910, Virginia Woolf singled out Butler's *The Way of All Flesh*, which Woolf well knew had appeared in 1903 and had been written many years before.[4] For Woolf as for Forster, Butler represented a new beginning, a modern who was openly contemptuous of nineteenth-century shibboleths, whether in families or other institutions, literature or morals. And if we grant that Butler's materials were all very much of his age, that he rebelled against a "Victorian" world on the basis of Darwinian and other contemporary ideas, there is no question about his novelty. But he was not new in the way that Woolf should have wanted, not new in his intimate portrayals, his sensitive handling of people, his understanding of "Mrs. Brown" (or any other woman, for that matter). His real modernity, beyond the ideals that Woolf espoused, centered in that obsession Butler shared with White and Tyrrell: the ambivalent sense of a writer's identity.

I can clarify this best by mentioning Maurice Merleau-Ponty and his description of the "modern" writer, the writer who struggles between the "self" and the "self" materializing in written discourse. "For a century now," he says "writers have always been more aware of what is singular and even problematic in their calling. Writing is no longer . . . the simple enunciation of what is conceived. It is working with a tool which at times produces more and at times less than one puts into it."[5] The new medium is likely to divorce us from ourselves without necessarily opening us to others.

Merleau-Ponty's remark applies doubly to Butler, in part because Butler suffered from his awareness of singularity and failed expression, in part because he argued along similar lines. He admits that *Luck, or Cunning?* turned out "very differently from the [book] I had in mind," as if it had a life of is own.[6] *Life and Habit,* he says, persuaded him as he wrote it: "I admit that when I began to write upon my subject I did not seriously believe in it."[7] Admirable that his world could be changed by pursuing ideas—but what a confession! Butler's comment on *The Way of All Flesh* is a little different, but clearly parallel. The book, he admits, is "full of contradictions—I having intended at one time to turn the thing in one way and then turned it in another."[8] Not only does Butler recognize the independent life or the shifting qualities of the books he writes, he insists that all books are of dubious origin. In the midst of argument he can interrupt himself to say, as he does in *Life and Habit,* "Above all things, let no unwary reader do me the injustice of believing in *me*. In that I write at all I am among the damned."[9] It is as though another self intrudes and appeals, mocking author, argument, and book. At issue are more than just contradictions, or what Kingsley Amis describes as saying one thing, meaning another, and doing a third.[10] The introduction of a religious vocabulary—*belief* and *damnation,* and elsewhere *grace*—implies a conflicting view, of the writing process and of the person who writes. For all his irony, Butler wants the unattainable while insisting that it cannot be found. Much as "faith and hope beckon to the dream"[11]—his words from *Life and Habit*—the dream can only be hinted at within the pages of a book. This does not of course stop him from writing.

What he did write, however, draws attention to the anomalous situation of the writer, who depicts conscious life by betraying something important. To put this another way, Butler raises questions about an author's identity that parallel recent discussions in such writers as Roland Barthes or Michel Foucault. "What Is an Author?" asks Foucault, and his answer is not dissimilar from Butler's. An author is no privileged, creative force, just as an author's function is "not defined by the spontaneous attribution of a text to its creator." "In short, the subject (and its substitutes) must be stripped of its creative role and analysed as a complex and variable function of discourse." Our inflated and misleading views of authorship have their roots in nineteenth-century conventions; they do not apply to the shifting modes of modern discourse.[12]

Much of Foucault's argument seems either implicit or overt in Butler, and with analogous applications. Butler similarly imagines that writing "unfolds like a game that inevitably moves beyond its own rules" and does so because it has freed itself from stifling views of "expression." "What matter," says Foucault, quoting Beckett, "what matter who's speaking?"[13]

Whether we see Butler as struggling, in Merleau-Ponty's sense, with intractable materials, aware of the oddities of his public self, or whether we see him aware, like Foucault, of historical conditions, of "author" as a fictional construct behind a given "text," the fact remains that he thinks independently about the problems of authorship. (I overlook the ironies of Butler-as-author in my own discussion.) And those problems are a direct consequence of his theories of memory.

Butler developed his ideas in books that are ironic in substance and engaged but impersonal in tone, that plead against individual consciousness with an often testy and unbending logic. The author who disparages authorship posits a scientific myth of development which seems to deny the development of an individual consciousness, and he does so, often enough, with works that are extended rejoinders to opponents real or imagined who have ignored or slighted Samuel Butler. It is in the context of Butler's paradoxical views that a work like *Ernest Pontifex; or, The Way of All Flesh* needs to be read. Butler's friend Eliza Ann Savage urged him to become the "novel-making machine" she thought his talents demanded.[14] Butler tired of the novel, convinced that he should tell the world about the derivative and erroneous features of Darwinism. Because I believe Butler's theories are often far more interesting than the novel he wrote to embody them, I begin here with a discussion of "unconscious memory" before turning to *The Way of All Flesh,* which is at once a fascinating experiment and an unrealized vision of Butler's ideas.

> Ideas . . . are more fully understood when their relations to other ideas of their time, and the history of their development are known and borne in mind.
>
> Butler, Luck or Cunning?

Butler's scientific ideas developed much as *The Way of All Flesh* developed, over many years and with sporadic new beginnings. From his first encounter in New Zealand with Darwin's *Origin of Species,* which he read in 1860, Butler appreciated the importance of evolution for matters of self and identity, indeed for basic questions about the nature and the growth of human life. He wrote essays and dialogues testing the implications of Darwin's theories and toyed, half facetiously, with speculative notions of his own. He also made a substantial amount of money. On his return to England, he spent five years as a student painter, setting aside his writing until the early 1870s and establishing his habits of privacy and well-to-do bachelorhood in Clifford's Inn.[15] *Erewhon,* which draws upon his New Zealand experience, also draws upon his speculation about evolution and applies his ideas to the satiric utopia of Ydgrunism and Musical Banks. After the religious satire of *The Fair Haven,* Butler addressed what Miss Savage had in mind: a novel to be more accessible than Butler's earlier fiction, and to outdo *Middlemarch.*

Butler began *The Way of All Flesh* in the summer of 1873, writing at it until he left for Canada (and financial losses) the following summer. When he got back to England he turned not to the novel again but to the matter of *Life and Habit* (1877; dated 1878), the first of his scientific books. Hence, the second stage of *The Way of All Flesh* (1878) emerges from the work on evolution. Butler had reached the unrecorded scene between Ernest and Miss Maitland by the time he once again took up his scientific studies. The final sections of *The Way of All Flesh* and the revisions of its early sections (May 1882–February 1883) followed the remaining scientific books, except for *Luck, or Cunning?* (1886; dated 1887), which offers new insights and reflects *The Way of All Flesh* in emphasizing consciousness and conduct.[16] Besides the chronological overlap, there is a tangled kinship between the scientific works and Butler's story of Ernest Pontifex, whose "priestly" functions "bridge" in a sense science and autobiography, polemics and fiction.

There are really two theses to Butler's scientific works: (1) that Darwin was right to affirm evolutionary development, but (2) he was wholly wrong about the means of change. To get a sense of Butler's own inflated sense of his achievement in these writings, we might glance at a summary statement from his *Note-Books,* later published in an essay for *The New Quarterly Review* (1885), two years before the appearance of *Luck, or Cunning?* Butler writes:

> To me it seems that my contributions to the theory of evolution have been mainly these:
> 1. The identification of heredity and memory and the corollaries relating to sports, the reversion to remote ancestors, the phenomena of old age, and the causes of sterility in hybrids. . . . This was *Life and Habit* [:*An Essay After a Complete View of Evolution,* 1877].
> 2. The re-introduction of teleology into organic life, which to me seems hardly (if at all) less important than the *Life and Habit* theory. This was *Evolution, Old and New* [1879].
> 3. An attempt to suggest an explanation of the physics of memory. [I] thus connected memory with vibrations. This was *Unconscious Memory* [1880].[17]

Few of Butler's contemporaries and few people since would have agreed with his self-estimate. Although the evolutionist Alfred Wallace had surprisingly high praise for *Life and Habit,* and although Shaw and the philosopher C. E. M. Joad, among others, have praised him since, Butler has never found widespread recognition from biologists or from the group he valued more highly, that "jury" of general readers, from whom he expected at least posthumous honor.[18] As he sometimes boasted, his ventures into science had little to do with his training, his sense of his real abilities, or his talents, for he had no direct scientific knowledge and expressed his disdain for what he did know.[19] It is hard to see how he could credit himself with informing theories about "the phenomena of old age" or "the sterility of hybrids," let alone the physics of memory. He was and remained an amateur, a gifted speculator, someone—as Wallace appreciated—with brilliant insights, but not a seminal theorist. With his lack of training or first-hand knowledge, how could it have been otherwise? Even putting aside Butler's understandable limitations, his statement implies clear and careful development, whereas most of his ideas occur fully in *Life and Habit*, and Butler tends in the remaining books either to repeat with variations (to use his own favorite phrase) or to restate his ideas in the form of attack. Again, *Luck, or Cunning?* is something of an exception.

Before dismissing Butler's writings, we should remember that while such fields as psychology were taking the shape and gaining the stature they have since enjoyed, they were often peopled by self-didacts and enthusiasts, who brought their learning from other disciplines and could boast of qualifications scarcely in advance of Butler's own. Only the rare early psychologist, Hermann Ebbinghaus or Wilhelm Wundt, conducted research in a laboratory or worked, for that matter, in any way differently from a philosopher or other speculative thinker.[20] Alexander Bain, often considered the first real force in English psychology, has had a wholly undeserved reputation for experimental research. Herbert Spencer, who was widely influential, wrote his *Principles of Psychology* (1855) as if to illustrate not only Spencer's disregard of empirical study but what appears to be his underlying reluctance to read books.[21] If there is a difference between Butler's speculations and those of a man like Spencer, it lies in Butler's aggressive amateurism, in his contempt for scientists and professionals who lack a necessary aesthetic appreciation of their subjects. By contrast, Butler thinks of himself as the representative of enlightened "uncommon sense" in a Laputan world.[22]

Butler's speculations reflect his awareness of diverse scientific activity in biology, physics, and chemistry, as well as psychology. His ideas about heredity and memory coincide, for example, with the conscious-automaton debate of the 1870s, which centered on the question of human consciousness as a more or less mechanical or independent and freely willed process. For Butler, the heart of the question was memory, which he construed as a basically unconscious force. He asserts that his views were independent of those of Ewald Hering, who, along with Carlyle and Eduard von Hartmann, helped to make "the unconscious" a substantive in English as well as in German. "Between the 'me' of today and the 'me' of yesterday," says Hering, in Butler's own translation, "lie night and sleep, abysses of unconsciousness; nor is there any bridge but memory with which to span them."[23]

Butler's sense of unconscious memory reaches in two almost opposing directions, one best described as spiritual, the other material. When Charles Radcliffe adapted Coleridge's distinction between the Platonists and the Aristotelians he made memory the agent for "unity in multeity" and, diverging from Coleridge, elevated memory to the status of imagination. Close as he comes to Radcliffe's hyperbole, Butler does not use Plato's analogies to clarify his own or invoke Plato's authority for a higher order of recollection. He differs in this from Frederic W. H. Myers, an advocate of the "survival" of human personality after "bodily death," who says his ideas parallel Plato's theory of "reminiscence," which he defends as an illustration of the continuity of memory. At the same time, much of Myers's commentary is so close to Butler's as to seem a paraphrase. Even the naïve spiritualism echoes Butler's desire for purposive and creative change, binding "our own intellect and some unseen intellect," which Myers associates with God.[24] Butler's theories rarely become the simple and uncontradictory longings of Myers. If he believes in unity in multeity or the continuity of memory, Butler also believes skeptically. Both men nevertheless seek from evolutionary theories a kind of spiritual system, drawn from but independent of the scientists. Myers says that "thought and Consciousness are not, as the materialists hold them, a mere *epiphenomenon,* an accidental and transitory accompaniment [to evolution] . . . , but are . . . the central subject of the evolutionary process."[25]

Perhaps because of his irony and his sense of contradiction, Butler lacks Myers's reliance on a transcendent intellect. In this respect, his obsession with "the evolutionary process" and with problems of memory and continuity more closely resembles Thomas Laycock, another pioneer thinker, whose concerns about inherited memory speak to a less personal continuity. Two years before Butler published *Life and Habit,* Laycock wrote, "I propose to show that organic memory consists in cerebral processes, regulated by the laws of evolution and reversion, and common as vital processes to both plants and animals." And, "heredity is an evolutionary reversion . . . as in like manner reminiscence is an evolutional reversion to antecedent modes . . . in the individual."[26]

As Myers's and Laycock's language suggests, the debates about memory and heredity, conscious and unconscious processes, grew directly out of issues raised by Darwin, who offered a rich system for speculative application. Butler's response to ideas of evolution was perhaps singular. Preoccupied like so many of his contemporaries with analogies between individual thought and collective theories, he invariably attacks the analogies of others. Whether he takes on psychologists such as Alexander Bain and William Carpenter, scientists like Alfred Wallace, or social philosophers like Herbert Spencer, he argues implicitly with Charles Darwin, who has, he thinks, done great disservice to evolutionary principles. Whatever his disagreements, it is odd that Butler should appropriate so much from Darwin, yet fail to see in him another explorer of diverse fields, a truly synthetic thinker.

Darwin at any rate provided Butler with his major premise along with a bemused and unwitting opponent.[27] At first he idolized Darwin, made his acquaintance, and appropriated his theories. Soon, however, he grew wary and skeptical, began to attack Darwin's ideas, and eventually accused Darwin of dishonesty and plagiarism.

The "Butler-Darwin Controversy" reached its climax when Butler published *Evolution, Old and New* (1879), urging the recognition of evolutionary pioneers.[28] Darwin glanced at the book and sent it on as a kind of nuisance to Krause, a German collaborator. Krause, who was revising an essay on Erasmus Darwin for English publication, read Butler's work, quietly added rebuttals of his arguments, but failed even to mention his name. Consequently, Darwin's little book on Erasmus Darwin, which included Krause's essay, left the impression that Butler's arguments had been discounted without Butler himself having been named. Butler saw as usual a conspiracy of silence about his work. His letters to Darwin and (when Darwin's response proved inadequate) to the press in turn hurt and dismayed Darwin, who shunned any controversy, and who acceded to Thomas Huxley's recommendation that he should not reply at all beyond the private letter he had sent to Butler. Insulted and hurt, Butler increased his polemics, attacked Darwin with renewed energy, and essentially wrote *Unconscious Memory* as a self-justifying assault on Darwin's manners.

Because of Butler's fierce attacks, the Freudian psychoanalyst Phyllis Greenacre sees *Evolution, Old and New* and *Unconscious Memory* as classic cases of oedipal rivalry: Butler the aggrieved and troubled son forcing Charles Darwin to play the role of father, so that Butler mocks at once the religious dogmas of his biological father and the scientific authority of Darwin.[29] Both men were, indeed, upset by the books, although Canon Butler—while banning his son from his home—stopped reading them and Darwin, after great discomfort, learned to dismiss them by silence.

Butler's conception of memory grows out of his response to Darwin.

He turned increasingly to Darwin's predecessors—Erasmus Darwin, Buffon, and especially Lamarck—rejecting the principle of natural selection in favor of the Lamarckian principle of "use and disuse," which allows for climatic and environmental influences on inheritable characteristics. Unaware that Darwin's adjustments were largely a response to the speculations of Lord Kelvin (about a much younger world), he points out that Darwin increasingly accepted use and disuse theories through the various editions of the *Origin of Species*.[30] What is fascinating about his scathing, often hyperbolic, attacks on Darwin is the intensity of his belief in an evolutionary process. *Belief* is an appropriate word, for like F. W. H. Myers, Butler was seeking more than mechanical explanations of growth and development. This "earnest atheist" of Malcolm Muggeridge's description wanted nothing more than an ethical and religious alternative to his father's easy dogma. In the theory of unconscious memory he discovered something close.

If the central concern throughout his books on evolution is the demonstration of intelligent purpose in all organic life, Butler's teleology substitutes a pervading power of memory, a god within, for a less vital god of conventional belief. The ways that a living being remembers allow the gradual shift to a fuller and more efficient future, and the individuals who live fully and efficiently exhibit what he likes to refer to as "grace" or "design." By proposing a willing force in evolutionary change, Butler affirms the continuity of the workings of the psyche. Often, he overstates his case. To imagine as he does a grain of corn content to be deployed for a hen's well-being would seem to reflect a whimsical humor, yet Butler, much as he laughs at the theories of others, laughs hesitantly at his own ideas.[31] His satire turns to something like self-parody when his favorite hobbyhorses are at issue.

Memory is, to Butler, so much an accepted part of our lives that we become conscious of it at our peril—like the person asking himself how he walks. To stop breathing, for instance, can only be a conscious or disruptive act. The human animal, like all organic life, performs as a unit of complementary memories, accrued over centuries and shaping individuals with a kind of genetic predetermination. Free will and the capacity for design are possible only within the constraints of our inheritance. We carry both the physical attributes and the psychic character of our forebears. One of Butler's favorite illustrations of the workings of unconscious memory is the analogy of the pianist who plays hundreds of notes a minute and who could not perform if he were to "think about" the process. He may have latitude, but he has learned too well to play except by habit. Any skill, any true knowledge, Butler argues, presupposes such total absorption, such conscious forgetting. Ironically, he charges Darwin with precisely the sort of memory lapses his own works defend, of having absorbed his sources, that is, to the point at which Darwin can no longer disentangle source from knowledge. Darwin might have quoted Butler's own words: "It is not too much to say that we have no really profound knowledge of any subject . . . till we have left off feeling conscious of the possession of such knowledge."[32]

Epistemological questions remained central for Butler throughout his long course of opposition to Darwinism. His scheme of achievements in *The New Quarterly* article tells of a wide range of inquiry, largely about topics raised by Darwin or elicited by Darwin's own unanswered questions. Whether in *Life and Habit* or *Evolution, Old and New, Erewhon* or *The Fair Haven,* Butler is asking about how and what we know, equating knowledge with a vast mnemonic inheritance, with forces and history that tend to dwarf the faculties of a given individual. Already in *Erewhon* the idea of the Unborn, who come into ignorance at birth, retaining only "a bare, vital principle" instead of prior knowledge, speaks of what people know and cannot know about their lives.[33] Implicit knowledge of former states or ideas bears on matters of personal identity, which is at most a reflection of the imperishable essence of continuing life.

The effect in Butler's thinking is of an underlying if inaccessible reality, divergent form Radcliffe's or Myers's, with their direct appeal to Platonic myth, but with the assumption of recurrent and ideal states (however construed) nonetheless assumed.[34] To speak of myth in Butler is to approach, in a different but related way, the matter of religious longing, the substitution of what he thinks an unassailable belief for something shop-worn and tired. Butler wants the energy of Darwinism channeled into satisfying alternatives, into purpose, meaning, happiness. His myth substitutes a collective for an individual awareness, with awareness, in fact, an anomalous necessity even for the announcement of the theories themselves. In *Life and Habit,* Butler speaks of knowledge as something to be lost with experience until experience becomes the legacy of previous generations. "Life . . . is memory," or inherited knowledge; death is the failure of memory to link past and present. "It is the young and fair," Butler says, "who are truly old and experienced; it is they alone who have a trustworthy memory to guide them; they alone know things as they are."[35] I shall suggest later what bearing such statements have on *The Way of All Flesh,* where Butler has to wrestle with conventions of development and education, while Overton tacitly burlesques not only emotional or intellectual growth but also the narrative which implies it. Myths of collective meaning remain, even in a work like *The Way of All Flesh,* distinct from the individuals they seem designed to serve.

By the time he wrote *Luck, or Cunning?,* which appeared a decade after *Life and Habit,* Butler had wrestled with the personal or dramatized applications of his theories in *The Way of All Flesh.* He continued to define life as memory, but with some differences. Expressing easy confidence, his *New Quarterly* article had promised a sure development of the ideas on memory:

> What I want to do now [1885] is to connect vibrations not only with memory but with the physical constitution of that body in which the memory resides, thus adapting Newland's law (sometimes called Mendelejeff's law) that there is one substance.[36]

Sounding much like George Eliot's Lydgate, Butler blithely set himself unattainable goals; and within *Luck, or Cunning?* he devotes only a few pages to the "one substance" or even to the physical properties of memory. Instead, he plunges once again into questions of knowledge. For the first time he seems to appreciate the anti-intellectual and potentially limiting nature of wholly unconscious memory. Whereas in *Life and Habit* he had argued a Carlylean view about the evils of self-consciousness, he now attacks Spencer and Huxley both for their advocacy of a chance and material universe and for their tendency to abolish "mind," with mind taking on new and unexpected virtues. "The main point with which I am concerned is the fact that Professor Huxley was trying to expel consciousness and sentience from any causative action in the workings of the universe."[37] "Professor Huxley" could stand perfectly well here for Butler himself, for whom thinking and consciousness are no longer proscribed words; the advocate for unconscious thought can say, "The more a thing knows its mind, the more living it becomes."[38]

As if to compensate for having rehabilitated consciousness, Butler speaks at length in *Luck, or Cunning?* not only about the cunning mind, but also about the "miraculous," which emphasizes the matter of belief by appeal to "design." "All, then, whether fusion or diffusion, whether of ideas or things, is miraculous. It is the two in one, and at the same time one in two, which is only two and two making five put before us in another shape."[39] Again the problem seems to be how to articulate the ineffable, how to construe scientific materials which both hint at and obscure the meanings of life. Miracle had been implicit in Butler's earlier writings when he spoke of willing purpose, evident if unprovable, in a universe of change. He now uses the term to express his faith in the process and to set the limits of conscious knowledge. If miracle lies in small, imperceptible change, it is subtly related to our sense of paradox. Very much like George Tyrrell, Butler thinks that we must be content with incomplete or contradictory truths, with faith on the one hand and a kind of negative capability on the other. For this reason, complexities of miracle and truth escape scientists like Darwin, those who cannot live with paradox and have "wrestled with the light and lost."[40]

Whatever advances *Luck, or Cunning?* makes over the earlier books, and however much conscious processes enter into Butler's understanding of knowledge, his fundamental principles remain. "Abiding memory" is no recapitulation of one's personal past, even in *Luck, or Cunning?* It is part of that unseen and finally inscrutable world of the unconscious. Indeed, Butler shows to what extent conscious thought can impinge on our lives when he says that only "a little margin of individual taste" remains over the vast part of ourselves determined by "the past habits of the race."[41] Design or any other concept with which we struggle intellectually is "like all our ideas, substantial enough until we try to grasp it—and then, like all our ideas, it mockingly eludes us; it is like life or death a rope of many strands."[42] Finally, then, memory has little to do with traditional notions of intellectual storehouses or even of personal identity as a function of private recollection. It remains our umbilical link with all "ensouled" matter. Ego and non-ego, life and death, are for Butler irreconcilable extremes only from the inadequate if now necessary vantage point of conscious thought.

In some of this thinking, Butler anticipates and intersects with another and better known mnemonic theorist. To introduce the implications of unconscious memory in *The Way of All Flesh,* it may help to think of Butler in relation to Henri Bergson, his younger contemporary.

A lengthy comparison of Butler and Henri Bergson, even on memory, would be inappropriate here, but a few points can be made. Claude Bissell has argued that, some apparent parallels notwithstanding, the two writers are far apart, and Bergson's own testimony that he had not heard of Butler let alone read his books before 1914 should be enough to close the discussion.[43] It is true that there are major differences. In his version of "creative evolution" Bergson flatly denies the possibility of acquired characteristics and he thinks of evolutionary process in terms of quantum leaps (as, nowadays, does Stephen Jay Gould),[44] whereas Butler imagines a process inching forward with microscopic steps. Speaking in *Matter and Memory* of two kinds of memory, "pure" memory and habit, Bergson makes a separation alien to Butler's thinking, for Butler insists on habit as essential memory and predicates it on physiological assumptions. Then, too, Bergson insists on the primacy of consciousness, which for Butler, as Bergson would say, diminishes to a mere "epiphenomenon"; Bergson sees conscious choice, which is made possible by remembering, as the necessary given for creative life. In spite of such differences and in spite of Bergson's ignorance of Butler, Beatrice Edgell was right to see the two as having much in common.[45] Similarities, after all, presuppose neither identity nor influence.

With their shared distaste for mechanistic thinking (associated for both with Darwin and Spencer), Butler and Bergson advocate a version of creative evolutionary change, however different the imagined means; both conceive of mind acting upon matter in an ultimately mysterious process, the laws of association always assumed; both emphasize action or doing as opposed to thinking, while insisting on the force of heredity; and both rely on memory as the key function, or what Bergson would call the privileged problem, in the understanding of human life. Memory gives continuity and meaning, while remembered states of mind achieve a kind of independent existence. "Memory," says Bergson, in language that seems to echo Butler's, "is the intersection of mind and matter."[46]

Bergson also illustrates what Butler does not do. Above all, Butler scoffs at tight definitions. He has little to say about perception as against reflection, personal against hereditary memory, instinct against intelligence, or — a pressing issue in Bergson, and one I have raised before — spatial against temporal recollection. Unlike Bergson, he is unimpressed by metaphysical argument. Yet Bergson indicates the importance if also the minimal effect of Butler's theories, which raise basic and urgent questions about a range of topics fascinating to his contemporaries. I want to quote one final passage from Bergson to indicate what Butler faced when he wrote *The Way of All Flesh*. In *Creative Evolution* (1907), Bergson says:

> Whenever we are trying to recover a recollection, to call up some period of our history, we become conscious of an act *sui generis* by which we detach ourselves from the present in order to replace ourselves, first in the past in general, then in a certain region of the past — a work of adjustment, something like the focusing of a camera. But our recollections still remain virtual; we simply prepare ourselves to receive it by adopting the proper attitude. Little by little it comes into view . . . and as its outlines become clear and its surface takes on colour, it tends to imitate perception.[47]

The recovery of the past in almost any autobiographical work would seem to involve the passive self-awareness, the slow unfolding or focusing, that Bergson describes. And perhaps Butler's recollective process worked analogously for *The Way of All Flesh*. Bergson's metaphor of the camera, however, implies his awareness of contemporary technology and its use for mnemonic and autobiographical thinking. Even writers like George Tyrrell, though they may avoid references to camera processes, speak of "reflexes" and reflections. At a key moment in *Father and Son*, for example, Edmund Gosse peers down into a sea pool, as if then and now, and sees himself and his father mirrored there. Butler has few such metaphors (none, I think, from technology) about reflection and self-reflection. His metaphors come from such processes as weaving and growing, which illustrate both his scientific assumptions as to complexities of self and his unassessed assumptions about his own past life. Butler's problem was to make his "perceptions" and his consciousness fit the theories of unconscious memory, which were inhospitable to full or dramatic self-awareness, in fiction or in autobiography, without some radical adjustment. The writing of *The Way of All Flesh*, in short, forced Butler to reconsider his sense of memory and self as personal recollection vied with an inherently untellable past.

> *Can we say that all lives, works, and deeds that matter were never anything but the undisturbed unfolding of the most banal, most fleeting, most sentimental, weakest hour in the life of the one to whom they pertain?*
> Walter Benjamin, Illuminations

Butler would have understood Benjamin's remarks, which fit so well with his own thoughts about the miraculous in the mundane and which explore the enigmas and contradictions inherent in memory. Benjamin is speaking about Marcel Proust and the complexity of memory in *Remembrance of Things Past*. Drawing attention to the importance of the banal and the fleeting in Proust's "Penelope work of recollection" or his "Penelope work of forgetting," Benjamin plays with the paradox of interwoven recollections, "in which remembrance is the woof and forgetting the warp."[48] Whatever he might have thought of Proust's novels, and he was rarely generous about fiction, Butler would have applauded Benjamin's sense that in a recollective work recollection itself becomes more important than the recollecting author, however much he would have sympathized with Proust's "quest for happiness," as Benjamin calls it. Butler would also have heard in Benjamin echoes of his own speculations about the process of memory, which include analogous notions of paradox — as well as overlapping metaphor. "I know that contradiction in terms lurk," he says, "within much that I have said, but the texture of the world is a warp and woof of contradictions in terms."[49]

The Way of All Flesh emerges from Butler's personal recollections and embodies as much as it expresses the paradoxes of his career. It may be too strong to call the book "an unconstruable synthesis in which the absorption of a mystic, the art of a prose writer, the verve of a satirist, the erudition of a scholar, the self-consciousness of a monomaniac have combined in an autobiographical work."[50] This is Benjamin on *Remembrance of Things Past;* and Butler is unquestionably no Proust. The ingredients of his book may be those of Proust's, though his "mysticism" is more asserted than real; what is lacking is the synthesis itself, in his own words, the weaving of the rope. In *The Way of All Flesh* another and unspoken text seems to hover behind the text Butler left unfinished.

Paradox is both the program and the condition of *The Way of All Flesh,* with its novelistic format, its autobiographical story, its satiric and detached tone, its historical references and dates, its appeal to memory which defies recollection, its sometimes documentary, sometimes "banal" detail. Like William Hale White's and Edmund Gosse's autobiographical works, it raises generic questions. Should we think of it as autobiography, autobiographical fiction, satiric autobiography? Is it an extension of the sort of self-dramatizing and self-exploration Butler attempted in *The Fair Haven,* in which an imaginary man tells the life of his brother, whose trials and thoughts are based upon Samuel Butler's? Or is it closer to *Erewhon,* albeit set at home, with an uncommitted narrator quietly toppling the institutions he knows?

Butler's theories seem to lead both toward and away from an understanding of autobiography, especially his own, even assuming *The Way of All Flesh* to approximate autobiography. (There are clear reasons why, given Butler's ideas, it should be so considered, as I shall suggest.) In a sense Butler takes away with one hand what he gives with the other. Identity, in his theories of unconscious memory, is the ultimate issue: who or what we are, within ourselves and in relation to others. But identity becomes most confused for a writer who sees all life as one, who equates any individual with his or her multitudinous ancestors, and who understands personality in a plural sense. While he sees "our conscious life [growing] out of memory,"[51] he essentially acknowledges conscious life as aberrant, so that memory informs our consciousness, but consciousness is suspect. What we remember has apparently little to do with "images" or tangible traces of the past; yet we remember by "association," by the traditionally conscious mechanisms, which Butler himself attributes to Hartley and other earlier associationists. The result is a version of self exquisitely difficult, perhaps impossible, to isolate, a combination of mechanical and deterministic forces, along with a faith in "cunning" and individuation, all made more confused by the testy, self-consciously paradoxical qualities of the proposing author.

Because of his shifting modes, his approaches to and retreats from fiction and autobiography, his insistent but peculiar assertions of his ideas, *author* is, as I have suggested, a problematic word for Butler. It implies a consistency he would not affirm and a sense of continuing identity teasingly removed from a writing self. It also implies conscious "authority" and control of processes requiring a different order of mental cunning. How, then, can Butler have imagined the contrivances and postures necessary for an autobiographical book? And how do *we* approach ideas of memory and identity as they emerge in *The Way of All Flesh*?

When R. A. Streatfeild, Butler's friend and literary executor, issued *The Way of All Flesh*, he wanted to make clear what he saw as the connection between the evolutionary scheme of Butler's theories and the self-portrait now appearing. "Samuel Butler began to write *The Way of All Flesh* about the year 1872 [actually 1873], and was engaged upon it intermittently until 1884 [actually 1883]. It is, therefore, to a great extent contemporaneous with *Life and Habit,* and may be taken as a practical illustration of the theory of heredity embodied in that book."[52] Immediate questions seem to leap out of Streatfeild's comment. What does it mean, for example, to say that a book is a practical illustration of ideas from another book? Butler himself knew how books take on a life of their own, bearing on other works, but always independently. If *Evolution, Old and New* repeats and develops the ideas of *Life and Habit,* can a self-dramatizing narrative simply "illustrate" without changing the ideas or forcing a reassessment? Or did Streatfeild mean only that Butler, obsessed by his evolutionary notions, had no choice but to introduce them even in a radically different sort of book?

In any case, the relationship between the treatises and *The Way of All Flesh*—and the novel overlaps with three of them—is more tenuous than Streatfeild suggested but also, as Claude Bissell puts it, more intimate and fruitful. Bissell argues that Butler's "scientific ideas were . . . inseparable from a moral philosophy that could find its fullest expression [only] . . . in the literary form that deals most directly with problems of human conduct."[53] This is a shrewd remark, since Butler consistently spoke of purposive life and reacted to Darwinism as ethically and religiously barren. However, while it is true that he cared about conduct, it seems far less true that the novel afforded him a favored medium. By contending that Butler's "scientific ideas had implications that could be expressed only in terms of human nature and conduct," Bissell has to overlook some awkward facts, among them that Butler wrote *The Way of All Flesh* at different stages, finally abandoning it after ten years of work.[54] If he thought of the novel as his medium, why would he not have continued it or written another? And if he thought of his scientific books as inadequate, why would he return to them while he worked on the novel, and after he had put it aside? Common assumptions that fiction is the highest form of writing or that it can help us, as D. H. Lawrence put it, "to live," may not have been Butler's, for Butler not only scoffed at George Eliot and Dickens, he told Miss Savage that she had a much higher opinion of his own fiction than he could have himself. He was prouder of *Life and Habit* than of *The Way of All Flesh*.[55]

The issue still remains about the intersection of theories of memory, admittedly paradoxical, and a work about an individual life, in which theory sits among the dust and details of daily remembered experience. Butler was quite aware of the problem, as his comment on turning the book one way, then another would suggest. Toward the end of his account, the narrator, Overton, says that "all philosophies that I have ever seen lead ultimately either to some gross absurdity, or else to the conclusion already more than once insisted on in these volumes, that the just shall live by faith—that is to say that sensible people will get through life by rule of thumb. . . . Take any fact, and reason upon it to the bitter end, and it will ere long lead to this, as the only refuge from some palpable folly."[56]

Butler appreciates that what is true of other theories is true of his own. Overton more than once cites an unidentified author—*his* author—to suggest the absurdity of theory without experience. He says, for example, "Theorists may say what they like about a man's children being a continuation of his own identity, but it will generally be found that those who talk this way have no children of their own. Practical family men know better" (77). The ironies here are many. Butler after all "believes" in his theory of continued identity, within *The Way of All Flesh* and throughout his scientific books. Elsewhere, Overton himself expresses versions of the theory; yet neither Overton nor Butler knows anything about "practical family men," whose point of view offers the corrective to Butler's ideas. What we need to remember about the scientific ideas within *The Way of All Flesh* is that they represent Butler's ambivalent sense of their worth, emerge through Overton's mind, and evidently conflict with the processes of Ernest's life. Although in a sense they point toward "a scientific *Bildungsroman*," as Jerome Buckley says, they also present more problems than Butler was able to handle and they illuminate less than they complicate the meanings of *The Way of All Flesh*.[57]

It is hardly an exaggeration to say that *The Way of All Flesh* includes or tries to include all that had concerned Butler, and nearly all that he had written about, in fiction or in science. Perhaps for this reason, U. C. Knoepflmacher says that the book "became a private experience, written and re-written to test Butler's theories about heredity, theories which were themselves an attempt to free himself from his personal doubts."[58] "Private" applies equally well to the assertive but elusive speakers in Butler's works, *The Way of All Flesh* included, and to the implied audience, which of course never received the book during Butler's lifetime. (Knoepflmacher's assumption seems right: that neither the novelistic autobiography nor the scientific treatises served the underlying purpose of setting personal doubts at rest.) To think about *The Way of All Flesh* as a "private experience" is, however, to appreciate its complexities, to see that its privacy is both exclusive and reticent and that, unlike Rousseau's, for example, it avoids almost totally a revelation of interior life.

The absence of emotional depth (and a corollary range of subtlety) struck William Butler Yeats, who condemned Butler along with Shaw in his nightmare of singing sewing machines. Butler, he wrote, in *The Trembling of the Veil,* "was the first Englishman to make the discovery, that it is possible to write with great effect without music, without style, either good or bad, [and] to eliminate from the mind all emotional implication."[59] If in *The Way of All Flesh* Butler wrote with intricate and maybe confusing masks, dramatizing his personality through the mouths of others and implying both a sense of wonder and a complexity of character that Yeats could have admired, his emotional range remained muted or limited. Some of this was willed, and some of it reflects an assumption dear to Yeats himself. When Yeats wrote, late in his life, that man can embody truth but never know it, he offered another clue to Butler, whose views on emotion grow directly out of his sense that we do, literally, embody truth, that knowledge *is* embodied memory or lived truth.[60] In theory, then, Butler might have agreed even with Yeats's strictures on his emotional imbecility. He says, in *Luck, or Cunning?,* "How strange the irony that hides us from ourselves."[61] Whether or not Butler dealt adequately with the implications of his insight in *The Way of All Flesh,* the irony of hidden selves is the underlying theme of the novel. Overton himself says:

How little do we know our thoughts—our reflex actions indeed, yes; but our reflections! Man, forsooth, prides himself on his consciousness. We boast that we differ from the winds and waves and falling stones, and plants, which grow they know not why, and from the wandering creatures which go up and down after their prey, as we are pleased to say without the help of reason. We know so well what we are doing ourselves, and why we do it, do we not?

(21–22)

Overton's part lyrical, part chatty statement indicates the problems Butler encounters in a book about self-knowledge which is dubious about self-knowledge and which assumes development while hiding its phases like a secret of nature. Evidently writing *The Way of All Flesh* convinced that "I am rather a disappointing person,"[62] Butler implies through Overton the conviction of purposeful life at odds with a private life-history. The original title, *Ernest Pontifex: or, The Way of All Flesh* addresses the identity of Ernest, but in Butler's scheme, and to some extent in his novel, personal identity is hardly separable from the winds and the waves and the falling stones. As in Mark Rutherford's "autobiography," the effect in *The Way of All Flesh* is a peculiar and indirect autobiographical study, in which Samuel Butler as Ernest Pontifex appears through the recording mind of the disinterested, satiric, complacent Overton, who is both Butler himself and not Butler, Ernest and not Ernest.

Unlike many autobiographers, who look back with either real or feigned assurance as to who they are now and how their lives have led to this moment and this awareness, Butler remains in continual debate about the status of Ernest's life. This may well be because of his notions of the self, his realization, like Sartre's, that the self is never fully formed and is, therefore, nothing in itself, less in written discourse. The problem seems to be that which Francis Hart identifies and which touches again on Butler and Bergson: "Access to a recollected self," says Hart, "begins in a discontinuity of identity or being." Yet only a sense of continuity gives meaning to a recorded life.[63] Overton's limited access to Ernest allows narrative continuity but disallows an intimate understanding of Ernest's inner growth, with the result that Ernest, who seldom approaches dramatic insight, also seldom understands or acts upon whatever it is he learns:

> For as yet he knew nothing of that other Ernest that dwelt within him that was so much stronger and more real than the Ernest of which he was conscious. The dumb Ernest persuaded with inarticulate feelings too swift and sure to be translateable into such debateable things as words, but practically insisted as follows. . . .
> "You are surrounded on every side with lies which would deceive even the elect, if the elect were not generally so uncommonly wide awake; the

self of which you are conscious, your reasoning and reflecting self, will believe these lies and bid you act in accordance with them. This conscious self of yours, Ernest, is a prig—begotten of prigs, and trained in priggishness; I will not allow it to shape your actions, though it will doubtless shape your words for many a year to come. Your papa is not here to beat you now, this is a change in the conditions of your existence, and should be followed by changed actions. Obey *me,* your true self, and things will go tolerably well with you, but only listen to that outward and visible old husk of yours which is called your father, and I will rend you in pieces even unto the third and fourth generation as one who has hated God; for I, Ernest, am the God who made you."

(115–16)

The heavy irony along with the biblical echoes and admonitions for conduct recall Carlyle, though with an important difference. Whereas Carlyle mocks the outer garments or false values, he also writes *Sartor Resartus* as a paradigm of negation, longing, and self-discovery. Butler creates analogous masks, but again like William Hale White, he sees the life of an individual in terms of no dramatic conversion or illumination, no consistent progression. Just as there is no Socrates or Christ or other such guiding ideal in Butler, there is also no Saul or Paul, because no chance for illuminating crisis. Knowledge must be attained slowly, piecemeal, and with the uncertainty of any conviction the one certainty of life. Except that he neglects his studies more after the lecture from his inner self, Ernest's life simply tumbles on.

A vision of life as slow accumulation or *accommodation*—Butler's word for an individual's response to his changing world—can fit the generic framework of a book about education and development, however little it might exhibit the clear phases or the moments of anagnorisis common to so many autobiographies. Butler's contradictory vision, quoted by Overton—"that it is the young and fair who are the truly old and truly experienced inasmuch as it is they who alone have a living memory to guide them" (125)—calls attention to the conflict between progressive nineteenth-century assumptions about individual growth as evidenced in the *Bildungsroman,* and Butler's retrogressive notions of remembering. To understand the novel in terms of the growth of an individual (Butler-Ernest) is not, then, to call it an autobiography in an ordinary sense. Butler admitted to substantial parallels between himself and Ernest, wanting at the same time the detachment of a narrator who, if an alter ego, could assess his life with unsentimental regard. Beyond the obvious facts that the book is told in the third person *by* another person, or that its events break that purported "autobiographical pact" between author and reader, we would have to stretch definitions to call it autobiography.[64]

And yet in ways that Butler might argue, it *is* autobiography. Setting aside reductive generic or biographical arguments, it makes sense to think of *The Way of All Flesh* as unabashed autobiography of precisely the kind Butler would have to have written. Delighting in one apparent corollary of unconscious knowledge, he conceives of all art in a fundamentally expressive way, frequently quoting Buffon about the style and the man and saying directly what he means through Overton:

> Every man's work, whether it be literature, or music, or pictures, or architecture, or anything else, is always a portrait of himself, and the more he tries to conceal himself the more clearly will his character appear in spite of him. I may very likely be condemning myself all the time that I am writing this book, for I know that whether I like it or no I am portraying myself more surely than I am portraying any of the characters whom I set before the reader.[65]

Although he may not know what he means by self or what self is possible, given his mnemonic theories, Butler does know that his ironies involve self-deception and blindness, for writing necessitates a self-condemning and unwitting confession, albeit less of conscious sins than of sins of the fathers. When George Tyrrell describes his familial "inheritance," he judges himself harshly, finding fault with his temper or wishing for the simple piety of his mother. Butler accepts a kind of determinism, for himself and for Ernest, which dispenses with the possibility of personal sin while defining personality in a genetic or otherwise extended sense. Overton reveals Butler, as does Ernest and Theobold, Pryor and Towneley, Christina and old Mr. Pontifex. All are part of divided and enigmatic self, of a self indistinguishable from the structures of recollection, whatever the masks or fictions of the written word.

Butler's understanding of personality in the scientific books posits art as autobiography in an even larger context. For if all life is one life, one individual life has to be understood from a dwarfing perspective. We are one with our ancestors, who are themselves one with rudimentary forms of life, and, again, only what amounts to an ailing consciousness brings division or recognition of difference. Perhaps when Butler read *Middlemarch* and pronounced it "not interesting," he objected to characters who are discrete and knowable, sure of their identities, however representative of universal characteristics.[66] Butler had shown his contempt for personality in the "flat" Higgs, narrator of

Erewhon, who records his own adventures without a trace of intense feeling. In *The Way of All Flesh* he creates Overton, whose name suggests, apart from his love of music (Handel is Overton's and Butler's touchstone), an elevated and perhaps amused perspective. Overton is at once the ironic mouthpiece for certain of Butler's scientific ideas and their embodied rebuttal. In his chapter, "Our Subordinate Personalities," Butler argues that "it is within the common scope of meaning of the words 'personal identity,' not only that one creature can become many as the moth becomes manifold in her eggs, but that each individual may be manifold in the sense of being compounded of vast numbers of subordinate individualities, which have their separate lives within him."[67] The idea helps explain Ernest's multiple roles — as student, clergyman, prisoner, businessman, writer, man of the world, as well as son, husband, father, friend, bachelor — and the role of Overton in recording his life. Like a latter-day Tristram Shandy, Ernest enters his own book well into the narrative, in fact, after three generations; by the close of the novel, the narrator can speak of Ernest and himself as *we*, even appropriating Ernest's children as "our own two" (339). Since Butler conceives of the individual enacting all the stages of life before him — going "through the embryonic stages an infinite number of times"[68] — he may want to diminish Ernest, making him representative and insisting on common failings. The descriptions of Ernest as "my hero" would thus become a means to further irony, heroes being impossible in Butler's evolutionary cosmos.

Butler may avoid a more obviously autobiographical method in order to diffuse the sense of personality, for himself or for Ernest. To put this differently, *The Way of All Flesh* is obviously not Butler's "described life," in the words Ruskin used for *Praeterita,*[69] but rather an essay about life, with illustration and argument as central as narrative and description. It is "oratorical," albeit tentative and exploratory.[70] Though the effect is reduction or limitation rather than greater complexity of the person, that, too, may be what Butler seeks, Ernest's unconscious knowledge working itself out in unpredictable and inexplicable ways, the banal and the mundane masking the miraculous, passivity and apparent purposelessness reflecting unknowable design. Conversely, Butler may imply a kind of programmed development, so that Aunt Alethea (her name meaning *truth*) and Overton, from before and after, so to speak, can await the unfolding of a largely determined life. "Embryo minds," in the words of Overton-Butler, "like embryo bodies, pass through a number of strange metamorphoses before they adopt their final shape. . . . Ernest however could not be expected to know this. Embryos never do" (207). Life is a "journey," as Butler says in *Life and Habit*, and Ernest seems a passive traveler, his life, in Bergson's terms, slowly coming into focus as Overton guides his looking back.

Overtone's profession as writer of historical burlesques—one of them based on *Pilgrim's Progress*—suggests his capacity for the parodic, low-mimetic point of view, with Ernest the hero and mock hero of his work. Overton seems to understand matters from a long-term, almost fatigued, vantage point, without being physically or temperamentally close enough to care; and at times when he approaches important moments in Ernest's life he tends to distance himself from his godson-subject. Conveniently, for example, he sees little of Ernest during the time Ernest spends in jail. In Schopenhauer's terms, it is as though Ernest performs as the hero of his own life while figuring in a drama foreign to him.[71]

From Overton's, and from his own later perspective, Ernest's life is not quite burlesque, yet its dramatic moments are short-lived and attenuated by Overton's calm of mind. We would expect theatrical metaphors from a writer of burlesque, however lacking in drama the story that he tells, and references to theater recur in *The Way of All Flesh*. In one of his dubious and witty entries into Christina's mind, Overton has her think: "How it would tell in a novel or upon the stage—for though the stage as a whole was immoral, yet there were doubtless some plays which were improving spectacles." And on she goes: "Oh it was sublime! What a roar of applause must follow . . . !" (159). Apart from the fun with Greek tragedians, the debunking of Shakespeare, and the reminders of his own trade, Overton insists on laughter consequent on social roles—along with the importance of not being earnest. Here again Overton's language reflects Butler's directly. In *Life and Habit* he says, "We must conceive of the impregnate germ as a creature which has to repeat a performance already repeated before on countless occasions, but with no more variation on the recent ones than is inevitable in the repetition of any performance by an intelligent being."[72] It does not strictly matter if the performance is biological or theatrical, for Butler, like his narrator in *The Way of All Flesh*, sees all role-playing as analogous on life's comic journey.

Within and apparently at odds with the metaphors of theater and comedy are metaphors of music, especially fugues, and the equally prominent Darwinian metaphors of war and struggle, as in *attack, annihilation, battles:* "It is one against legion," Butler writes,

> when a creature tries to differ from his own past selves. He must yield or die if he wants to differ widely, so as to lack natural instincts, such

as hunger or thirst, or not to gratify them. . . . [Our] former selves fight within us and wrangle for our possession. Have we not here what is commonly called an *internal tumult,* when dead pleasures and pains tug within us hither and thither? Then may the battle be decided by what people are pleased to call our own experience. Our own indeed![73]

Whether Butler conceived of personal identity as farcical role-playing or musical variation on "one life" or a sort of Darwinian Psychomachia, he allows their mutual claims in the story of Ernest. A passive actor in a world he cannot understand (until, like Overton, he copes by simple reduction), Ernest is defined by his narrator rather than by his world. The very nature of his self and self-understanding are a function of Overton's skeptical, if mildly sympathetic, account. As Butler sometimes pointed out, any story can be told from a different point of view; though he refers to "my story," "my narrative," and to Ernest as "my son," Overton is simply one possible voice, neither privileged nor profound.

It is, then, difficult to speak about *The Way of All Flesh* without emphasizing Overton and his role as storyteller. He perhaps gives a consistency to the book that it would otherwise lack, as William Marshall suggests, and his role as "Ishmaelite" commentator may provide the kind of distancing Butler needs.[74] My own sense is that Overton afforded a narrative mask, useful for some of the novel, an impediment for the rest. If Butler felt that he needed an intermediary, that it would not do "to make Ernest a direct replica of himself," he clearly did not understand how to use Overton to depict, for example, Ernest's qualities as a writer, or his later independent thoughts, or the nature of his final maturity.[75] In a story about memory, it is Overton's recollections which recur through the narrative, ("When I was a small boy at the beginning of this century," etc. [3]), Ernest's memories creeping in later as additions to Overton's second-hand account. Only periodically, and as prompted by Overton, does Ernest himself "remember": " 'And then, you know,' said Ernest to me, when I asked him not long since to give me more of his childish reminiscences for the benefit of my [sic] story, 'we used to learn Mrs. Barbauld's hymns'" (90).

Overton's slow introduction of Ernest allows a wry distancing, and it compounds the traditional, autobiographical separation between older narrator and younger self by developing at least two perspectives on the events or nonevents of Ernest's life. Ernest can correct Overton, insisting that he wants even a discrediting document to be included, and he periodically discusses with his mentor-friend-father the shape of his lived and his recorded life. As the book progresses, Ernest serves

Overton as a present authority, correcting or supplementing facts about his past: "'Shall I cut it out?' said I, 'I will if you like.' 'Certainly not,' he answered, 'and if good-natured friends have kept more records of my follies, pick out any plums that may amuse the reader'" (199). Or, "Again I asked Ernest whether he minded my printing this [embarrassing letter]. He winced, but said, 'No, not if it helps you to tell your story; but don't you think it is too long?'" (209). The differences between Ernest and Overton are mainly those of knowledge (neither seems to have acute insight), which is, however, external to Ernest rather than intrinsic to his growing up. Overton says, for example, "In the spring of 1859 I find him writing . . ." (211), as though Overton is editor, alert to the importance of 1859, even if Ernest was not. Overton seems to be waiting for equipoise between himself and his godson, who attains his "wisdom" with time and who becomes, in essence, himself.[76]

Yet the losses are real. Ernest often seems to vanish behind what Butler elsewhere calls "inexorable conventions." He means by the phrase the tyranny of parents and ancestors over children, but he might well be speaking of novelistic demands forcing their way on Overton. *The Way of All Flesh* may invert typical nineteenth-century sentiments about orphans (who are to be envied), or about money (an end in itself), or marriage (from which Ernest fortuitously escapes), or social resolution (essentially burlesqued in the paradise of bachelors). Ernest insists that his childhood was not so bad, after all, his suffering being necessary, oppression—at home or school—to be expected. But as a self-satisfied man of the world, Overton loves many of the worst sorts of narrative conventions, indulging in asides and tangents, addressing his reader in almost parodic ways. As if to emulate Jane Eyre he says, "Reader, did you ever have an income at the best none too large?" (34), and "Have you, oh gentle reader, ever loved at first sight?" (273). Since, with the presumably passionless attraction for Alethea expected, it is unlikely that Overton himself has loved at all, the question is as absurd in substance as in phrasing.

"Reader" and "gentle reader" and other such phrases recur throughout the narrative and have as their equivalent Overton's increasing reference to Ernest as "my hero" or "my unhappy hero." Overton at once coaxes us into sympathy and intrudes between us and the immediacy of Ernest's experience. What makes matters worse is that the narrator and the god-from-the-machine are one and the same, since Overton can always supply Ernest with the money he needs and, in effect, bring about the happy ending he delays.

Overton's acceptance of inadequate, even reductive, conventions seems especially ironic when he speaks of Ernest's development as a writer. Even assuming that development would have to be "unconscious," its permutations scarcely known by the writer himself, let alone by a detached narrator, still, Butler could have done much to explore Ernest's writing career, which in some respects parallels his own, and which Overton scarcely understands. "I did not know that he was actually publishing till one day he brought me a book and told me that it was his own. I opened it and found it to be a series of semi-theological, semi-social essays" (341). With an autobiographical touch, Butler allows Overton to say, "He still therefore stuck to science instead of turning to literature proper as I hoped he would have done" (287). Whereas Butler made himself unpopular in perfectly explicable ways, it is hard to imagine Ernest writing with any energy, let alone addressing the coming "generation rather than his own." This, like the following, seems far truer of Butler than of the Ernest we know:

> With the public generally he is not a favourite. He is admitted to have talent, but it is considered generally to be of a queer unpractical kind, and no matter how serious he is, he is always accused of being in jest.
> (355)

Apart from these wry allusions to Butler's own career, there are in *The Way of All Flesh* scant signs of Ernest's achievement, saving the silly undergraduate essay or Overton's paraphrasing, in a book about the growth of a writer. And what about Butler's preoccupation with the anomalies of authorship in a narrative written by one writer (whose theories emerge in the text) and told by another writer about a third? Where *is* the author here? Where is the double application of mnemonic theory to narrative and to "personality"?

Butler creates in Overton a professional "jester," a man whose easy values sometimes overlap his own, but who is a sort of literary Towneley, the good-looking nonentity "worshipped" by Ernest and himself for qualities of ease and grace, "the very best man I ever saw in my life" (314). Towneley and Overton are the "Nice Persons" of Malcolm Muggeridge's description, the representatives in Butler's theories of unselfconscious, evolutionary accommodation.[77] "For he is the most perfect saint," says Overton, "who is the most perfect gentleman" (260). Unfortunately, such gentlemen are mindless conformists, predictably, and like Butler himself, politically conservative, but without Butler's or Ernest's complexities. With his conviction that nothing is worth doing that is not done easily, Butler creates an empty ideal in Towneley and an unengaged narrator in Overton.

For all his worldliness and knowledge, Overton's knowledge is superficial, at a great remove from either his author's ideas about memory and identity or the related notion of design. He can mouth the statements about "our less conscious thoughts and our less conscious actions which mainly mould our own lives" (22), and he refers persistently to "instinct" and heredity, along with the inherited voice within. Yet his own memories are all conscious and predictable, as though the theories have no bearing on his life, whether or not they are pertinent for Ernest's. It may be that if design is that rope of many strands, purposeful but mysterious, Overton is the ideal combination of the uninquisitive and uninvolved observer, the one who provides us with the materials to weave. The cost is that Butler's preoccupation with offspring and generation, memory and continuity, finds only ironic testimony in his confirmed and self-protective bachelor. Since Overton provides a model as well as tells the story for Ernest, he can only mock the continuity from generation to generation or nod in passing to Butler's paradoxical view that "everything is so much involved in and so much a process of its opposite that, as it is almost fair to call death a process of life and life a process of death, so it is to call memory a process of forgetting and forgetting a process of remembering. . . . Everything is like a door swinging backwards and forwards."[78] As a "subordinate personality" of Ernest, Overton may suggest a complexity of character and of character in time, yet the useful and provocative ideas of his author (here anticipating Genette and Benjamin) are blurred in the narrative.

To put this another way, Butler's paradoxes are present but not sufficiently dramatized by Overton. If life, or the understanding of life, as Butler says, centers on largely unconscious intelligence and cunning opposing a Darwinian nightmare of waste and luck, Ernest's development begins to seem like an exception or anomaly. The inheritance from his great-grandfather, another sun-worshipper, may be clear enough, but the sense of inherited wisdom, the semi-Platonism of the scientific books eludes Overton and leaves Butler with an incomplete portrait. "The book [rings]," as Overton says of Ernest's work, "with the courage alike of conviction and of an entire absence of conviction" (343). Whether or not Butler's conclusions are "conservative" and "escapist,"[79] they lack the energy and the ingenuity of, say, *Life and Habit* — and the passion or depth of emotion in novels like *Fathers and Sons*. Passion may not have been necessary. Missing is the exploration, the full testing of unconscious memories in the incidents of a child's rebellion or "the vagaries . . . it will now be my duty to chronicle" (201). What has occurred to make his adult life tolerable? Moneyed leisure and idle travel may have been a part of Butler's ideals, but they had little to do with the speculations about life in his studies of human memory.

Theodore Dreiser called *The Way of All Flesh* a "very great" book because "it presents and perfectly . . . , this brooding, semi-poetic thinker, almost entirely absorbed by his own life."[80] Certainly few other books before Butler's dealt so openly with apparently private questions as well as honored conventions of family and church: these were the innovations that appealed to Woolf and Forster, as well as to Dreiser and Shaw. But the book itself, as I have tried to show, deals obliquely with such issues, in part for theoretical reasons, in part because Butler could not equate a private life with the theory and the myth of unconscious forces. His unfinished work was as "future-piercing" as Shaw realized, but it left Butler himself uncertain and dissatisfied, knowing perhaps that he had not achieved the kind of "unconstruable synthesis" that Walter Benjamin was to associate with Proust. While his own work of recollection put together strands of personal experience and mnemonic theory in an experimental and paradoxical form, the final design is lacking, as if foreseen by Butler when he spoke about the weaving of a rope, the meaning or form of which "mockingly eludes us."

4 The Consciousness of Self: Edmund Gosse's *Father and Son*

> *Every individual human being . . . carries within him, potentially and prescriptively, an ideal man, an archetype of a human being, and it is in his life's task to be . . . in harmony with the unchanging unity of this ideal.*
> Friedrich Schiller, On the Aesthetic Education of Man

By the time he published *Father and Son*, in 1907, Edmund Gosse was fifty-eight. He had written many books of poetry, criticism, and literary history, and he was acquainted with most of the best-known English and American writers of his time. Beyond this, he knew French writers like Mallarmé—and was soon to befriend Gide. He had long been recognized as a major English spokesman for Ibsen and other Scandinavian writers. As Clark Lecturer of English Literature at Cambridge, he had established academic ties denied by his education; and his lectures in the United States had drawn large and responsive audiences from the universities as well as the general public. Gosse was a man of letters in Carlyle's sense—an important arbiter of literary taste—but also a man of letters in its new sense—a faintly ineffectual and amateur commentator on any and all topics for the reviews of his day.[1] Although he was friends with Tennyson and Browning, Gosse's own attenuated, if skillful, poetry set him apart from the writers he cultivated. This man who knew Hardy and Henry James, Arnold and Yeats, Conrad and Wilde, wrote little that outlived the moment and nothing that ranked him with his great contemporaries. Nothing, that is, except *Father and Son*.

> *[I]n an autobiography it is so difficult to dissimulate, that there is perhaps not a single one that is not, on a whole, truer than any history ever written. The man who records his life surveys it as a whole; the individual thing becomes small, the near becomes distant, the distant again becomes near. . . . He is sitting at the confessional, and is doing so of his own free will.*
> Arthur Schopenhauer, The World as Will and Idea

The world described by Schopenhauer is one of strife, conflict and war, both within the individual and without; it illustrates an inexorable clash of unconscious will and conscious desire. Written long before *The Origin of Species, The World as Will and Idea* describes a similar struggle for survival and development, albeit in a human context and with differing assumptions about the nature of time. Gosse's *Father and Son* relies on metaphors from Darwin, whose theories are also central topics of Gosse's life, but Gosse begins his book with an epigraph, two brief lines from Schopenhauer, and Schopenhauer's metaphoric vision informs much of Gosse's presentation:

Der Glaube ist wie die Liebe:
Er lässt sich nicht erzwingen.[2]

Behind Schopenhauer's lines lie an entire philosophy of force and power. Belief and love may be independent of force, but only in a certain sense, for life as Schopenhauer describes it is life subjected to a powerful *will,* while will itself is a drive, if not to "love," certainly to sex and reproduction. And belief seems little more than a conscious gesture in a struggle for understanding and freedom, the latter always illusive in a world of necessity. Even granting the possibility of either love or belief in the conditions he describes, Schopenhauer is convinced that all satisfaction is only apparent, that "attainment of ideals is fatal to pleasure."[3] Temporary relief from pain is perhaps all that can be hoped from any fulfillment, any self-realization, excepting the attenuated consciousness of the self-denying philosopher.

Gosse's vision is not apparently so negative as Schopenhauer's, but it shares a realization of the tragic nature of life (mitigated by the awareness of comedy), and it implies throughout an unresolved determinism in a book that speaks to independence and achievement, to belief and love. *Father and Son* is very much about pain and suffering in a world seen to be hostile. Like Butler's *The Way of All Flesh,* it seems to draw on Schopenhauer while applying his skepticism to what is in a sense a Darwinian plot of evolution and growth.[4]

Gosse's response to Butler's autobiographical study bears on his reading of Schopenhauer and particularly on Schopenhauer's categorical defense of autobiographical "truth." It may be that Gosse wrote *Father and Son* with *The Way of All Flesh* as both model and warning. His book followed Butler's by four years (and is therefore contemporary with the early stages of Proust's *Swann's Way* and Joyce's *Portrait,* another study of parents and rebellious offspring).[5] Gosse also published an essay on Butler, calling him that "very remarkable man" who "is historically notable as the earliest anti-Victorian."[6] Although written long after the appearance of *The Way of All Flesh*, Gosse's commentary on Butler speaks implicitly about his own autobiographical study and about the relation of fictional means to purportedly factual accounts.[7]

The essay on Butler is a review of Henry Festing-Jones's *Memoir* (1919), a book that Gosse admires for its specificity and candor. Gosse admits his delight in secret diaries and otherwise private documents, and he is intrigued by Butler's scrupulous preparation for posterity. The man who systematically hurt his career "recovered as many of his . . . letters as he could and annotated them; he arranged the letters of his friends; he copied, edited, indexed, and dated." Perhaps "no one ever laboured more to appear at his best . . . to the world after his decease" (57). Without thinking the efforts wasted, Gosse wishes that Butler could have put the same effort into his published works, especially into *The Way of All Flesh*. Gosse is in fact ambivalent about Butler, whom he praises for veracity and self-revelation and criticizes for reticence and self-deception. His keys are Miss Savage—Butler's muse and best critic—and Canon Butler, who provides the essential test of Butler's strengths.

Because of his failure to love, to take risks, this "self-tormenting man of extraordinary talent" was "out of harmony with the world *and* cut off from his own strengths" (76). Gosse is puzzled that Miss Savage, who guided Butler to a more directly autobiographical version of *The Way of All Flesh*, figures in the narrative, as the idealized Alethea, to illustrate its failures. "In spite of warnings from Miss Savage, and, oddly enough, most of all in the person of Miss Savage herself, Butler was incapable of confronting the incidents of his own life without colouring them, and without giving way to prejudice in the statement of plain facts" (63). Instead of writing a "story in flesh and blood," he writes something neither autobiography nor novel: "*The Way of All Flesh* is . . . romance founded on recollection" (63).

For Gosse the essential relationship in *The Way of All Flesh* is that between Ernest and his father, and it is here that the real failure lies. Just as in life "Butler would sacrifice his father, and actually tell falsehoods," so in the novel he caricatures Theobald. "It is impossible to avoid hoping that if he had studied his father, as at the age of fifty he studied his grandfather, he might have relented a little" (69). How closely this reflects Gosse's values when he first read *The Way of All Flesh* would be hard to pin down, but it does clearly echo those matters of self-understanding and what might be called "emotional facts" which concerned him in *Father and Son*. The opposing constraints of accuracy and kindness must have put Gosse to the test, the more so since Philip Gosse instilled in his son the absolute if unrealizable ideal of "Truth." According to Edmund, the elder Gosse "utterly despised that species of modern biography which depicts what was a human being as though transformed into the tinted wax of a hairdresser's block."[8] Unlike Butler's indictment of his father, Gosse's more probing but more generous portrait came with the distance of half a century, but also with Butler's example to guide him.

While he is probably right about Butler's failures, Gosse sets up impossible and contradictory standards. "The best of autobiographies," he says, "can never be the 'real life,' because it can never depict the man quite as others saw him" (62). An appeal to "exterior" rather than to an "interior study" oddly enough characterizes Gosse's position on fiction, which should not, he argues, dwell on "the life of the soul."[9] At the same time, if internal honesty or "self-revelation" is what matters, the public aspects of autobiography would presumably be incidental, the private account essential. Gosse wants at least two conflicting ideals: a vision generous and unfanatical, that borrows Arnold's injunction "to see life steadily, and see it whole" (69); and the kind of radical risk-taking he appreciated in Rousseau.[10]

There is, however, another way of thinking about Gosse's assessment. He may imply that the underlying failure in Butler's work is his timid acknowledgment of unconscious memory or *will,* which Schopenhauer sees driving all else, which works within the individual, but also within all natural things, from stones to human races. Under the conscious intellect, says Schopenhauer, is an unconscious, striving, vital force, and only when we separate things in space and time do we become conscious, individuated persons. By flirting with such a theory in *The Way of All Flesh,* Butler trivializes his subject, becoming the "miniaturist" of Gosse's description. On the one hand he scarcely acknowledges the power of his essential myth; on the other hand, he fails to report honestly his own troubled emotions. Because he himself had long been accused of inaccuracies and of superficial insights (not to mention lifeless poems),[11] Gosse may have been acutely sensitive to Butler's problems in *The Way of All Flesh.* It was Gosse, not Butler, whom Virginia Woolf accused of an "innate regard for caution," because he was "always a little afraid of being found out."[12] In any case, Gosse's ambivalence about autobiographical purposes and autobiographical truth, implied in the motto from Schopenhauer, emerges unresolved and prominent in the opening pages of *Father and Son.*

Beginning with strictures on contemporary fiction for its "ingenious" and "specious" forms, the preface to *Father and Son* asserts the careful, the "punctilious attention" of the work at hand as another kind of writing.[13] Gosse may or may not have known as he wrote *Father and Son* how much of *The Way of All Flesh* had been fictional, but the essay on Butler draws attention to the elderly narrator as an instance of artifice and contrivance. There is no Overton in *Father and Son*. There is, at the beginning, an impersonal appeal from "the writer," who offers a "document, as a record of educational and religious conditions which, having passed away, will never return." The "document"—or "narrative," "record," "study," "recollections," as well as "diagnosis" and "examination"—"is scrupulously true." Only in the matter of names, says the anonymous speaker, "has there been any tampering with precise fact" (i).

What kind of book does Gosse promise? Well, in addition to being "a record of educational and religious conditions," specifically a "diagnosis of a dying puritanism," it is "in a subsidiary sense, a study of the development of moral and intellectual ideas" (i), though we do not for the moment know whose. If Butler equivocates with a meddling narrator, Gosse seems at first to introduce a treatise, a balanced, dispassionate book about historical conditions, yet warranted to be true because based on first-hand knowledge.[14]

This emphasis on truth, which I have mentioned in connection with such writers as Francis Newman and William Hale White, as well as with Schopenhauer, seems anomalous in an autobiographer, the more so when, like Newman and Gosse, the writer asserts that he is not writing autobiography at all. It is traditionally from writers of novels that we hear such protestations. "Truth," as the narrator of *Erewhon* blithely pronounces, "bears its own impress, and . . . [the] story will carry conviction by reason of the interval evidences for its accuracy." And: "No one who is himself honest will doubt my being so."[15] This is of course typical of the appeal of countless stories, from Lucian's "True Story" to Butler's, which deal with unlikely happenings. Autobiographers are more ready to assume the reader's acceptance of their veracity and to worry about effect. Rousseau advertises himself as one of a kind, challenging us to judge; John Stuart Mill doubts that his life will prove interesting; Wordsworth fears that his "drift" will be less than obvious. Gosse's preface hints at the indeterminate quality of the story he will tell, which is autobiographical in form, yet "true" just as novels are "specious." After settling on his purpose as "the narrative of a spiritual struggle" (ii), Gosse ventures to call his book a "tragedy," albeit with a touch of "comedy," since laughter and pathos mix in our lives, "and this book is nothing if it is not a genuine slice of life" (ii).[16]

No doubt Gosse was unaware of his mixed "metaphors of self"—to adapt James Olney's useful phrase[17] — but could he also have been unaware that the self he introduces in the preface figures only in the one reference to "the Son," everything else being relegated to impersonal constructions? Because *Father and Son* incorporates or dramatizes most of the contradictions of the preface, the question remains as to why Gosse struggled with his public definitions of the book, why, for example, he would invoke the already hackneyed critical trope about "the slice of life." I suspect that several things are going on here. Most obviously, Gosse wants to present his book with as many credentials as possible, not realizing that one of his definitions would suffice or that none was essential. Hence he appeals to the authority of separate genres: naturalistic novels provide a slice of life; tragedies evoke emotional anguish along with dignity and possible catharsis; narratives of spiritual struggle lend importance to the person struggling; and studies of development sound sober and reliable, though not too sober if softened by touches of "merriment and humour" (ii).

Behind the confusion lies the larger generic question faced by any autobiographer: the nature and the status of a book about ourselves, which tacitly asserts the narrator-subject as hero, which uses methods of fiction to re-create personal history. Gosse's dilemma is that of Dilthey, Tyrrell, or White, who think of autobiography caught between the competing poles of unchecked egotism and formal history, unsure where it belongs and apprehensive about its value. Dickens allows David Copperfield to wonder, in his fictional autobiography, whether he will turn out to be the hero of his own book. There is perhaps no alternative. Even Jean-Paul Sartre, denouncing his younger self and confessing to a hatred of his childhood, knows that his "words" are a tribute to himself.[18] No one equivocates more than Gosse, who asserts that he is *not* writing an autobiography (212) but rather telling of the relationship between himself and his father, to whom he tries to give the last word: "This narrative . . . must not be allowed to close with the Son in the foreground of the piece" (233). The final words are, however, "for himself" (250), and appropriately, since the focus on almost every page is on the feelings and the thinking of Edmund Gosse. The process of looking back invariably entails the task of sorting out and selecting, of making both an envisioned whole and a satisfactory self out of that chaotic past that we alone can know. "Nothing," as Gosse says, "abides in one tense projection" (241); what can and should abide in the construction of personal history?

His cross-purposes notwithstanding, Gosse is sure of one thing. For all its overlap with various literary genres, *Father and Son* is not a "romance." Behind the distinction between romance and truth — a distinction only implied in the preface to *Father and Son*—lies Gosse's impatience with *The Way of All Flesh* as romance and his own previous attempts at prose fiction. *The Unequal Yoke* (1886) and *The Secret of Narcisse: A Romance* (1892) are, to my mind, deservedly forgotten, and *The Unequal Yoke* emerged from the pages of *The English Illustrated Magazine* a few years ago only by an act of scholarly generosity.[19] In an introduction to *The Unequal Yoke,* James Woolf has high praise for Gosse's fiction, suggesting that the treatments of dissent in *The Unequal Yoke* and of aesthetics in *The Secret of Narcisse* anticipate *Father and Son* and deserve attention. Arguing against the contemporary reader for Macmillan, who found *The Unequal Yoke* uncontrolled, emotionally unbalanced, and replete with solecisms, Woolf says that the novel "made use of the best theory and practice of the time regarding plot," and that its "romantic ideal is such that it embraces, in its truth to humanism, the values in all religious and social endeavor toward good."[20] There is no doubt that the friend of Henry James was aware of novelistic theory and sophisticated novelistic practice, or that he expressed ideals, "romantic" and social, in his novel. The novel is probably none the better for all that. If the Macmillan reader misread Gosse's attitudes toward nonconformity, he was right about the solecisms: not in the sense of bad grammar, but in the sense of bad literary "etiquette" or decorum, as he might have put it. For example, after discussing with his friend Leyoncrona his intention to jilt his betrothed, Jane Baxter, Frank Capulet leaves the room:

> And he went to bed much easier in his mind than he left Mr. Leyoncrona, who nevertheless had neither prevaricated, nor written a selfish letter, nor betrayed the traditions of his class. But it is the privilege of youth to be callous.[21]

Gosse can hardly have recalled the arch narrator and his easy values with pride. Nor is there much point in speaking about the story in relation to Hardy's tragic vision, or describing its characters as "carefully and symbolically drawn."[22] Neither *The Unequal Yoke* nor *The Secret of Narcisse* is more than inadequate "romance," though the one is set in contemporary London and the other in medieval France. My guess is that Gosse's memory of these works, along with the admonitory lessons of his father, forced him to think differently when he came to write *Father and Son.* What had evaded him in the past and what he saw missing and hinted at in *The Way of All Flesh* became his ideal: a book of psychological and historical verisimilitude, which would deal generously with the difficult topics and the conflicting people it introduced.

Gosse's preface, hesitant or defensive as it may be, promises the *development* of that unnamed speaker from dissenting darkness (invoking Matthew Arnold's prejudice) to a kind of personal and aesthetic freedom. To a limited extent this is what happens. But just as John Stuart Mill and Matthew Arnold do not entirely overthrow the convictions of their fathers, Gosse unknowingly remains in the thrall of his. The careful and impersonal writing of the preface are, in a sense, testimony to the father whose values Gosse needs to transcend but whose influence clearly remains. Like *The Way of All Flesh,* this is an epistemological study, a book about the elements and the limits of knowing in a world as difficult for the present teller as for the self of his distant past. Gosse's language will suggest some of the complexities or confusions with which he struggled in *Father and Son;* it will also suggest his ideal of growth, an ideal like Schiller's, quoted above, in *The Aesthetic of Education of Man.* Without mentioning and perhaps without knowing Schiller, he writes:

> The recollection [of various incidents] confirms me in my opinion that certain leading features in each human soul are inherent to it, and cannot be accounted for by suggestion or training. . . . What came to me was the consciousness of self, as a force and as a companion.
>
> (32)

Here is a more or less benevolent view of Schopenhauer's "will," a philosophical position allowing progress as well as skepticism. In Gosse's world inherited characteristics (his mother's capacity for fiction, his father's for scientific understanding, his own for personal freedom) struggle for realization, a "force" against "forces," stasis against growth. Gosse's study is a retrospective account of those "leading qualities" that Schiller calls both goal and archetype, and though the narrator may remain as unaware as Butler's Ernest as to what his ideal is, or what it means, his book will explore its meaning.

> *"Ah! . . . you do not know how unaccountable is the development of the soul, and what is the meaning of any given form of character which presents itself to you. You see nothing but the peaceful, long since settled result, but how it came there, what its history has been, you cannot tell. It may always have been there, or have gradually grown . . . from seed to flower, or it may be the final repose of tremendous forces."*
>
> Miss Arbour, in The Autobiography of Mark Rutherford

To some extent the first chapter of *Father and Son* continues the expository quality of the preface. Speaking of people and times before his birth and during his earliest years, Gosse introduces the forces and the strife that underlie the entire book and that enter into its first sentence:

"This book is the record of a struggle between two temperaments, two consciousnesses and almost two epochs" (9). The self-conscious abstracting and weighing goes on, with the circumstances of his parents' meeting, their social and economic backgrounds, their professional aims, and, above all, their religious commitments and affiliations. The relatively dispassionate preamble to matters that would end in heartrending "disruption" attests to the distance of fifty years but no less to Gosse's strong if inconsistent desire to be fair.[23] Even his sentences have a deliberate, Gibbon-like counterbalance, "certain spiritual determinations" opposing "happy animal instincts" (14), "praise of the learned world" opposing "very little money" (15), love against loneliness, dull monotony against quiet happiness.[24]

But the balances are a rhetorical accounting, strife the historical reality. We know because the opening paragraph says so, but we know, too, from the revealing metaphors. Whether drawing from Darwin or Schopenhauer, Gosse like Butler thinks of the human organism alone in a dangerous and competitive world. With details of conflict more often implied than described, he recurs throughout his narrative to battles of wills. His mother has struggled with her family and even more with her mother-in-law. Gosse's parents themselves have had difficulties, though their relationship is built on trust and love. The father's strong opposition to his independence depends in part on the power of Gosse's mother, who exerts a life-long control "over the will and nature of my father" (16). "Hence, while it was with my Father that the long struggle which I have to narrate took place, behind my father stood the ethereal memory of my Mother's will" (17).[25] The will of both mother and father has been directed against fellow religious enthusiasts or chapel members, and because of their commitment as Plymouth Brethren, the two have also clashed with the society around them. Philip Gosse will later struggle with Sister Paget, who "became almost a terror to him" (203). Poverty, too, requires rigorous self-expression and struggle, as Edmund discovers in accompanying his mother to depressing lodgings near the doctor who treats her illness. This is a story not only about the puritanical world into which Gosse was born but about the clash of wills, about "magnetic power" and "unswerving purpose" (16–17), all related in metaphoric terms with which Schopenhauer would have sympathized. And Philip Gosse's grim fight with evolutionary doctrine epitomizes both the family's isolation and the powerful forces his son sees underlying all human activity.

While depicting in this first chapter a world not his own, or not yet tangibly his own, Gosse moves sporadically in and out of exposition. "It is not my business here," he says, "to re-write the biographies of my parents" (17). Instead, he gives brief glances, thumbnail histories, a few anticipatory details. If he is not offering biographies or "another memoir of public individuals," he is still sorting out his purposes as he sets the "scene." His task now emerges as "the record of a state of soul" (18), but a soul that develops from and is intertwined with the puritanical convictions of his parents. For this reason his language of balance and mediation echoes *their* language, which Gosse apparently distinguishes from "specious" fiction or romance, however much Gosse thinks of his life in terms of literature or writes, for that matter, what his parents would have deplored. Indeed, while *Father and Son* records an "aesthetic" development, the life of an artist, the early years of a *Künstlerroman,* its underlying emphasis is on spiritual rather than artistic growth, as if, in Ruskin's words, "a dutiful offering at the grave of parents."[26]

Gosse's "document" is a kind of mnemonic palimpsest, early voices sounding in the mind of the man of letters now writing. Diverse voices unfold in the narrative, including, for example, Wordsworth's, whose moments of insight lend value to Gosse's own and who seems more prophet than poet. Other voices contend as well, and Gosse establishes an early parallel between his own account and that of confessing puritans, "once not uncommon in Protestant Europe, of which my parents were perhaps the latest consistent exemplars among people of light and leading" (18). Without yet mentioning Bunyan and Wesley, Gosse wants them in his reader's mind, for this is a story that inverts the usual record of the discovery of grace while grounding itself in religious issues and remaining throughout a spiritual confession.

When Samuel Butler–Ernest Pontifex illustrates the inhibiting religion of his parents, he quotes self-damning letters from his mother or ludicrous messages from an unloving father. Gosse quotes from his mother's "secret notes," but these reveal a saintly, loving, if similarly parochial woman: not a fool or an enemy who can easily be rejected, but someone with conviction and the will to be a force after she dies. Gosse is careful to present both his parents, in these opening pages, with understanding and compassion.

After a few intermittent flickers of narrative, Gosse concludes his first chapter in two divergent ways. He presents a final, magisterial overview of his parents and their situation when he was born, then turns to a kind of conceit or extended metaphor, which foreshadows the promised record of the growth of his "soul." Here are sections from the two paragraphs.

The peculiarities of a family life founded upon such principles, are, in relation to a little child, obvious; but I may be permitted to recapitulate them. Here was perfect purity, perfect intrepidity, perfect abnegation; yet there was also narrowness, isolation, an absence of perspective, let it be boldly admitted, an absence of humanity. And there was a curious mixture of humbleness and arrogance; entire resignation to the will of God and not less entire disdain of the judgment and opinion of man. My parents founded every action, every attitude, upon their interpretation of the Scriptures, and upon the guidance of the Divine Will as revealed to them by direct answer to prayer.

(18)

Saving the personal pronoun, this passage reads like a paragraph from Arnold's *St. Paul and Protestantism*. It precedes other related statements of incarceration, of lives trapped in "an intellectual cell" (19), before Gosse concludes with an astonishing leap of rhetoric:

This, then, was the scene in which the soul of a little child was planted, not as in an ordinary open flower-border or carefully tended social parterre, but as on a ledge, split in the granite of some mountain. The ledge was hung between the night and the snows on one hand, and the dizzy depths of the world upon the other; was furnished with just soil enough for a gentian to struggle skywards and open its stiff azure stars; and offered no lodgement, no hope of salvation, to any rootlet which should stray beyond its inexorable limits.

(19)

Here are two competing idioms. The one reports with the kind of dead rhetoric of his father, with studied detachment, what are countervailing and stalemating forces; the other overflows (to use one of his own tropes) with hyperbole and metaphor, telling of painful, precarious growth. Although much of the late narrative subsumes the essayist manner or relegates it to short commentary, Gosse maintains the terms and the tone of his early passage, and to good effect. That quality of stalemate suggests how little his parents, especially his father, ever changed or ever could change, within themselves or in relation to others. Gosse mentions later his father's confidence in the second coming of Christ, about which, like so many fundamentalists before and since, his predictive arithmetic was repeatedly mistaken. This confidence epitomizes his father's belief, but it also makes clear how rooted and limited he had become, how unadapted to any future. Out of the static world of his parents Gosse measures his growth.

The conceit of the gentian (with its pun on birth and family), if close to self-pity and preciosity, introduces several strands of the narrative. Much like William Hale White, Gosse contrasts the dark, entrapping city, or room, or school with the freedom of hills and seashore.[27] The move of Philip Henry Gosse and his son to Devon (recorded at the end of chapter 4) reminds the older narrator of Wordsworth's encounters with a redeeming nature and prompts him to speak of both imagination and of growing up. "I was a town-child no longer" (81). Earlier, father and son make an expedition to Primrose Hill, where Edmund expects to see endless fields of flowers and untrammeled countryside. He learns the power of words to mislead, but he has, if anything, gained in his appreciation of natural beauty, though as a child of a zoologist he often describes natural beauty with either a taxonomic stiffness or a loose hyperbole.

The gentian metaphor suggests the abundance of figurative language throughout *Father and Son,* including flowers, bright colors, streams, journeys, and frightening depths. Often they come together in the figures of light and dark, with light assuming all the traditional connotations of learning and understanding. It is in spite of the darkness of his parents' world and without, presumably, choosing a merely hedonistic alternative, that Gosse finds his way, and the way is as much backwards as forwards, the narrator redescending, in Pater's words, into his own past while using the past to understand his present.[28] Gosse's opening to his second chapter suggests how metaphors of light imply both past awareness and present discovery. "Out of the darkness of my infancy," he says, "there comes only one flash of memory" (21). Freud might have called this flash of memory a screen-memory. The baby, unattended, watches a large animal (Gosse thinks a greyhound) slip into the room and leave with the meat for dinner. Not being old enough to talk, he has no words to explain the event to his family, and it is only in later years that they can laugh together about what happened. It is appropriate that they do laugh, because Gosse never denies either the good laughter that his family shared or the partly comic perspective from which he looks back at such events. As for the theft of the meat, it does not matter whether Gosse remembered an actual event or imagined another to cover something repressed. What he remembers tells a great deal about the workings of his mind and the process of his book, so much of which emphasizes the metaphoric "light" of his parents' vocabulary.

Consciousness of words plays an important part in Gosse's account of his life, and the finding and learning about words helps to accomplish his growing up. From the "secret diary" of his mother to the late letters of his father, words of various documents matter enormously.

Why, for example, should Gosse quote those secret diaries? They are, on the face of it, quite innocuous:

> We are happy and contented [she writes at one time], having all things needful and pleasant, and our present habitation is hallowed by many sweet associations. We have our house to ourselves and enjoy each other's society. If we move we shall no longer be alone. The situation may be more favourable, however, for Baby, as being more in the country.
>
> (16)

His mother's dispassionate weighing—characteristic of his preface and of his critical essays—may appeal to him; and most people enjoy references to their own childhood and infancy, even if they figure as the unnamed "Baby." Beyond this, I think that Gosse appreciates his mother's attempts to sort out her soul's journey, the more so in documents that have been sealed for sixty years and reserved for his private reading. He knows, too, that her ordinary words had a strength difficult to fathom, for he records several times how her graceful, quiet talk could convert the most unlikely people to her faith and zeal. At one time a young soldier, about to leave for the Crimea (where he died), listens with eagerness to her prayers and exhortations. Gosse's sense of his book as a document means that he cares about words, the memory or recording of which honors his past. Whether or not he actually remembers the words of his father's conversation, he presents a few quotations and says a great deal indirectly, contrasting his father's stern and measured phrases with his own "childish language." In addition to the later letters to Edmund in London—"Let me know more of your inner light" (236)—bits of his father's words are recorded from sermons, prayers, and conversations heard and overheard. Throughout his life Gosse could tell anecdotes, mimic people's talk, and record conversations; still, after many decades, the vivid transcriptions of *Father and Son* are obviously "truth" in an imagined more than a recollected form.

The remembering of spoken and written words is indispensable in the re-creation of "scenes," as Gosse calls them, indispensable for the "record" or "document" he offers, even if the words re-create more than they actually report. But words do far more than authenticate in *Father and Son*. They are a measure of understanding and a means to understanding. The young boy who excels in geography loves the sound of names, which "have always appealed directly to my imagination" (39). Primrose Hill disappoints him so intensely because its name has promised so much; for the first of many times he is forced to see the discrepancy between a squalid reality and words invested by his solitary imagination. Even the young boy's dreams, or nightmares, center on words. One distressing nightmare recurs and leads to "frenzied despair." Beginning as a "vision," the dream resolves itself in a singular fashion: "Far away, in the pulsation of the great luminous whorls, I could just see that goal, a ruby-coloured point waxing and waning, and it bore, or to be exact it consisted of, the letters of the word CARMINE" (119).[29] Gosse's explanation of the dream has to do with the rarity of a pigment among his father's illustrative paints, something he was not allowed to play with, yet as his introductory comments make clear, he sensed larger meanings in his nightmares:

> I had hardly laid my head down on the pillow, than, as it seemed to me, I was taking part in a mad gallop through space. Some force, which had tight hold of me, so that I felt myself an atom in its grasp, was hurrying me on, over an endless slender bridge, under which on either side a loud torrent rushed at a vertiginous depth below. . . . It seemed as if we,—I, that is, and the undefined force which carried me,—were pushing feverishly on towards a goal which our whole concentrated energies were bent on reaching, but which a frenzied despair in my heart told me we could never reach, yet the attainment of which alone could save us from destruction.
>
> (118–19)

Here as elsewhere, Gosse's metaphors compound each other, one "force" defining and increasing another, with torrents or waves or streams paired with heights and insecure footing. The gentian of the early passage suggested a similar solitude and precariousness, with force the underlying condition and despair its emotional correlative. "We" also stands out in this passage, and whereas in other places the "we" may be father and son, or Gosse and his two selves (39), Gosse here associates himself with the "undefined force," with unconscious will. In what emerges as an apocalyptic vision, words become both extreme and uncertain, "scarcely adequate to describe" (23).

Whether recollected or dramatically re-created, other words affect Gosse with similar power. When, as a very young boy, he realizes that his father has said something that "was not true," "Nothing could possibly have been more trifling to my parents, but to me it meant an epoch. Here was the appalling discovery, never suspected before, that my father was not as God" (33). At different moments in his childhood he emphasizes the shock of such insights, examining words and silences against a shrinking absolute. Even God comes in for scrutiny when Edmund, defying his parents, attempts the worship of an "idol" in the form of an ordinary chair. No angry Jehovah smites him when he says, "Oh Chair!" (44). Here, too, the boy learns a lesson, not just about his parents' God, but about language, which he tests as well as records, defines as well as describes. The young Edmund is as obsessed by words as Stephen Dedalus, his younger, fictional contemporary.[30]

Another and wholly different indication of the power of words in *Father and Son* occurs in one of its most moving scenes. When his mother becomes ill and visits a physician, Edmund tells of her return home:

> While I was wondering at all this [his father's preparations for dinner], the door opened, and my Mother entered the room; she emerged from behind the bedroom curtains, with her bonnet on, having returned from her expedition. My Father rose hurriedly, pushing back his chair. There was a pause, while my Mother seemed to be steadying her voice, and then she replied, loudly and distinctly, "He says it is——" and she mentioned one of the most cruel maladies by which our poor mortal nature can be tormented. Then I saw them fold one another in a silent long embrace, and presently sink together out of sight on their knees, . . . whereupon my Father lifted up his voice in prayer.
>
> (48)

As Gosse recounts this episode, his father's question doesn't get asked, and his mother's reply gets abbreviated, though she herself speaks "loudly and distinctly." When the episode continues to the next morning, Gosse still withholds the word: "With my eyes on my plate, as I was cutting up my food, I asked, casually, 'What is —?' mentioning the disease whose unfamiliar name I had heard from my bed" (48–49). We learn after the account of his mother's illness, what agonies of suffering *cancer* evokes for him, how much it still fills him with dread. The effect of the record is to give the unspoken or unwritten word the power of taboo. It is too real, too powerful to spell out. And yet, oddly enough, Gosse had been quite able to write about "breast cancer" in his biography of Philip Gosse. Here is his matter-of-fact account from that book:

> Late in April my mother became conscious of a local discomfort in her left breast. . . . But on May 1 . . . Miss Mary Stacey persuaded her to consult a physician, who rather crudely and roughly pronounced it to be cancer. She returned very calmly to her home, and in the course of the evening she quietly told her husband.[31]

Allowing for different narrative purposes and focus (which in this passage carefully omits the child), what seems to happen in *Father and Son* is that the reliving, rather than simply recounting, of the scene charges the dramatic moment with the power of new language.

When Gosse tells us late in his story that "the great subject of my curiosity at this time was words" (215), he is only emphasizing what has long become clear. The best indication of his obsession with words is, predictably, his growing sense of literature, which becomes a major sign of his emotional and intellectual development. Early in the book he speaks about the effect of hymns, which continue to move him and which he is unable to judge beyond the scope of his own remembered emotions. In this increasingly allusive book, Gosse quotes Scripture, John Donne, Rousseau, Pascal, and others among the dozens of writers he encountered later as a critic and literary historian. Like William Butler Yeats, he comes to distinguish his taste from his father's by emphasizing his reading of Ruskin who, along with Carlyle, soon competes with the diet of Scripture.[32] He has always enjoyed reading, from the days his parents allowed him the *Penny Cyclopaedia,* and the progress of the narrative is to great extent a record of the indulgence of his literary curiosity. His mother's strong convictions as to the dangers of fiction, and his father's less adamant but hardly less restricted literary judgments limit his readings for many years. Dickens wins approval, but not Walter Scott. Few books make their way into the Gosse household, unless they are scientific. But slowly, Edmund gets hold of the "Graveyard Poets," Blair, Young, Gray. His father's surprising recitation of Vergil staggers him with the beauty of poetic rhythm; and a chance encounter with Marlowe's "Hero and Leander" moves him sensually, before his father can take the book away. At several points in the narrative, Gosse quotes Wordsworth, and though he does not say when he encountered Wordsworth, *The Prelude* and other poems evidently help in the review of his own life. Again, after the move to Devon, Gosse describes the pristine beauty of the sea and shore and quotes Wordsworth, not Scripture, on light and inner light, because he has Wordsworth's sense of wonder in mind. He also invokes Wordsworth to define "the infirmity of love for days disowned by memory" (81), implying that his own record is a testimony to imagination earned through acts of recollection.

Important as Wordsworth and other writers are, they are not as important as two unlikely bedfellows: Shakespeare and Michael Scott. Because of its geographical information, Gosse's father oddly allows his son *Tom Cringle's Log,* and for the young boy it comes like "a glass of brandy neat to some one who had never been weaned from a milk diet" (160). Gosse is reminiscent here of John Stuart Mill, whose recovery from his emotional crisis is eased by Wordsworth and Coleridge, but also by Marmontel, whose memoirs have a similar effect on his emotions. Gosse, however, is speaking of himself as a young boy, reading as Coleridge read, voraciously and indiscriminately. In the long run, Shakespeare does matter more to him than *Tom Cringle*, though he came to Shakespeare relatively late. I quote the passage on Shakespeare, putting the statement about Gosse's curiosity for words in a fuller context:

> The great subject of my curiosity at this time was words, as instruments of expression. I was incessant in adding to my vocabulary, and in finding accurate and individual terms for things. Here, too, the exercise preceded the employment, since I was busy providing myself with words before I had any ideas to express with them. When I read Shakespeare and came upon the passage in which Prospero tells Caliban that he had no thoughts till his master taught him words, I remember starting with amazement at the poet's intuition, for such a Caliban had I been:
>
> > I pitied thee
> > Took pains to make thee speak, taught thee each hour
> > One thing or other, when thou didst not, savage,
> > Know thine own meaning, but wouldst gabble, like
> > A thing most brutish; I endow'd thy purposes
> > With words that made them know.
>
> For my Prosperos I sought vaguely in such books as I had access to, and I was conscious that as the inevitable word seized hold of me, with it out of the darkness into strong light came the image and the idea.
>
> (215–16)

The passage epitomizes *Father and Son*. Gosse begins the paragraph that follows with "My Father," but his father is notably absent from the discussion of *The Tempest*, which treats of another powerful father, Prospero, himself a teacher, albeit of a creature nurtured in vain. Gosse has spoken throughout his story of the lessons learned from his father: lessons of observation, patience, hard work, and accuracy, for his father "taught him words." In spite of all this, Philip Henry Gosse has lost his magic, or his magic has died within, victim of a religion that divides "heart from heart" (246). With confused emotions, Edmund sees himself not as Miranda or Ferdinand but as Caliban, the ungrateful son of a loving father, a monster after all. Then with new insight he senses that he is no monster, because he has been, unlike poor Caliban, lifted up by the words he has learned. He is himself a Prospero, the wizard with the book. Finally, however, his imagery comes not from Prospero, or Shakespeare, but—as so often in this story—from the world of his parents, where the "Word" is everything and where grace is light.

> *I was standing, just now, thinking of these things, where the Cascine ends in the wooded point which is carved out sharply by the lion-coloured swirl of the Arno on the one side and by the pure flow of the Mugnone on the other. The rivers meet, and run parallel, but there comes a moment when the one or the other must conquer, and it is the yellow vehemence that drowns the purer tide.*
>
> Gosse, Father and Son (84)

Gosse makes this statement in the middle of a paragraph about his father, his father's naturalistic researches in Devon, and the "exquisite journeys" father and son take to the seashore. He has just described the "uncouth majesty" of Devon in those times, and he will say a little later that the shore was a kind of Eden to him: untouched and unspoiled. His descriptions sound like those of George Henry Lewes, scouring the lovely sands and rocks at Tenby, where he took a holiday with George Eliot and paid his tribute to geology.[33] John Fowles has drawn a similar picture in *The French Lieutenant's Woman,* in which the amateur naturalist, Charles, clambers across the Lyme Cobb in search of fossils. Fowles catches the double vision of Gosse, who looks back on an Edenic world, but who writes with all the consciousness of loss and change. Describing his father and himself at the shore, Gosse recalls the "shallow tidal pools," his most conspicuous reflective image:

> Those pools were our mirrors, in which, reflected in the dark hyaline and framed by the sleek and shining fronds of oar-weed there used to appear the shapes of a middle-aged man and a funny little boy.
>
> (109–10)

The middle-aged narrator here sees himself as his own father and his former self, real and unreal, in that "Garden of Eden" now no more. Not only has the shore been plundered (and Gosse says that his father's obsession inspired many collectors), but, in his own idiom, the waves or the currents of change have left nothing untouched. Darwin, Wallace, Hooker, Lyell, and Gray have irreparably altered the world we see.

It is not surprising that Gosse focuses on evolution, using it as a metaphor as well as a sign of change, since his father's career became so sadly connected with the new scientific discoveries. In his zeal to acknowledge the new findings and to protect the authority of the Bible, Philip Henry Gosse wrote his *Omphalos,* a work scorned alike by true believers and the scientists.[34] That short period of relative happiness in Devon, some time after the death of Gosse's mother, was soon to be "darkened . . . by disappointments" (84), that is, by his father's anguish and professional isolation. Even his friend Charles Kingsley wrote that "he could not 'give up the painful and slow conclusion of five and twenty years' study of geology, and believe that God has written on the rocks one enormous and superfluous lie'" (88). That "honest hodman of science" (96), as T. H. Huxley called Gosse's father, had lost his way in theory, satisfying no one. He had "allowed the turbid volume of superstition to drown the delicate stream of reason" (84).

The reference to "now" in the passage written, or thought, by the banks of the Arno stands apart. It is not like Gibbon's pointed recollection of that October day in 1764, when he first contemplated writing *The Decline and Fall.* Gosse's "now" opens his present consciousness, allowing belated insight into a distant and previously indistinct past. Though in a sense buried within a larger paragraph, it involves a radical shift in references and in the sense of narrative time. Presumably, we accept a "now" in any autobiography, changing as it may with the growth of perception through the book or during different periods when the book is written (see, for example, the later discussion of George Moore's *Memoirs of My Dead Life*). Gosse's reference to Tuscany is a pointed and for him unusual look back from a named place as well as a definite moment. "Looking back" is itself a phrase he uses repeatedly: he looks "back at this time as upon a cantankerous, ill-tempered and unobliging child" (93); and he looks back as "the stream of my spiritual nature spread out into a shallow pool" (214). But at no point does he specify both time and place except on the banks of the Arno, where he is far from England, far from the anguish (and occasional joys) of his childhood.

However singular in quality, the reference to "I" writing "now," "here," near the Arno, helps to clarify the sense of time and memory throughout *Father and Son.* In the first place, Gosse resorts easily and often to the cliché of time's stream or river. With or without Heraclitus in mind (Heraclitus was a favorite with Yeats, Hopkins, and other contemporaries), he is obsessed with the hopeless flow of time, which he tends to see in both large and personal terms. When he speaks about the clear and the yellow stream, he speaks almost literally of the same streams within his father's mind. History is a stream no less than the life of an individual, and, like Wilhelm Dilthey and F. H. Bradley, Gosse tacitly understands the individual life in terms of great historical forces. His father is at once a tragic and representative example. Beyond this, the "yellow tide" has emotional attributes: its vehemence drowns the purer water. Since Gosse assumes the implacable power of Darwin's theories in other contexts, he seems to twist his usual metaphors of power and will, associating his father's stubborness with the unstoppable force. So within the larger categories of science and historical development, there is also a further allusion to his own situation, to his quest for reason in opposition to the force and vehemence of his father's belief. In the long run, the small child may be on the side of the scientists and progress, but for the moment his older self sees him as human driftwood in the flow of time.

Gosse does not mention a book about rivers with which he must have been familiar: his father's *Sacred Streams* (1850), a kind of meditation on "Rivers of the Bible." His own writing seems to parody his father's enthusiastic work, which brings together Bible lore, delight in topography, and easy reflections about time and history. "Sweet it is," writes Philip Gosse, "in the heat of a summer's noon, to sit on the mossy bank, and watch the meandering stream . . . [and] admire its clearness."[35] Despite his son's dismissal of his literal readings, Philip Gosse assumes a metaphorical understanding of rivers, which he connects with biblical events and with present meditation. Like *A Naturalist's Rambles on the Devonshire Coast* (1853) and other books about the seashore, *Sacred Streams* is an engaging and popular work. It emphasizes a shared pleasure in streams and rivers, especially in "crystal streams," which Gosse associates with great public events and with private satisfaction.

Rivers can be, says Philip Gosse, not only emblems of beauty and peace, but also of division and suffering. "In such lands [as Mesopotamia], nothing is more natural than that fresh streams and flowing rivers should be constantly used by the inspired poets and prophets, as emblems." But, he says, in anticipation of his son's metaphors, "utter confusion is the immediate consequence [of Babel], an undistinguishable jargon of sounds." In the struggle between "the powers of light and darkness," rivers are the central symbol, albeit the "pure river of the water of life" can never flow "on earth."[36]

Whether Edmund Gosse was aware of the irony, his placing himself near the Arno (in the midst, that is, of Renaissance instead of biblical history) is a wonderful commentary on himself and on his father's life. Troping his father's tropes, as Harold Bloom might say, Gosse also looks back on a prelapsarian world, his youth in Devon, his father's happiness. His contemplation now almost echoes his father's "sweet it is" while mocking the view of history that allows biblical paradigms to renew individual lives. His own sense of history is manifest in the sullied stream, the lost clarity, the breached love. At the same time, the Arno gives him the distance from his loss and the implication at least of his aesthetic independence, which draws on his father's myths and his father's work while pointing in a new direction.[37]

The combination of biblical myth and assumptions about evolutionary change bears on the sense of time and memory in a narrative about the development of an individual life, all the more so when an author sees his life as inextricable from larger social and intellectual forces. Time and memory in *Father and Son* are for this reason both public and private. On the question of progress or ameliorative development, for example, Gosse seems of two minds. In a peculiar way, he is most optimistic when speaking about the death of his mother. Just as the professional disgrace of his father calls up thoughts of violent change, so the death of his mother reminds him of time's "mitigations":

> Everywhere, in the whole system of human life, improvements, alleviations, ingenious appliances and human inventions are being reproduced to lessen the great burden of suffering. . . . If we were suddenly transplanted into the world of only fifty years ago, we should be startled and even horror-striken by the wretchedness to which the step backwards would re-introduce us.
>
> (55)

Throughout his narrative, Gosse repeatedly steps back and makes us aware of time having passed: "Time moves smoothly and swiftly, and we do not perceive the mitigations which he brings in his hands" (55). In the passages about the professional "death" of his father and the actual death of his mother, he does something more. Here as nowhere else he speaks at length about scientific and technological advances, while speculating about the changes of fifty years. He also reiterates that his focus *is* fifty years ago, with the implication that the two events of his eighth year were the crucial events of his lifetime. Another way of putting this is to say that, although *Father and Son,* as its title makes clear, is the record of the struggle between Edmund and Philip Henry Gosse, the book is also a tribute—after fifty years—to his dead mother.[38] This raises further questions about his personal history and its literary shape.

The full term of *Father and Son* extends from Gosse's birth, with a few backward glances at his parents' backgrounds, to his first years in London, which means the years of his early manhood, from seventeen, when he left home, to perhaps twenty-one. The final years are extremely uneventful; again, Gosse has affirmed his desire that the book should not dwell on himself, and his final chapter consists largely of excerpts from his father's letters with a description of his own gradual independence. The early years seem fuller, but here again there is little direct narrative, only those brilliant scenes like that of the dog stealing the meat, or of his mother returning with her terrible news. Essentially, then, Gosse's narrative covers his life in detail from just before his mother's death to the time he left home, only ten years later, for his his life in London. The span is roughly that used by D. H. Lawrence when, in describing Paul Morel's upbringing, he emphasizes the adolescent years and the events prior to his move toward independence and the city.

Gosse's term "history" is appropriate for the years he describes. Only during this span does he care about dates, for example, and he gives many: he notes specifically his own age, in relation to "fifty years ago" (1857), or to the discovery of anaesthetics, or the publication of Darwin's major books. For a few weeks after his mother's death, Edmund stays with an aunt in Clifton, and it is in reference to this one interlude that he speaks of having "no history," living for a brief time the ordinary life of a child (66). History otherwise seems a record of events he may not want to remember, events he associates with suffering, death, or estrangement. Perhaps he has Gibbon in mind, and Gibbon's comment about history as a record of crime and misfortunes.[39] When Gosse looks back on his past, he comes to important insights about his sense of time. Twice in the narrative he says, for example, that his memory, "so clear and vivid about earlier solitary times, now in all this society [school] becomes blurred and vague" (65), and "once more I have to record the fact . . . that precisely as my life ceases to be solitary, it ceases to be distinct" (176). What remains clear are the times with his father, in the laboratory or at the shore, and times by himself, which he describes as solitary in the extreme. That Gosse was not as solitary as he remembered, that he "forgot" meetings, aquaintances, and even protracted company—as Ann Thwaite's comprehensive biography makes clear—is fascinating to consider.[40] We know how much, and Gosse says how much, he came to love company, how he needed to be with other people. His narrative describes a boy who with rare brief exceptions was indifferent to people other than his parents, who only learned to appreciate, even to crave, company as an older man. Was it a lapse of memory or the exigencies of drama that led him to see his life as he did? What does his claim to be "scrupulously true" mean for a narrative that conflated different periods, omitted significant people, and obviously bent facts to fit the needs of the story? And if Gosse selected and altered facts, what differentiates his story from a novel such as *Portrait of the Artist* or *Sons and Lovers*?

I shall return to this question, or an aspect of the question, a little later. Here I want to glance at one more passage, perhaps the central passage in *Father and Son* dealing with time and memory.

In chapter 4, after speaking of the interlude in which his "hard-driven soul was allowed to have for a little while, no history" (66), Gosse pauses in his narrative, both to sum up his experience of childhood temporality and to cover a tract of time he equates with that experience. The effect is a little like that in *David Copperfield,* when David introduces the "Retrospects," with their analogous reminder that nothing abides in one tense projection.

> The life of a child is brief, its impressions are so illusory and fugitive, that it is as difficult to record its history as it would be to design a morning cloud sailing before the wind. It is short, as we count shortness in after years, when the drag of lead pulls down to earth the foot that used to flutter with a winged impetuosity, and to float with the pulse of Hermes. But in memory, my childhood was long, long with interminable hours, hours with the pale cheek pressed against the window-pane, hours of mechanical and repeatedly lonely "games," which lost their savour, and were kept going by sheer inertness. Not unhappy, not fretful, but long,—long, long. It seems to me, as I look back to life in the motherless Islington house, as I resumed it in that slow, eighth year of my life, that time had ceased to move. There was a whole age between one tick of the eight-day clock in the hall and the next tick. . . . There was no past and no future for me, and the present felt as though it were sealed up in a Leyden jar.
> (66)

This brilliant evocation of a sort of living death after a death works, as Gosse's prose usually works, by compounding metaphor. Against the morning cloud and the winged Hermes, he gives a sense of pulseless, empty life. As a child he must have been unaware of the pale cheek, but the adult looking back looks at and with the child, seeing what he will soon call the "theater" of the street through the windowpanes or playing the flavorless, lifeless, mechanical "games," which epitomize the entire futility of the boy's life. If "long,—long, long" recalls the reiterative cadences of Dickens, that may not be accidental: a few pages later Gosse will describe his governess, "Miss Marks," as a combination of Dickens's types, and he will tell us that Dickens was one of a handful of fiction writers allowed him when a boy. That sense of *duration* or personal time is particularly acute in relation to the ticking of the clock, and the sense of suspended time may be reminiscent of another novelist, Sterne, who understands human consciousness in terms of psychological time and who makes his pages reflect an inner clock. At any rate, Gosse evokes the child's reality of time slowing to stillness or racing with a happy and ineffable speed; he catches "the illusory and fugitive" nature of time, and of time in memory, and he records the "child's" history with uncanny precision.

> *Eh quoi! vous me demandez si je connais "Father and Son"—!!! un livre que j'ai lu et relu, et fait lire je ne sais combien de fois; un livre avec qui j'ai vecu, que j'ai senti écrit pour moi et qui put reveiller les échoes les plus indiscret dans mon coeur.*
>
> André Gide, 1926 letter to Gosse

In the section on William Hale White I mentioned Susanne Langer's distinction between a kind of "concrete" or flashback memory and a memory that is "biographical." Langer suggests that memories of our past lives are of these two basic sorts: those from childhood, which we experience selectively, intensely, and with strong emotions; and those from our later lives, which we more obviously re-create, re-cognize along a line of historical or biographical intention. The later memories are characteristically less vivid, less compelling, than those of our childhood. Without pursuing the distinction—obvious to a writer such as Wordsworth—I would suggest that the power in Gosse's story comes from his emphasis on the early years, which are for him as for his reader invested with energy and passion.

When Gosse says that he is not writing "a regular autobiography" (212), he may mean that his emphasis is on two (or including his mother, three) people, and that he has selected incidents and patterns that a different focus would have changed. He may also mean that his book deals only with the early, formative years of his life, ignoring almost completely the development of the older man, who looks back over almost forty years to the last events of his story. *Father and Son* is more tightly written than Ford Madox Ford's *Ancient Lights,* but it shares with Ford's book the intensity of childhood memories and the vision of a life untrammelled by adult complications, problems of career or marriage, or for that matter any of the real consequences of emotional and intellectual crises dramatized in the account of childhood events.

Such a focus, as Gide recognized in his letter to Gosse, allows a distinctive resonance, *echoes* in the heart, of the sort that Gide himself could elicit, and that somehow bind together writer and reader in a world they can share. It is not only that memories of early years remain invested with power; they also have a public appeal that can be inversely proportionate to their common ground. Gosse evokes the same kind of feelings about his mother as, for example, the Russian Serge Aksakoff (in *A Russian Schoolboy,* 1917), although provincial life on the Steppes has nothing on the face of it to do with Gosse's boyhood. Aksakoff speaks of "the Golden Age" of childhood, the recollection of which "has power to move the old man's heart."[41] As with Gosse, that golden age is not necessarily a happy time, but it is remembered with such love, such passion, that any recollected event can matter.

Vivid childhood recollections take on, in writers like Aksakoff and Gosse, Wordsworth and Proust, the qualities of fairytale and myth, in which, again, a nonheroic figure becomes almost preternaturally important. Trifles can make the sum of life if early life can be seen in a coherent or integrating way. And this is what happens in Gosse, who transforms the anguish and loneliness and struggles of his boyhood into the materials of a compelling book. "Corresponding power," which Wordsworth called for in his reader develops almost inevitably in a work that catches the visionary quality so many people see in their early lives and so few in their later. Hence, the rightness of Gide's word *echoes,* the aptness of his conviction that the book had been written for him.

Let me return for a moment to Gosse's insistence that "this is not an autobiography" (212), which seems to echo Charlotte Brontë's similar comment in *Jane Eyre.* What Brontë seems intuitively to know is the distinction between types of memory as distinguished by Susanne Langer. Although *Jane Eyre* is a novel written in the mode of autobiography, it disclaims any attempt to be autobiography, though not at the outset of the book. In chapter 10 Jane says that her intent is quite different. She can omit large tracts of time because she is not writing "a regular autobiography."[42] But why, having emphasized the personal validity of her own recollections, and hence the reliability of the narrative itself, should she step back at this point and, essentially, enter into another arrangement with her reader? After chapter 10, Jane's story continues in the first person, but with a different and looser emphasis on the word *memory.* The bulk of the novel, coming after chapter 10, changes both its use of recollected time and its employment of fictional devices. The autobiographical disclaimer may or may not be the immediate point of change, but it signals a change. The adult Jane, who emerges as capable student and even teacher, begins to look at her past from another perspective.

When she prepares an adult life for her character-narrator, Charlotte Brontë tacitly acknowledges another need, which is at once a new "biographical" reporting and an increased use of common, fictional devices. Nineteenth-century autobiography does not shun coincidence, foreshadowing, as George Moore and John Henry Newman might suggest ("I have a work to do in England"); and as Butler and White have shown, autobiography soon slips into novelistic modes (just as novels like Brontë's draw on autobiographical materials). And autobiographical ordering has much to do with novelistic conventions. Can we really say at the outset whether *Robinson Crusoe* or *David Copperfield* or *Jane Eyre* is autobiography or novel? Can we be any surer about the generic boundaries of *Father and Son*?

In any case, Charlotte Brontë seems to work a double bonus. She purports to write autobiography, with its attendant sympathy, pathos, and vividness; she then shifts the emphasis, not away from Jane as her controlling character, but to a world in which people can meet in unlikely places, can inherit wealth and identity, can "hear" the call of people they love over great distances, and can resolve their lives before they die. Brontë has vouchsafed the authenticity of Jane's voice, which is "now," even when it speaks of childhood, long before she has to test it. She has also prepared the way for the lonely orphan to discover self and love in a world that remains in fact as hostile as Jane's early environment even when Jane's own life turns into the wish-fulfillment of fairytales. We would not believe the Cinderella without the vivid cinders of Jane's childhood memories.

Jane Eyre helps to suggest the nature of Gosse's book, which stands somewhere between the lives of David Copperfield or Jane Eyre and the lives of Stephen Dedalus and Paul Morel. By ignoring or implying his adult life, Gosse preserves the embryonic power of his narrative. He does not risk, like Butler, the difficult task of sorting out years too close for understanding, years that need to be dealt with "biographically," which in fact means fictionally or at least novelistically, a prospect which frightened Gosse as much as it frightened White or Tyrrell or Butler. The long gestation may not lead, as the book implies, toward the perfect artist or the fulfilled man, but then it doesn't have to. It suggests like *Portrait of the Artist* what is ahead, and Gosse wrote no *Ulysses* to temper myth with irony.

I began this chapter with Gosse's response to Samuel Butler; I close with a few brief remarks on Gosse and George Moore, one of Gosse's many friends. A glance at *Father and Son* and Moore's *Memoirs of My Dead Life* illustrates how differently contemporary writers can look at their past and how differently they would define what the past involved. Instead of the childhood world of Gosse's book, Moore's explores the complexities of adult longings, his retrospections avoiding childhood until, finally, he is compelled to see himself in fuller and more troubling ways. In a sense, Moore was interested in the kinds of issues Gosse pointedly omitted (in his *non*-autobiography), the issues that J. A. Symonds tried to deal with in his *Memoirs,* now recently published for the first time.[43] Gosse himself was involved in the supervision of Symonds's book, which emphasizes sexuality as a primary topic in Symonds's growing up, and which dwells on that "interior" quality which Moore also seemed to want. In the violent and turbulent world of *Father and Son,* there is no sexuality, just as there is no coming to terms with career or adult self.[44] All is implied. But in Moore as in Symonds, it is the nature of the adult self that matters most, the dramatic present, through which the narrative of past events may by understood.[45]

5 Contemplations of Time: George Moore's *Memoirs of My Dead Life*

> *My contemplations are of Time*
> *That has transfigured me.*
> W. B. Yeats, "The Lamentation of the Old Pensioner"

Like his countryman W. B. Yeats, George Moore was consumed by thoughts of time and by the transfigurations of time within his own life. He, too, wrote "autobiographies," contemplative reminiscences no one of which could be definitive, all of which try to articulate the changes time has made. At his death in 1933, Moore was at work on yet another autobiographical study, an addition to the list that included *Confessions of a Young Man* (1888), *Memoirs of My Dead Life* (1906), *Avowals* (1919), and the monumental three-volume *Hail and Farewell* (1911–14).[1] The range of Moore's autobiographical books is wide. He moves from the Baudelairean young man of *Confessions*, who loves to shock a prudish reader, to the self-sufficient narrator of *Hail and Farewell*, who seeks self-understanding as much as theatrical effect. *Ave, Salve,* and *Vale* blend memoir with autobiography: in these works, Moore's acquaintances, Yeats, AE, Edward Martyn and others, come to life historically and personally, while Moore considers his own role in the Irish Renaissance.

Between *Confessions* and *Hail and Farewell* there came *Memoirs of My Dead Life*, a book that is not a memoir and not a full life-story, but rather a subtle exploration of past loves and past episodes in Moore's adult life. *Memoirs* is a book that shows Moore, if not at his best—and *Hail and Farewell* would be hard to surpass—at least at his most contemplative. In this work he is self-absorbed and fully aware of the disruption of selves. He has grown out of the buffoonery of *Confessions*, but he is neither writing accounts of historical movements and personal friends nor indulging in the long, conversational, if not tedious dialogues as the sage of Ebury Street. *Memoirs* explores a variety of past experiences, all with a view toward Moore's present state of mind. While introducing his retrospection at different times and in different places, he addresses his reader from a shifting and conversational "now," creating a kind of dialogue with the reader about time and loss and recovery.

> For all his novels are written, covertly and obliquely, about himself, so at least memory would persuade us.
> Virginia Woolf, "George Moore"

Before turning to *Memoirs of My Dead Life*, it would help to glance back at that extraordinary book in which George Moore lambasted English tastes and proclaimed himself a needed apostle bringing tidings from France. *Confessions* is contemporary with Tennyson's *Idylls of the King* and Arnold's (posthumous) *Essays in Criticism, Second Series*, but also with more nearly related works: Hardy's *Wessex Tales*, Gissing's *Life's Morning*, and the anonymous *My Secret Life*. Moore shared with Hardy and Gissing concerns about censorship. Hardy had tampered with the final story of *Wessex Tales*, substituting a happy or a conventional ending for his original version; and Gissing spent much of 1888 in Italy, hiding from reviews of *A Life's Morning*, which he had altered at his publisher's insistence with what he thought to be ruinous effect.[2] Moore's desire to "épater" the middle classes is different from Gissing's or Hardy's attempt simply to write what should be written. With its irony and scorn, *Confessions* comes closer to Butler's onslaught on Victorian conventions in *The Way of All Flesh*, however insular Butler's perspective; and in his later books Moore speculates about a form of cultural memory akin to that of Butler.

Another peculiar relative of Moore's *Confessions* is *My Secret Life*, which apparently began its history of private printing in 1888, and which shares with Moore's work a self-indulgence and self-assertion of a radically new sort.[3] What Moore might have thought about *My Secret Life* at this point in his life would be hard to say. Probably he would have found it artless (in more than one sense) and uninteresting. His own book proclaims the values of French literature, symbolist and realist, to reluctant English readers, whereas the author of *My Secret Life* publishes his book clandestinely and with misgivings, his re-creations almost masturbatory. Yet when Moore describes *Confessions* as the testimony of a man consumed by art, he speaks of comparable obsession as well as alienation. The author of *My Secret Life* relives his experience from an older perspective than Moore's, focusing entirely on his sexuality. Moore actually speaks with reticence about sexual matters, but he does boast that "I am ashamed of nothing I have done, especially my sins" (185).[4] His sins seem rather unimposing, although he cultivates what he evidently thinks of as a satanic pride, as if justifying the dislike he found in others. Both Moore and the author of *My Secret Life* expect to be misunderstood; both, in a sense, "confess" a past that is at once their professional interest and their consuming avocation. Both are looking ahead to the less narcissistic but no less publicly shocking works of a D. H. Lawrence or James Joyce.

Moore saw himself at once as the new truth-telling Zola and as the aesthete and decadent, the Des Esseintes of English literature. Important as Huysmans, Verlaine, and Rimbaud may have been to Moore when he wrote *Confessions,* the pre-eminent English aesthete was probably just as important. I mean of course Pater, whose essay on "Style" appeared in the same year as *Confessions,* and who served for Moore as for Tyrrell as a kind of benchmark.[5] Moore's study, *Impressions and Opinions* (1891), looks at the French symbolists by drawing on Pater, for whom "impressions" was a central word. Impressions involved the interiority, the privacy of experience, which defined an individual's response to the world of art. "Every one of those impressions," as Pater wrote in the conclusion to *The Renaissance,* "is the impression of the individual in his isolation, each mind keeping as a solitary prisoner its own dream of the world." Moore apparently owes much to Pater's aesthetics, his desire to speak about large cultural movements, and his sense of the "weaving and unweaving of ourselves" necessary in our personal response.[6] Pater was one of few English writers for whom Moore had much respect. Behind *Confessions* may also be the oblique model of *Marius the Epicurean* (1886), which predated Moore's book by two years and which offered a portrait of someone who, as Pater wrote, lived self-consciously in reminiscence. In his 1904 and later prefaces to the *Confessions,* a book which Moore continued to love, he quotes a letter about the work that he received from Pater. It spoke with kindness if not of kinship:

> MY DEAR, AUDACIOUS MOORE.—Many thanks for the "Confessions," which I have read with great interest and admiration for your originality—your delightful criticisms—your Aristophanic joy, or at least enjoyment, in life—your unfailing liveliness. Of course, there are many things in the book I don't agree with. But then, in the case of so satiric a book, I suppose one is hardly expected to agree or disagree. What I cannot doubt is the literary faculty displayed. "Thou com'st in such a questionable shape!" I feel inclined to say on finishing your book; "shape" morally, I mean; not in reference to style.
>
> You speak of my own work very pleasantly; but my enjoyment has

been independent of that. And still I wonder how much you may be losing, both for yourself and for your writings, by what, in spite of its gaiety and good-nature and genuine sense of the beauty of many things, I must still call a cynical, and therefore exclusive, way of looking at the world. You call it "realistic." Still!

With sincere wishes for the future success of your entertaining pen,

Very sincerely yours,
Walter Pater.[7]

Moore comments on this "delightful" letter from "a great artist," indeed "the last great English writer" (42–43), at some length. Whether he took Pater's criticisms seriously is hard to know, but his later autobiographies are markedly less "cynical," and at once more and less exclusive, because they involve a wholly new attitude to the reader. *Memoirs* will take on some of the deliberative "weaving and unweaving" of Pater's own writing.

Of Moore's "originality" and "literary faculty" in *Confessions,* the most seminal example might be his borrowed notion of the "echo-augury." He took the phrase from Thomas De Quincey, who described the echo-augury as a state of mind in which "a man, perplexed in judgment, and sighing for some determining counsel, suddenly heard from a stranger in some unlooked-for quarter words not meant for himself, but clamorously applying to the difficulty besetting him . . . the mystical word always unsought for."[8] In adapting De Quincey's garbled idea, Moore defines *his* echo-augury as "words heard in an unexpected quarter, but applying marvellously well to the besetting difficulty of the moment" (72–73). His language here is obviously from De Quincey, with the difference that De Quincey focuses on emotional sustenance and Moore on aesthetic significance. In fact, his use of the term subsumes both De Quincey and Wordsworth, whom Moore reads and respects.

For Wordsworth (whose *Recluse* appeared coincidentally in the same year as *Confessions*) the spots of time differ in at least one respect from De Quincey's echo-auguries. De Quincey's notion emphasizes words, whereas in the scenes Wordsworth depicts, words are in a sense stifled, images paramount. The woman with the jug, the gallows scene, the drowned man, the "woods decaying, never to be decayed," and the vision from Snowdon are elemental moments in which no one speaks, as if a remembered silence finds belated equivalent in the voice of the poet. Moore's epiphanic moments are about words, about the discovery of books, in fact, but share with Wordsworth's spots of time the private discovery and the larger sense of renovation. Moore applies the term *echo-augury* to only a few situations in *Confessions*. From the shock of recognition when he first read Shelley to the later awareness of useful novelistic techniques in Zola, Moore charts his education in a series of encounters with writers who contribute to his artistic growth: Shelley, Gautier, Zola, Anatole France. (He speaks of an even more sympathetic writer, Balzac, as though he had always known him.)

Because Moore emphasizes writing techniques and ideas, Susan Dick concludes that his retrospection usually begins with and mainly records the pursuit of intellectual threads.[9] By contrast she cites Proust, whose senses lead him via sounds and tastes to a hitherto buried past. Moore's re-creations of his memories certainly include intellectual experiences, and the echo-auguries of his first autobiography tell of the discoveries of writers more than the discoveries of a forgotten self. But this is only partly true of other recollecting in *Confessions* and hardly at all true of the later autobiographies. Even in *Confessions* Moore places his intellectual and aesthetic pursuits in an emotional and sensual context. When he describes early in *Confessions* his infatuation with Shelley, his preliminary comments are of a childhood memory.

> I was eleven years old when I first heard and obeyed this cry, or, shall I say, echo-augury. Scene: A great family coach, drawn by two powerful country horses, lumbers along a narrow Irish road. The even recurrent signs—long ranges of blue mountains, the streak of bog, the rotting cabin, the flock of plover rising from the desolate water. Inside the coach there are two children. They are smart, with new jackets and neckties; their faces are pale with sleep, and the rolling of the coach makes them feel a little sick. It is seven o'clock in the morning. Opposite the children are their parents, and they are talking of a novel the world is reading. Did Lady Audley murder her husband? Lady Audley! What a beautiful name; and she, who is a slender, pale, fairy-like woman, killed her husband. Such thoughts flash through the boy's mind; his imagination is stirred and quickened, and he begs for an explanation. The coach lumbers along, it arrives at its destination, and Lady Audley is forgotten in the delight of tearing down fruit trees and killing a cat.
> (50)

The appreciation of Shelley comes after the reading of Elizabeth Braddon's romance, but, more importantly, after the episode in the coach, which is an apparently trivial flashback, an epiphany, in Joyce's fuller sense of that word, by which minor, remembered events consolidate whole ranges of feeling. This echo-augury not only anticipates the ironic growth of the writer in Joyce's *Portrait of the Artist,* it resembles the way to knowledge in Proust's *Swann's Way,* which is contemporary in early drafts with the *Portrait* and with Moore's *Memoirs*.[10] Like Proust, Moore believes that we can only know in retrospect, but also that we can only know in a combined, partly physical way. In his later autobiographies, as in certain passages of *Confessions,* sensual nudging or uninvited recollection begins a whole train of association. Ideas are central for Moore, but they are characteristically—in the works after *Confessions,* if not always in the early book—part of an indefinable complex of new awareness and recollected sensation.

In his comments that *Confessions* generated many of his later works, Moore testifies to more than the powerful autobiographical impulse behind his writing. If genius is, as he says in *Evelyn Innes,* "the power of assimilation," and if "only a fool imagines he invents," then Moore honestly saw the importance of retrospection for his own writing and recognized his need to return to autobiography apart from the less personal but not less assimilative tasks of the novels and plays.[11] Moore acknowledged the autobiographical underpinning of his fiction; did he similarly recognize the fictive nature of his autobiographies? Evidently he did. In *Confessions* he fuses various periods of his life, as the partly imaginary and unchronological section on the Impressionists shows, and this latitude with memory continues through his later autobiographies. What largely disappears with *Confessions* is the "deceitful, stage-Irish" hyperbole, which Patrick Kavanagh found so obnoxious in his first "so-called autobiography," and which Moore tacitly rejected in his own.[12]

Moore's title for his first autobiography should have come from Rousseau, whom he later read with pleasure. His notions about confession seem like Rousseau's to center on idiosyncracy and full disclosures, as if what are sins to others and failings to himself must be recounted. (This is, as Lionel Trilling points out, more a French than an English mandate for autobiography.)[13] As a young man, however, Moore said that he did not know Rousseau's *Confessions,* admitting that, had he read Rousseau, his own venture might have been impossible.[14] He *had* read Saint Augustine, hater of Catholicism as he was. Inasmuch as Augustine had written "the story of a God-tormented soul," he said, "would it not be interesting to write the story of an art-tortured soul?" (1). Apt as this is for *Confessions,* it may be less apt for Moore's later autobiographical ventures than Augustine's brilliant speculations on memory. When Moore came, almost twenty years after *Confessions,* to write *Memoirs of My Dead Life,* what he evidently kept in mind from Augustine was the famous dictum about how we remember: that we only experience a present of things past, a present of things present, and a present of things future. "Resurgam" and other episodes form *Memoirs of My Dead Life* seem to be narrative explorations of Augustine's idea.

> There were times when it appeared to Dorian Gray that the whole of history was merely the record of his own life, not as he had lived it in act and circumstance, but as his imagination had created it for him. . . .
> Oscar Wilde, The Picture of Dorian Gray

There is at least one refrain running through *Memoirs of My Dead Life*: "Twenty years have passed."[15] Unlike *Confessions*, which describes, like a more conventional autobiography, the years intervening between an arbitrary beginning and a moody but relatively stable present consciousness, *Memoirs* looks back to episodes that usually took place twenty years before the indeterminate "now" of the present episode. Moore might be in London, as in "Spring in London," or Paris, as in "A Waitress," or on the way between them as in "Flowering Normandy." It is as though the present place guides the retrospect, which is spontaneous, arbitrary, sometimes unwanted. How much time elapses during the present consciousness of the book would be hard to say. *Hail and Farewell*, a much longer work, covers about twelve years. *Memoirs* might cover a writing time of anywhere from a few months to a few years. The result is apparently disparate recollections, told in overlapping but sometimes distinct ways. What holds the book together is a combination of Moore's illusion of a unified present and his insistence on a few basic themes. Apart from memory, this is a book about love and about death.

Moore recalls an afternoon's thoughts in London, tells the story of his encounters with artists' models in Paris, describes a fruitless walk to a friend's house in Montmartre, or his meeting with an old lover in another part of Paris. Only "The Lovers of Orelay" is more than a few dozen pages in length, and this story, in the center of the book, is something of a novella among anecdotes. With its initial patronizing of the young woman, its seaside setting, its record of unexpected love, it reads like George Moore's personal version of Chekhov's "Lady with a Dog." No less than Chekhov's story, "Lovers" is a meditation on time, in which the acknowledgment of passion forces new understanding, as a reluctant, middle-aged lover contemplates his own past life, love and death defining his retrospect.

"The Lovers of Orelay" is one of several accounts of Moore's meetings with former mistresses. Doris has gone to the south of France for her health. Moore follows her. Although the story itself is fairly banal, the development of Moore's emotions becomes increasingly complex.

He says in another section of *Memoirs* that he knows he has one strength as a writer: to engage readers, to establish an intimacy with them (303). He does this in "The Lovers of Orelay" by several means, the most remarkable of which turns us, "the reader," into the main object of his discourse as well as the confidante about his affair.

In *Confessions,* Moore makes a repeated point of pushing his reader away. Like T. S. Eliot, he invokes the "hypocrite reader" of Baudelaire, writing as if angry with his reader because his reader accepts what he attacks. The rhetoric is borrowed:

> You, hypocritical reader, who are now turning up your eyes and murmuring "horrid young man"—examine your weakly heart, and see what divides us; I am not ashamed of my appetites, I proclaim them, what is more I gratify them; you're silent, you refrain.
>
> (185)

This is not at all the manner of *Memoirs of My Dead Life.* Moore seems to have changed radically by the time he writes the new book; without doubt he has changed his rhetorical approach. Instead of affirming himself as a sinner, he quietly implies that we all sin, although his use of the word is neither so dramatic nor so simple as it is in *Confessions.* Throughout most of *Memoirs,* Moore assumes a listener, seems confident that what he says must be of interest, but emphasizes the genuineness of his memories rather than their improprieties or idiosyncracies.

Contemplative and self-sufficient as he is in *Memoirs,* Moore cultivates his reader. Sometimes he reaches beyond the apparent boundaries of his meditations, using self-conscious narrative devices. In "The Lovers of Orelay," for example, Moore employs a Victorian narrative convention he would have scorned in *Confessions.* Like Butler and Gosse, he seems at times to parody Jane Eyre: "If I could innoculate you, reader, with the sentiment of the delicious pastoral, you would understand why . . . I looked upon myself as a hero of legend" (132); or "The sympathetic reader will not have forgotten this avowal" (207). Throughout the story Moore appeals to a "reader," not to insult or to establish moral distance or to implicate by assumptions of hypocrisy, but to entice and involve. Fascinated by his own rememberings, he seems to want to show how he thinks, how his own memories can concern the reader as much as himself. The appeals are seldom exclamatory or hyperbolic. Moore enjoys a kind of lyrical meditation, as if he had learned the mystics' recollection but limited his thoughts to memory, time, and physical love. In "The Lovers," unlike the other episodes, the humor more directly involves the reader, who may be addressed as "dear, dear reader" and asked to imagine a scene: "I am sure you can see me" (183).

One effect of such appeals is the extension of the reader's role. Invited to "imagine" and "understand," the reader must also oblige by remembering. This is a complex element in any narrative. As Paul Alkon has shown in regard to Defoe's narratives (and Wolfgang Iser and others with respect to fiction in general), a reader necessarily does remember throughout a narrative, so that incidents slight in themselves can become charged by what we know, a repeated statement can gain incrementally, a scene can become a part of our own as well as of the narrator's memory, judgments can become at once more difficult and more imperative.[16]

Moore evidently thinks about the complexity of his reader's remembering as he considers his own, and the appeals to the "reader" in "The Lovers" accentuate what takes place throughout this book. As if sorting out or trying to anticipate a reader's response, Moore suggests that "some readers will doubt" the appropriateness of a digression, for example, and like Sterne or Byron, whom he sometimes echoes, he will play with digressions or even make an apparent digression the final focus of a chapter. The effect is an informality like Ford Madox Ford's, an admission of the reader into both intimate detail and intimate thought, a kind of literary disrobing. (In "The Lovers" Moore makes a rather large to-do about his silk pajamas.) Although Moore leaves much out, he nevertheless demands complicity from his readers, who must work to organize and make sense of his experience.

Here is a comment from "The Lovers," which typifies Moore's concern with memory and digression and incidentally recalls Byron's *Don Juan*:

> And as I write the sad thought floats past that such expectations will never be my lot again. The delights of the moment are perhaps behind me, but why should I feel sad for that? Life is always beautiful, in age as well as in youth; the old have a joy that the youths do not know—recollection. It is through memory we know ourselves; without memory it might be said we have hardly lived at all, or only like animals.
>
> (184)

Memory provides a solace or alternative joy, an "abundant recompense," in Wordsworth's phrase; it also distinguishes us from animals, as Augustine had said, and Schopenhauer more recently, essentially civilizing us. Moore praises memory throughout *Memoirs,* and acts of remembering in this book are more functional than they are in *Confessions.* One surprising development in *Memoirs* is the absence of the term "echo-augury," perhaps because Moore associates the idea with discoveries of youth, perhaps because he found the term, after all, to be too restrictive. He has become more concerned with present speculation, with the nature of the remembering mind rather than with the remembered materials as such.

Hence, while he puts aside the echo-augury, Moore probes deeper in *Memoirs* into theoretical aspects of memory, just as he emphasizes the word itself. He interests himself in a number of questions: the essential importance of his memories; their relationship to narrative; the ways that personal memory point to racial or archetypal memory; and the connections among recollection, emotional well-being, and thoughts of death.

Apart from the quotation above, in which he uses memory to distinguish men and women from animals and speaks of it as the joy of old age, Moore makes constant reference to the process of remembering. With his usual assortment of metaphors, he comments on "the gross, jaded, uncouth present," which has slipped from him "as a garment might," leaving the past like a stage play or show illuminated in his mind (76). He says that "the passing of things is always a moving subject for meditation" and that "it is strange how accident will bring back a scene, explicit in every detail" (94). Moments of contemplation often elicit both distance and regret, as if they were mountaintops "from which we survey our dead life" (96). All the episodes of *Memoirs* begin with a description of how Moore reminisces; all emphasize the centrality of reminiscence to any kind of personal or aesthetic understanding.

I have mentioned the importance of the reader's participation in the *Memoirs,* occasioned if nothing else by Moore's constant reminder that we should remember with him, as though with enough imaginative effort we might make his memories our own. Just as he expects his reader to bear in mind the recollections he has told us, pulling them together in our understanding, he also emphasizes the interworking of his and our memories in the art of telling stories. At the "end" of "The Lovers" he plays with what he knows to be a reader's desire for closure, describing a few nearly final scenes with Doris as they travel back to Paris. Then he begs off. "These stories," he says, moving away from the one at hand, "are memories, not inventions, and an account of the days I spent in Paris would interest nobody; all the details are forgotten, and inventions and remembrance do not agree any better than the goat and the cabbage" (221). What he achieves here is an emotional break from the love story that could have gone on, whatever the factual background, to a conventional marriage or could have been treated in novelistic detail, with Moore looking ahead through months and years of intermittent relations. But if "my mind is no longer engrossed with the story" (221), the story as story no longer matters. Moore says that he can in fact remember details; he cannot remember with passion. ("Passion" is a recurrent word for him as, with a different emphasis, it is for White and Tyrrell.) The story of Doris has been day-by-day, hour-by-hour. A summing-up would damage the story because it would spoil what amounts to his tacit, emotional recapitulation. If this leaves things indeterminate—and Moore does say elsewhere that he is "writing the quest of a golden fleece" (106)—it also charges the stories with a kind of exploratory energy, a "passion" of reminiscence, which gives *Memoirs* its distinctive character.

"Things are interesting" Moore says, "in proportion to the amount of ourselves we put into them" (133). In contrast to the self-assertiveness of *Confessions, Memoirs* focuses on a meditative and ironic speaker, someone aware of the complexity of self or selves, whose speculations about issues of identity and change become a conscious part both of his recreation of the past and of the text which records it. Sometimes he finds himself in a waking dream so strong that to return from it is to be shocked by present reality. "My mind is dark [again] . . . I hear a horse trotting in the Strand" (94–95).

For Moore there is, then, a compelling bond between memory and the type of literature he feels it necessary to write. "We are all impressionists to-day," he says, "and we are eager to note down what we feel and see" (24). Moore means to argue for a kind of indulgent but charged metonymy, a whole imagined from what may seem the dregs of recollection. "All this," he says, "is twenty years ago, and is it not silly to spend the afternoon thinking of such rubbish [as an unfulfilled love affair]? But it is of such stuff that our lives are made" (64). He could have said "our books and our lives," for he relates his fictional progress to his emotional explorations. One carefully realized illusion in *Memoirs* is the recurrent way that late afternoon daydreams turn into the substance of the retrospective episodes, any slight memory begetting another. Since "memory may not be beckoned," "a memory or a shadow of a memory" can "fret" his mind "like a fly on a pane" (118). "Why am I thinking of it [a trivial recollection]? Only because a more interesting memory hangs upon it" (225). Moore suggests that after a day of other writing, these memories rise unbidden and in competition before him. The effect is that we are witnessing the daydream recollections rather than reading the work that has, presumably, been the day's labor.

Perhaps the best illustration of this process is "Bring in the Lamp," a short episode in which Moore, bored and lonely after a day's work, invents a story to be told, a story that is, in fact, another of his recoveries of "twenty years ago." In this section Moore begins by thinking of a hypothetical writer as he in turn thinks of his own (but really Moore's) life. His stories are "among the trivial things that compose the tedium that we call life" (270). In his imagined text the writer will, says Moore, using the future tense, "flit back over the past, and his own life will hardly seem more real than the day's work" (270). It is in these contexts that Moore approximates Pater, for whom dreams lend "awe" and "mystery" (269) to perception, while perception and recollection merge in the writing process. The apparently trivial takes on significance as the "solitary prisoner" creates his "own dream of the world," his own *impressions*,[17] albeit in concert with an independent muse. "What—is the story coming now? Yes, it is forming independently of his will" (272).

When the vision begins once more to fade, Moore apparently contradicts his claim about the work being "memories, not inventions": "The situation my fancy creates is ingenious; and I regret it did not happen. Nature spins her romances differently" (283). What we have here is at least a double process: a seeking out or receptivity to remembered material and a simultaneous desire "to modify reality, . . . to author a new fictional entity."[18] These words of Edward Said are meant to describe the impetus behind novels, but they bear directly on a novelist-autobiographer such as Moore. For though memory is the imaginative force, memories remain illusory, as untrustworthy as they are inescapable. "Nothing endures; life is but change" (285). With this recurrent thought, the tone becomes Keatsian: "I have come to the end of my mood, an ache in my heart brings me to my feet" (285). Like Keats, Moore has thought of his imagined-remembered vision in terms of music as well as of sight, projecting himself forward and backward and through envisioned love to a kind of hopeless and embalmed darkness: "There is no hope, not a particle. . . . Bring in the lamp" (285).

"Bring in the Lamp" involves a further question of narrative that is for Moore at once a departure from his novels and a development from *Confessions*, wherein he compressed and toyed with but largely followed chronological sequence. Throughout *Memoirs*, sequence obtains quite loosely within individual episodes. There may be an emotional development to the entire book, but Moore obviously has no interest in following traditional patterns of *bios* in presenting his materials. Whatever he intended by the term *memoirs*, the term here does not apply as it would to *Hail and Farewell* as a sign of the author's interest in other people. Perhaps a few people emerge as identifiable individuals in *Memoirs*, yet the women are quite obviously disguised, and Moore's interest, in any case, is not with things external to himself.[19] Even

Confessions, despite its assertive egotism, speaks at length about Zola, Manet, Cabaner, Mallarmé, and so on, as Moore (or "Dayne," as he calls himself) retails his aesthetic apprenticeship. But *Memoirs* seems almost a deliberate misnomer, recording only past loves or past scenes, evoked—despite the appeals to the "reader"—in a kind of narrative privacy: indulged, enjoyed, and presented as if for a final time. As with George Tyrrell's *Autobiography,* the idea of finality underlies the entire work, and there is, as "Bring in the Lamp" makes clear, a tendency to remember the joy in relation to Moore's sense of his own ending or of endings in general. *Memoirs* might be read to illustrate some of the *fin de siècle* emotions that we have seen in White or Tyrrell and that Oscar Wilde may have best expressed:

> "*Fin de siècle,*" murmured Lord Henry.
> "*Fin du globe,*" answered his hostess.
> "I wish it were *fin du globe,*" said Dorian, with a sigh. "Life is a great disappointment."[20]

If *Memoirs* is no conventional memoir, it is, again, no conventional autobiography. Apart from its break with chronology, it is a book about adult life: the middle-aged man looks back, not to childhood, but early manhood. This is in sharp contrast to Ford Madox Ford's *Ancient Lights,* which maintains an almost absolute distance between Ford as a young child and Ford as the mature man and writer (and which deals so fully with the named individuals of Ford's childhood). Moore nevertheless writes, like Ford, a book that seems created as it goes, memory begetting memory, memory dying, as in "The Lovers" and "Bring in the Lamp," when the writer's energy or remembered vision wanes. "Fled is the music . . . do I wake or sleep?"

Unlike *Confessions* and *Hail and Farewell, Memoirs* is remarkably undated, free of historical and contemporary reference. It is true that some things can be tied to events, modes of transportation, fashions (like the wearing of white scarves or silk pajamas), but Moore's preoccupation with time takes him, paradoxically, away from chronological placing just as it takes him from chronological ordering. There is good reason for his new emphasis. In this book as in the later *Hail and Farewell* he interests himself with various "contemplations" of time and of memory, ranging from details of his own life—the potential "rubbish" of impression and recollection—to history and to myth. In the midst of a conversation or personal reverie, Moore can break away, or rather shift his memory into another context. He can speak of himself descending "the Champs Elysées a thousand years hence" and, more characteristically, he can imagine a landscape carrying "me back into past times when men believed in nymphs and satyrs" (65).

In addition to his memories within memories, he thus "remembers" other times. "Is it not strange," he says, "that all this [a scene on the Mediterranean] is at once new to me and old? I seem, as it were, to have come into my inheritance" (116). As he extends his vision of personal self into remote, often mythical times, Moore characteristically shifts into present tense. He seems to explore the kind of double sense of time or recognition that Freud spoke about as "déjà vu" and Jung as "synchronicity," although his mythological implication brings him closer to Jung. In this passage, where he emphasizes enormous gulfs of time, he speaks about a present consciousness, as if to say, I am here now, looking back on my own life, speculating about love and death, and I am in a sense reliving a moment that vanished thousands of years ago. The farther he reaches, the more immediate the memory may seem to him, as the use of the present tense suggests. And there is another illusion here: Doris is for him a Greek goddess of mythical beauty as well as a woman of exquisite fashion; and she, too, for a moment, seems to share his concerns about time. Moore believes that at a pause in their conversation both are looking back and looking ahead, envisioning themselves as figures in myth while considering the prospect of their own deaths.

Moore seems entirely conscious of the way that verb tenses reflect and occasion our awareness of time. At one moment in "The Lovers" he records a request made to a friend for information about French tenses:

> I remember last year I wrote to him saying that I did not understand the three [sic] past tenses in French, and would he explain why—something, I have forgotten what—and he answered *"Avec mes pieds sur des glaciers* [he is a mountaineer] *je ne puis m'arrêter pour vous expliquer les trois passés."*
>
> Doris laughed and was interested . . . ; and then we discussed the *fussent* and the *eussent, été,* etc.
>
> (152)

Moore himself then laughs, bringing the narrative back to their lovemaking, but he is obviously intrigued by the ways that languages determine what and how we think and what bearing our own language has on memory. Since Moore knew French well enough to write his first draft of *Confessions* in the language, he has in mind a fairly sophisticated question, however much he makes light of it. He is thinking, in other words, of what is a kind of Whorffian hypothesis: that we are constrained by our culture and by the language that defines our culture.

Moore is not explicit on this, but he would probably have understood the kind of thinking that engages George Steiner in *After Babel:*

> Does the past have any existence outside grammar? No raw data from the past have absolute intrinsic authority. Their meaning is relational to the present and that relation is realized linguistically. Memory is articulated as a function of the past tense of the verb. It operates through a deep-seated, intuitively obvious, yet in a large measure conventional application of past tenses to a scanning of "stored material." . . . If a characteristic discomfort arises over such a phrase ["it happened tomorrow"] . . . , if the instantaneous metamorphosis of present into past attaches to our every word and act, the reason is that the inflection of verbs as we practise it has become our skin and natural topography. From it we construe our personal and cultural past, the immensely detailed but wholly impalpable landscape "behind us." Our conjugations of verb tenses have a literal and physical force, a pointer backward and forward.[21]

Steiner goes on to illustrate his argument: "French knows a *passé défini,* a *passé indéfini,* a *passé antérieur,* a *parfait.* . . . " *Memoirs* is a book about such matters. "Bring in the Lamp" posits something like "it happened tomorrow." The entire book deals with metamorphoses of present-into-past-into present, a landscape emerging which is at once of the moment and in the mind. Consciousness becomes a kind of scanning process, either active or passive, which memory articulates by tenses. And memory, however personal, self-indulgent, and private in origin, becomes—through narrative—historic, archetypal, and ultimately public.

> *That garden sweet, that lady fair,*
> *And all sweet shapes and odours there*
> *In truth have never pass'd away—*
> *'Tis we, 'tis ours, are changed—not they.*
> Shelley, "The Sensitive Plant"

The most complex of Moore's chapters is the last of the book, "Resurgam," with its echo of *Jane Eyre* and *Vanity Fair.* An account of Moore's return to his birthplace at the time of his mother's death, "Resurgam" both pulls together and extends his speculations about time and memory. As with the episodes "Flowering Normandy" and "The Lovers of Orelay," the materials of "Resurgam" develop through a train journey. Moore imagines the end of the journey before he sets off, foreseeing his mother at the moment of death. He also refers back to "A

Remembrance," the story of another woman's death, recalling her slow dying, while reminding us of his own telling. Then, quickly, he crosses to Ireland and takes the train home: "It is impossible, at least for me, to find words to express adequately the agony of mind I endured on that journey. Words can only hint at it" (324). But words do very well. A little like Coleridge in "Dejection," who writes about the impossibility of writing, Moore excels himself in this episode. Not only does he play down the matter of earlier episodes, memories of sexual love, he focuses the thoughts on death that underlie all the rest of the book. The death of his mother involves Moore in another order of speculation, prompted by the journey on the train.

It is a somber journey. "How shall I tell it?" he says, for the process beggars description, and the feelings return with force: "Indeed, he says (anticipating Proust), "we can only see clearly when we look back or forwards" (324); reality is otherwise intolerable. For the first time in *Memoirs* Moore introduces significant flashbacks to childhood, most of them painful confrontations with a past he has withheld or ignored. He later becomes "seized by an unaccountable dread or shyness" (338) about meeting people he has known as a child. All this emerges in the journey by train, the moving panorama opening him to a "terrible" vista which is both past and present. Even the conventional "one is bound on a wheel" emphasizes the sense of fatality elicited by that anxious backward trek.

> The familiar country evocative of a great part of my childhood, carried my thoughts hither and thither. My thoughts ranged like the swallows; the birds had no doubt just arrived, and in swift, elliptical flights they hunted for gnats along the banks of the old weedy canal. That weedy canal along which the train travelled, took my thoughts back to the very beginning of my life, when I stood at the carriage window and plagued my father and my mother with questions regarding the life of barges passing up and down. And it was the sudden awakenings of these memories that were so terrible; the sudden thrust of the thought that I was going westward to see my mother die, and that nothing could save her from death or me from seeing her die.
>
> (325)

The horror grows as the train moves on:

> How many times did I say to myself, "Nothing can save me unless I get out at the next station," and I imagined myself taking a car and driving away through the country. But if I did such a thing I should be looked upon as a madman. . . . I began to think how men under sentence of

death must often wonder why they were selected especially for such a fate, and the mystery, the riddle of it all, must be perhaps the greatest part of their pain.

(325)

Compounding his own sympathetic sense of pain is the apparently mocking beauty of the weather and landscape, a theme which continues beyond the journey and through the time of the funeral:

> The morning was one of the most beautiful I had ever seen, and I used to catch myself thinking out a picturesque expression to describe it. It seemed to me that the earth might be compared to an egg, it looked so warm under the white sky, and the sky was as soft as the breast feathers of a dove. . . . A moment afterwards I found myself plunged in reflections regarding the impossibility of keeping one's thoughts fixed on any one subject for any considerable length of time.
>
> (326)

These passages indicate how Moore has come to understand the interworkings of his experiences and his writing. Often while speaking of his work he will comment on the intrusions of thoughts of love; often while speaking of love he will be reminded of his age and the passing of time. The inversion here, beauty intruding on thoughts of death, is really the same pattern. And the sense of an inevitable journey, reluctantly taken, as even his journey to Doris had been, obviously becomes a metaphor for his life. In spite of his work, his travels, his assumed emancipation, "I could not put the past behind me" (329). When he reaches home (to find his mother dead), he continues to think in the same essential way, except that now his own death rather than his mother's, which remains poignantly in the background, becomes his preoccupation. For returning home means returning not only to his ancestors, but also to the troubling beauty of the landscape and the sad burden of his own mortality.

Moore's writing in "Resurgam" often sounds like that of his contemporary (and Yeats's friend), Arthur Symons, whose assessment of some contemporary literature, above all the writings of Pater and the works of the French symbolists, paralleled Moore's own. Symons speaks of the need for spiritual answers through literature, of new and uncataloguing descriptions of nature, of the centrality of "magic" and "mystery" in a symbolic view of nature.[22] All this may come to Symons as to Moore directly out of Pater, but the two have nonetheless learned a similar wisdom. In the conclusion to *The Symbolist Movement in Literature* (1899), Symons might have been imagining the underlying topic of

Moore's *Memoirs:* "The lovers who have quickened the pulses of the world," he says, "have really . . . been fleeing from the certainty of one thought, that we have, all of us, only our one day." We are always, in short, conspiring to forget death.[23]

No doubt Symons touches on a quality in many autobiographies, which look back as a way of not looking forward, if only because no autobiography can deal simply with the death of its subject. At any rate, Moore seems to arrive inadvertently at a similar conclusion, as if throughout his book he has introduced but toyed with thoughts of death and must now do his accounting.

Moore thinks about his death as he contemplates the family vault, already full of the remains of his ancestors, already waiting nonetheless for him. The thought of that vault takes him inexorably in new directions. In addition to the disquiet of reliving moments of childhood, Moore discovers an intenser understanding of himself in time. He has prided himself throughout *Memoirs* on his honesty. In "Resurgam" he pushes himself to a kind of confession unimagined in his earlier book, confession that reveals him lonely, lost, and frightened. He admits that the parting from a young woman competes in his mind with the death of his mother, and "a man cannot lament two women at the same time" (339). The young woman, Nancy Cunard, had married shortly before the death of Moore's mother, in 1895.[24] Oddly, even these events are couched in the general frame of "twenty years ago," though they happened about ten years before the publication of *Memoirs*. Whatever the actual distances in time, both losses are heartbreaking, and both can only be addressed, in a sense, "now," many years later. The narrative is a tribute to both women, which, impossible to be paid at the proper time, must be paid at last in the memory. Guilt for the first time overwhelms nostalgia, conflating time and loss and blurring differences:

> When I am alone in the evening [his constant refrain], when the fire is sinking, the sweetness of her presence steals by me, and I realize what I lost in losing her. We do not grieve for the dead because they have been deprived of the pleasures of life (if this life be a pleasure), but because of our own loss.
>
> (341)

Although one may forget "how one thought twenty years ago" (347), one is forced to reassess, and for Moore this involves places as much as people. The return to his native land is apparently unlike the later return recorded in *Hail and Farewell,* in which Moore describes Ireland as "a fatal disease," while acknowledging ancestral ties. "I became possessed by a sentimental craving for the country itself," he was to write. "After all, it was my country."[25] This, however, came after the beginnings of the Boer War, which for Moore represented England's capitulation to folly and aggression and prompted him into self-imposed exile. At the time remembered in *Memoirs,* Ireland offers no lure, no call to the proud emigré; Moore simply returns because of his mother's dying.

There is a way, however, in which Moore's homecoming parallels that of the later book, without the impetus of the war or the lure of the Irish Renaissance. As if unconsciously, Moore seeks here what he was to seek later: some better understanding of himself in relation to the homeland he both needs and hates. Anticipating some of the "dryness," the restrained emotion, of a book like *The Untilled Field* (with its evocation of the Irish countryside and peasantry),[26] the Irish descriptions in *Memoirs* are understated and precise, as though, in compensation for his pain, Moore is seeing with renewed eyes, with physical and emotional intensity.

> The water there is so shallow that our governess used to allow us to wander at will, to run on ahead in pursuit of a sandpiper. The bird used to fly round with little cries; and we often used to think it was wounded; perhaps it pretended to be wounded in order to lead us away from its nest. We did not think it possible to see the lake in any new aspect, yet there it lay as we had never seen it before, so still, so soft, so grey, like a white muslin scarf flowing out, winding past island and headland. The silence was so intense that one thought of the fairy books of long ago, of sleeping woods and haunted castles.
>
> (336)

Such description, based upon Moore's remembering his remembering, entails a more subtle form of the earlier notion of "echo-augury" along with a myth of collective remembering quite distinct from the earlier vision of Hellenic beauty. The remembered landscape suggests the satisfaction and the magic "one thought of" with fairy books, personal memory blending with a collective literary or even folk memory, and unfolding now on native ground. Moore's recollective process touches on the relationship argued by Charles Radcliffe about the protean qualities of natural scenery, the meanings of which lie so much with the interpretive (and reminiscing) mind. Our memories are compounded of matters personal and inherited and are intimately linked to a privileged view of landscape.

For Moore, on the other hand, there is a toll. "How terrible," he says in "Resurgam," "was all this resurrection" (338). If there is a kind of eternal recurrence, our own lives a part of some larger scheme of history, the recognition comes with pain and reluctance. Involved is an unwanted and almost unacknowledged crisis. What comes to life both resurrects the anguish of past times and demands a vision, not less "terrible," of a possible future.

In his own way, Moore is worrying that idea of "repetition" described by Kierkegaard, by which the past may be transformed into a richer future. Complicating the process is his attempt at the same time to imagine his own death—and to compose his own funeral. The Irish Catholic rituals seem to him barbaric (he invokes various kinds of paganism as desirable alternatives). Thinking ahead "twenty or thirty years," just as he has been thinking back in increments of twenty years, he imagines his own death and wills himself an appropriate send-off. His burial is not to be in the tomb of his forefathers, which frightens him with its closeness, but cremation: he wants to be "burned" (353). Finally, Moore imagines a kind of immortality in a Greek urn, his ashes surviving the run of history and the drying of oceans. He reaches even farther forward in his imagination than he has ever looked back.

Moore's achievement in "Resurgam" is intellectual as well as emotional and literary. He creates in this episode intense feelings, links those feelings to landscapes of memory, and speculates about his own life as if preternaturally occupied with its "trivia," its losses, and its pleasures, while no less occupied with the idea of himself as a dying animal. His language, which once again echoes Keats, often sounds in "Resurgam" like some of Yeats. The swans, the lake, the symbolic birds—all mock that tattered coat upon the stick. Moore's appeal to Irish and Greek myth, his recognition of personal cycles intersecting with historic and mythic cycles, and his profound concern with the landscape of his homeland, recall Yeats and remind us that *Memoirs* was written in the period covered by *Hail and Farewell*, a work that as much as anything else offers an account of Yeats and the Irish Renaissance.[27]

> *It is hard to analyse a spiritual transformation; one knows so little about oneself; life is mysterious.*
>
> George Moore, Hail and Farewell

For George Moore as for Samuel Butler, that weaving and unweaving of the self is primarily a function of memory, of forgetting and remembering in a world no less mysterious than it was for Pater. In this final section, however, I would like to consider how Moore's "ideas" about the mysteries of time and memory coincide with those of a very different kind of writer, the contemporary psychologist, James Sully.

What is at stake in so much writing about memory is not merely the process of recollection as a defining human attribute, but the sense of conservation as a fundamental principle. The mind is able to conserve, with memory its primary instrument. Sully is explicit about this:

> The mystery of memory lies in the apparent immediateness of the mind's contact with the vanished past. In "looking back" on our life, we seem to ourselves for the moment to rise above the limitations of time, to undo its work of extinction. . . . Memory is a kind of resurrection of the buried past: as we fix our retrospective glance on it, it appears to start anew into life.[28]

Perhaps it is inevitable that contemporaries writing about the same topic will employ the same terms. Still, there is real kinship between Sully's thinking and that of Moore. Moore's own use of the terms *mystery* and *resurrection* in "Resurgam" assume the same sort of power that Sully ascribes to memory. Thinking that memory throws "a gleam into the mystery of life, without destroying the mystery" (255), Moore also speaks about rising above time as we look back with that feeling of immediacy on our past. Immersion in and rising above suggest a power or faculty of extraordinary strength, and Moore conceives of memory, as Yeats does, emerging from some archaic source. He speaks of a heard melody as coming "from the heart, or out of some unconscious self, an ante-natal self that . . . only emerged in music" (251). Tapping that unconscious self and that prenatal memory involves an imaginative as well as recollective act, and in this respect, too, Moore's thinking parallels Sully's. It is evidently Sully's phrase "reproductive imagination" that the authors of the OED used to define one function of memory, and reproductive imagination, a combination of symbolic and abbreviated but emotionally authentic recreation, is precisely Moore's understanding of the process of recollection.[29] In sum, we do not invent at all, but recover what we have absorbed.

Moore's ambivalent sense of the privacy of memory, which nevertheless becomes publicly available in literature, is paralleled in Sully, who speaks about the past not only as subject to the caprice of memory but also as reflective of individual needs. Our memories are indelibly our own; imagination is the means by which we move, regressively, along the lines of our experience. Sully speculates like Moore about a movement that keeps doubling back on itself, redescending the past, as Pater wrote. Related is William James's and Sully's use of the phrase "stream of consciousness" to describe that regressive and returning, public and private, spatial and temporal process at work whenever we engage in acts of remembering.

There is a further point to be mentioned here. Sully's comment about memory as resurrection and our rising above the limits of time includes the statement that, in looking back, we can seem "to undo [time's] work of extinction."[30] Implicit in this remark may lie another fundamental reason for autobiographical writing, as George Moore himself suggests: a conscious or unconscious denial of death by the revitalizing of moments from the past, themselves reminders, often enough, of our mortality. This is not a simple matter for Moore. He speaks resignedly of futility and failure, for which memory offers small compensation. "Nothing endures; life is but change. What we call death is only change. . . . Twenty long years ago, and there is no hope" (285). But the "mood" passes, and Moore usually does return to the notion of memory as muse or as "a shrine where we can worship" both love and life (269).

The phrase "time's work of extinction" also speaks to one of the major issues of late-nineteenth-century intellectual life. We are used to thinking about the arguments between Darwinians and their opponents, Darwin, Wallace, and Huxley lined up against the marshalled ranks of bishops or Oxford dons; or about Darwin's opponents—such as Samuel Butler—who basically accepted evolution while they rejected "natural selection" or some other facet of Darwin's arguments. The more important opposition may have been that between Darwin's great theory of life and growth and a competing scientific hypothesis: the notion of entropy.

In the universe posited by Darwin, life may be brutal, nature remorseless, God lamentably missing. But life for Darwin goes on, and time is on the side of life. For Rudolf Clausius, William Thomson (later Lord Kelvin), and other physicists, speculation about thermodynamics led to frightening conclusions about time. Time could mean, with a future more horrifying than Darwin's past, the failure of energy, the burnout of the universe, on a scale which dwarfed mankind as much as anything in *The Origin of Species*.[31] Oddly enough, though perhaps understandably, it was Darwinism more than thermodynamics that captured imaginations. But Darwin himself, as I have mentioned, worried excessively about Kelvin's theories, for which he had, in fact, no rebuttal, except to nibble at his own evolutionary time scheme in an attempt to make things fit. Relatively few people in the late nineteenth century speak directly about the problems of entropy or theoretical responses to it, perhaps because few people equated physical with emotional or intellectual energy. But the debates about "degeneration" and "disintegration" (in William Hale White, for example), suggest that implications of entropic theory fed *fin de siècle* notions of chaos and disorder, with consequences for literature as well as society. Hardy and Conrad are cases in point. Only in our century, nevertheless, with such thinkers as Rudolf Arnheim and Ilya Prigogine, do we have basic questions asked about the relation of artistic order to the disordered physical world or do we hear about the mind (by and large on computer analogies) being in essence anti-entropic.[32]

Without pushing too far into a massive subject, I would suggest that Moore and Sully—in their very different ways—seem to be anticipating later responses to entropic arguments. If the memory can, as both Sully and Moore believe, at least offer an emotional counter to time's work of extinction, then the mind is far more than just our distinguishing human feature or a mere physical stage in a long, evolutionary process. The remembering individual mind is, in a collective sense, history and civilization, all that need not die by the workings of time.

I have elsewhere quoted Miguel de Unamuno, who speaks for psychologists, novelists, philosophers, novelists, philosophers, when he says in *The Tragic Sense of Life:* "Memory is the basis of individual personality, just as tradition is the basis of the collective personality of a people. We live in memory and by memory, and our spiritual life is at bottom simply the effort of our memory to persist, to transform itself into hope, the effort of our past to transform itself into our future."[33] What is pertinent about Unamuno's passionate regard for memory is the way he fuses public and private. As with Moore, private recollection becomes through myth, presumably, or literature whatever we understand by tradition, and tradition itself is a form of conservation with promise of a future. Suspicious of "theory," Moore nonetheless recognized the kind of paradox that Unamuno expresses, the conflict between private introspection and public history, the desire to go beyond personal indulgence to imaginative recollection of another order. This is, again, the assumption behind Dilthey's view of history. Moore was wise enough to know not only that his conscious understanding might be inadequate, that there were powers within him he could only intuit, but also, as Dilthey argued, that the autobiographical process as literary memory touched on spiritual insight. Hence his increasing emphasis like Butler's or Symons's on words such as "mystery" and "magic."

What happens unannounced in *Memoirs* is a slow unfolding of understanding, and the understanding is at once of and beyond the speaker, who emerges from a kind of narcissism and self-indulgence. To put this differently, Moore's obsessive autobiographical writing begins with easy assumptions or values but moves unexpectedly to a kind of spiritual awareness. Butler appreciated the process without realizing it in *The Way of All Flesh;* Moore was maybe more daring or less troubled by his insights. In *Hail and Farewell* he was to write, "But an autobiography, I said [to myself], is an unusual form for a sacred book. But is it? My doubts quenched a moment after in a memory of Paul, and the next day the dictation of the rough outline . . . was begun."[34]

I shall suggest in the following chapter how Ford Madox Ford resurrected *his* buried past and dealt analogously with what Ford calls "growing up," the process of accepting adulthood, of coming to terms with a difficult past amidst a less than simple present. Both men perhaps knew a road to Damascus, and whether or not they experienced a conversion like Paul's, they used a biblical vocabulary to define their state of mind. Ford disliked Moore personally as he disliked Samuel Butler, but he recognized that, as a writer, "Moore was wolf-lean, silent, infinitely swift and solitary," not to mention a "high priest" in the world of art.[35] Ford came to think like Virginia Woolf that "*Ave, Salve, Vale* was much more imaginative" than most of Moore's fiction, but he said of the fiction itself, "the technical excellences of Mr. Moore are probably unsurpassed in the world at the present time."[36] Although anything but wolf-like and lean himself, Ford had much in common with Moore, whose place as England's pre-eminent writer he thought he would take. Both men were engrossed by issues of "style," which they found lacking in English fiction and which seemed to be found at its best in Turgenev, whom Ford describes in *Ancient Lights* as a part of his re-creation of a Pre-Raphaelite past. For related reasons, painting matters to both writers, and both will phrase descriptions in terms of a particular artist, a Corot or a Madox Brown, whose perspective informs the recollecting eye. To each of these men, the Boer War marked the end of an England they could admire and precipitated a crisis in their personal lives. Ford went off to the English countryside; Moore, as I have said, went off with Yeats and Edward Martyn to attend to Ireland.

Moore and Ford are writers of fiction with at least two main preoccupations in common: a compulsion to explore their own lives in a series of autobiographies; and a desire to chronicle while they redefine the world of art. In a sense, *Ancient Lights* is to the Pre-Raphaelites what Moore's *Confessions* is to the French impressionists and symbolists, except that Ford concentrates on himself as a boy rather than as a young man, writing with the nostalgia and the sense of mystery that Moore first achieves in *Memoirs*. *Ancient Lights* grows out of Ford's vision of London "gloom," and like Moore's re-creations, it works dramatically both to conserve and to transform.

6 The End of an Epoch, the Closing of a Door: Ford Madox Ford's *Ancient Lights*

> *All good autobiographies are in some sense the story of a calling.*
> Roy Pascal, Design and Truth in Autobiography

When he published *Ancient Lights* in 1911, Ford Madox Ford was thirty-seven years old. Although he was to write until the time of his death in 1939, he could already look back on a busy career. He had been editor of the famous *English Review*, which published Conrad and Galsworthy, Pound and Yeats, Lawrence and Henry James. He had published poems and fairy stories, as well as novels, and while *The Good Soldier* (1915) and the novels by which he is best known were to come later, he had written *The Fifth Queen* trilogy (1906–8) and other significant books. The collaborative work with Conrad, including *The Inheritors* (1901) and *Romance* (1903), was already behind him, and in spite of horrendous personal problems, severe ill health, and financial hardships, his writing continued, as it always did, without serious interruption.[1] In the same year that *Ancient Lights* appeared, Ford published two novels and a collection of critical essays.

Appearing in America with the more generic title of *Memories and Impressions, Ancient Lights* is an account of a late-Victorian boyhood, a historical meditation on the *fin de siècle,* told from the perspective of someone suddenly aware of his own middle age and middling success in an era indifferent to the arts and given to mediocrity. But while the implications of change and the consciousness of present time underlie Ford's memoir, his eye is largely on the personalities who shaped his past. "Fordie who wrote of giants" — in Ezra Pound's words — cared passionately about those giants, however painful some of them made his childhood.[2] They included his grandfather Ford Madox Brown, his uncles William and Dante Gabriel Rossetti, Swinburne, Morris, Ruskin, Holman Hunt, even Franz Liszt and Ivan Turgenev. Another prominent foreigner in Ford's life was his own father, Francis Hueffer, who came to England with a degree from Göttingen, was a correspondent for numerous papers, and music critic for *The Times*.

Ancient Lights is Ford's early attempt at sorting out, to decide who or what matters, after the literary feuds, after the lives and the personalities have gone. As if opening its doors to uninvited as well as expected guests, Ford's book is full of people; it is a record of lives and times, an exuberant memoir, a celebration of the past. "Frankly, garrulously, at ease," as Ruskin says of *Praeterita*,[3] it differs from Ruskin's or Gosse's autobiography in speaking of a lonely but not a solitary childhood. Of the characters who enter this book, most perform on its central stage, the household of Madox Brown, which was for a time Ford's own home and which serves him as the focus for all the life and vitality of his boyhood.

> *What he really or if he is really, nobody knows now and he least of all; he has become a great system of assumed* personae *and dramatized selves.*
> H. G. Wells, Experiment in Autobiography, *on Ford*

Wells's comment on Ford, included in his own autobiography, speaks to the enigmatic and complex "selves" apparent throughout Ford's voluminous writing and perhaps especially in those "fictional reminiscences" of which *Ancient Lights* was the first.[4] The phrase "ancient lights" itself implies Ford's ambivalent representations of himself and his world, his contradictory vision of historic and personal change. "Ancient lights" are at once the illustrious personalities of Ford's boyhood and the possessive rights of the person looking back, for the legal phrase has to do with the protection from new building, with the continued privilege, that is, of window light that has been enjoyed for at least twenty years. Ford announces the eminence of the individuals he will introduce, but he is at least as concerned with his own proprietal looking.

Almost everything in *Ancient Lights* turns on contrary ways of seeing. No less than Samuel Butler, whom he disliked as a waster of words and admired for *The Way of All Flesh,* Ford attended to his boyhood past with feelings still unsettled or unresolved, so that opposing moods — let alone facts or statements of opinion — alternate throughout.[5] I want to sort out some of the qualities of *Ancient Lights,* not to make pronouncements about Ford himself but to reach a better understanding of the distinctive memoir-autobiographies he began with this volume to write. *Ancient Lights* bears, as I shall suggest, on much of the later fiction. To think about the book itself, it may help to begin with two interwoven questions: Ford's vision of his boyhood-adult self and his described relationships with the giants of his past. I shall touch in later sections on

Ancient Lights as a fictional as well as retrospective work and comment more directly on what I see as Ford's urban and ambivalent pastoral.

In a limited sense, *Ancient Lights* reads like George Moore's *Memoirs*, as a pagan book that celebrates the almost mythical qualities of the Pre-Raphaelites, with Madox Brown (who was not strictly speaking of the Brotherhood) serving as a benign and lovable Jove. For all their follies, Ford's giants represented for him that heroic conception of literature which emerges in much of his writing and which makes his retrospections so vital and so forgiving. But to call his book *pagan* and to see it delighting in the life of the arts is to ignore another emphasis, the world of guilt and emotional darkness, which contends in *Ancient Lights* with the remembered pleasures of his childhood and the implied satisfactions of his adult life. Ford draws attention (as he does obliquely in *The Good Soldier*) to his Roman Catholic belief, which remains, however, at once prominent and anomalous in the rest of the narrative. On the first page he says:

> My own childhood was a thing so vivid that it certainly influenced me, that it certainly rendered me timid, incapable of self-assertion and as it were perpetually conscious of original sin until only just the other day.[6]

If the consciousness of sin runs through the book, consciousness is separate from acceptance, separate almost from belief. Unlike George Tyrrell's autobiography, Ford's seems only loosely related to confession or penance. While gladly asserting his timidity or lack of confidence, he never comes close to assessing his life or reviewing the story of his life in terms of faith. Yet he will often draw on assumptions about sin and suffering and other legacies of his Catholic upbringing. There is no easy optimism in this book, but there is also no intense self-criticism, very little regret, and only small hints of remorse. The sense of self that emerges may be unsure and contradictory, but it is as elastic as the narrative itself.

For the most part, Ford's historic and narrating selves emerge as if detached or neutral; instead of expressing the self-hatred common in religious autobiographers, or otherwise dwelling on his personal failings, he reports what he has seen or heard with his own qualities neither prominent nor ignored. Ford projects the kind of balance that Gosse wanted and could not achieve, although he clearly lacks the passion and the conviction of purposeful growth that inform Gosse's book. George Tyrrell may laugh at himself or confess his weaknesses, but he also never manages what is Ford's habitual manner, a kind of deflection from self, which can involve either self-mockery or a sudden shift to another and perhaps less troubling topic.

When H. G. Wells tried to characterize Ford and decided that neither he nor anyone else could, he described someone whose personality vacillated between different poles, a kind of chameleon writer with competing and inexplicable qualities. Ford always elicited extreme reactions. Ezra Pound could praise him for his generosity (and call *Ancient Lights* a book in which every word mattered), and Ernest Hemingway could write about him as if he were merely contemptible.[7] Aware of his conflicting values or even selves, which he knew how to exploit, Ford uses *Ancient Lights* as a kind of conversation with himself about himself. He does not seem to be in search of resolution or closure. Indeed, he seems determined to avoid it. Just as at the outset he can imply that his book is a sort of religious confession, later, and no more accurately, he can speak of it as a *jeremiad* (287), feeling that his convictions and self-assertions have become tracts for the times, lectures to his readers about the values of literature and the inhospitability to literature of the world in which he now writes. From the first page there is a sense of a writer who lives with contradictions, who is content with his book as a series of anecdotes and equally content to lecture on what he holds to be sacred, who delights in the scenes he depicts and emphasizes his boyhood unhappiness, who can speak of original sin and praise the Pre-Raphaelites for their gusto. Although he recurs to the topic of his childhood unhappiness, imagining a world that is on balance "sad," Ford looks back on himself with some of the same detachment and humor that he finds for Rossetti, say, or Ruskin, whom he dislikes. It is as if, like Moore, he had read Keats's injunctions about negative capability and applied them to the account of his own boyhood—just as he would later apply them to the lives of Edward Ashburnam and the entire cast of *The Good Soldier*.

The effects of Ford's noncommittal writing are sometimes harmful. In the first place, he seems to write *Ancient Lights* as he writes even some of his best novels, with an irritating carelessness, although haste and the exigencies of deadlines are no doubt partly to blame. *Ancient Lights* is replete with hyperbolic statements, for example, which clash so much with the understated tone of other sections. "Vast" is a common word, as well as "great" and "absolutely," "extraordinary," and "enormously." The world of Ford's childhood has, as a consequence, a large-scale or fairytale quality, but much of the overstatement is repetitive and finally unemphatic. Ford says that "I . . . am told sometimes that I am the first—or let us say most precious—stylist now employing the English language" (155), but Henry James and Conrad, to name only two, would not have allowed themselves the loose and garrulous prose which mars too many pages in *Ancient Lights*.

Related to the uneven style is Ford's readiness to introduce passages that, because they seem gratuitous, verge on gossip; and while gossip is for Ford (as for Jane Austen and others) indispensable to his social vision, I mean here a quality of casual writing. His anecdote about Oscar Wilde is a case in point. Ford agrees with Richard Garnett, who pronounced, at the time of Oscar Wilde's arrest, that the scandal would prove terribly harmful for English poetry. (The likely "death" of English poetry had been a common lament through the previous generation.) What he relates is unflattering, though Ford seems careful to avoid malice:

> I found him exceedingly difficult to talk to, and I only once remember hearing him utter one of his brilliancies. This was at a private view of the New Gallery. Some one asked Wilde if he were not going to the soirée of the O. P. Club. Wilde, who at that time had embroiled himself with that organization, replied: "No. Why, I should be like a poor lion in a den of savage Daniels."
>
> I saw him once or twice afterwards in Paris, where he was, I think, rather shamefully treated by the younger denizens of Montmartre and of the Quartier Latin. I remember him as, indeed, a tragic figure, seated at a table in a little cabaret, lachrymosely drunk.
>
> (150)

Ford's account, which allows Wilde only the dullest of quips, seems less insightful than that of two other memoirists: Yeats, who was ambivalent but sympathetic to a fellow Irishman and a "tragic" figure; and William Rothenstein, the painter, whose diaries record, like Ford's book, encounters with a faintly disquieting and self-destructive man.[8] Ford forgets his own injunctions about "precision," which is, he says, a necessary counter to "the fortuitous materialism of a bewildered world" (62), a world hostile to careful writing, and he seems to struggle against his own lack of generosity. Such easy and even careless anecdotes occur in *Ancient Lights,* but they remain peripheral to the main interests of the book, which re-create scenes of boyhood with the excitement and pleasure of rediscovery.

Most of Ford's self-portrayal occurs in remembered scenes, wherein his childhood self fears and confronts larger-than-life adults, almost all of whom seem to have made him suffer. Ford's troubled memory of his father is particularly noticeable, although his father died while a relatively young man and before Ford had been able to convince him that he had either talents or promise. Several times in *Ancient Lights,* Ford recalls that his father called him "a patient but extremely stupid donkey" (ix), and while he tells this with apparent amusement, his insistence on the phrase obviously speaks to the problem of his father's memory. That brilliant, German-educated intellectual, journalist, apologist for Schopenhauer, represented for his son all that was not clumsy, limited in intelligence, or otherwise incapable. Along with the other proponents of "genuis," Francis Hueffer implicitly taught his son that he was likely to fail.

Whatever the later consequences of being raised as a donkey who ought to be a genius (perhaps a "golden ass"), Ford can speak categorically about his childhood:

> To me life was simply not worth living because of the existence of Carlyle, of Mr. Ruskin, of Mr. Holman Hunt, of Mr. Browning, or of the gentleman who built the Crystal Palace. These people were perpetually held up to me as standing upon unattainable heights, and at the same time I was perpetually being told that if I could not attain to these heights I might just as well not cumber the earth. What then was left for me? Nothing. Simply nothing.
>
> (xi)

Ford does not in any way try to lessen the achievement of the people he names, except that "Mr." usually creeps in when he wants to be critical and that "the gentleman who built the Crystal Palace," Joseph Paxton, has lost a touch of stature in Ford's neat bequest of anonymity. Even in Ford's memory, Ruskin and Tennyson, Browning and Carlyle, and all the rest of the "ancient lights" are "twenty-five feet tall" (vii); he could not and he will not try to emulate them. With the exception that he borrows a criterion of sincerity from those times, he wants to attain something different from whatever the mentor-geniuses of his childhood attained. He also wants to present them now with their lost eminence. This makes for a number of ironies.

In retrospect Ford is usually small, at fault, and in an untenable situation. He describes as the worst night of his life escorting a prominent musician back to his hotel. The musician is furious because an equally prominent composer has been allowed to play on the same platform, and he vents his anger on Fordie. Given to the habit of carrying chocolates in one pocket and diamonds in another, the musician thrusts his hands in his pockets and, with a wild gesture, scatters his diamonds along the platform of an Underground station. When the last train of the evening arrives, he steps into the train, leaving the small boy torn between his responsibilities to the musician, who knows no English, and to the diamonds, the loss of which seems unthinkable.

The End of an Epoch, the Closing of a Door 155

He chooses the diamonds, then spends the rest of his night tramping around London in search of the musician. How old he was or how helpless or why he was required to assist the musician he does not say. As if with the distance of Overton, in *The Way of All Flesh,* he emphasizes the impossibility of the situation, with its unfair burden on the child, along with the laughable, farcical nature of the circumstances. The musician is not at all grateful for his diamonds, simply miffed that Fordie has caused him trouble, including detainment by the police.

Victimized by usually benevolent or otherwise harmless people, the "singularly shy" little boy finds himself situated in circumstances which he simply cannot control.

> Miss [Mathilde] Blind frightened me out of my life. And rising up and gathering her proof-sheets together, the poetess, with her Medusa head, would regard me with indignant and piercing brown eyes. "Fordie," she would say with an awful scrutiny, "Your grandfather says you are a genius, but I have never been able to discover in you any signs but those of your being as stupid as a donkey." I never *could* escape from being likened to that other useful quadruped.
>
> (51–52)

Excepting the brief reference to Madox Brown's generosity (Ford makes clear that his grandfather thought of nearly everyone as a genius), this is characteristic of his remembered encounters. Never does he enjoy revenge or report later acknowledgment of his success. Failure seems to be as final as it is inevitable. After describing the episode with the musician or Miss Blind, Ford distances himself from its effect and slides into another anecdote, leaving the reader to piece together what his own reticence has omitted.

Not always a laughable victim, Ford occasionally allows himself a vision of the small boy which puts aside the poor donkey. In different memoirs, for example, he records an encounter with the novelist Turgenev, who remained for him the world's finest writer. I quote first a description, not from *Ancient Lights,* but from *Mightier than the Sword* (1938):

> I was conscious . . . of a singular, compassionate smile that still seems to me to look up out of the pages of his books when—as I constantly do, and always with a sense of amazement—I re-read them. I felt instinctively that I was in the presence of a being that could not but compassionately regard anything that was very young, small, and helpless. The year was 1881. He, sixty-three.

> But I certainly can't have been awed, for I brought out in a high, squeaky voice and with complete composure, the words:
> "Won't you and your friends be seated, Mr. Ralston?"[9]

Obviously entranced by his anecdote, Ford introduces it carefully (and with a typical string of adverbs), giving a sense both of the moment in the past and the endurance of his values. He still loves Turgenev, because the qualities he sensed as a child come through Turgenev's pages on every re-reading; adult judgments corroborate childhood impressions. At least in literary matters, life offers meaning in continuity. Beyond this, Ford recalls, not only what must have been told to him by adults in his family, to whom Ralston or Turgenev presumably spoke, but also the historical framing of the anecdote. Turgenev was, in 1881, sixty-three. So much time has passed, so much has changed, if not his judgment on Turgenev's novels. In his remembering, Ford has the capacity, like Gosse or Moore or Yeats, to record sounds as well as sights, words and phrases, emphases and omissions (none seems to recall smells), but whereas they profess to remember best the scenes when they were alone or with another person, Ford remembers himself in a social context.

Asked whether he really remembered, Ford would probably have wondered whether the question made sense. And perhaps it does not. As a matter of fact, however, the Turgenev passage I have quoted differs appreciably from the account in *Ancient Lights,* and the differences are revealing:

> I must have been alone in the immense studio that had once been the drawing-room of Colonel Newcome. At any rate it is recorded as the earliest incident of my chequered and adventurous career, and moreover as evidencing the exquisite politeness that at that time had been taught me—I hope I may not since have lost it—that my grandfather, coming into the studio, found me approaching the two giants and exclaiming in high treble: "Won't you take a chair?" I must have been one, two or three years of age at the itme.
>
> (186–87)

At the beginning of *Ancient Lights* Ford is careful to point out that impressions are far more germaine than facts, and that his business is with impressions. "Just a word," he says, "to make plain the actual nature of this book. It consists of impressions" (xiii). What, then, are we to make of impressions that are asserted as though they were facts? "It is recorded that" shifts the burden of reliability from the narrator to someone unidentified, someone buried away in a passive construction.

In the Turgenev accounts, Ford is not only inconsistent, altering his story to suit different purposes in different books, he stretches facts in a most peculiar way. The young child of "one, two or three years of age" nicely fits Ford's pattern of the tiny and helpless waif who plays such an ambiguous role with the literary giants around him. But if his older self is right about the year, 1881—as he specifies in *Mightier than the Sword*—Ford must have been about eight, rather than two or three, when he offered Mr. Ralston and friend a chair, in which case there was little remarkable about his gesture. What is remarkable is the need for twisted fact, the insistence on the pathos of the child by a storyteller who is still performing in another world.

But perhaps the point of the anecdote is not so much its verifiability as its verisimilitude, the product of intimate detail and what is, again, a kind of double vision: the child's and the grown man's. Although careful not to commit himself too far, and perhaps incapable of certain kinds of self-commitment, Ford wants his book to seem both new and authentic. To suggest the immediacy—the authenticity—of his writing, Ford comments on a critic who has responded to one of his anecdotes published earlier in a magazine. "My impression was and remains that I heard Thomas Carlyle tell how at Weimar he borrowed an apron from a waiter and served tea to Goethe and Schiller, who were sitting in eighteenth-century court dress beneath a tree" (xiii). No matter that facts tell otherwise, that the scene could not have taken place; his "impression" is the final arbiter.

At the time he wrote *Ancient Lights,* Ford had not yet become famous for his defense of "impressionism"; nor was he dismissing contemptuously the factual accuracy associated with scholarship or, for that matter, with ordinary social and business dealings. Yet he was clearly anticipating his later novelistic concerns while trying to establish easy intimacy—between himself and his past and himself and his reader. What his critic lacks, says Ford, is a saving sense both of humor and of imagination. For reader as well as writer, the past only comes to life when it escapes the dullness and sterility of the literal-minded. This is Ford's good-humored but blunt hint to his readers, about whom he seems to think a great deal, and from whom he expects both laughter and intelligence, quite apart from his unstated need for sympathy.

Ford's relationship with his reader, at once genial and circumspect, illustrates further qualities in the complex and shifting narrator of *Ancient Lights*. The epitome of Ford's entire book is his prefatory dedication, possibly the wittiest and most idiosyncratic introduction ever written for an autobiography. Ford writes a letter—offering his book as a present—to his children, who are, he says, his immediate but not admittedly his only audience. Such a letter implies close ties and affection, but in Ford's case things are not quite what they seem. He does not mention the fact that he no longer lived with either his wife or his children or that his relationship with his children had been badly disrupted. Obviously he can ignore facts as conveniently as he can arrange them.

Among its more evident peculiarities, his letter begins with an echo of those many religious autobiographies that confer on doubtless needy heirs the lessons gleaned from a life of sin and redemption. Describing the preposterous standards set by his elders, Ford says:

> We were to give not only all our goods, but all our thoughts, all our endeavours; we were to stand aside always to give openings for others. I do not know that I would ask you to look upon life otherwise, or to adopt another standard of conduct, but still it is well to know beforehand that such a rule of life will expose you to innumerable miseries.
>
> (xii)

This is, in a sense, the obverse side of admonitions requiring self-sacrifice and single-minded belief; but it is no less what Ford would call a "sincere" and reflective comment as to the conduct of life. Little else in Ford's letter to his children has this tone or takes this approach, although, again, he insists in later passages on the burdens placed on his own youth and makes an implicit appeal for his daughter's sympathy. He deals affectionately with his children, laughing at little jokes, poking fun at himself, offering his sympathies about the absurdities of growing up, yet he seems resigned to the obvious: that his advice is no doubt wasted on young people and that it reflects, in any case, only his own peculiar life. He recalls here the conclusion of the more somber William Hale White, who also looked back to a dark and troubling childhood and who knew the limits of his own knowledge. D. H. Lawrence, who called Ford "everybody's blessed Uncle," recognized in the mercurial Ford an avuncular interest, a generosity toward the work and the frailties of others.[10] Ford's address to his children has more of the quality of the benevolent uncle than of a father—of someone, that is, both detached and affectionate. He seems to want to avoid the kind of categorical or peremptory judgment so hurtful from his own father, but the cost is his evasion and disengagement. The tone of his letter is, in any case, precisely the tone Ford adopts toward his larger audience. This is how he justifies the reason for his book:

> I made for myself that somewhat singular discovery that I can only be said to have grown up a very short time ago—perhaps three months,

perhaps six. I discovered that I had grown up only when I discovered quite suddenly that I was forgetting my own childhood.

(viii)

With an inconsistency for which Ford was and is notorious, he can later speak to all his readers who, like himself, are still essentially children, who may forget details of their childhood but who carry with them the qualities of children which he tries to reach in his opening chapter. To begin his narrative, nonetheless, it makes sense to suggest a "singular discovery," his growing up, which is arbitrary and humorous (was it three months ago or six?), and the forgetting of the past that requires its immediate recollection, with the grown-up narrator speaking of far away and long ago to his children, those real and those imagined.

As the discerning but usually uncommitted commentator, Ford is, as I have been suggesting, both the recorder of past times and the boy to whom he looks back. The needs of the adult, particularly the adult writer, require a continuing revision of the life of the child. In imagining his past for his daughters, Ford begins with an apparently conventional introduction of his first memory.

> The earliest thing that I can remember is this, and the odd thing is that, as I remember it, I seem to be looking at myself from the outside. I see myself a very tiny child in a long blue pinafore looking into the breeding-box of some Barbary ring-doves that my grandmother kept in the window of the huge studio in Fitzroy Square.[11]

If we think of this passage in terms of Gaston Bachelard's "poetics of space," we may be reminded of the importance of "intimate" space for writers, space associated with the intrinsic needs of childhood, but also perceived in the present with astonishing energy and vividness. The passage may well be, as Thomas Moser calls it, "a Freudian's delight," and with good reason.[12] Ford's troubled sense of losing his boyhood home, his painful relationship with a talented and evidently unsympathetic father, his almost determined overlooking of his mother—quite apart from matters of sibling rivalry, fear of sex, awareness of guilt, and others—suggest a concentration of the themes of the book in this basic image of nest or home. The small and unknowing boy (described from a somewhat naïve vantage point) disrupts the intimate space within the "vast" surroundings of the Madox Brown household. Images of intimate space, as Bachelard argues, are the product of language emerging into meaning; they are also, emotionally, "abodes for an unforgettable past."[13] Ford's passage suggests the complexities of language in such acts of creative remembering. He writes, as it were, in two almost contradictory ways. His emphasis on "I" calls attention to the intimacy of his re-creation; at the same time, the "I" is the older writer more than the remembered child, as the dominant present tense would suggest. Ford realizes like Pater the importance of *objects* in children's lives, but also how our sense of ourselves as the object seen dissociates us from past selves even while we seek out those selves to understand the present.[14] Ford remembers the "long blue pinafore" as precisely as "some Barbary ring-doves."

In observing the remembered scene, Ford is aware of proportions as well as details, the window appearing "to be as high as a house, and I myself as small as a doorstep" (viii). Whereas Dickens might describe from a similar perspective, Dickens would also dwell on the emotional intensity of the scene, evoking the child's feelings as accurately as his observations. Ford does say that (having disturbed the bird's eggs), "I thought I had destroyed life, and that I was exceedingly sinful" (viii–ix). Direct but unexpansive in such observations, his tendency is to move on, as he does after the episode with the musician or with Miss Blind, to comment on his grandmother, who had been angry with him, but who was, he says, the most genial of people. The effect is to relate the individual child's remembered suffering to what Ford elsewhere calls the "tragedy of childhood."[15]

Such disconnected or unglossed passages occur in a book that isolates the boy while describing the profusion of people whom he meets. What seems implied here is an odd competition, not so much between Ford's younger self and his historic world, but between Ford the recorder of his past and Ford the historian, or better, between Ford the compulsive self-historian and Ford the creator of evasive and protective selves. I am speaking of the privacy of Ford's autobiographical account. Notorious for his reticence, Ford writes even reminiscences with a clear regard for his own confessional limits, however much he tells about detached, intimate happenings. In other words, while Ford will praise his own style or tell of a childhood prank or record some strong conviction, he is perhaps just as self-protective as Gosse or White or, in a different way, Yeats. Unlike George Moore who increasingly allows an unacknowledged and previously unknown self to materialize as he writes, Ford is both circumspect and consistent. Much of his life is missing from this book. There is little of his intervening relations with Henry James and Conrad, of his professional activities, his work as editor, his dealings with agents, his success (or lack of it) with the public.[16] Nor does he speak about his marriage, his relationship with his children, his love affairs, his entangled divorce, or—excepting those admissions of inadequacy—his adult problems, including at least one major breakdown. Granted that the focus of his book is largely on Ford's boyhood, the omissions seem conspicuous, because, as I have suggested, Ford goes into some detail about the social world he lives in. He may imply the history he does not write, and like Gosse, Ford acknowledges social and technological developments, which have mitigated some suffering and made life better for more people; but he essentially pays tribute to a richer past. A hint of his attitudes toward private revelations can be seen in his declaration that "the influence of Jean-Jacques Rousseau . . . is on the wane" (65), a remark with which Edmund Gosse would have disagreed but which would be as pertinent for Gosse as for Ford himself. Detailed and exploratory as it is, *Ancient Lights* remains a carefully circumscribed book, in which an amused and sometimes skeptical middle-aged man describes intimately only limited aspects of himself from a limited time in his life.

If Gosse's dominant perspective is fifty years and George Moore's is twenty years, Ford's is twenty-five. He seems to compress the years that have elapsed since his boyhood into a pliable historic era so that Ruskin and Carlyle, Rossetti and Wilde, Turgenev and Liszt, Browning and Whistler are, so to speak, performing together twenty-five years before. Ford gives a number of indexes of chronology (Meredith lived only a short time with Rossetti at Cheyne Walk; Madox Brown's diary entry preceded later estimates of Morris; Turgenev must have been sixty-three in the year 1881), but he offers no paradigm of development or evolution. Except for the large hiatus between his days as "Fordie" and the "now" of his writing, Ford's effect is to blur distinctions of time. Accentuating the disparity between then and now, between the large hulking man and the very small child, he alternates habitually between "when I was a small boy" and "just the other day." When, after all, did he stop thinking of himself as a small child? How did the patient, stupid donkey overcome or at least learn to live with the pain of his childhood? Ford offers nothing akin to George Tyrrell's lines of demarcation, nothing to separate the layers of his "growing up." When he mentions Christina Rossetti responding to his first book and saying she could no longer refer to him as "Fordie," he emphasizes, untypically, the stage in his life; he has not built up chronologically from preceding scenes to this one any more than he will go on to account for his writing career after the success of the first book. He does report that *The Brown Owl* was a fairytale, an appropriate work for a writer fascinated by the status of children in an adult world and by the sensuous wonders of his own boyhood.

The creativity which drives Ford and about which, implicitly, he is always writing, forces his constant re-evaluation of his own talents. If at least one definable condition of "modern man" is that he (or she) recognizes that he is not a genius, Ford seems quintessentially the modern man.[17] Like Diderot's Nephew, who perhaps first thought of himself in such terms, he plays the buffoon with parts of his own life, skirting the very achievements which make his life matter; hence his preoccupation with the "geniuses" of another era, his need to sort out his own beginnings in a world that demanded and disallowed the talents he wants. He projects his present dilemmas into the still unresolved but somewhat more manageable world of the smaller boy.

> The man in me revolts against the fictionist.
> Vladimir Nabokov, Speak, Memory

At the heart of Ford's letter to his "kids"—which speaks of the end of an epoch and means by it both a phase of Ford's life and a major shift in literature and society—is the conflict between a private if reticent account of childhood and a public and historical document. No less than Edmund Gosse or William Hale White, Ford sees himself depicting a historical era from a perspective that only he can know, as if history must be seen from a personal vantage point or re-enacted on the bright stage of his own childhood. This brings us back to "impressions" and their connection to historical facts, but also raises the question as to the bond between autobiography and fiction, which in Ford's as in George Moore's case is particularly intimate. We can approach all this by looking at Ford's portrait of Christina Rossetti, which he evidently includes for two main reasons: to elevate Christina in the Pre-Raphaelite pantheon; and to show how she anticipates modern literary developments that he himself advocates.

Ford's sympathetic portrait of Christina tacitly equates his own distinctive childhood with her isolation, his writing with hers. Along the way he can imply that Ruskin was to Christina's talents what the admonitions of his father and the Pre-Raphaelites were to his own. Ford writes in the following passage with more acerbity than usual, and for reasons that will be apparent:

> Mr. Ruskin pooh-poohed and discouraged Christina Rossetti's efforts at poetry. For there is extant at least one letter from the voluminous critic in which he declares that the *Goblin Market* volume was too slight and too frivolous a fascicule to publish, and to the end of his days Mr. Ruskin considered that Christina damaged her brother. It was not good for Gabriel's fame or market, he considered, that there should be another

Rossetti in the field. And I must confess that when I consider these utterances and this attitude I am filled with as hot and as uncontrollable an anger as I am when faced by some more than usually imbecile argument against the cause of women's franchise.

(55)

Ironic and scornful Ford is in this passage and throughout his discussion of Christina Rossetti closest to his *jeremiad*. His contempt for Ruskin is evident without the direct statement about his anger, as the "Mr." and the "fascicule" suggest. Since "Mr." Ruskin also represents blindness to the ambitions of creative women, Ford's scorn for the "imbecile" arguments of those opposing women's suffrage offers not just a comparison but also a larger comment on the world in which Christina Rossetti had to work. Ford describes her writing, in "cloistral seclusion," alone and "in pain" (59), her "tragic" life representing the darker side of the shining Pre-Raphaelite stage. Although he has to imagine much of Christina's life, his imaginative sympathy makes this portrait at least as vivid as those of the other eminent characters, most of whose reported activities he either observed or read about in such documents as his grandfather's journal. Without any overt connection, he implies his own relationship, his deeper kinship, with Christina than with her more famous brother.

Much as Ford admires Dante Gabriel Rossetti, he thinks that "The Blessed Damozel" (written, he points out, when Rossetti was still an adolescent) introduced obscurity and false medievalism into English poetry, doing damage on a par with that resulting from Wilde's arrest and trial. He conceives of Christina's poetry as medieval in another way: "Christina Rossetti's nature was medieval in the sense that it cared for little things and for arbitrary arrangements" (61–62). Whatever the merits of this view of medievalism, Ford makes a central point about Christina Rossetti's and his own writing. Several times in *Ancient Lights* he speaks of little things constituting the reality of life, and it is the power to deal with little things that distinguishes modern writing, whether poetry or fiction. (William Hale White, George Tyrrell, and George Moore all make similar comments.) The Pre-Raphaelite generation loved, he says, to generalize, generalizing himself with a Blake-like contradiction. Christina Rossetti was a conspicuous exception. With her painful honesty, her sensitivity to human suffering and self-isolation, above all with her "introspective" nature, she anticipated the conditions of modern literature as Ford understands them. To Ford, then, Christina represents an example of both personal dignity and artistic integrity. He may not explain why her modernism necessitates a "medieval" attention to detail, and he only touches on matters of "arbitrary arrangement." At the same time, for all its emphasis on people and the clutter of their lives, his vision of modernism parallels that of T. E. Hulme, Wilhelm Worringer, and other contemporaries, who also invoked medieval ideals in their attempt to define a modernist aesthetic.[18]

In the passage I have mentioned about Christina's response to his first book, Ford quotes her letter:

> My dear young relation (if you will permit me to style you so, though I am aware that I should write more justly "connection." Yet you are now too old for me to call you "Fordie") . . .
>
> (58)

Ford does not comment on his evident delight to have been addressed, finally, as a grownup, though this manifestly weighed with him. What intrigues him is Christina's "precision," a quality lacking among the other writers in her family or among the larger family of the Pre-Raphaelite circle, which was given to hyperbole and what he calls "Romantic" perceptions. Oddly, he quotes phrases about "golden spires" and "golden days" to illustrate imprecision, overlooking his own heavy use of "golden" (of which more later) throughout this memoir.

Ford's understanding of "precision" relates to his overall purpose in *Ancient Lights,* which he has already implied is a modern work dealing though it does with a past generation. While arguing, in the dedication to his children, the value of impressions over facts, he says, "I have for facts a most profound contempt" (xv). Promising to be "sincere" in his presentation—truthful, that is, to the spirit, the essence, of his memories rather than to some verifiable background—he even boasts about "inaccuracies as to facts" (xv). By the time Ford was writing *Ancient Lights,* terms such as *impression* and *impressionism* had already become commonplace, if not hackneyed. "Nowadays," wrote George Moore, echoing Pater or Arthur Symons, "we are all impressionists."[19] Apart from being timely or representative, Ford's early and passionate commitment to impressionism has important implications for his own writing.

Intentionally or not, impressionism means in *Ancient Lights* something necessarily piecemeal. Ford is not at all apologetic about introducing his episodes as *anecdotes* and makes no protestations about underlying unity or formal coherence. Some of the episodes had appeared serially in magazines, and few would seem crucial to the overall shape of the book, which is roughly but by no means rigorously chronological. Ford seems to appreciate that the main difference between nineteenth- and twentieth-century versions of narrative time had to do with chronology, with "arbitrary" or seemingly arbitrary arrangements that did away with what Forster describes as the "then, and then, and then" of earlier narrative. As so many of his novels illustrate, Ford was clear about the uselessness of linear story, which implied cause and effect and which imposed on characters an inescapable pattern of externality. *Ancient Lights* precedes the novels in which Ford experiments most radically with the materials of disrupted lives, but it suggests that he was already quite aware of what he wanted from fiction and what, apart from matters of "precision" and "sincerity," he considered desirable ingredients of modern literature. His paradoxical emphasis on social and cultural "changes" since his youth, without parallel emphasis on sequence or development, reflects the hand of the theorist or the "fictionist" manipulating personal time, dispensing with narrative continuity.

"Impressionism" as discontinuous narrative bears on *Ancient Lights*, its assertive "lack of architecture"—to use Turgenev's phrase—a consequence of a fully realized literary work. Turgenev appreciates the heterogenous nature of his own writing as a function of his open-mindedness, his availability to the richness of life. (I refer to comments quoted by Henry James in the 1906 preface to *The Portrait of a Lady*.)[20] Ford's kinship with earlier novelists such as Turgenev or contemporaries like James may be, however, more apparent than real. For him, impressions are a useful defense when he wants them, but something to be put aside when he does not. As Carol Ohmann points out, "In *Ancient Lights* [Ford] scorns reality and implies that his 'impressions' as a creative writer are more true than literal truth. But in *No More Parades* he claims to speak not as a creative artist but only as a scrupulous observer of what has actually happened."[21] Ford's statement in *No More Parades* is, "I present therefore only what I observed or heard."[22] The evident contradiction belongs, according to Ohmann, to the same pattern. "In either case he disclaims responsibility; he separates himself from what he has written. He announces, in effect, that he will not anywhere reveal himself."[23]

Ohmann's shrewd comment points to what might be evasion on the one hand and brilliant understanding on the other. Open, as Turgenev says of himself, to wide experience, Ford is also suspicious of his own limits, of himself as an artist. As *Ancient Lights* suggests, Ford was deeply concerned with the limits of knowing and the paradoxes associated with knowing long before he wrote the Tietjens books—or even *The Good Soldier*. The polarities of facts and impressions, self-revelation and reticence, distance and immediacy, the precise and the arbitrary, underlie his writing, whether memoirs or novels. He appreciates with

Conrad's Marlow how difficult it is to know another person, how difficult to know oneself as another person, and how inescapable knowing is from subjectivity or consciousness. "The heart of another is a dark forest" (xi), he says, anticipating the famous lines from *The Good Soldier:* "Who in this world knows anything of another heart—or of his own?"[24]

Ford's fascination with paradox involves him in some of the same visual oppositions as Conrad's, and paradox seems to define his peculiar brand of modernism beyond the hints implicit in the portrait of Christina Rossetti. Like Conrad, he wants to "make you see." "My business in life . . . is to attempt to discover, and to try to let you see, where we stand" (xv). Ford speaks repeatedly of the "vivid" nature of his memories, and he is able to re-create the vividness for his readers, as if he were present in a past scene or could obliterate, not the past tenses themselves, but the boundaries they prescribe between past and present. On the other hand, his emphasis on the words "plain" and "actual" suggest his underlying desire for veracity as well as verisimilitude and what Ford, no less than Tyrrell, say, or Gosse, asserts as "truth." Again, Ford's sensual immediacy (like Conrad's) goes hand in hand with a certain emotional distance, whether he speaks about his own life or about someone else's, or about life, panoramic and public, which he seeks to evoke: "I try to give you what I see to be the spirit of an age, of a town, of a movement" (xv).

When David Daiches distinguished between the nineteenth- and the twentieth-century novel, he spoke of values: the nineteenth-century novel, he said, emphasized public values, the novel of our own century private values.[25] Hence, perhaps, George Eliot against Virginia Woolf, Dickens against D. H. Lawrence. The distinction would be, in Ford's view, a typically nineteenth-century argument, rather neat and convincing, except in application. Is Charlotte Brontë a twentieth-century novelist? And C. P. Snow a nineteenth-century novelist? Lawrence would seem in one sense no more private than a mentor like Hardy, and Joyce would certainly seem to be concerned with more than private matters in *Ulysses* or *Finnegans Wake*. Virginia Woolf herself addressed such questions in "Mr. Bennett and Mrs. Brown," wherein the argument against Bennett and Galsworthy and Wells, while assuming faulty values or interests, focuses on their methods: Mrs. Brown cannot be understood from the outside, even perhaps from any perspective, but at least she must not be approached as an object, a thing-like character who, on such and such a date, wearing such and such an outfit, set off down such and such a street.

Woolf's half-facetious remark that human nature changed in December, 1910 is a reminder at least that human nature within the boards of fiction had begun to change;[26] and though Woolf did not have Ford in mind, Ford himself draws attention not only to the date of his writing — prior to Christmas, 1910 — but also to the place, which is Bloomsbury, or close enough. His own sympathetic portraits of people as well as his arbitrary arrangements of chronology imply an understanding similar to Woolf's, not least of which is that the truth of fact may be opposed to the higher truth of fiction, as Woolf suggests in *Granite and Rainbow*.[27] For both writers, an understanding of a Mrs. Brown, a Christina Rossetti, or a Ford Madox Ford lay through the explorations of personal consciousness and the necessary distortions of narrative time.

Behind Virginia Woolf's essay lies another important assumption she seems to share with Ford Madox Ford: that the novelist, in treating her characters, deals with them as she would with herself, fiction becoming a sort of extended biography or autobiography, which guarantees a full humanity, whatever the apparent dullness of the public exterior. Since consciousness presupposes a remembering, novels, like autobiographies, lend themselves to the vagaries and the subjectivity — the lack of traditional "architecture" — in a re-created past. Despite more recent theories of fiction, which supplant character by text, autobiography remains as an affirmation of character, or rather, of people's lives as they are converted in texts. Words are not people, and autobiography no less than novels may occupy fictional worlds, but texts remain statements about people, however oblique the presentation may be.[28]

If Ford seems to anticipate Woolf's version of modernism in *Ancient Lights*, he also points to major differences. However much, for example, both writers emphasize the centrality of "scenes," their sense of scene, or of the writer within the scene, seems quite distinct. "Scenemaking" for each is a "natural way of marking the past," but their scenes have an altogether different weight.[29] In *Moments of Being*, Woolf describes her necessary return to key scenes from the past, especially her mother's death, which she either "makes whole" or exorcises by writing. Beginning with apparent superficialities, Woolf works through to unconscious or hidden aspects of her "exceptional moments," while Ford, as I have said, approaches emotion only to retreat. Ford contentedly skirts topics such as death, or passion, and few of his scenes are charged with emotion, just as few are explored beyond the immediate needs of narrative. Obviously, various scenes mattered greatly to Ford, as his compulsive repetition indicates, yet he did not explore so much as describe anew when he did return. To some extent, his descriptions are those of an aesthete, someone fascinated by surface, uninterested for the purposes of this work either in the unconscious or the tragic dimensions of his material, which he touches without probing. Conrad's collaborator was of course aware of other writing methods, and would turn to them himself; *Ancient Lights* preserves an affable almost surface freedom—not impersonal, but not dissatisfied with the sensuous appearance of things.

"Moments of being" nevertheless suggest for both Woolf and Ford an intensity of vision, although here, too, Ford's moments are assertively cultural or broadly *historical* as well as private. Ford imagines the individual as enacting history, his view of history perhaps wider than Woolf's, or more acknowledgedly public. Again, Ford cared deeply about history. He had written biographies (Ford Madox Brown) and historical novels (*The Fifth Queen* trilogy), and his fictional ideals included characters who are representative of their times, immersed in history. This helps to explain the distinctive attributes of *Ancient Lights* and the ways in which for all its frankly evocative quality, Ford's first, personal reminiscence anticipates his later fiction. Malcolm Bradbury has described recurrent processes of Ford's novels, addressing their "historical" character, their reliance on public "spots of time," which seem increasingly bound to World War 1:

> The techniques, then, are techniques for presenting large-scale dispositions of time, of characters, of moods and insights, of bringing the large and the small into relation—in the interests of giving not only a sense of psychological verisimilitude but social accuracy.[30]

Although directed at *Parade's End* and Ford's later novels, much of what Bradbury says pertains to *Ancient Lights,* even Ford's tendency to see the world of his novels culminating in war. "That was the end of everything—of the Pre-Raphaelites, of the Henley gang, of the New Humour, of the Victorian Great Figures" (235). In *Ancient Lights* the war happens to be the Boer War, which Ford early recognized as a major index of change: both likely and futile, on whatever scale, war was the supreme reminder of the kinship between public events and private lives.

No less than Virginia Woolf—or Joseph Conrad or D. H. Lawrence or James Joyce—Ford is essentially an autobiographical writer, someone who draws habitually on his own experiences or, in the sense that I have suggested, makes other people's experiences analogous to those of his own. We have seen in Butler and Gosse, White and Moore, how inextricably linked are private life and public book, how difficult it becomes to separate autobiography from fiction; or how close so much late-nineteenth-century and early-twentieth-century fiction remains to autobiographical studies.

Whether Ford saw within himself that division between "man" and "fictionist" which Nabokov mentions in *Speak, Memory,* he is working with similar ideas. Nabakov's title recalls traditional invocations to the muse, whether Clio, say, or Urania, and in his case the appeal is to Mnemosyne, mother of the muses, who figures large in so much twentieth-century writing and who had become, in the late nineteenth century, the presiding muse for autobiographers and novelists dissatisfied with tired conventions.[31] I have mentioned Memory as muse in earlier sections, and she is just as pertinent for Ford.

For many of Ford's contemporaries, the invocation of memory suggests the artificiality of those common nineteenth-century polarities between memory and imagination, the "creative" and the "meditative," which no longer seem appropriate for authors who predicate imagination on the remembered or who see in remembering a creative act. (Although I am speaking of personal narrative, one could argue analogously even for naturalistic works, which imply the full extent of Mnemosyne's powers in an effort to re-create vast amounts of social facticity: what is true of Virginia Woolf, in other words, could be potentially true of Arnold Bennett or Zola.) Memory, whether collective or private, conscious or unconscious, has for Ford and his contemporaries both an important voice and a protean shape. And if memory is subject to the inspiration of a muse or is the muse, it need not follow rules or prescriptions any more than another form of writing. This seems to be Ford's assumption throughout *Ancient Lights*. Like George Moore, he might say that his impressions are the precise images of recollection, presented in their own order rather than in the order of the passing of time, and moving backward and forward like the workings of memory itself. Ford implies that memory is not—as Coleridge and others had charged—a subordinate faculty, but a form of imagination as important as Wordsworth would have it and with essential qualities for modern literature.

Ford's incorporative memory blurs distinctions between sources just as it overruns genre and batters facts. It is as if, without overt comment, he posits a special memory in the writer, which is both personal and collective, albeit collective would mean social or historical rather than unconscious. Drawing on his father, for example, he can tell about a singer, Mme. B——, who, because she is denied an operatic role, kills her rival's parrots both to punish and to incapacitate her. Just as he elsewhere claims to use "the exact words" that he has heard (11), so here, too, he quotes the singer as if he overheard her triumphant claim: "Mme. C—— has fits for a fortnight, and I—I sing *Dinorah*. I sing it like a miracle; I sing it like an angel, and Mme. C—— has never the face to put her nose on the stage in that part again. Never!" (76). The final "never" sounds very much like Ford himself, and so does the business about singing like an angel. But there is really no discrepancy between the scenes observed by "the small boy" and those told by his father. "This was," he says, "perhaps the mildest of the stories of the epic jealousies of musicians with which my father's house re-echoed, but it is the one which remains most vividly in my mind, I suppose because of the poor parrots" (76). Since the parrots recall the doves he had been accused of killing, the memory fits well with the rest of the anecdotes, and the repetition of "vividly" vouches in Ford's vocabulary for its authenticity if not for its historical accuracy. Indeed, the assertion that the anecdote comes from his father and blends with his own emphasizes the plastic quality of his memories and implies that the fictionist can make almost any material his own, if it works.

To put this differently, *Ancient Lights* should perhaps be read as a work of fiction, in which memory adapts itself to suit a variety of narrative ends. Ford meant what he said when he called his memoir of Conrad "a novel, not a monograph."[32] He might also have said, with Paul De Man, "that the distinction between fiction and autobiography is not an either/or polarity but . . . is undecidable."[33] Ford's instincts were right, for he knows that there are and can be no fixed lines. He seeks freedom from conventional restraints, whatever the ostensible genre. Whether he creates a historical past, as in *The Fifth Queen,* an impressionistic present and past, as in *The Soul of London* (his first successful book, of 1905); whether he speaks about his own life or that of Madox Brown, he writes with overlapping aims. *The Good Soldier* (1915) mixes apparently personal reflection with social commentary, as memories unfold and compete, present consciousness combining a shifting past with a complex and troubled now.

> *To say that on an average in the last 25 years there have been in Bloomsbury per 365 days, 10 of bright sunshine, 299 of rain, 42 of fog and the remainder compounded of all three would not seriously help the impression. This fact I think you will understand, though I doubt whether my friend the critic will. F.M.H. [Hueffer]*
>
> P.P.S. *I find that have written these words not in Bloomsbury but in the electoral district of East Saint Pancras. Perhaps it is gloomier in Bloomsbury. I will go and see.*
>
> P.P.P.S. *It is.*
>
> Ford, Ancient Lights *(xvi)*

I have been speaking of Ford Madox Ford as the author of *Ancient Lights,* which would seem to make sense, except that, as the initials F.M.H. suggest, Ford's name in 1911 remained Ford Madox Hueffer. It was not until after the First World War, and all the pressure to change a German name, that Ford did change it, the fictionist revolting against the man. Ford himself would have appreciated the irony of his first autobiography (the later ones were written by "Ford") having been published as if by an earlier or created self, a certain Hueffer of German extraction, another character in his vivid past. And as someone who made dramatic changes in his life—an officer in the army during the war, an American citizen and part-time resident of France after the 1920s—Ford appropriately dissociated himself from a past that he had dealt with in his books.

In this section I want briefly to touch on ways that memory lends itself not just to historical inquiry or to narratives of self-history but to pastoral, in the sense of a re-created past emerging as counter to adult sufferings or disappointments. Such pastoral takes different forms, as W. H. White, George Tyrrell, Edmund Gosse, even George Moore, have indicated; and Yeats will offer a yet more radical version. Ford's is different again, and far more problematic. "Pastoral" may not in fact be the right word at all. What I have in mind, however, is Ford's sense of space and the ways he associates space with comfort, say, or pain with disclosure or with silence. I have mentioned Gaston Bachelard's *The Poetics of Space,* and Bachelard's assessment of spatial images in literature speaks implicitly about the world of *Ancient Lights.* Bachelard discusses a variety of places by a method he calls *topoanalysis,* the assessment of places within the literary imagination.

For Bachelard, topoanalysis is the "study of the sites of our interior lives."[34] Sometimes he seems to mean the writer's own self-analysis, sometimes the reader's, but the confusion may reflect the situation of literature, which requires both. Bachelard is particularly insightful for Ford, because he is interested in the separateness of images, in their connection with "past moments of solitude" of childhood, and in their spatial qualities. Rooms are especially important to him: rooms, houses, and other examples of what he calls "felicitous space."[35] Ford's "pastoral" involves the adult writer's creation of felicitous space out of the world of his boyhood. It is a singular creation.

To begin with, Ford's pastoral is conspicuously removed from the country; then too, it seems denied by descriptions of childhood that emphasize discomfort and awkwardness more than pleasures and joys. Ford associates his past with so much gloom and darkness that his footsteps, it would seem, scarcely left Bloomsbury for East Saint Pancras, let alone Chelsea and beyond. There is little of Gosse's longed-for excursion to Primrose Hill or his real discovery of rural beauty in Devon, and there is none of the almost caressing love of countryside that Ford (like Conrad) admired so much in W. H. Hudson. Yet the man who wrote affectionately about "the soul of London" knew another kind of remembered beauty, even as he seemed to ignore it.[36]

We can get a good sense of Ford's implicit pastoral by a brief comparison with another autobiographer-novelist, George Gissing, who created his remembered past under the pseudonym of Henry Ryecroft. Ryecroft and Hueffer both address the question of vocation, their "calling" as writers, in relation to a troubling past, but whereas "Ford" dwells on his childhood and distances himself from it, Gissing uses Ryecroft to describe his development as a writer and his hopes for the future.[37] In *The Private Papers of Henry Ryecroft*, Gissing drew on his own earlier life for more or less fictional ends and, like William Hale White before him, killed off his self-hero for reasons best known to himself. Written only a few years before *Ancient Lights*, *Henry Ryecroft* (1903) is perhaps as different from Ford's book as another autobiographical work could be. Gissing looks back on a life of almost uninterrupted work, on poverty, on London life from a Grub Street perspective. He allows Ryecroft what he never achieved himself, a retirement to leisure and rural peace, escaping from semi-starvation as well as from the gloom of London.

Mesmerized as he is with country living, Gissing shapes his book—purporting to be Ryecroft's editor—around the four seasons, and Ryecroft lives out the few last years of his life in a kind of bucolic privacy, a modern Columella, who puts aside city and all that it entails for a simple, untroubled existence. Gissing shares with Ford the rearrangement of "facts" or events; he is similarly interested in the ways that a novelist looks back on his youth from an entirely new perspective, Ryecroft's emerging from the pastoral life he has found, Ford's from the awareness of having grown up or grown away from the circumstances of his youth. But whereas Gissing emphasizes Ryecroft the novelist, as if other people scarcely mattered in his life, Ford, as I have suggested, plays down his own career, except for brief references to his present activities.

Despite the striking differences between the two books, both are creating a version of pastoral. Ryecroft frequently comments on the beauty of flowers and sunsets or other items that he has missed during his years on Grub Street. Ford does none of this. He does, toward the end of his book—and with the advent of the Boer War—speak about escape, feeling ill at ease in London and needing to be elsewhere:

> I fled—into the country. . . . I did not know then, but I know now that my brain was singing to me:
> "Under the bright and starry sky

Dig my grave and let me lie."
Only I wanted to have some tussles with the "good brown earth" before that hill-top should receive me. Well, we have most of us found the "good brown earth" part of a silly pose—but I am not sorry. . . . I am very glad that the intolerable boredom of a country life without sport or pursuit taught me better in time.

(241–42)

Unlike Gissing, in short, Ford laughs at easy pastoralism, dismissing it with the other "romanticisms" of the past century. Yet the pastoralism remains in muted and peculiar ways. In Ford's own life, the country loomed large. "Atque ego in Arcadia vixi" (230). He longed to own land, which he identified inconsistently with certain Tory ideals, and at the least he was always an ardent kitchen gardener. For a time he did live in a rural area, and in later memoirs he describes his life there along with the lives of people he met with a sharp understanding of what the "intolerable boredom" (242) and harsh realities of country life really entail. Whereas for Gissing the country place has all of the trappings of Gilbert White's Selborne, without evils and distractions or real sufferings, Ford knows better. Yet he omits his life in the country, only remarking on his escape and his return.

What does recur throughout the book is the emphasis on "the gloom of central London," (34) now somewhat mitigated, he says, since the days of his boyhood, but a characteristic of Bloomsbury—or East Saint Pancras—that one cannot avoid. Madox Brown's house was, he says, the house Thackeray describes in *The Newcomes,* with its "gloomy" stables and kitchens, and "with a funeral urn in the centre of the entry." It had "great black passages; cracked conservatory; dilapidated bath-room, with melancholy waters moaning and fizzing from the cistern . . . ; but the Colonel [Newcome] thought it perfectly cheerful and pleasant" (1), and so did Madox Brown. The quotation from Thackeray begins *Ancient Lights,* and not inappropriately; it suggests the incessant conflict in Ford between the pleasures and the pains of childhood, the pagan and the sinning, the illumined and the dark.

There is, as Thomas Moser makes clear, good reason for Ford's hesitant praise of the country, or, rather, for his insistence on the enclosed world of his grandfather's house.[38] Agoraphobic, he suffered terribly in the country that he loved, just as he suffered in the open streets of London. His *Soul of London* speaks of those moments of terror when a tourist (like himself as a boy) experiences the "odd sensation of being very little, of peering around the corners of gray and gigantic buildings."[39] Only in open space broken by the line of the sea could Ford feel comfortable or avoid the terror of "the pitiless stars."[40] Perhaps this is why, in *Ancient Lights* he speaks about so many closing doors, referring even to the book itself as marking "the end of an epoch, the closing of a door" (x).

Doors tell a great deal about *Ancient Lights* and about Ford's pastoral creations. Ford's contemporary, Edith Wharton, had spoken of a woman's world (like Ford's description of Christina Rossetti's) as "a great house full of rooms . . . handles of whose doors are never turned; no one knows the way to them, no one knows whither they lead; and in the innermost room . . . , the soul sits alone and waits for a footstep that never comes."[41] One might say of *Ancient Lights* that Ford's own footsteps never reach the inner door and that the surface narrative only allows us, the reader, to approach its meanings. Intimate, spatial images at once entice and conceal.

Bachelard almost echoes Edith Wharton's sense of interior space. He says, "If one were to give an account of all the doors one has closed and opened, of all the doors one would like to re-open, one would have to tell the story of one's entire life."[42] Ford's choice is for a limited number of doors, including and above all the door (with its funerary urn and lasting threat) to Madox Brown's household, just as his choice is for a circumspect narrative. He does not tell the entire story. Since his acute sensitivity to open places seems sadly complementary to his intimidation by adults, he essentially creates an emotional and fictional landscape in which he can be comfortable, an interior landscape that allows a limited investigation of the spaces of childhood. Hence the importance of the nest of ring-doves, of Madox Brown's studio, of his own violated privacy.

At any rate, instead of describing natural scenery or rural retreats, Ford's pastoral alternative in *Ancient Lights* resides in his inner world of "golden" lights (what George Tyrrell called the hackneyed yet elusive "golden haze" of childhood).[43] He speaks for example of Rossetti's "golden crown," of the "golden glow of candles" (26). It is almost as though his remembered world is illuminated, like the theater he attends as a small boy, left abandoned by another well-meaning adult, amid its dignitaries and fanfare. Appropriately, Ford insists that his grandfather was "the first painter in England, if not the world, to attempt to render light exactly as it appeared to him" (2), as if Brown the painter, like Conrad the writer, turned on the lights. Just as Madox Brown lives in the gloomy Newcomes' house and makes it unpredictably cheerful, Ford insists on a world that was continually gloomy, with dark rooms and dark days and dark moods, while presenting scenes of a very different sort.

He describes Dante Gabriel Rossetti, for example, lying on a couch—"the king" in state. "Thus," he says, with a favorite introductory word:

> I remember, in a sort of golden vision, Rossetti lying upon a sofa in the back studio with lighted candles at his feet and lighted candles at his head, while two extremely beautiful ladies dropped grapes into his mouth. But Rossetti did this, not because he desired to present the beholder with a beautiful vision, but because he liked lying on sofas, he liked grapes, and he particularly liked beautiful ladies.
>
> (5)

What Rossetti escapes by sheer power of personality, Ford escapes by the "vividness" of his impressions. However unhappy his childhood may have been in fact, and however gloomy Bloomsbury may have seemed, Ford's memories work like rekindling and re-creating ideas, transforming as they record, improving as they fade. Their light is not the sunlight of Provence, which Ford later came to know, nor even the open and fresh light of the English countryside, which both delighted and discomforted him. It is, at once, the artificial light of the theater, which intensifies and falsifies, which points repeatedly to a world of escape and of illusion, and the "ancient light" suggested by Ford's title. "Ancient lights" are again, not just the "giants" of Ford's past, but also the prescriptive rights of an owner, of someone who has enjoyed the privileges of light and air for a minimum of twenty years. Ford uses the legal phrase to imply his own, inherited vantage, but also to suggest the continuing power of the world he describes, which has, in a sense, its own natural light filtered through magic casements.[44] This bears again on Ford's concern for Christina Rossetti, who, with her profound love of the country, never makes any move to leave London. The implication is that her writing, like his own, creates an alternative world within the gloom of Bloomsbury, illuminating those darkened halls of memory, and remembering—if the paradox works—as to make a dark world golden.

One final point about *Ancient Lights* will connect Ford's book with those of Moore and Yeats. There is a sense in which the artifice of Ford's retrospects implies the underlying values of pastoral while pulling together some of the other observations I have made. If we think again about Ford's better-known novels, *The Good Soldier* and the Tietjens tetralogy, we might say that they involve men of fixed principles (Tietjens, Ashburnam) who live in worlds of shifting intrigues and gossip. Victims, even anachronisms, in the society around them, they are finally defeated, learning about new selves while losing the possibility of an ethical self. They are, like Ford himself in *Ancient Lights*, men who look back for an ethical alternative and who look around them with a certain bewilderment.

Like his own characters, Ford appears to think of himself as a victim of malice, although his response in *Ancient Lights* is relatively mild. And he upholds even if questioning the values of an earlier generation. Fascinated here and in his novels by the destructive effect of lies and gossip, he sees such fictions as constituting the environment of fixed or permanent truths, which they subvert and belittle. Someone like Christina Rossetti has been reduced by the calumnies of Ruskin and by the folly of later critics. Implicitly, Ford Madox Ford has been similarly treated. Christina may have been a "modern" writer, like himself, but she also embodied a kind of nineteenth-century ideal (of genius, duty, sincerity) now lost in a shifting and diminished world. Like Ashburnam, she was doomed.

The irony of all this is that Ford himself was a notorious gossip and that even *Ancient Lights* builds on the zest and the energy of something very close to gossip—not to say, given the defensiveness about impressions, close to lies. Perhaps accepting malice and false accounts as a necessary part of the "modern" world, Ford also accepts his kinship with the characters he would create. In the complex interchange of unhappy childhood and valuable childhood ideals, of a socially advanced world awash with rumor and inauthentic selves, Ford seeks through anecdote both his own version of pastoral and an understanding of who and what he is.

His recollection of the banal and the personal recalls that of Moore (another gossip who suffered from the gossip of others) and of Yeats, who seems to struggle with similar issues. What is the relationship, these men apparently ask, between the trivia of life and the essence, both of which are the matter of art? Ford disparaged Yeats for his emotional reticence and ridiculed "the dreary shibboleth that literature must be written by those who have read the *Cuchulain Saga* or something dull and pompous" (254).[45] If Ford found Yeats to be provincial or parochial, because he himself sought a large audience, he probably misread what Yeats was about. The theatrical visions of "felicitous space," of a bygone Bloomsbury are not altogether different in intent from Yeats's depictions of a resurrected Sligo. Like Yeats, he seeks from his remembering, not a mere recapitulation of a past life or recording of development; not the intrinsic truth of memory itself, but the creation, through memory, of a shared sense of truth between writer and audience.

7 Fragments of a Great Confession: W. B. Yeats's *Reveries over Childhood and Youth*

> [A]ll drawing necessitates choice; but what hampers me most is having to represent states that are really one confused blend of simultaneous happenings, as though they were successive.
>
> André Gide, If It Die

It was typical of Yeats that he wanted his various autobiographical writings to be his "autobiography," the title pulling together what are, in fact, separate and distinct works rather than any realized whole. My emphasis here is on the first of his autobiographies, published privately in 1915, its preface dated Christmas Day in the year the Great War began.[1] I concentrate on *Reveries* because it is a self-sufficient work, quite different from the other "autobiographies," and because it draws together so many of the topics I have raised in the previous chapters.

Reveries is at once a peculiar and an apt title for Yeats's little book. At first glance, the title would seem to have come from Rousseau, whose own *Reveries of a Solitary* speaks of calling in a context of isolation and disenchantment; but the differences are profound.[2] Despite his apparent confidence in his readers, Yeats preserves a kind of reticence, avoiding the self-indulgence, "all that defacement, degradation and almost madness" that Carlyle describes in the revelations of Rousseau.[3] While disarmingly frank at times or surprisingly intimate, *Reveries* is not at all a full apology, and certainly no "surrender to history";[4] it is "private" in only a provisional sense: private until shared by responsive readers, who themselves hear echoes of their own remembered lives—and echoes beyond those lives of life itself.

"Echoes" is the word Gide found to describe the effect of Gosse's *Father and Son,* and it applies in a related way to *Reveries*. While Yeats is concerned with the sounds of words—with the difference, for example, between poetry and rhetoric—his reveries are largely visual. His first title for the book was, appropriately, *Memory Harbour: A Revery of Childhood and Youth,* and *Memory Harbour,* the painting by his

177

brother of Rosses Point, suggests the ways in which a poet's eye works analogously with that of the painter. Proper seeing is, I believe, Yeats's major task in *Reveries,* and it carries with it the attendant task of eliciting from his reader a comparable vision. In an essay from the turn of the century, Yeats quotes from Shelley: "Those who are subject to the state called reverie, feel as if their nature were resolved into the surrounding universe or as if the surrounding universe were resolved into their being." Yeats takes Shelley as the model not only of such a "dreamer" but also of the process he has in mind. The crux here is memory, for whether Shelley did or did not draw from Plato, he assumes the synecdochic relation between "our little memories" and "some great Memory that renews the world and men's thoughts age after age."[5] *Reveries* would seem to be Yeats's exploration as to how "little memories" conjoin with the underlying memory shared by all, or at least by all those given "to the state called reverie."

Memory is of immense importance to Yeats, but memory is more complex than it is for Gosse, say, or Butler, for whom "fictions" or imaginative freedoms were a threat to achievable truth. For Yeats, the images of memory are the materials for what memory alone cannot finally provide. "Real images," as Bachelard says in *The Poetics of Space,* "are *engravings,* for it is the imagination that engraves them on our minds."[6] The state of mind necessary to the poet, says Bachelard, is *revery,* which mixes memory with imagination and works through the engraving of images, for the poet himself and for the sympathetic reader. I suggest that for Yeats even more than for Ford or Moore, the imaginative vision, its moments privileged and surprising, is indivisible from a life immersed in time. Images of a private and collective memory become themselves "the artifice of eternity." Brooding on that paradox, Yeats is inclined to give up on the kind of spiritual authority sought by White or Tyrrell, say, and to look elsewhere—perhaps to the surrounding universe, perhaps more deeply within. The authority he seeks depends on memory, but not on its historical truth so much as on the created truth memory makes possible between writer and reader or the community implied by reader. Having said this, I want to approach *Reveries* by thinking of it as an experiment that is itself a reworking of older autobiographical traditions, by looking back, that is, to another poet who anticipated Yeats's concerns.

All, therefore, that has been confessed by me, consists of fragments of a great confession; and this little book is an attempt which I have ventured on to render it complete.

Goethe, Dichtung und Wahrheit

When the psychoanalyst Theodor Reik set out to write his autobiography, he returned to Goethe, thinking of Goethe as the paradigm of confessional writers. To show his identification, Reik called his book *Fragments of a Great Confession,* a title that recalls Goethe's power over him while it promises a selective presentation of Reik's own remembered past.[7] In borrowing from and struggling against Goethe, Reik illustrates some of the complex relations between authors of different ages, especially when, like Goethe, earlier authors exact that "agony of influence," that toll of authority, which Harold Bloom sees as crucial to the understanding of authorship.[8] Because Reik has spent a career analyzing himself and others, he comes back to Goethe with a large awareness of the complexities of the bonds between himself and the master. Goethe is to his writing self what Freud had been to his psychoanalytic self: a presiding force, a burden as well as an inspiration.

There is not, I believe, any comparable figure for William Butler Yeats. Blake matters, and so does Shelley, who was as important to Yeats as he was to George Moore. Yeats knows the power (to Yeats the stunted power) of Wordsworth's confessional work. And he has read the social prophets of a former generation, including Ruskin, along with the new voices of his own. None of them—including even Pater— serves the purpose in his works that Goethe serves in Reik's reflexive study of himself and the author of *Dichtung und Wahrheit.*

Nor does Yeats himself especially identify Goethe as a model. Although he often cites Goethe, particularly Goethe's remarks on the Irish, he often dissociates himself from Goethe as from a destructive legacy. After speaking in "The Autumn of the Body" (1898) about his shift from external to internal concerns, he lumps Goethe with Wordsworth and Browning as "modern poets" whose work "gave up the right to consider all things in the world as a dictionary of types and symbols and began to call itself a critic of life."[9] Yeats also distrusts Goethe's temperament, as he suggests in *The Trembling of the Veil,* for in *Wilhelm Meister* Goethe seeks Unity of Being "intellectually, critically, and through a multitude of deliberately chosen experiences . . . as if for a collector's cabinet." Goethe's temperamental mixture of "objectivity and subjectivity" is "at the eighteenth Lunar Phase" and therefore at odds with his own creative personality.[10] If Yeats had read *Dichtung und Wahrheit,* a very different kind of book, he seems to have avoided any reference to it, unless his assessment of Goethe's personality comes also from a reading of the autobiography. In any case, I am not about to offer Goethe as either a model for Yeats or as an influence with which he perennially contended.[11] There are, however, revealing parallels between Goethe's autobiography and Yeats's, which put in perspective Yeats's first autobiographical study.

About a century before Yeats ventured on his *Reveries,* Goethe began *Dichtung und Wahrheit* (it appeared between 1811 and 1833, piecemeal like Yeats's autobiographies). Citing a request from a probably fictitious friend, Goethe says that he tried to put his works in chronological order and to comment on their "inner relationships" as well as the state of his mind when he wrote them. All this proved beyond his powers. He could, to some extent, meet the second request, which subsumed the editorial chore, by writing his own life. Yet here again complexities arose. Goethe recognized that in the process of writing he

> was driven from my circumscribed private life into the world outside. A hundred significant persons who had had a greater or lesser influence upon me came to mind; the portentous motions of the world's political course, which had had such an immense impact on me as well as on the great mass of my contemporaries, demanded major attention. For the principal task of [self] biography, I believe, is to present a man in the conditions of his time, and to show to what extent those conditions, taken as a whole, thwart him or favor him, . . . and how, if he is an artist, a poet, or a writer, he then takes that view and projects it back into the world. It is, however, an almost impossible task, for what is demanded is that the individual know both himself and his century.[12]

Goethe offers here a kind of temporal equivalent for Shelley's idea of the self and the external world (the substance of "Mont Blanc"), with historical conditions, the century, at once influencing the creative artist and responding to the artist's work. Yeats seems to have seen his own role in a similar way. More so in the later autobiographies but to a great extent in *Reveries* as well, he concerns himself with his era, especially with the personalities characteristic of the era: he will speak of great numbers of people, from artists to philosophers, statesmen to novelists. The limited cast of *Reveries* includes above all his grandfather and father, along with people like Edward Dowden whom his father knew. But even in *Reveries,* other people tug at Yeats's private life, "demanding" attention. No less than Ford Madox Ford, Yeats appreciates the special qualities of his childhood and of the people he encountered, and the definition of his own life involves a retrospective confrontation similar to Goethe's.

Yeats would probably have agreed with Goethe that "ten years earlier or later" could make a different person with a different perspective, a different sense of both personal and national history.[13] For history is a direct challenge to both these writers. Wilhelm Dilthey, Yeats's early contemporary and a sympathetic reader of Goethe, wrote of *Dichtung und Wahrheit:* "A man looks at his own existence in the context of the literary movement of his age." Almost paraphrasing Goethe, he speaks directly about Yeats's concerns: "To the person looking back, every moment in his existence is doubly significant, both as an enjoyed fullness of life and as an effective force in the context of life. . . . The significance of life lies in its shaping and its development."[14] Both Goethe and Yeats appreciate the public extensions of their lives, acknowledging themselves as major innovative poets and playwrights, and both look at their lives with a sense of their place in history. Hence both are writing a special form of *memoir*, in which their own development intersects with and bears upon significant literary and political events of the age. If, however, we bear in mind Yeats's and Goethe's known reticence, their notorious tinkering with facts, we can see that both have in mind a partial but significant revelation: a symbolic presentation of what they want known. "I have an historian's rights" (74), says Yeats; but "I am no stickler for the fact."[15]

Goethe subtitled his work "Poetry and Truth," although he changed the order of the words, for euphonic reasons, from "Truth and Poetry." The full title, *Aus Meinem Leben: Dichtung und Wahrheit*, puts the opposition of truth and poetry into a full context. Opposition may not really be accurate, because Goethe does not mean to imply the falsity of his account, or that he has written about imagined events, but rather like Yeats that facts are not paramount, and that any "biography" requires selection, retelling, and imaginative re-creation. (This is really Pater's or Ford's or George Moore's sense of "impression.") The process of remembering is selective; it is to make "poetry," in the fuller sense of the German word. Following, as it does, "out of my life," the phrase "poetry and truth" announces the selective and creative nature of Goethe's looking back.

> And thus began . . . the tendency to turn into an image, into a poem, everything that delighted or troubled me, or otherwise occupied me, and to come to some certain understanding with myself upon it, that I might both rectify my conceptions of external things, and set my mind at rest about them. The faculty of doing this was necessary to no one more than to me, for my natural disposition whirled me constantly from one extreme to the other.[16]

Like Goethe, Yeats felt himself whirled from one extreme to the other, and indeed his whole system of masks and phases in *A Vision* reflects the need to cope with contrary visions of his life and personality. Goethe's figure of whirling describes exactly Gérard Genette's understanding of the autobiographical situation, the revolving door of emotion and genre touched on earlier.[17] What is "internal" or "external" in such a work is often hard to decide: AE dismissed *Reveries* as a record of "pure externalities," saying that "the boy in this book might have become a grocer as well as a poet."[18] Yet the kind of self-explanatory, linear process that, for example, Darwin imposes on his past is the antithesis of what either Goethe or Yeats thinks of a written life having to do. Expressive in a more complex way, it must show how a life evolves, exploring its medium as well as its subject.

> I tried from that [time] on to write out my emotions exactly as they came to me in life, not changing them to make them more beautiful. "If I can be sincere and make my language natural, and without becoming discursive like a novelist, and so indiscreet and prosaic," I said to myself, "I shall, if good luck or bad luck make my life interesting, be a great poet."
>
> (68–69)

In what sounds almost like a direct commentary on someone like George Moore, Yeats may be a little disingenuous, the more so since he read—in the year he wrote *Reveries*—Joyce's "discreet" and undiscursive *Portrait,* a novel that rivals in compression and selectivity his own retrospective work. Still, as "Among School Children" would suggest, there is no doubt that Yeats saw what he called "personal utterance" as unavoidable and that he argued, like Goethe, for a relationship between the expressive poet and the public who read him, as if his autobiography ratified his public self. He had written in "Friends of My Youth" (1910): "A poet is by the very nature of things a man who lives with entire sincerity, or rather the better his poetry the more sincere his life; his life is an experiment in living and those who come after have a right to know it."[19]

To what extent readers have a right to know, or how far a poet's "sincerity" translates into confession, or what kind of literary bargain may actually be struck—these are questions, the answers to which we can only surmise. But that both men would write several autobiographical studies (as well as autobiographical novels: *Wilhelm Meister, John Sherman*), exploring and explaining, editing and refining, says much about their desire to address their public; it also says something about the intensely personal, reflexive nature of their art, of which each was aware.

Yeats's "reverie" approximates Goethe's "urge to reflect": It is a concrete, musing, unhurried conjunction of past and present, with a sense of recurrence and heightening significance. Past for Goethe emphasizes Germanic, for Yeats Irish traditions, each writer inquiring into native folklore and national history. Beyond this, each imagines an ideal land, or landscape—"Kennst du das Land . . . ?"—which is, finally, a landscape of the imagination, even in the song from *Wilhelm Meister*. I shall come back to Yeats's ideal landscape a little later. Among other parallels are the reverence both writers had for the aristocracy (to the chagrin of younger contemporaries), the extent to which each searched for materials about his life for the autobiographies, the importance each ascribed to family and ancestors, the importance they placed on architecture and buildings, the way they explored symbolic or symptomatic love affairs while turning everything into the primary subject: growth of the imagination, training for the life of a poet. There is also, of course, a shared interest in magic.

Dichtung und Wahrheit opens with discussions of the horoscopes and confident astrology at Johann's birth. Later in volume 1, Goethe says that he was cured of a mysterious illness by "universal medicine," by a cabbalist that is, and at a time when he was exploring the "secrets" of nature and experimenting with alchemy (1:372). Alchemy appeals to Yeats (as to his contemporary, Karl Jung) because of the potential elevation of base metals into gold, ordinary experience, in the alembic of a poet's mind, transformed by the imagination. In addition to the recognition of supernatural powers—which alert us to Goethe's more than symbolic use of them in *Faust*—Goethe expresses a faith in "daimons" and demonic powers, those bridges between the natural and an unknown world.

Yeats also experimented with hermetic and cabbalistic materials, but his commitment to magic and the supernatural went even beyond Goethe's, as we see in studies like Mary Catherine Flannery's *Yeats and Magic: The Early Works* and George Mills Harper's collection *Yeats and the Occult*.[20] James Olney has shown how Yeats's reading in the perennial philosophy led to theories of "daimons" and intermediary symbols, which he drew from Greek philosophers as well as from hermetic societies. Yeats's essay on "Magic" (1901) testifies to his commitment. "I believe in the practice and philosophy of what we have agreed to call magic, in what I must call the evocation of spirits."[21] Throughout *Reveries* Yeats often turns to magical or supernatural matters: "At Ballisodare an event happened that brought me back to the superstitions of my childhood" (50). "Brought back" suggests that quality of recurrence and remembering which goes even beyond childhood and beyond one individual's life. For Yeats the "great confession" would stretch beyond the individual to tap that "great Memory" or "the memory of Nature."[22] I shall return to this. Here it is enough to say that Yeats, like Goethe, emphasizes remembering as a creative agency, which clarifies his own development in relation to a prophetic and evocative past. "Hope and Memory," as Yeats put it, "have one daughter, and her name is Art."[23]

> My first memories are fragmentary and isolated and contemporaneous, as though one remembered some first moments of the Seven Days. It seems as if time had not yet been created, for all thoughts connected with emotion and place are without sequence.
>
> Yeats, Reveries over Childhood and Youth (1)

So begins the first of Yeats's autobiographical books, a reverie reaching back to and beyond the contours of personal time. Yeats's two sentences set the pattern for much of this brief work while hinting at the speculations about time characteristic of all his writing. The simple shift in the first sentence from "I" to "one" accompanies a like shift from "my memories" to hypothetical "moments" of original creation, which for Yeats remained mythical and symbolic as much as historical.[24] Time not yet created may mean only that sequence has vanished from the memory, for it is the adult's, not the child's, consciousness making the perception. Nor can it be the child's consciousness that is aware of "the Seven Days" and a world before the Fall.[25] "Seems" and "as if" speak of the gulf between the child and the remembering adult that memory can scarcely bridge. As with Nietzsche, failure to remember becomes a paradoxical value, transforming the fragments of memory into signs of greater insight.[26] When, at the conclusion of *Reveries,* Yeats speaks of his present sorrow, the effect of looking back, he knows that the sadness he feels is more than the awareness of unfulfilled promise, more than the recollection of childhood "pain" (5). The "breaking of the dream of childhood" (16) is the recognition of a mythical fall or of a rupture from an imagined whole.[27] In terms that William Earle employs, Yeats's narrative plunge into chaos is a necessary condition for the understanding of self, and the process is both within his present consciousness and in the life he describes.[28] No less than for Tyrrell, there seems to be an unawaited sorrow attendant on retrospection, a recognition of what Yeats and Tyrrell both come to acknowledge as tragedy.

Much as Yeats speaks of childhood pain and unhappiness, he tells a great deal about early joys. In fact, he seems to include in his musings both the unhappiness which Edmund Gosse and Ford Madox Ford unearth from their childhoods and the sense, in writers such as Henry Vaughan, of those "happy" "early days! when I / Shined in my angel infancy."[29] He speaks of growing "happier with every year of life as though gradually conquering something in myself" (5), but it is those same years which bring recognition of loss and inadequacy. He remembers with ambivalence, and he speaks of himself with ambivalence, too. Most of the time Yeats does not shift to a third-person account, as Goethe often does; he never refers to himself as "the boy," for example. But his introduction of "one" and his frequent moving from "I" to "one" point to an understanding of himself as object as well as subject of his autobiography, so that appeals to a faith in magic or the supernatural can jostle with humorous recollections of the child's misunderstanding or innocence. Despite its emotional reserve, *Reveries* has little of the self-distancing that Henry Adams erects between himself and the child he remembers, the almost alien "he" of an era gone by, and it has as a consequence little of the stylistic distancing between author and reader.[30] Yeats confronts his childhood with both irony and intimacy, disarming with an often colloquial or at least unimpassioned style, while writing a book that is deeply emotional. "One" remembers, yet "I have lived with my own youth and childhood, not always writing indeed but thinking of it almost every day, and I am sorrowful and disturbed" (71). The final paragraph follows by a page a quotation that recalls the beginning paragraph once again: Yeats's version of Milton's opening to *Paradise Lost*:

> Of man's first disobedience and the fruit
> Of that forbidden tree whose mortal taste
> Brought death into the world and all our woe . . .
> Sing heavenly muse.[31]

With its reference back to "the Seven Days," and to a mythical scheme at odds with some of the anecdotal tone of *Reveries,* the passage from Milton suggests how much Yeats has invested in his brief testament of childhood and youth and what weight he gives to his own remembering.

The immediate sense of *Reveries* is not only of myth-making and "eternal returns" (Miltonic or Nietzschean) but of something true to each individual childhood. Yeats has been cited, by psychologists, for the shrewdness of his insight that early memories are divorced from sequence, that they re-emerge, "fragmentary and isolated," into consciousness.[32] The dislocation of biographical or historical time, however, is one small part of Yeats's appeal to readers, which rests far more on the sharpness of remembered scenes, that "engraved" quality which retains shadows or unfilled spaces, which elicits the reader's own "oneiric situation."[33]

Perhaps to emphasize his sense of the fragmentary and atemporal quality of his recollections, Yeats divides his book into relatively brief, discrete sections, identified by Roman numerals. (In fact he repeats the pattern, which is also that of his journals, when moving beyond his youth in the later *Memoirs* and autobiographies.)[34] Apart from avoiding discursiveness or the illusion of novelistic completeness or transition, narrative and imagistic fragments allow the feeling of contemporaneity; each episode, few of which run for more than a page or two, can flick back and forth at the whim of the recollecting mind, without the framework of dates or of other temporal milestones. From childhood to youth, from Dublin to London, from father to grandfather, from Sligo back to Sligo. Let me anticipate a little by saying that Sligo is Yeats's promised land, while Ireland as a whole recurs throughout, and that Yeats's "daydream" compresses past time into the imagined or remembered landscape. His sections move in evidently different directions toward the same end, and the end is a form of unity in memory that history has denied.

My question here is not just how that memory of Ireland emerges, and what the phrase means, but how Yeats thinks about remembering and how his memories arise in the text. The range of his remembering is, first of all, large. On a simple level it includes the almost hackneyed signs of the recollected vulnerability of childhood: What approximate David Copperfield's memories of black, hairy dogs paired with black-haired and imposing fathers (stepfather, in David's case) occur with other, now standard, indexes of suffering in psychoanalytic studies of children. Otherwise, not much of Dickens's semi-autobiographical novel anticipates *Reveries,* although some of David's "remembering" does. The common shift to present tense in both authors conjures the perception of a relived past. Both offer the detailed remembering and appropriate perspective of houses and topography, the affectionate portraits of eccentric and recurrent individuals, and the indication, however muted in Dickens, of the relationship between the growing child and the reconstructing man of letters. David, who often speculates about memory—"caverns of memory," "depths of memory," his "written memory"[35]—might have included a sentence such as, "We lived in a villa where the red bricks were made pretentious and vulgar with streaks of slate colour, and there seemed to be enemies everywhere" (55). For both authors the evocation of childhood depends on an indelible, almost mythical sense of childhood loneliness and solitude, which is the shared and defining condition of their lives and work. Since Yeats affirmed the symbolic and therefore partly collective nature of his past, even "discursive" explorers of their own lives such as Dickens participated in the formulation of his memories. It is worth noting a few contrasts, however, since Yeats's *Reveries* share none of

Dickens's careful and intertwining narrative, no sustained story as such, no re-creation of days he could not remember. Yeats does recount many stories and anecdotes related to his life, but none—from other people—*about* his life. He introduces no quaint Aunt Betsie pushing her nose against windows. Yeats's story emerges from representative scenes or images, from bits of remembered conversation, from all the shards of bygone events deciphered from innumerable sources and from his own pointed and sensual powers of recollection.

Yeats's impressions might seem more immediately to recall those of Ford, say, who moved without transition from one anecdote to another, his narrative arbitrary, cumulative, unfixed by chronology. Yeats's sections share the implied continuity behind the fragmentary narrative, and they deal analogously with the evident trivia of boyhood and youth, out of which emerges some larger "impression" or "image." Perhaps in both cases, that apparent glee in surface detail characteristic of late-nineteenth-century aesthetes is the initial matter of composition. But it is obvious that Yeats's writing is more deliberate, his juxtapositions integrated, his informality contrived. Ford himself complained, according to Ezra Pound, that Yeats so used his emotions as to deplete emotion from his writing, artistry overwhelming spontaneity or personal energy.[36] Close to Yeats's own complaint about Samuel Butler, this criticism points to the peculiar piecemeal nature of *Reveries,* which partly conceals the author while showing forth the author-as-poet. "Fragments of a confession" as applied to Yeats would mean something different than Goethe's fragments, as if—in Thomas Burnet's seventeenth-century cosmology—fragments are evidence of a larger, vanished and probably unattainable whole rather than just signs of careful omission.

Much does, however, remain omitted. In the following section (xx), Yeats creates a typically isolating and emblematic effect. Occasionally in *Reveries* he mentions his age at the time of a remembered event, but in this account, which would seem to need some such guidance, he gives none. The passage occurs after a discussion of "exchanged wives and immoral horse dealings" and comes, without transition, before a commentary on the supernatural.

> I was climbing up a hill at Howth when I heard wheels behind me and a pony-carriage drew up beside me. A pretty girl was driving alone and without a hat. She told me her name and said we had friends in common and asked me to ride beside her. After that I saw a great deal of her and was soon in love. I did not tell her I was in love, however, because she was engaged. She had chosen me for her confidant and I

learned all about her quarrels with her lover. Several times he broke the engagement off, and she fell ill, and friends had to make peace. Sometimes she would write to him three times a day, but she could not do without a confidant. She was a wild creature, a fine mimic and given to bursts of religion. I had known her to weep at a sermon, call herself a sinful woman, and mimic it after. I wrote her some bad poems and had more than one sleepless night through anger with her betrothed.

(50)

With such laconic, incidental language, Yeats records his first infatuation, again after mentioning early awareness of sex and imagining the wife-exchanges of the English aristocracy. When was he at Howth? How old was he? Why does he introduce the girl without giving her name? When *had* he known her to "weep at a sermon"? What happened to his feelings of love? Indeed, what was there about her that made him love? How did the relationship end? There are of course no answers to these and other questions we might ask. The understated tone characterizes some of the other sections of *Reveries,* but by no means all. Here Yeats clearly establishes a distance from his adolescent love, blending the hackneyed ("pretty girl," "soon in love") with sympathetic, if ironic understanding, then dismissing the episode with the almost predictable bad poems and sleepless nights. The tone is surprising if we remember that "the great event of a boy's life is the awakening of sex" (40) and that this is his only discussion of a relationship with a girl or woman in the entire *Reveries.* On the other hand, the encounter and its aftermath, which amount to a self-contained story, reflect both Yeats's autobiographic method and the life he is trying to understand. By his own accounts, so many of his later relations with women involved a kind of passive role as confidant or patient lover, into whose life women entered dramatically and unexpectedly.[37] The brief anecdote in *Reveries* leaps back over intervening experiences, subsumes at least part of the relationship with Maude Gonne, and speaks at once cryptically and directly. What it leaves unsaid suggests something mysterious, for who is the young woman, "la belle dame," come to whisk him away, emerging with only hints of context ("She was a wild creature") and disappearing without closure? Yeats tells only enough to hint or entice.

A very different section (vii) plays in another way with the arbitrary nature of time and memory. Just as the scene with the girl at Howth follows comments on adultery, so this passage begins with exulting and ends in awkward sorrow, all within the one brief section. Here Yeats offers a kind of "union of contraries," two opposing visions working inexplicably together. Once more he is climbing:

Fragments of a Great Confession 189

> Two pictures come into my memory. I have climbed to the top of a tree by the edge of the playing field, and am looking at my school-fellows and am as proud of myself as a March cock when it crows to its first sunrise. I am saying to myself, "If when I grow up I am as clever among grown-up men as I am among these boys, I shall be a famous man." I remind myself how they think all the same things and cover the school walls at election times with the opinions their fathers find in newspapers. I remind myself that I am an artist's son and must take some work as the whole end of life and not think as others do of becoming well off and living pleasantly. The other picture is of a hotel sitting-room in the Strand, where a man is hunched up over the fire. He is a cousin who has speculated with another cousin's money and has fled from Ireland in danger of arrest. My father has brought us to spend the evening with him, to distract him from the remorse that he must be suffering.
>
> (26–27)

The passage emphasizes how much of Yeats's remembering is visual, but also how conversation, even with himself, emerges from the visualized scene. Typically, "pictures come into my memory" as if unbidden, although Yeats makes clear that his concentration on the past of his boyhood has allowed the flow of memory, which moves in unpredictable and evidently opposing directions. In this passage the re-creation unfolds in the present tense. Neither episode gets an introduction, neither a summary comment. In the first, there is a young boy in the tree top (a little like Theodore Roethke on his father's greenhouse), aware of his powers, aware of his father and his father's sense of life, who is *reminded*, even then, of what he wants to consider now. Since so much of the book points to the importance of creative work, the exhilaration of the climb and the sense of looking down obviously approximate some act of creation, but they also illustrate to the boy and to the remembering adult the relation of space to time: I have climbed up and remember; if I remain distant and exultant, I shall be famous. Yeats offers both the image and an interpretation, albeit the interpretation occurs within the vision of the memory itself, within the child's awareness. And why the shift to the remorseful cousin? Here we have an effect like those in Joyce's *Portrait,* a deflation of the poet by the introduction of failure, flight, and poverty, a recognition, without gloss, that we do not stay atop the trees or contrive our escape at will. What to such a hater of commerce as Yeats would be an especially crushing sort of failure reflects on the artistic ambitions of the poet himself. For if Yeats has "grown happier with every year of life" (5), he repeatedly confronts his sense of "misery" and unfulfilled powers. "I am melancholy," he says, after looking at his brother's painting, *Memory Harbour,* "because I have not made more and better verses. I have walked on Sinbad's yellow shore and never shall another's hit my fancy" (33).

We might pursue these questions and their relation to *Memory Harbour* by considering two qualities in *Reveries:* the kinship of vision and paintings, which he speaks of like his own recollections as "pictures"; and the ways that Yeats's remembering intersects with the age-old notions of "artificial memory," a method of recollection based on "masks" and "places."

As his essay, "Symbolism in Painting" (1898), makes clear, Yeats found in the primacy of visual arts not only an analogue for the "mind's eye" of the poet but also a reminder of a heritage he wants to rekindle. Out of a "variable and capricious world," the poet, like the painter, "sees" his tradition.[38] "Even today," he says in *Reveries,* "I constantly see people as a portrait painter" (55). Yeats's later poem, "The Municipal Gallery Revisited" (in *Last Poems*) speaks of the importance of portraits, "this hallowed place" recalling to the poet more than "the images of thirty years," or his own role in a real and imagined Ireland:

> Heart smitten with emotion I sink down,
> My heart recovering with covered eyes. . . . [39]

The process here, with its Hopkins-like pun, approximates that in *Reveries,* which also deals with a poet's painful acceptance of loss and gain, his heart recovering, but "smitten" by the retrospective process. Yeats's involvement with paintings (portraits or landscapes) recalls Wordsworth's response to his friend Beaumont's *Peele Castle,* with its combination of remembered seascape, depicted in paint by another man, but haunting as if a feature of the writer's own "consecrated" vision.[40] Like Yeats, Wordsworth is cast down by the sense of loss (largely but not exclusively personal in "Elegiac Stanzas") which the scene has prompted.

Whereas Wordsworth's scene is unpeopled, Yeats mentions a blue-coated pilot, who dominates the painting and who occasions specific memories. Yeats's figure stands, however, as another of those strong, singular men who appealed to the imagination of both poets, who helped to define their sense of history and of place. The presence of such solitaries appears to emphasize Yeats's revelation (which was also Edmund Gosse's) that "what I saw when alone is more vivid in my memory than what I did or saw in company" (41).

In the text of *Reveries,* Yeats makes only perfunctory remarks about his brother's painting and its meanings for him; in notes accompanying the plates of the first edition, he says much more about its importance. To begin with, he identifies *Memory Harbour* as the village of Rosses Point, albeit he says, "with the distances shortened and the houses run together as in an old-fashioned panoramic map." He then describes the rest of the painting, actually omitting commentary on the solitary sailor, and emphasizing the symbolic qualities of the remainder of the painting. "The coffin, cross-bones, skull, and a loaf at the point of the headland are to remind one of the sailor who was buried there by a ship's crew in a hurry not to miss the tide. As they were not sure if he was really dead they buried him with a loaf as the story runs."[41] Clearly, Yeats's interpretation of his brother's painting offers an emblem of his own method. The foreshortening, which runs things together, as if on an old, pictorial and panoramic map, suggests his manipulation of temporal events, which can be pieced together or distorted for symbolic and presentational ends. He, too, will "remind" his reader of the meanings of his text, which is analogously visual, composite, and intimately related to the old stories of the region or the country. (What is peculiar, however, about Yeats's description is that he does not mention color, and Jack Yeats's painting has the vivid color of a Cézanne or a Mönch.)

The emphasis, first on the solitary man, then, in the account of *Memory Harbour*, on the abandoned sailor, confirms that Yeats remembers even peopled scenes with the consciousness of separateness or singularity. This is particularly clear in the accounts of school days:

> On one side [of the school in Hammersmith], there was a piano factory of yellow brick, . . . on the fourth side, outside the wall of our playing field, a brick-field of cinders and piles of half-burned yellow bricks. All the names and faces of my school-fellows have faded from me except one name without a face and the face and name of one friend, mainly no doubt because it was all so long ago, but partly because I only seem to remember things dramatic in themselves or that are somehow associated with unforgettable places.
>
> (19)

If Yeats asserts the selective and "de-facing" quality of his remembering, he also associates it with sharp seeing, and those yellow bricks stand out like the houses the family lived in, or the visions of Lough Gill and Ben Bulben. Instead of contrasting his memory with that of his painter-brother, Yeats could have written of himself as he wrote of Jack Yeats: "His memory seems as accurate as the sight of the eye" (45). In a painting such as *Memory Harbour* or a poet's description of landscape, perception and recollection merge as vision, the one inextricable from the other.

The intimacy between vision and memory suggests also the tradition of the "artificial memory." With the possible exception of Ford Madox Ford, Yeats comes closer than the other writers I have mentioned in this study to the practice of artificial memory, that method of storing and recollecting which associates memory "with unforgettable places" for the purpose of retrieval and audience effect. There is a kind of mnemonic recovery in *Reveries* that is indistinguishable from named places, as though the author had merely to open his "inner" eye to a recollected impression, and as though, too, he had a choice as to what to recover from a profusion of available, fragmentary materials.

At first glance, the artificial memory might seem remote from Yeats's ideal of writing that is "as cold and passionate as the dawn," that disdains "oratory" or rhetoric, which the artificial memory originally served, and which usually emphasized a specific inner space. Yet there are surprising connections. The notion that memory can be expanded almost indefinitely—for whatever "rhetorical" purposes—may be different from Yeats's sense of memory as selective, shared, or symbolic, but it suggests parallels. In the first place (a phrase apparently deriving from the process of artificial memory), even the vocabulary of mnemonic theorists bears on Yeats, as *places* (*topoi*) and *masks* would indicate. *Topoi* are in the tradition of the artificial memory visual models for recollecting. Whether a house or a theater (a municipal gallery or a grandfather's home), the *topoi* of the systems reflected places in the "natural" memory that might be augmented or layered, so that a given mask or image could hold innumerable memories of things, people, or words. "Inner writing," as Frances Yates describes the artificial memory, was the process of remembering, and remembering became a deliberate unpeeling or unfolding of the various masks, all within those caverns or storehouses of mnemonic materials.[42] Surface masks were the bridge between what George Tyrrell called the "now-self" and the "then-self" and also between what Yeats preferred to think of as "the self" and "anti-self" of our lives.[43]

Yeats's developing notions of masks as aspects of moon phases and an elaborate theory of personality (or escape from personality) differs from that in the tradition of artificial memory; in fact, however, his "Anima Mundi" or *Great Memory* comes close to the old mnemonics. If nothing else, it establishes a personal and visual mnemonic order, which invites a closer relationship with a reader. Notwithstanding his dismissal of the insincere and the rhetorical, Yeats came to approximate a theory of remembering and of writing that had long served public ends.

Within *Reveries* itself, it is clear how much Yeats emphasizes the connections between the apparently arbitrary and the wholly meaningful. We might say that for Yeats symbolic memories, personal and collective, reside within certain masks or images, each of which has the potential for almost infinite recall, however much may seem forgotten, lost, or destroyed. "Symbolic memory," as Ernst Cassirer wrote, "is the process by which man not only repeats his past experience, but also reconstructs his experience."[44] Hence any small image expands to include other images, other meanings, connected by association in the remembering mind, itself a new source of meaning and power.

Daniel Harris has said that Yeats's places in *Reveries* are largely houses or rooms.[45] This is certainly true for Ford Madox Ford, whose rooms approximate the remembering mechanisms of the artificial memory; it is far less true of Yeats, whose recollections are equally of open spaces: lights rising across Ben Bulben, ships leaving Liverpool, solitary figures standing (in paintings or in graveyards). Sligo and the physical topography of Sligo are, in a manner of speaking, Yeats's mnemonic *topoi,* places and images that symbolize his own rich past along with the richer past of family and Ireland. Here, too, the artifical memory seems pertinent, for in its later, Renaissance phases, it became associated with hermetic lore, as Giordano Bruno and Robert Fludd testify, so that the remembering process itself as well as its constituent elements combine alchemically for new awareness. This *would* have appealed to Yeats, who perhaps creates a modern version of Fludd's memory theater.[46]

An experienced event is finite—at any rate, confined to one sphere of experience, [while] a remembered event is infinite, because it is only a key to everything that happened before it and after it.
                                        Walter Benjamin, Illuminations

In his brilliant analysis of Proust's remembering, Walter Benjamin addresses larger questions of modern literary memory in very different kinds of writers. His comments seem especially apt for Yeats. Both Proust and Yeats seem to think of remembered things (scenes, events, voices) as keys, although Yeats would prefer the word *symbol,* and places are the central key. Moore's ancestral home and its surrounding landscape, Ford's grandfather's house, and so many other powerful settings work, like Proust's Cambrai, to find meanings in recollection. In *Reveries,* Sligo is at once the locus of memory and a "paradise lost" for Yeats, providing keys to before and after.

Yeats is, in Benjamin's terms, detached from experience, preoccupied with memory. As he looks back on family, birthrights, landscape, and legend, his mind, as I have suggested, moves back and forth between England and Ireland, weighing Dublin and London, Irish and English. But Sligo seems to represent a state of mind beyond antinomies and a place beyond all places. When, by contrast, George Moore returns in *Memoirs of My Dead Life* to Mayo, he is overwhelmed by its beauty, broken by its grandeur. Only in this one section does Moore admit to a loss of self-possession, the death of his mother and lover working together with the alien, ineluctable topography. Moore's ambivalent response reflects his feelings about Ireland, which he hated more than he loved, and which he is forced to confront at the end of *Memoirs* as he does glancingly in the "echo-augury" that begins *Confessions*. Yeats's love of Sligo grows out of a perspective similar to Moore's, or at least out of comparable passion complicated by a distrust of easy provincialism. Sligo is no less Ireland for Yeats than Mayo is Ireland for Moore, whose family, after all, had an even older Anglo-Irish tradition. Yeats focuses his remembering there, forgets other "experiences," and uses Sligo as a measure and an ideal of his art.

Late in *Reveries* Yeats pulls together some of his hints about the "idea" of Ireland, thus far symbolized by Sligo and touched on in a variety of conversations with and about John O'Leary, John Taylor, Edward Dowden, his father, and other men. Excepting brief and sometimes cryptic accounts of his grandmother and mother (whose own nostalgia anticipates his) the women in his life are not yet dominant. This is what he says:

> I began to plot and scheme how one might seal with the right image the soft wax before it began to harden [wax tablets are a common metaphor in various mnemonic traditions]. I had noticed that Irish Catholics among whom had been born so many political martyrs had not the good taste, the household courtesy and decency of the Protestant Ireland I had known, yet Protestant Ireland seemed to think of nothing but getting on in the world. I thought we might bring the halves together if we had a national literature that made Ireland beautiful in the memory, and yet had been freed from provincialism by an exacting criticism, an European prose.
>
> (68)

Blending some of Yeats's favorite platonic myths and metaphors with what sounds like Matthew Arnold on culture, this passage illustrates both Yeats's large ambition and the underlying ideals of his autobiography.

What does he mean, however, by making "Ireland beautiful in the memory"? I want to approach this question by thinking again about

Bachelard's speculations in *The Poetics of Space*, where, by locating the study of poetic language in "the sites of our interior lives," Bachelard points to the importance of landscape in literature and appreciates "felicitous spaces" as the essence of literary and psychological processes. Bachelard focuses initially only on closed spaces such as rooms, houses, shells, cupboards; but if "the space we love" cannot "remain permanently enclosed," perhaps "intimate" landscapes can be as important as interiors, in the realm at least of "reverie and memory," that "oneiric" state which characterizes poetry.[47] Bachelard is thinking of poetry as emergent language, and perhaps *Reveries* needs to be seen, if not *as* poetry, then working *like* poetry in its evocation. It may be true, as David Lynch says, that Yeats wrote his best autobiography when he wrote poetry;[48] *Reveries* is itself a kind of poetry and is among his best autobiographical writings.

Topoanalysis seems an appropriate way of looking at section xvii of *Reveries*, which emphasizes the vision of landscape in relation to an "unforgettable past." The section is unusually long (about four pages) and deals with a variety of "topics," each of which in other contexts might have its own entry, each of which bears on a larger topography. At first glance, it seems inchoate and tangential. Yeats speaks of returning to Sligo for his holidays, after the retirement of his grandfather. Without dates, he suggests the passage of time, and with quotations from the old man anticipates his grandfather's dying. From his grandfather's own thoughts of death and tombs and after yet another anecdote about sailing prowess, Yeats moves on to his brother, who "had partly taken my place in my grandmother's affections" (44), and who had begun to draw. It is here that Yeats speaks of his brother's keen visual memory. From Jack Yeats, Yeats turns to his uncle, George Pollexfen, a gentle, patient man, full of melancholy. The paragraph ends with another reminder of landscape and death:

> In some Connaught burying-ground he had chanced upon the funeral of a child with but one mourner, a distinguished foreign-looking man. It was an Austrian count burying the last of an Irish family, long nobles of Austria, who were always carried to that half-ruined burying-ground.
> (45–46)

Although he gently mocks his uncle's eccentricities, his lack of passion and energy, Yeats finds in him important virtues. First, Yeats cites him for his horsemanship, which Yeats values highly, then for his association with his servant, Mary Battle, "who had been with him since he was a young man, [and] had the second sight" (46). Yeats illustrates Mary Battle's second sight and anticipates the uncle's and Yeats's own immersion in "ceremonial magic." "Much of my Celtic Twilight," he says, "is but [Mary Battle's] daily speech." Crazy Jane and later characters in the poems grow out of lessons learned from George Pollexfen and Mary Battle, as the words *ceremony, history, common people,* and *strange belief* seem to promise.

George Pollexfen is appropriately privileged to witness the strange funeral of an older aristocracy of Ireland, because he serves in a sense as the caretaker of what Yeats would resurrect. His attenuated but genuine ideals allow him historical as well as "second sight," for he appreciates "the common people" of Sligo, who return his esteem. "He gave to all men the respect due to their station or their worth with an added measure of ceremony," and they in turn gave him respect "as few Sligo men have had it" (46). Even beyond the magic, the mutually respectful relations with other people, and the understanding of traditions, George Pollexfen serves an important purpose. Within one paragraph, Yeats moves from his uncle's relations with Sligo's "common people" to recollections of Thoreau's "Walden" and his own, admittedly derivative, "Innisfree," his first imagined landscape. Clearly, his uncle provides an important link:

> When I said to him, echoing some book I had read, that one never knew a countryside till one knew it at night he was pleased (though nothing would have kept him from his bed a moment beyond the hour); for he loved natural things and had learnt two cries of the lapwing, one that drew them to where he stood and one that made them fly away.
>
> (46–47)

Described thus in terms of contraries or opposites, Pollexfen anticipates the poet's own later understanding. He can sympathize, for example, with the boy's attraction to the "little island called Innisfree" and his compulsion to spend the night in its vicinity. Whereas a servant of the house (not Mary Battle) laughs at the antics of a young man, believing "I had spent the night in a different fashion" (48), his uncle's natural modesty apparently lets him be sympathetic.

The night in Slish Wood prompts Yeats to another recollection of a night spent out of doors, this time on the sea.

> I called upon a cousin towards midnight and asked him to get his yacht out, for I wanted to find what sea birds began to stir before dawn. He was indignant and refused; but his elder sister had overheard me and came to the head of the stairs and forbade him to stir, and that so vexed him that he shouted to the kitchen for his sea boots.
>
> (48)

Once again, Yeats's remembering takes him from the sublime (the lapwing's cry) to the trivial (sea boots in the kitchen), and the crowding of such images characterizes the entire book. Yeats always seems to remember how such apparently dysfunctional images work together in the poet's reverie. As he writes elsewhere:

> Those masterful images because complete
> Grew in pure mind, but out of what began?
> A mound of refuse or the sweepings of a street,
> Old kettles, old bottles, and a broken can.
> . . . .
> I must lie down where all the ladders start
> In the foul rag-and-bone shop of the heart.[49]

Without the urgency of "The Circus Animals' Desertion" or even of other sections in *Reveries,* the description of the night in a boat suggests the same insight. Yeats says that in an effort to look respectable, he and his cousin pretend to have fished, then look for money to buy from returning fisherman. From "empty pockets," he shifts abruptly: "I had wanted the birds' cries for the poem that became fifteen years afterwards 'The Shadowy Waters,' and it had been full of observation had I been able to write it when I first planned it. I had found again the windy light that moved me when a child" (48). More than this, he has in a sense found the entire meaning of his craft: whence it comes, what it must do, how it must speak. Disdaining transition from the nocturnal adventure and the calls of the birds, he talks about a "histrionic" but genuine "passion for the dawn." Then he says:

> Years afterwards when I had finished *The Wanderings of Oisin*, . . . I deliberately reshaped my style, deliberately sought out an impression as of cold light and tumbling clouds. I cast off traditional metaphors and loosened my rhythm, and recognizing that all the criticism of life known to me was alien and English, became as emotional as possible but with an emotion which I described to myself as cold. It is a natural conviction for a painter's son to believe that there may be a landscape that is symbolical of some spiritual condition and awakens a hunger such as cats feel for valerian.
>
> (48)

This passage fuses two intimately connected ideas: that of style or language, and that of the symbolic landscape. Stylistically, Yeats seems to illustrate his own values, as the matter-of-fact and deliberate language moves from descriptive images of the cold light to the surprising metaphor of cats and valerian. This is, to use Bachelard's terms, "language in a state of emergence," defining both the poet's life and the literary work itself. Here an Irish poet seeks out a new style, a new and "unrhetorical" rhythm, albeit with another, unwitting nod to Matthew Arnold on poetry as "the criticism of life." (Arnold would have sympathized with a self-consciously urbane and Celtic poetic voice.) The opposition to English rhetoric and English poetic models is an underlying theme of *Reveries,* and it bears directly on the ways that Ireland is to be made beautiful in the memory. Even Yeats's friends knew that he was making a deliberate choice. AE wrote in his *Memoirs,* "He began about the time of *The Wind Among the Reeds* [1899] to do two things consciously, one to create a 'style' in literature, the second to create or rather re-create William Butler Yeats in a style which would harmonize with the literary style."[50] *Reveries* gives Yeats the opportunity to present a literary style that accords with his private life, or emerges in the record of that life, but it does something more.

Throughout the book, Yeats emphasizes the importance of language and its extension in style as a national as well as personal accomplishment. The tacit dismissal of Matthew Arnold in the passage above, and the explicit dismissal of other English models, leads him to that vexed question of an Irish style in English. This is of course related to his discussions in the later autobiographies about the writings of Synge, the meaning of national culture, and other such matters. It is also related to George Moore's almost parallel discussions in *Hail and Farewell.* In *Reveries,* Yeats tends to speak indirectly about the issue of culture, but he emphasizes language. Without making a distinction between spoken and written English, he usually expresses dissatisfaction with his public speaking or conversation, his interior world infinitely more valuable than the public world he still feels compelled to record. On the other hand, he insists on the importance of oral traditions and the language of nonliterary people. The secret for Yeats was to find a way of making the best of Irish speech a literary and radically non-English form of writing. What this means for *Reveries* is a process of discovery and an increasing association between Yeats's personal style and the memory of Ireland. In the account of his father and Edward Dowden, Yeats describes his growing skepticism about Dowden, and he has this to say about the *Life of Shelley* (invoking Arnold once again):

> When it was published, Matthew Arnold made sport of certain conventionalities and extravagances that were, my father and I had come to see [agreeing, indeed, for almost the first time], the violence or clumsiness of a conscientious man hiding from himself a lack of sympathy.
>
> (58)

Behind the lack of sympathy, however, is Dowden's insecure status in a literary no-man's-land: he is neither Irish nor English, but an alien writer who has lost his tongue. By contrast, Yeats cites his own family (although not in direct relation to Dowden), whose uncommercial and "powerful" status appeals to his historic sense. Earlier, with his usual appeal to "pictures" and his self-consciously present vision of past people and things, he has spoken of the Yeats's family portraits:

> Two eighteenth-century faces interest me the most, one that of a great-great-grandfather, for both have under their powdered curling wigs a half-feminine charm, and as I look at them I discover a something clumsy and heavy in myself. Yet it was a Yeats who spoke the only eulogy that turns my head: "We have ideas and no passions, but by marriage with a Pollexfen we have given a tongue to the sea cliffs."
>
> (13)

These final words, which John Butler Yeats says he found for his son,[51] anticipate the irony of the next page, which comments mundanely of the father's having forbidden teachers to try to teach the young boy how to sing. But as Yeats's innumerable birds will testify, there is no question that he means to make music, his own voice giving a tongue to those sea cliffs. At one point he quotes John Stuart Mill to the orator John Taylor: "Oratory is heard, poetry is overheard" (65). Discussions about poetry, its origins and significance, occupy Yeats and his father throughout *Reveries*. The father read a great deal of poetry together: "All our discussion was of style" (43). In a sense all Yeats's discussion throughout *Reveries* is of style, and style cannot be dissociated either from his audience or, relatedly, from his conception of Ireland. Nor can it be separated from his accounts of his father and Yeats's discussion throughout *Reveries* is of style, and style cannot be dissociated either from his audience or, relatedly, from his conception of Ireland. Nor can it be separated form his accounts of his father and their relationship. Whether or not Yeats's conception of "intensity" came from his father's theories, most of those remembered discussions bear on his developing sense of art and its context.[52]

When, some time after his son's suggestion that he do so, John Butler Yeats began an autobiography, he emphasized the importance of his own father: "Why I became an artist is a question which every artist must sometimes put to himself. It was my father who made me an artist, though his intention was that I should become a barrister."[53] The respect for his father and the implied struggle between father and son characterizes *Reveries* as much as *Some Chapters of Autobiography*. John Butler Yeats's always outspoken views on art and literature challenged the young man, often eliciting his strongest positions, especially on the issues of the supernatural and of personality in art. *Memoirs* (the autobiographical work which followed *Reveries* and remained unpublished) begins with near fights between father and son about Ruskin:

> I began to read Ruskin's *Unto This Last,* and this, when added to my interest in psychical research and mysticism, enraged my father, who was a disciple of John Stuart Mill's. One night a quarrel over Ruskin came to such a height that in putting me out of the room he broke the glass in a picture with the back of my head. Another night when we had been in argument over Ruskin or mysticism, I cannot now remember what theme, he followed me upstairs to the room I shared with my brother. He squared up at me, and wanted to box, and when I said I could not fight my own father, he replied, "I don't see why you should not."[54]

With this slightly ludicrous portrait of his father, Yeats establishes the importance of the difference between them, which—though often less great than he implies—serves as a measure of the son's independence and of the development of his own positions on writers and their work. Their struggles are about art, about poetry or painting, and William Butler Yeats like his father before him becomes an artist because, in a sense, his father "made" him.

For all the emphasis on his father, Yeats rarely associates him, as he does his grandfather and mother, with Sligo, and in a tacit way he dissociates himself from his father, just as he hints at a closer bond with his mother. In any case, he pulls together his own writing career with the developed sense of place or landscape concentrated in Sligo. From mother and uncle, grandfather and common people, he has learned not only what kind of language he needs, but also what symbolic landscape he has to use. The focus on Sligo—in his own past, his brother's paintings, his uncle's sympathy—reflects his hunger for an absolute beauty and incorporates audience as well as vision. And audience has been a concern throughout the book. The preface tells of Yeats having bored his friends with tales of childhood, then casts the reader in the role of a friend, with the reminder that this friend can set the book down at will. Here as throughout *Reveries* there is a different introduction to what is passionately felt, with *passion* itself a recurrent word. Yeats mixes his own compulsive telling about his compulsive remembering with a kind of hoped-for catharsis: "Now that I have written it out, I may even begin to forget it all" (preface). But the wandering about "till I have somebody to talk to" implies a tale like the ancient mariner's, which cannot be disburdened. Those powerful visions are addressed here to the reader-as-friend, the audience Yeats has created (assuming the preface to have been written last) in the course of telling.[55] Yeats's other audience is implied in the text and assumes a different role. Early in *Reveries* he writes:

> All the well-known families had their grotesque or tragic or romantic legends, and I often said to myself how terrible it would be to go away and die where nobody would know my story. Years afterwards, when I was ten or twelve years old and in London, I would remember Sligo with tears, and when I began to write, it was there I hoped to find my audience.
>
> (10)

The progression here from early intuition to what amounts to present conviction is typical, not only of *Reveries,* but of other writings of Yeats as well. In "The Fisherman," for example (in *The Wild Swans At Coole* [1919]), Yeats remembers by seeing "The freckled man who goes / To a grey place on a hill / In grey Connemara clothes," who casts his flies at dawn. "To write for my own race / And the reality" involves a remembered ideal, a man instead of hated men, someone, like Wordsworth's silent poets, who lives his poetry. Then, in the poem's final lines, Yeats posits his ideal audience: "A man who does not exist, / A man who is but a dream...." Imagining this man is remembering too, grey Connemara cloth and all, and it is for him that Yeats will write:

> "Before I am old
> I shall have written him one
> Poem maybe as cold
> And passionate as the dawn."[56]

The fisherman suggests again that recurrent figure in *Reveries,* Yeats's grandfather, who serves like comparable figures in Butler's *The Way of All Flesh* and Ford's *Ancient Lights* as a model of vigor and independence, and whose practical competence and unread wisdom, in Yeats's case, link the young boy with ships and brave deeds, providing an "image" that "is always before me." "I often wonder if the delight in passionate men in my plays and in my poetry is more than his memory" (4). This proud old man suggests in his way an Ireland of strength and romance; appropriately, his "image" is before us at various times in the text, and his death is recorded on the final page. Indeed, Yeats leaps ahead in his narrative to include his grandfather's death, which happened several years after the other incidents he records.[57]

Such powerful men are a part of Yeats's retrospective vision when he speaks of keeping Ireland "beautiful in the memory." But *memory* needs a further word. Again, in *Reveries,* Yeats turns often to questions about magic and the supernatural. He records stories he has heard and his own experiences with supernatural events. His arguments with his father sometimes revert to this divisive issue, since his father's allegiance to the rationalism of Mill precludes a sympathetic understanding of his son's growing interest in things irrational or logically inexplicable. Yeats makes clear his dedication to supernatural forces, but in *Reveries* he only implies the link between such forces and memory. Elsewhere he had already made connections, just as he would in later works like "Anima Mundi" and *A Vision*. The two early essays on "Shelley" and "Magic" bear directly on the topic. In "Magic" (1901), Yeats asserts his belief in supernatural powers and claims that such a belief involves three interrelated "doctrines":

1. That the borders of our mind [and even here he thinks of landscape images] are ever shifting, and that many minds can flow into one another, as it were, and create or reveal a single mind, a single energy.
2. That the borders of our memories are as shifting, and that our memories are part of one great memory, the memory of Nature herself.
3. That this great mind and great memory can be evoked by symbols.[58]

My sense is that *Reveries* tries to evoke "one great memory" out of tradition, history, and Irish folklore, all of which fuse in the landscape of Sligo, bringing together Yeats's own personal memories with the memories of others *and* with his own imaginative or symbolic perception of "shifting" borders. Yeats expresses the same sense of memory in "The Philosophy of Shelley's Poetry," where he relates it to Platonic memory:

> It may be that [Shelley's] subconscious life seized upon some passing scene, and moulded it into an ancient symbol without help from anything but that great Memory; but so good a Platonist as Shelley could hardly have thought of any cave as a symbol, without thinking of Plato's cave.[59]

Because of the great Memory, he seems to find in Shelley an even more kindred spirit than in Blake, and he makes an astute observation about Shelley that undercuts dozens of complaints about unbridled egotism: he imagines Shelley growing

> perhaps dizzy with the sudden conviction that our little memories are but part of some great Memory that renews the world and men's thoughts

age after age, and that our thoughts are not, as we suppose, the deep, but a little foam upon the deep.[60]

In this essay, too, Yeats speaks of the great Memory as "the memory of Nature" (74), a transcendent and almost Platonic power, which informs and underlies "the memory of Ireland," as the phrase appears in *Reveries*. That sense of "reverie," which Shelley sees as bringing the "surrounding universe . . . into [one's] being"[61] is precisely Yeats's ideal in his own *Reveries*. The apparent conflict between an egotistical "I" of autobiography and "the deep" of the sea or "the memory of Nature" is for Yeats a useful dialectic, akin to those between Irish and English culture, father and son, Yeatses and Pollexfens, abstract and concrete, "truth and poetry." Like Shelley—and Goethe—Yeats knows his power as a poet, his ascendant mastery of language, his isolation as a man. He also knows about a profound connection between himself and other people, living and dead.

Shelley's *being* suggests two final points, both brief. Earlier, I quoted Goethe about the importance of living at a particular historical time rather than, say, ten years before or after. Yeats's dialogue with himself about language, art, culture, and Ireland all belong to his era, and while Yeats scrupulously avoids dating his life's activities, he makes clear his historical grounding. It is worth emphasizing, however, how singular this grounding is. Yeats says nothing about technology: motion pictures, Marconi radios, airplanes, express trains, and all the paraphernalia of a rapidly changing world—a world, by the time he finished his book, at war—seem banished from his world, or at least from his consciousness. I think the reasons for this are clear from what I have said before, but they are perhaps most concisely expressed in a sentence from Dilthey's *Meaning in History*: "The objects of the physical world are as changeable as self-conscious life; but only in the latter does the present embrace ideas of the past in memory and the future in imagination."[62] Yeats's self-conscious mind seeks in his past the relatively timeless ideas he needs for his poetry.

My second point also takes us back to Goethe. I mentioned earlier Theodor Reik's fascination with Goethe's phrase, "fragments of a great confession." Confession is, once again, a rather inappropriate term for Yeats's autobiographies because his selective and symbolic presentation is so self-conscious and self-creating, as George Russell noticed and Yeats himself was well aware.

The friends that have it I do wrong
whenever I remake a song,

Should know what issue is at stake:
It is myself that I remake.[63]

What we find in *Reveries* is little different in aim from what we find in Yeats's autobiographical poetry, which is of course what Goethe was saying about the entirety of his confessional, that is, intensely personal, work. *Reveries* is about *being,* about the creation of "ontological fictions" in propositions about the past.[64] Why, then, does Yeats end his book "sorrowful and disturbed" (71), as though profoundly troubled or broken by the process? Like Gosse, Ford, and Tyrrell, he limits his self-account to his boyhood and youth and seems unwilling to move on, though of course he will move on in later years and add to his accounts. Was it the horrors of an unmentioned war that troubled him, informing his book as it did, say, Lawrence's *Women in Love?* Was it the sense, as in Tyrrell, of a profound failure, the recognition that he had indeed "walked on Sinbad's yellow shore" for a final time? Or did Yeats find the conflict between remembered time and a desired stasis — again like Tyrrell — reconcilable in theory alone? "The soul cannot have much knowledge," he was soon to write, "till it has shaken off the habit of time and of place."[65] Yet memory, collective or personal, must dwell on time and place, while Yeats's own sense of "reveries" implies the culling of disjunctive images from a vital and informing past.

Images themselves may be indistinguishable from acts of remembering and acts of remembering from fragmentary and partial "knowledge": after all, "we select our images from past times."[66] Moreover, as Yeats came to understand, men and women cannot know truth, they can only hope to embody it, which is to say live it, and life is lived on the ladder of time. Hence, to "find myself and not an image" involves an inherent contradiction, for myself is unknowable except through image, its vision a function of retrospective acts.[67] "Unity of being" is probably an unattainable ideal, promised by a compulsive memory for a purifying but recalcitrant imagination. Perhaps there can be no setting the past in order, no adequate arrangement of image and fragment — only an exploratory search and a disquieting resolution.

8 Recollecting Selves: The Province of Memory

There is a dual will to happiness: a hymnic and an elegiac form. The one is the unheard of, the unprecedented, the height of bliss; the other, the eternal repetition, the eternal restoration of the original, the first happiness. It is this elegiac idea of happiness — it could also be called Eleatic — which for Proust transforms existence into a province of memory.
                                                    Walter Benjamin, Illuminations

For any autobiographer, existence becomes necessarily a province of memory, an act of deliberate repetition and, to the extent possible, of restoration. Proust, whether or not technically an autobiographer, may be the most autobiographical of novelists. Benjamin understands Proust to be both singular and normative, a writer who represents the major literary tendencies of his day, but not without painful dismantling both of past life and past books. Such a writer "dissolves" genre in the act of exploring himself, his retrospective books an extreme case of forgetting and remembering, of that "Penelope work of recollection" and "the Penelope work of forgetting" so characteristic of the modern literary synthesis.[1]

Benjamin's terms, as I have suggested earlier, bear on the mnemonic theories of Samuel Butler and on the literary practice of Yeats. Indeed Benjamin speaks to the issues of self and genre underlying this book. He makes clear, through his analysis of Proust, how crucial autobiographical processes are to modern literature, but also how "radical" experiment involves roots as well as change. Ralph Harper's comparison of Proust and Saint Augustine illustrates Benjamin's argument as to the underlying power of autobiographical works such as Proust's: that they speak to "eternal" questions of faith and hope, seeking happiness through that elegiac rather than hymnic mode, but seeking nonetheless.[2]

What is true of Proust in Benjamin's understanding is true not only of such conspicuously religious writers as W. H. White and George Tyrrell, but equally of Ford Madox Ford, William Butler Yeats, Edmund

Gosse, and even George Moore. "It is," says Moore in *Hail and Farewell,* "hard to analyse a spiritual transformation; one knows so little about oneself; life is mysterious."[3] Samuel Butler's religious phraseology is as important as his scientific, and Butler wants a spiritual alternative to Darwin's "nightmare" vision, wants precisely the sense of eternal return made possible by unconscious processes and hereditary habits. To find one's present and future one relives and probably remakes an elusive past.

The elegiac is as much a modern mode as the ironic, and for comparable reasons. To look back on one's past involves the recognition of lost dreams and hopes, false starts and misdirections. Whether this leads to self-mockery or to rededication depends of course on the way that one's life is interpreted, recognized in those articulations of tense and selections of memory inevitable to any autobiographer. But what Proust and the writers I have discussed have in common is a greater incentive to "eleatic" hopes, generated by both a tragic and ironic awareness of their lives. When private and public seem irreconcilable, the private life may be at the same time inconsequential and absolute. And this, I think, is the paradox we encounter in self-deprecating and self-asserting writers such as Ford, Tyrrell, and White.

Benjamin argues that in Proust's retrospective novels remembering becomes, through unexpected inversion, more imperative than the person doing the remembering; the unity of the text somehow emerging from "the *actus purus* of recollection itself, not the author or plot."[4] Nietzsche, while apprehensive about "the loss of self," had something related in mind when he spoke of enlightened forgetting in any historical ordering, the author's freedom essentially re-creating the author, refining him into something new. Hence, though Wilhelm Dilthey accused Nietzsche of introspective malaise, Nietzsche shares with Dilthey and with Kierkegaard the desire to rewrite the past for future purposes. I have argued an analogous revisionary process in William Hale White's edited "autobiography," in Yeats's selective rememberings, in Ford's anecdotal but symbolic episodes, and in George Moore's painful anagnorisis in the final chapter of *Memoirs of My Dead Life.* A narcissistic involvement with past selves often leads to unawaited and disquieting new awareness.

If Proust's religious quest moves backward instead of forward, finding the only paradise in the paradise we have lost, and if the past he explores is a fabrication of "forgetting" as much as of "recollecting," the remembering author seems blessed with total freedom on the one hand and limited possibilities on the other. His own life, in Nicola Chiaromonte's terms, is a contradiction of the public world and his recollection a kind of escape from self into a web of his own making.[5] Benjamin describes poignantly the kind of dilemma I have commented on in previous chapters, his speculations touching directly the strands of confrontation and evasion, the double perspectives of autobiographical discourse.

In spite of historical threats to individual freedom or importance, the status of self in autobiography would seem to be unassailable. Autobiography is implicitly an affirmation of self, and it is etymologically a history, *bios,* of the self, an unraveling in time of whatever constitutes an individual identity.[6] Even David Hume, who discarded theories of soul or easy notions of personal unity, wrote his own autobiography as if all were well, as if memory provided not just our only guarantee of identity but a reasonably certain one.[7] In fact, Hume's philosophical doubts are more material to the understanding of autobiography than his own model. Hume's fear, in the *Treatise,* that he has created a philosophical monster suggests the true nature of the remembering mind, which questions its own integrity while pursuing its constituent parts. Autobiography, then, may be both an assertion of self and a likely route to the doubting of self.

Because of the radical exploration of self in modern autobiography and in autobiographical novels such as Proust's, the ideas of self or identity or "author" have succumbed to another kind of doubting, as Michel Foucault makes clear in *Language, Counter-Memory* or Roland Barthes in "The Death of the Author." In so much contemporary theory the self of the writer gets subordinated to the power of the text, as if texts or reader alone mattered, a "someone," perhaps, but a someone for Barthes who is distinctly not "the author" as historically assumed.[8] Whether the effect is the demise of autobiography in traditional or recognizable forms, it may mean that autobiography is more vulnerable as a preserve of self than, say, another kind of fiction like the novel, wherein there can only be fictive projections of character. This is Kierkegaard's assumption in the distinction between aesthetic and ethical or religious states of mind, and Kierkegaard assumes the necessity of fictional projections in that absurd endeavor of writing about essential matters. Michael Sprinker has followed some of the implications of Kierkegaard's assumptions in an essay he calls "The End of Autobiography." Citing also Foucault, along with Nietzsche and Freud, Sprinker posits the end of autobiography because it cannot sustain a credible notion of self.[9] And certainly, if Nietzsche's theory of forgetting or Kierkegaard's understanding of repetition were carried to an extreme, an autobiographical self would be as dubious as Hume's actual self, so that the writer would be neither privileged nor real.

The problem with such arguments is their absoluteness. Although they speak to the fictional nature of any narrative, and hence help in the reading of writers who, like Rousseau, tamper unflinchingly with events, they also remind us of what is obvious in any act of reading. No written life approximates the lived. Informed as an autobiographer is about the events of his own life, his task of writing involves the editing, choosing, and changing required for the completion of any text. And any text will reflect the needs and wishes of the person writing. André Gide speaks of being "defrauded" by truth when finding out that he could not have experienced certain events.[10] But whether a writer is accurate, or even whether he or she gains any obvious self-knowledge, may be beside the point. The fact is that it is the person we seek. To put this differently, autobiographies remain human documents however slippery their medium. The continued and growing curiosity about autobiography is not just a matter of new pastures in a crowded discipline or a spillover from studies of other narrative forms. It reflects a direct interest in the lives and passions of individuals, in the ways they come to terms with their calling, their past lives, their imagined deaths. To say that their written lives are only texts is perhaps to be right in a technical sense, but it probably denies every fundamental reason for the reading of autobiographical works.

A persuasive approach to the status of the autobiographical self may be implicit in the thinking of Maurice Merleau-Ponty, who accepts the problematic nature of a public text without denying the importance of the writer within and behind the text. In any act of writing, says Merleau-Ponty, a long process of assimilation and thought leads to statements at odds with what one wanted or meant to say. The translation of private into public discourse inevitably mistranslates, as if the text emerges independently of the writer even while it reflects his deepest convictions.[11] This is, as I have mentioned, precisely what Samuel Butler was driving at, and it is a view of the writing process that Tyrrell or Ford or Moore would have understood.

What distinguishes Butler and the others from our contemporaries is their assumption as to the "truth" of their documents, albeit they imply by "truth" not a dispassionate account of their lives but a complex, interpretive act. "Sincerity" and "veracity" still obtain as standards for writers who see themselves as historians of their childhood worlds as well as of their earlier selves. To "be sincere," says Yeats, is the first requisite of being "a great poet; for it will be no longer a matter of literature at all."[12] Self exists and functions within the finished book, to be interpreted and re-cognized in Charles Radcliffe's terms. Yet self for these writers is also no simple construct, no easy extension of the lived experience.

When George Tyrrell wrote to Maude Petre about his prospective autobiography he said that perhaps ten selves might emerge, selves that could be created by his story, which he knew tended to fiction, and selves that would be discovered *in* story (as a projection of "truth").[13] One of Tyrrell's main concerns throughout his autobiographical fragment is the problematic nature of the person he looks back on, although his past selves seem to him immeasurably superior to the man who writes. Selves for Tyrrell are on the one hand the historical creations elicited by acts of recollection and on the other the divided person he feels to have experienced the events of his life.

What is true of Tyrrell is no less true of William Hale White or Samuel Butler, who essentially divide their projected "I" into the categories of narrating subject and object, both made distant by a fictional editor or a dispassionate storyteller. Although White and Butler only hint at the essentially ironic circumstance of their writing at all, they are fully aware of the limiting qualities of language, the need for and the impossibility of "silence"; and hence their understanding of selves is more complex than the narrative voices they create. Butler speaks meaningfully of "our subordinate personalities," construing individuals in terms of ancestral inheritance and of local history, with "luck or cunning" and other "contradictions" working in the warp and woof of quintessentially inchoate lives. For someone like Butler, problems of self are paramount, and they are inescapably a function of remembering.

Multiple selves occur in other writers, too. When Edmund Gosse begins his long course of alienation from his father, in a sense he divides his consciousness, creating or discovering an independent and a skeptical "I." "There was a secret in this world and it belonged to me and to a somebody who lived in the same body with me. There were two of us, and we could talk with one another."[14] Gosse's larger sense of self involves other divisions: the historical and the ahistorical, the young boy and the observing older man; the writer of a chronicle and the passionate actor in his own carefully edited past. This is equally the case with Ford Madox Ford, whose anecdotal history takes assertively unsequential courses, and who knows himself to be, whether genius or "patient stupid donkey," as complex as his own novelistic characters or as unknowable as Pound and Wells and other acquaintances found "Ford" to be. Ford and Hueffer are in a way but two conjectures about a largely inscrutable writer.

Both George Moore and William Butler Yeats seem consciously to create the selves of their autobiographies, and for both the figure of Ireland is a shaping and complicating force.[15] In *Hail and Farewell,* Moore was to think of Ireland in mythical terms, seeing himself as the instrument of his country's muse though expressing himself with reluctance or difficulty: "A trilogy, if ever there was one, each character so far above anything one meets in fiction that the reader's thoughts will return to Banva as the author, thinly disguised by the puerile name of George Moore, of this extraordinary work."[16] In *Memoirs,* Moore comes with painful awakening back to his ancestral home, to roots he has tried to cut and to emotions he did not want. Moore's County Mayo is not Yeats's mythical Sligo, yet in "Resurgam," Moore appreciates his roles as novelist, son, patriot, exile, and atheist, in terms of the confrontation with his birthplace. Earlier in *Memoirs of My Dead Life,* he has looked back almost with smugness on a series of loves and sexual encounters, but even in "The Lovers of Orelay" or "Bring in the Lamp," the personae of George Moore have shifted to meet the needs of story, just as story has been created to dramatize the complexity and at times the puerility of the recollecting self.

Moore himself might illustrate Walter Benjamin's assumption about Proust: that he engages in a kind of spiritual quest, which is, again, an important element in so many autobiographers, as important as (and related to) the idea of a "calling." While Tyrrell may see his life as failure, a long, increasingly dark night of the soul without final reward, Tyrrell, like White and Gosse or, again, even Butler and Moore, searches within his past life for spiritual answers, for the meanings of the events he describes in terms of some ultimate belief. Indeed, like Proust, Tyrrell speaks definitively of a return, if not to the conditions of a lost childhood, to its values and innocence, and to the faith implicit in his mother's life. It is as if for Tyrrell recollection replaces what the mystics call *Recollection* as the way to spiritual happiness: the elegiac supplanting the hymnic, in Benjamin's terms, though finally with little satisfaction for the man who recollects.

That act or process of Recollection is pertinent for some of the autobiographical writers I have written about and speaks to more general issues of autobiography. To address a few last questions about self and memory, I shall glance at two books which are, in their assumptions, diametrically opposed, but which help to clarify the topics at hand: one is Evelyn Underhill's *Mysticism* (1911); the other is Sigmund Freud's *Psychopathology of Every-Day Life* (1901).

In her popular and influential study of mystical experience, Underhill wrote a long and passionate apology for what Benjamin calls the "hymnic" approach to happiness. Her book, which is almost contemporary with Yeats's *Reveries* and *is* contemporary with Ford's *Ancient Lights,* recalls the heavy emphasis on "mystical" qualities in Pater, who proved so important for the writers I have discussed, and in other Paterian acolytes such as Arthur Symons. In his 1899 dedication to Yeats of *The Symbolist Movement,* Symons says: "I speak often in this book of Mysticism," which he sees as escape from a trivial and a means to a profounder self.[17] Underhill's book epitomizes a generation of such thinking. She defends various sorts of inspired processes of thought and offers unexpected insight into self-history. Underhill defines Recollection, a stage in the mystical experience, as follows:

> The unfortunate word *Recollection,* which the hasty reader is apt to connect with remembrance, is the traditional term by which mystical writers define . . . a voluntary concentration, . . . a first collecting or gathering in of the attention of the self to its "most hidden cell." That self is as yet unacquainted with the strange plain of silence which so soon becomes familiar to those who attempt even the lowest activities of the contemplative life; where the self is released from succession, the noises of the world are never heard, and the great adventures of the spirit take place.[18]

Within the progression of mystical states, Recollection is still an early step in which the mystic sees "in a natural way," without ecstasy, without "the lifting up of the soul," though on "that strange plain of silence." Granting Underhill's distinctions and the special meanings of the term, I would suggest that the state of Recollection has much in common with recollection as generally understood, except that its "gathering" or meditative power may focus elsewhere than on the writer's or the mystic's life. Obviously writers such as Saint Teresa and Saint Augustine see their lives in stages of progression that can be compared with those of nonmystical or even antireligious individuals. But the point I would make lies elsewhere. Underhill's phrase "released from succession" implies on the face of it a quality unlike that of any autobiographer, who would seem to recount a succession of events in his or her life, with reflective silence paramount and chronology inescapable. As a matter of fact, the release from succession is very much what autobiographers achieve, however different their meditative process.

My point is implicit in the earlier discussion of tenses, which organize memories rather than simply imitate the sequence of events. When Berdyaev says that "the beauty of the past is the beauty of creative acts in the present," he adds a further dimension, for without the creative mind, the past is inert and meaningless.[19] Perhaps most autobiographers assume historical progression, with narrative an analogue for the passing of time. Implicitly, however, they know better. George Tyrrell's three heavy lines, demarking past stages from one another and past stages from his present self, reflect contradictory impulses of development and of return, of chronological ordering and atemporal understanding. Gosse similarly differentiates between phases of his life, conflating episodes, revising "history," partially undercutting his own tropes of development or evolution when he calls a scene timeless or without history.

Almost any autobiographical reconstruction demands a process of conversion or transformation, wherein sequence gives way to epiphanic scenes or moments, which, though experienced and remembered in historic context, recur as if to stop the movement of time. The alternative is the "biographical" memory, in Susanne Langer's terms, which adheres to sequence without vividness or intensity. Even when memory is sequential, moreover, it is still a choosing from an already selective repository, with memories controlled by our capacity to think in terms of spatial or tense relationships. Hence, simple sequence is a biographical ordering more than a mode of memory, for the workings of the recollective mind, as Rudolf Arnheim and others have suggested, involves the preservation of sequence in a spatial form, the mind "translating" episodes of time "into the synoptic condition of space."[20] Arnheim is speaking implicitly of Wordsworth and Wordsworth's generation, but his thesis seems to make even more sense for writers in the generation of Einstein. As I have suggested, someone like Bergson construed the "spatializing" of time as a negative process, his judgment akin to Samuel Butler's disdain for making things conscious. Both the making conscious and the making spatial essentially "stop" the sequence of time, whether for desirable or undesirable ends.

In fact, as Thomas Reid had suggested in the eighteenth century and as Gestalt and other thinkers have suggested since, the process of stopping time or translating time into space is an unavoidable condition of remembering. It is also a common attribute of literature since Wordsworth, as the spatial/temporal pun of the "spots of time" would suggest. For Gaston Bachelard the "image" is the timeless essence of creative thinking, although for Bachelard as for Yeats, images seem finally to emerge from an unhistoric view of a personal and collective past.[21]

The spatial realization of what are usually visual memories is, again, a symbolic or synecdochic way of "looking back" at the past, of investing past moments with power, the power emerging, as Nietzsche, Berdyaev, and Benjamin testify, from a fortuitous forgetting, a choosing of a significant part over a meaningless whole. It may also imply the attempt at spiritual recovery so important to a George Tyrrell or a

William Hale White. Inspired moments are, for Wordsworth's followers as for Wordsworth himself, potentially renovative as well as liberating. But at the same time, recollection as meditative re-creation, as revision of the past, points to both the problems of twentieth-century psychoanalysis and the methods that a thinker like Freud established to deal with mnemonic complexities. Tyrrell himself speaks of the "analysis" of his life, which involves the probing, the facing of things unpleasant, the self-awareness of the Freudian recovery of the past, and the Freudian recovery also in a sense moves from recollection to Recollection.

Tyrrell's autobiography is contemporary with Freud's *Psychopathology of Every-Day Life* (1901), a work with which it has surprisingly much in common. David Bakan has spoken of *The Interpretation of Dreams* as a new kind of scientific work, because it deals so extensively with the writer himself.[22] One could argue similarly for the *Psychopathology,* which is a much more intimate or revealing book and which explores memory through private experience, that of Freud's patients, of course, but also his own. It has become relatively common to think of Freud in terms of "Freudian analysis": Paul Ricouer and Jacques Lacan have extended Freud's methods to Freud himself or addressed his work as part of the large field of interpretation claimed by hermeneutics.[23] In *Psychopathology,* Freud anticipates this process. His self-analysis, at times confessional, assesses his topics through the medium of his own complicated psyche.

From the outset, Freud's metaphysics, his oedipal theories, his world of id and ego, *déjà vu* and the uncanny, pre- and unconscious, enthralled as much as they have surprised or enraged his readers. But perhaps more intriguing than Freud's *Psychomachia,* his battling forces within the mind, is his awareness of the mind as a remembering and forgetting organism, a maker of secrets and a teller of tales. As a commentary on such matters as *déjà vu* and slips of the tongue, *Psychopathology* explores ways of forgetting without announcing any formal view of remembering, although recollection, including Freud's own recollection, is its central topic.

As with Ford Madox Ford or Edmund Gosse, it is difficult to know whether Freud, with his tenacious memory, actually remembered conversations or recollected them for his narrative, giving the illusion of full recall, just as he gives a sense of drama within his accounts. In any case, his analytical theories involve him in a process of reconstruction: fragments of confession, to use the phrase he would know from Goethe, come together in the remembering mind of the analyst, who acts as a kind of repository. Perhaps it was the assessment of his own remembering that led Freud to explore the relationship of private to public or collective remembering, his speculation analogous to Samuel Butler's theories of the unconscious memory, for example, and Yeats's idea of the Great Memory:

> If we assume the survival of . . . memory traces in the archaic heritage, we have bridged the gulf between individual and group psychology: we can deal with peoples as we do with an individual neurotic.[24]

Although, as Carl Schorske has shown, Freud is very much a product of *fin de siècle* Vienna, his interests cut across national boundaries and ethnic backgrounds.[25] Freud was contemporary, after all, with Bergson in France, with Richard Semon and Husserl in Germany, and was a late contemporary of James Ward and James Sully in England. For Freud no less than for Proust, existence is clearly a province of memory and the workings of memory provide keys both to individual and collective lives. Freud may not be interested in the recapturing of a lost paradise; he is concerned with the recapture of an elusive and misleading past, the fuller knowledge of which leads to fuller identity or health of the remembering individual. And the wisdom of Freud's book seems to lie in his recognition that the memories of his patients have become his own and that sorting them out has much to do with his own psychic health. He knows, in Schopenhauer's words, that each individual is the hero of his own drama while figuring in a drama foreign to him, and that the analyst plays that double role in a variety of ways.[26] Hence, when he speaks with the fellow Jew, who has forgotten Dido's lines from the *Aeneid,* Freud works through a long line of association about authority, race, and children, which have not only become a part of his clinical memory but also figure directly in his own life.

Out of his meditations come some of the most seminal analyses of childhood memories in our literature. Freud announces his theory of displacement, arguing that "the indifferent memories of childhood . . . are substitutes . . . for other impressions," and that it is only through analysis—"psychical analysis"—that resistance can be overcome and the original content revealed. Freud's rhetoric in this chapter almost parallels the process he describes. "I only touched on and in no way exhausted," he says, the meanings implicit in the analysis.[27] So his present discussion restates, recovers richer meanings, continuing the analysis from a fresh vantage point of understanding, which is also self-understanding. The process is that of an autobiographical writer such as George Moore, who asks a series of questions about past events, each new question affecting the status of what has gone before, each requiring of the writer a new response to present circumstances.

Freud came to regret his candor in *Psychopathology,* and his later, Darwin-like formality in the official autobiography is a measure of his early openness about his own childhood memories and developing self.[28]

Freud's self-exploration raises two final points about *Psychopathology.* In the first place, the book is, like so many of the autobiographies I have touched on, the story of a "calling." Freud's delicate professional and social status recurs as a theme in his book, which comments on the future of Jewish professionals and so much that concerns the ambitious Freud himself. Freud is also, like Gosse or Ford, a professional writer and someone who uses his own life to illustrate the problems of his calling. How did I arrive at my present position? What kind of man am I? What is the profession that I have chosen? Yeats on the calling of poetry or Tyrrell on the calling of the Jesuit priest is closely related to the *fin de siècle* uncertainty and the search for a larger historical context of which Freud continually speaks.

Freud also points to the importance of the recovery of the past, not only for his patients, but for so many writers and thinkers in diverse fields. On the other hand, recovery of the past entails more than re-creation; for the analyst it involves presentation, the shift from what one thinks one remembers to a narrative account that is both as accurate as it can be and as false as the medium requires. Theodor Reik touches on this problem in *Listening with a Third Ear,* in which he deals with matters of fragmentary confessions and wishful remembering. Reik believes, like Samuel Butler, that too much conscious recollection is almost certainly fictitious; but while the unconscious may be more trustworthy, it is also not directly available for the writing process. One fascinating quality in *The Psychopathology of Every-Day Life* is that Freud added great amounts to later editions, as if the book were in some sort of constant revision. But even of the first edition it is not too much to say that Freud, like Samuel Butler or George Moore, "dissolves" genre, his medium reflecting the recollective process to which his theory is addressed. Once more, Paul De Man's word for this process is "de-facement," which implies the paradoxical nature of self-revelation and the necessarily anomalous quality of autobiographical discourse, which laughs at categories and easy definition. In any case, Freud's exploratory writing, his underlying sense of *Heimlichkeit* in all facets of the human psyche, parallels Proust or Yeats or Joyce or Virginia Woolf, whose works depend on similar preoccupations.[29] *Psychopathology* is not, of course, autobiographical in format, but it does employ autobiographical methods in its unraveling of experience. It seems to illustrate in an unlikely way Benjamin's conviction that modern literature demands altogether new kinds of texts, new weavings of past and present in books that break down conventions.

To say that for modern writers "experience becomes a province of memory" is to assert what must be clear to any reader of early twentieth-century fiction. Autobiographers such as Ford and Moore, Yeats and Gosse, create very different kinds of self histories and speak about the perceptions of radically different lives. They share with Proust and Freud that obsession to understand and to recover a personal past, and they appreciate the past in terms of collective and incorporative theories of the workings of memory. Writing about their "calling," they also write about a spiritual calling, which autobiography seems to elicit out of the chaos of personal history. The recollective process may not lead to Recollection in Underhill's sense; and it may not involve the same kind of analysis advocated by Freud. It does demand a wholesale rethinking of generic boundaries, which tests the self in the process of discovery. It also involves the wrestle between remembering and forgetting, that web and warp of memory which reminds its teller of paradox and mystery, of life lost and life found.

Notes

Preface

Epigraph: Jane Austen, *Mansfield Park,* ed. James Kinsley and John Lucas (New York: Oxford Univ. Press, 1970), 188.

1. See, e.g., George Steiner, *After Babel: Aspects of Language and Translation* (New York: Oxford Univ. Press, 1975), 134, who speaks of "ontological 'fictions' in propositions about the past."
2. Saint Augustine, *Confessions,* trans. and intro. John K. Ryan (Garden City, N.Y.: Image Books, 1960), 246.
3. David Hume, *A Treatise of Human Nature,* ed. L. A. Selby-Brigge (Oxford: Oxford Univ. Press, 1955 [1881]), 264, 261–62.
4. Clifford Geertz, *The Interpretation of Cultures* (New York: Basic Books, 1973). See esp. the introductory chapter.
5. Stephen Kern, *The Culture of Time and Space, 1880–1918* (Cambridge: Harvard Univ. Press, 1983).
6. James Olney, *The Rhizome and the Flower: The Perennial Philosophy, Yeats and Jung* (Berkeley and Los Angeles: Univ. of California Press, 1980).
7. Wilhelm Dilthey, *Meaning in History: Wilhelm Dilthey's Thoughts on History and Society,* ed. H. P. Rickman (London: Allen & Unwin, 1961), 85, 66.
8. James Olney, "Some Versions of Memory, Some Versions of *Bios:* The Ontology of Autobiography," in *Autobiography: Essays Theoretical and Critical,* ed. Olney (Princeton: Princeton Univ. Press, 1980); and Olney, *Metaphors of Self: The Meaning of Autobiography* (Princeton: Princeton Univ. Press, 1972).
9. Dilthey, *Meaning in History,* 97. It may be true, as A. O. J. Cockshut argues, in his informed and insightful *The Art of Autobiography in Nineteenth- and Twentieth-Century England* (New Haven: Yale Univ. Press, 1984), 3, that "'Augustan,' 'Romantic,' 'Pre-Raphaelite' and the like, have no equivalents in the study of autobiography," but this does not mean that autobiographies written at the same time are likely to have little in common. Cockshut's title itself implies the importance of historical considerations, which should preclude easy categories and allow for important continuities.
10. An especially lucid discussion of psychological theories and their backgrounds is Daniel L. Schachter's *Stranger behind the Engram: Theories of Memory and the Psychology of Science* (Hillsdale, N.J.: Erlbaum Assocs., 1982).
11. Alice Miller, *Prisoners of Childhood* (New York: Farrar, Straus, & Giroux, 1981); Jeffrey M. Masson, *The Assault on Truth: Freud's Suppression of the*

Seduction Theory (New York: Farrar, Straus, & Giroux, 1984).
12. Estelle C. Jelinek, ed., *Women's Autobiography: Essays in Criticism* (Bloomington: Indiana Univ. Press, 1980). Jelinek's introduction is probably the best discussion of male assumptions about autobiography. See also Patricia Meyer Spacks, *Women's Imagination: History and Criticism* (New York: Knopf, 1975); Carol Hurd Green and Mary Mason, eds., *Journeys: Autobiographical Writings by Women* (Boston: G. K. Hall, 1979); and Margaret Homans, *Bearing the World: Language and Feminine Experience in Nineteenth-Century Women's Writing* (Chicago: Univ. of Chicago Press, 1986).
13. Stevenson's fragmentary autobiography [1880] was published as *Memoirs of Himself by Robert Louis Stevenson,* ed. Harry E. Widener (Philadelphia: privately issued, 1912).
14. See Richard Sorabji's fine introduction to *Aristotle on Memory* (Providence: Brown Univ. Press, 1972), a translation of *De Memoria et Reminiscentia,* with notes and summaries. Sorabji comments on various aspects of Aristotle's work that influenced later thinking about memory, especially "the principle of association" (43). See also Norman Gulley, *Plato's Theory of Knowledge* (London: Methuen, 1973) on *anamnesis* and other aspects of Platonic remembering.
15. This is Barrett J. Mandel's argument in "Full of Life Now," in Olney, *Autobiography,* 49.

1 Of Memory and Imagination

Epigraph: Thomas Mann, Foreword, *The Magic Mountain,* trans. H. T. Lowe-Porter (New York: Knopf, 1958).
1. Frank Kermode, *The Sense of an Ending: Studies in the Theory of Fiction* (New York: Oxford Univ. Press, 1967). Kermode, who explores apocalyptic sensibilities, calls his book "a paradigm of crisis" (16).
2. William Hale White [Mark Rutherford, pseud.], *The Autobiography of Mark Rutherford and Mark Rutherford's Deliverance,* ed. Basil Willey (New York: Humanities, 1969), 12. Cf. e.g., Annie Besant's *An Autobiography* (London: T. Fisher Unwin, 1893). Besant speaks about "this restless and eager generation" and of "troublous times like ours" (5).
3. *The Autobiography of William Butler Yeats Consisting of "Reveries over Childhood and Youth," "The Trembling of the Veil," and "Dramatis Personae"* (New York: Macmillan, Collier Books, 1965), 74. Gerda Lerner says, in *The Female Experience* (New York: Bobbs Merrill, 1977), that "the periods in which basic changes occur in society and which historians commonly regard as turning points are not necessarily the same for men and women" (xxiv). Estelle Jelinek quotes Lerner's comment to suggest that women's autobiography is usually less public, less "historical," than men's (*Women's Autobiography* [see preface, n. 12], 5–7).
4. Karl J. Weintraub, "Autobiography and Historical Consciousness," *Critical Inquiry* 1 (1975): 821–48; also Weintraub, *The Value of the Individual: Self and Circumstance in Autobiography* (Chicago: Univ. of Chicago Press, 1978); Ortega y Gassett, *Concord and Liberty* (New York: Norton, 1946), 50, 95. See also John Gunnell's fine study, *Political Philosophy and Time* (Middletown, Conn.: Wesleyan Univ. Press, 1968), which speaks of "the complete historization

of existence accomplished in the nineteenth century" (252).
5. Dilthey, *Meaning in History* (see preface, n. 7), 92. In his pioneering study of *Autobiography in Antiquity,* George Misch quotes Dilthey's comments on the Renaissance, which apply to turn-of-the-century thinking: "Every time a culture dies out and a new one is to arise, the world of ideas that proceeded from the older cultures fades and dissolves. The individual experience is, as it were, emancipated for a time from the fetters of conceptual thought" (*History of Autobiography in Antiquity,* 2 vols., trans. E. W. Dickes, Cambridge: Harvard Univ. Press, 1951, 1:72).
6. Nicola Chiaromonte, *The Paradox of History,* foreword by Joseph Frank (Philadelphia: Univ. of Pennsylvania Press, 1985).
7. Paul Fussell, *The Great War and Modern Memory* (New York: Oxford Univ. Press, 1975). Chapter 1 begins with Hardy (3–7).
8. Daniel J. Levinson, *The Seasons of a Man's Life* (New York: Ballantine, 1978).
9. See my brief discussion of Freud's *The Psychopathology of Every-Day Life* [1901], vol. 6 in *Complete Psychological Works,* 24 vols., trans. James Strachey (London: Hogarth, 1953–66), in the Conclusion.
10. Havelock Ellis, *My Life: Autobiography of Havelock Ellis* (Boston: Houghton Mifflin, 1939), vii. Although Ellis completed his autobiography years later, he emphasized its beginnings around the turn of the century. Another autobiographer fascinated by the turn of the century is Richard Church, *Over the Bridge: An Essay in Autobiography* (London: Heineman, 1955).
11. Ford Madox Hueffer [later Ford], *Ancient Lights and Certain New Reflections: Being the Memoirs of a Young Man* (London: Chapman Hall, 1911). See esp. the chapter, "Changes."
12. Northrop Frye, *The Anatomy of Criticism* (Princeton: Princeton Univ. Press, 1957). Hayden White draws on Frye's various categories (of fictional forms and tropes) in *Metahistory: The Historical Imagination in Nineteenth-Century Europe* (Baltimore: Johns Hopkins Univ. Press, 1973).
13. William C. Spengemann, *The Forms of Autobiography: Episodes in the History of a Literary Genre* (New Haven: Yale Univ. Press, 1980). Spengemann's specific analyses are illuminating, and he is certainly right in saying that "the more [autobiography] gets written about, the less agreement there seems to be on what it properly includes" (xi). For comparable groupings of autobiography, see William L. Howarth, "Some Principles of Autobiography," in Olney, *Autobiography* (see preface, n. 8), 84–114. Janet Varner Gunn discusses problems with "taxonomical strategies" in *Autobiography: Towards a Poetic of Experience* (Philadelphia: Univ. of Pennsylvania Press, 1982), 11.
14. Roman Jakobson, "Two Aspects of Language and Two Types of Aphasic Disturbances," in Jakobson and Morris Halle, *Fundamentals of Language* (Gravenhage: Mouton, 1956), esp. "The Metaphoric and Metonymic Modes," 76ff.
15. Burton Pike, "Time in Autobiography," *Comparative Literature* 28 (1976): 326–42. See Avrom Fleishman's distinction between a narrative past and a dramatic present in "Personal Myth: Three Victorian Autobiographers," in George P. Landow, ed., *Approaches to Victorian Autobiography,* (Columbus: Ohio Univ. Press, 1978), 216, and Wayne Shumaker's divisions of a static present, a static past, and an intervening development in *English Autobiography: Its Emergence, Materials, and Form* (Berkeley and Los Angeles: Univ. of California

Press, 1954), both of which tacitly rebut a chronological impetus behind autobiography.
16. Theodule Ribot, *English Psychology* (London: Henry King, 1873), 50. Edmund Gosse, *Father and Son: A Study of Two Temperaments* (New York: Norton, 1963), 241.
17. On diachronic and synchronic, see, e.g., George Lewes, *Problems of Life and Mind, 3rd Series: The Study of Psychology* (London: Trubner, 1879), 161. Much of Lewes's speculation anticipates later theories. He speaks of racial memories, of a "collective consciousness," as well as of the determining qualities of language. See also Ribot on "successive" as against "synchronic order" (*English Psychology*, 50).
18. Marcel Proust, *Time Regained: Remembrance of Things Past* trans. C. K. Scott Moncrieff, T. Kilmartin, and A. Mayor, intro. J. W. Krutch (New York: Random House, 1981), 3:903. See also Nicolas Berdyaev, *The Beginning and the End*, trans. R. M. French (Westport, Conn: Greenwood, 1976): "In art and poetry there is a memory of paradise. But in his attitude towards the future man is painfully divided" (239).
19. Charles Darwin, *The Autobiography of Charles Darwin, 1809–1882*, ed. Nora Barlow (New York: Norton, 1969), 21. Darwin himself, of course, was a pioneer in psychology, as *The Expression of the Emotions in Man and Animals* (1873) makes clear. On kinds of memory and the complexity of detailed versus gestalt-like memories, see Arthur Koestler, *The Act of Creation* (New York: Macmillan, 1964), esp. the chapter, "Perception and Memory."
20. On James and Wordsworth, see, e.g., Ralph Barton Perry, *The Thought and Character of William James*, 2 vols. (Boston: Little, Brown, 1935), esp. 1:320, 332, 337–39.
21. Francis Galton, *Hereditary Genius: An Inquiry into Its Laws and Consequences* [1869], intro. C. D. Darlington (New York: Fontana Library, 1962). See his *Memories of My Life* (London: Methuen, 1908) with its fascinating account of Galton's introduction to medicine and science.
22. Lewes, *Problems of Life and Mind*: "The higher form of Memory called Recollection may safely be said to be exclusively human" (119). As with Bergson, memory (conscious and unconscious) is for Lewes essentially "an act of orientation" (116).
Epigraph: Emily Dickinson, poem #1498 [1880?], *The Complete Poems of Emily Dickinson*, ed. Thomas H. Johnson (Boston: Little, Brown, 1960), 630.
23. Charles Bland Radcliffe, *Proteus; or, The Unity of Nature* [1850] (London: Macmillan, 1877), 171.
24. Roy Park, *Hazlitt and the Spirit of the Age* (Oxford: Clarendon, 1971), 209. On Plato in the universities, see, e.g., M. L. Clarke, *George Grote: A Biography* (London: Athlone, 1962), 146.
25. See Thomas Weiskel's brilliant analysis of memory and the sublime, in *The Romantic Sublime: Studies in the Structure and Psychology of Transcendence* (Baltimore: Johns Hopkins Univ. Press, 1976): "The unmanageable distance between Wordsworth and his theme becomes the manageable distance between present and past" (153). Weiskel speaks of "the regressive necessity of the poetic imagination" in Coleridge as well as Wordsworth (160).
26. Radcliffe, *Proteus*, 6. Among Radcliffe's classical sources, Plotinus was ob-

viously important, with his emphasis on unity in multiplicity, nature and contemplation, order and power. Plotinus was of course a major influence on the Romantic poets. See his *Enneads,* 3d ed., trans. S. McKenna, intro. Paul Henry, S. J. (London: Faber, 1980). Proclus's allegorized interpretations of Homer also emphasized unity in multiplicity. See M. H. Abrams, *Natural Supernaturalism: Tradition and Revolt in Romantic Literature* (New York: Norton, 1971), 149–50.

27. Radcliffe, *Proteus,* 185.
28. Dugald Stewart, *Elements of the Philosophy of the Human Mind,* 3d ed. (London: Cadell & Davies, 1808), 403. Locke says that memory "is of so great moment, that when it is wanting, all the rest of the faculties are in a great measure useless" (*Essay Concerning Human Understanding,* 2 vols., ed. and annotated A. C. Fraser, New York: Dover, 1959, 1:198).
29. Radcliffe, *Proteus,* 187.
30. Thomas Hobbes, *Leviathan,* ed. A. R. Waller (Cambridge: Cambridge Univ. Press, 1935), part 1, chap. 2, p. 4. See also James Beattie's enlightened discussion, "Of Memory and Imagination," in *Dissertations Moral and Critical* (London, 1783), wherein he summarizes earlier theories and, anticipating Coleridge, emphasizes the superiority of imagination to memory; and James Mill's influential *Analysis of the Phenomena of the Human Mind,* 2 vols. (London: Baldwin & Cradock, 1829), with its chapter, "Memory": "Memory . . . has in it all that Imagination has; but it must also have something more" (1:241).
31. Hume, *A Treatise* (see preface, n. 3), 261–62. Elsewhere (262) Hume says that personal identity is a matter of grammatical rather than of philosophical difficulty.
32. Ibid., 264.
33. See, e.g., John Ruskin, *Modern Painters* 3, *Works of Ruskin,* ed. E. T. Cook and A. Wedderburn, Library Edition, 39 vols. (London: George Allen, 1903), 5:205; and [W. E. Gladstone], "Works and Life of Giacomo Leopardi," *Quarterly Review* 86 (1850): 310. John Stuart Mill spoke of the "morbid self-consciousness" in Browning's *Pauline.*
34. For a discussion of Coleridge and memory, see Thomas Lockridge, *Coleridge the Moralist* (Ithaca, N.Y.: Cornell Univ. Press, 1977), 177–78.
35. Bernard Bosanquet, *Essays and Addresses* (London: Swann & Sonnenschein, 1889), 175. With German Romantic philosophers in mind, Bosanquet says, "Unity in multiplicity . . . is the essence of identity."
36. F. W. Colegrove, *Memory: An Inductive Study* (London: Bell; New York: Henry Holt, 1901), 3.
37. See particularly F. W. H. Myers, *Human Personality and Its Survival of Bodily Death,* 2 vols. (London: Longmans Green, 1903). I turn briefly to Myers when discussing Samuel Butler in chapter 3.
38. James Sully, *Illusions: A Psychological Study* (New York: Appleton, 1881), 241; also Sully, *Outlines of Psychology* (London: Longmans, 1884).
39. John Ruskin, "The Lamp of Memory," in *The Seven Lamps of Architecture* (1849); Arthur Symons, *The Symbolist Movement in Literature,* ed. Richard Ellmann (New York: Dutton, 1958), 11 and passim.
40. Søren Kierkegaard, *Fear and Trembling and Repetition,* ed. H. V. Hong and E. H. Hong, in *Kierkegaard's Writing,* vol. 6 (Princeton: Princeton Univ. Press, 1983).

Epigraph: Henri Bergson, *Matter and Memory* [1896], trans. N. M. Paul (London: Allen & Unwin, 1913), xii–xiii.

41. See William Earle, *The Autobiographical Consciousness* (Chicago: Quadrangle Books, 1972); also Earle's provocative "Memory," *Review of Metaphysics* 10, no. 1 (September 1956): 3–27.
42. Bergson, *Matter and Memory*, xiv and passim. Some of Bergson's ideas had been anticipated by Henry Calderwood (*The Philosophy of the Infinite, with Special Reference to the Works of Sir William Hamilton,* Edinburgh: Constable, 1854), whose analysis of "duration" and purposeful memory emerge in a critique of Hamilton's influential theories. For an attack on Bergson and his followers, "the time-spacers" (everyone from Proust to Freud to Gertrude Stein), see Wyndham Lewis's *Time and Western Man* [1927] (Boston: Beacon, 1957). Lewis says that the entire generation after Bergson was obsessed by *duration*. Lewis advocates the "spatializing" denigrated by Bergson.
43. Rudolf Arnheim, "Space as an Image of Time," in *Images of Romanticism*, ed. K. Kroeber and W. Walling (New Haven: Yale Univ. Press, 1978), 2.
44. Proust speaks of "the passion" he felt for Ruskin's thought in "John Ruskin" (*Marcel Proust: A Selection From His Writings*, ed. Gerard Hopkins, London: Wingate, 1948, 96).
45. Virginia Woolf, *Moments of Being: Unpublished Autobiographical Writings,* ed. and intro. Jeanne Schulkind (London: Sussex Univ. Press, 1976).
46. See, e.g., Jonathan Swift, "A Digression on Madness," in *Tale of a Tub*, 2d ed., ed. A. C. Guthkelch and D. Nichol Smith (Oxford: Clarendon, 1958), 170–72.
47. F. H. Bradley, "Why Do We Remember Forwards and Not Backwards?" *Mind* (October 1887), in *Collected Essays*, 2 vols. (Oxford: Oxford Univ. Press, 1935), 1:243. See Abrams's discussion of "Moments," in *Natural Supernaturalism*, 385–89; also Søren Kierkegaard, *The Concept of Anxiety*, trans. and intro. Raidar Thomte and Albert Anderson (Princeton: Princeton Univ. Press, 1980): "Precisely because every moment, as well as the sum of the moments, is a process (a passing by), no moment is a present, and accordingly there is in time neither present, nor past, nor future" (85).
48. Cf. also Bertrand Russell's "specious present." Russell accepts a basically behaviorist view of memory; see "Memory Objectively Regarded," in *Philosophy* (New York: Norton, 1927), 197ff. He objects like Nietzsche to the high stature given to memory in his time, but his own views are often questionable. He says, for example, that "memory does not, like imagination, involve a rearrangement" of chronology (195).
49. F. H. Bradley, "Some Remarks on Memory and Inference," *Mind* 8, n.s., no. 30 (April 1899): 147. For commentary on the larger context of Bradley's thinking, see Garrett L. Vander Veer, *Bradley's Metaphysics and the Self* (New Haven: Yale Univ. Press, 1970).
50. James Ward, *Psychological Principles* (Cambridge: Cambridge Univ. Press, 1918), 31–36, and elsewhere.
51. Sully, *Illusions*, 241.
52. See, e.g., Ira Progoff, *Depth Psychology and Modern Man* (New York: Julian, 1959), 10. However, Henri Ellenberger's *The Discovery of the Unconscious: The History and Development of Dynamic Psychiatry* (New York: Basic Books, 1970) will suggest how much had taken place before Freud.

53. Miguel de Unamuno, *The Tragic Sense of Life* [1912], trans. J. E. C. Flitch (New York: Dover, 1954 [first English trans. 1921]), 8–9. Unamuno is usually associated with "the generation of '98," the Spanish equivalent of Yeats's "tragic generation" in England.
54. Berdyaev, *Beginning and the End*, 215.
55. A. R. Luria, *The Mind of a Mnemonist*, trans. L. Solotaroff (New York: Basic Books, 1968).
56. George Moore, *Memoirs of My Dead Life* [1906] (London: Heinemann, 1919), 312.
57. Miguel de Unamuno, *Essays and Soliloquies*, trans. J. E. C. Flitch (New York: Knopf, 1924), 164.
58. Robert Wallis says that "*mermeros* in Greek means anxiety, and is also the root of the word *memory*" (*Time: Fourth Dimension of the World*, trans. B. B. and D. B. Montgomery, pref. by Marshall McLuhan, New York: Harcourt Brace, 1968, 102). According to Professor William Scott of Dartmouth, the etymology is strained since *mermeros* means "'baneful, captious, fastidious.' But *merimna* does mean 'care, anxiety,' and is said to be related to Latin *memor* (hence to *memoria*) through the Sanskrit root *smart-*." The OED confirms the Sanskrit base but does not go back to the Greek.
59. Jean-Paul Sartre, *Words*, trans. Irene Clephane (Baltimore: Penguin, 1967), 97.
60. Roy Pascal, *Design and Truth in Autobiography* (London: Routledge & Kegan Paul, 1960), 112.
61. Lionel Trilling, *Sincerity and Authenticity* (Cambridge: Harvard Univ. Press, 1971), 29.
62. Yeats, *Autobiography* 128. Cf. Richard Le Gallienne, *Vanishing Roads and Other Essays* (New York: Putnam, 1915), who speaks of "a tragic charm" and "melancholy . . . when we summon up shapes and happenings of the vanished past" (104).
63. Friedrich Nietzsche, *The Use and Abuse of History*, trans. Adrian Collins, Library of Liberal Arts (New York: Bobbs-Merrill, 1949), 5. Cf. Tolstoi's character, Platon Korataev (in *War and Peace*), who, Pierre realizes, is happy because he lives in the present—so much so that if he says something he immediately forgets his own remarks; also Plotinus, *Enneads*, 287, and the idea of "happy forgetfulness."
64. Nietzsche, *Use and Abuse of History*, 21.
65. Ibid., 72.
66. Ibid., 7.
67. Phyllis Grosskurth, "Where was Rousseau?", in Landow, ed., *Approaches*, 26–38. Early studies of autobiography emphasized the importance of Rousseau while granting his personal failings. See, e.g., James Field Stanfield, *An Essay on the Study and Composition of Biography* (Sunderland: Gale, Curtis, & Fenner, 1813), 34–40, with its discussion of Rousseau's example for "self-biography."
68. George Moore, Preface to 1917 American ed., *Confessions of a Young Man* [1888], ed. and intro. Susan Dick (Montreal: McGill Univ. Press, 1972), 42.
69. Herbert Lindenberger, *On Wordsworth's Prelude* (Princeton: Princeton Univ. Press, 1963), 277ff.

2 Transforming the Past

Epigraph: Dilthey, *Meaning in History* (see preface, n. 7), 80.
1. Ibid., 138. William Hale White (as "Mark Rutherford") says that "if we desire peace we must get beyond the notion of personality" (*More Pages from a Journal,* London: Oxford Univ. Press, 1910, 238). Tyrrell is perhaps the one autobiographer I deal with who mentions Dilthey. See *George Tyrrell's Letters,* selected and ed. M. D. Petre (London: T. Fisher Unwin, 1920), 58.
2. *Autobiography and Life of George Tyrrell,* 2 vols., ed. with vol. 2 written by M. D. Petre (London: Edward Arnold, 1912), 2:26 (letter of 30 June 1900).

Epigraph: W. B. Yeats, *Explorations* (London: Macmillan, 1962), 308; White, *More Pages from a Journal,* 224.
3. White, *Letters to Three Friends* (London: Oxford Univ. Press, 1924): "Shall think two or three times before consenting [to meet Tyrrell], as I dread argument or even conversation with a Jesuit on religion, especially as he is learned and pious" (240; letter of January 1904).
4. Catherine M. Maclean argues that White was neither a solitary thinker nor a recluse and "that his philosophy of life was not wrought in the leisure of his study but amidst the pressures of public affairs" (*Mark Rutherford: A Biography of William Hale White,* London: Macdonald, 1955, xiii). White did, nonetheless, seek his privacy, and there is no doubt that he thought of himself as a solitary and isolated figure.
5. White, *Autobiography of Mark Rutherford* (see chap. 1, n. 2), 47.
6. White, Introduction to Benedict de Spinoza, *Ethic, Demonstrated in Geometrical Order and Divided Into Five Parts, Translated form the Latin by William Hale White* (London: Trubner, 1883), x. White is paraphrasing Spinoza. Cf. George Tyrrell, *The Soul's Orbit; or, Man's Journey to God,* compiled with additions by M. D. Petre (London: Longmans, 1904): "Action is the only remedy" (11). Both White and Tyrrell seem to have Carlyle's many comparable statements in mind.
7. William Hale White, *The Early Life of Mark Rutherford, by Himself* (London: Oxford University Press, 1913), 5.
8. Maclean, *Mark Rutherford.* Wilfred H. Stone, *Religion and Art of William Hale White ("Mark Rutherford"),* Stanford University Series in Language and Literature 12 (Stanford: Stanford Univ. Press, 1954). On his failure to continue his friendship with George Eliot, White writes, "It is a lasting sorrow to me that I allowed my friendship with her to drop" (*Early Life,* 83).
9. See White, *Early Life,* 5.
10. Ibid.: "It would be a mistake to suppose that the creed in which I had been brought up was or could be cast away like an old garment" (77). The Carlylean metaphor was probably intended.
11. See Susanne Howe, *Wilhelm Meister and His English Kinsmen* (New York: Columbia Univ. Press, 1930). Howe does not mention White in her discussion of Meredith, Lewes, Disraeli, and others.
12. White, Introduction to Spinoza, *Ethic,* xxxv. White says, "The world is alarmed now at the various portents which threaten it. On every side are signs of danger" (xxiv). Cf. again Tyrrell, *The Soul's Orbit,* with the warning about immense changes and "the storm" which "is surely coming" (4).

13. On the *Confessions* as a novel, see C. D. E. Tolton, *André Gide and the Art of Autobiography* (Toronto: Univ. of Toronto Press, 1975), 58. One of the first insightful discussions of the facticity issue was Pascal's, in *Design and Truth* (see chap. 1, n. 60). See also Mandel, "Full of Life" (preface, n. 15).
14. See Elizabeth W. Bruss, *Autobiographical Acts: The Changing Situation of a Literary Genre* (Baltimore: Johns Hopkins Univ. Press, 1976), esp. the introduction, with its appropriation of John Searle's notion of "illocutionary acts." Also Philippe Lejeune, "The Autobiographical Contract," in T. Todorov, ed., *French Literary Theory Today* (Cambridge: Cambridge Univ. Press, 1982).
15. Gérard Genette, *Figures III* (Paris: Editions du Seuil, 1972), 50; quoted by Paul De Man, "Autobiography as De-Facement," *The Rhetoric of Romanticism* (New York: Columbia Univ. Press, 1984), 69.
16. White wrote a review, "The Genius of Walt Whitman," in *Secular Review* (20 March 1880), quoted by Irving Stock in *William Hale White, "Mark Rutherford": A Critical Study* (Stanford: Stanford Univ. Press, 1956), 76. White obviously had reservations about any fictional projection. He says, "The tyranny of the imagination is perhaps that which is most to be dreaded" (*More Pages from a Journal*, 227).
17. Walter Pater, "Coleridge," in *Appreciations: With an Essay on Style* (New York: MacMillan, 1907), 105–6.
18. Stone, *Religion and Art*, 43.
19. *Letters to Three Friends*, 173 (letter of December 1897).
20. Ibid., 107 (letter of September 1900).
21. Ibid., 7 (letter of April 1882).

Epigraph: Sartre, *Words* (see chap. 1, n. 59), 113.

22. Ibid., 71.
23. White's emphasis on aloneness, or at least on being without parental help, connects his books not only with those of Dickens and Charlotte Brontë but also with those of Byron, Bulwer, Thackeray, as well as Carlyle ("Wherein is my case peculiar?" *Sartor Resartus*, II, 1), who portrayed characters (or selves) as orphans. A surprising favorite of White was Borrow's *Lavengro*, in which the hero as gipsy is "orphaned" dramatically, from family and ordinary society. For a discussion of orphans in English fiction, see, e.g., Nina Auerbach, "Incarnations of the Orphan," *English Literary History* 42, no. 3 (Fall 1975): 395–419.
24. Susanne Langer, *Mind: An Essay on Human Feeling*, 2 vols. (Baltimore: Johns Hopkins Univ. Press, 1972), 2: 339. See also Koestler, *Act of Creation* (see chap. 1, n. 19), Chap. 10, on "cinematic memory"; and Paul Brockelman, "Of Memory and Things Past," *Int. Philosophical Quarterly* 15, no. 3 (September 1975): 310, on "concrete memory."
25. For a discussion of Wordsworth and "crisis autobiography," see Abrams, *Natural Supernaturalism* (see chap. 1, n. 26), esp. 71–140. Abrams comments on White's indebtedness to Wordsworth, but says that "the book, like Mill's *Autobiography*, was written before *The Prelude* was published" (137). In fact, of course, it followed *The Prelude* (in composition and publication) by about thirty years. Whatever his reservations about Wordsworth, White thought of him as one of those elite writers, superior to the mere "literary man" (*More Pages from a Journal*, 200).

26. Willey, ed., Introduction to White, *Autobiography of Mark Rutherford* (see chap. 1, n. 2), 9.

Epigraph: Kierkegaard, *The Concept of Anxiety* (see chap. 1, n. 47), 85.

27. Dorothy V. White, *The Groombridge Diary* (about W. H. White) (London: Oxford Univ. Press, 1935), 195.
28. White writes in January 1886 that his "admiration of Dickens grew almost to a worship" (*Letters to Three Friends*, 31). Most of the autobiographers I deal with in this study praise Dickens (as even Tyrrell does; see below). Barbara C. Gelpi's essay, "The Innocent I: Dickens's Influence on Victorian Autobiography," in *The Worlds of Victorian Fiction*, ed. Jerome H. Buckley (Cambridge: Harvard Univ. Press, 1975), discusses neither White nor Gosse, but Gelpi rightly emphasizes the importance of *David Copperfield* for later narratives about childhood and growing up. See Virginia Woolf's astute assessment of *David Copperfield* and its influence in *The Moment and Other Essays* (New York: Harcourt Brace, 1948), 75–76.
29. C. S. Lewis, *Surprised by Joy: The Shape of My Early Life* (New York: Harcourt, Brace & World, 1955). As his title suggests, Lewis, no less than White, thinks of his retrospection in relation to Wordsworth's.
30. White, Introduction to Spinoza, *Ethic*, lxiii. Stuart Hampshire, in his study of *Spinoza* (Harmondsworth: Penguin, 1976), 9, praises White's translation, which is still used in at least one modern edition.
31. White, *Letters to Three Friends*, 160 (letter of 30 Nov. 1878).
32. William Hale White, *John Bunyan, by the Author of "Mark Rutherford"* (London: Thomas Nelson, 1922), 13. In *Letters to Three Friends*, White says, "Elstow and the Ouse in a measure the temper of the man [Bunyan] are in my blood" (328; letter of January 1905).
33. Fussell, *The Great War and Modern Memory* (see chap. 1, n. 7), esp. 137–44.
34. Willey, ed., Introduction to White, *Autobiography of Mark Rutherford*, 15.
35. W. L. Sperry, "Mark Rutherford," *Harvard Theological Review* 7 (April 1914): 170; White, *Early Life*, 38.

Epigraph: Ellis, *My Life* (see chap. 1, n. 10), vi.

36. Paul Delaney mentions the importance of Job to seventeenth-century confessors, in *British Autobiography in the Seventeenth Century* (London: Routledge & Kegan Paul, 1969), 28–29; Saint Paul (as for many later autobiographers, including even George Moore) was, however, the exemplary figure.
37. De Man, "Autobiography as De-Facement," 70. De Man speaks eloquently about the "inherent instability" of autobiography. "Our topic deals with the giving and taking away of faces, with face and deface, *figure*, figuration and disfiguration" (76). De Man also draws on Lacan's *Ecrits*, speaking of "specular images" in autobiography.

Epigraph: Berdyaev, *Beginning and the End* (see chap. 1, n. 18), 212.

38. Tyrrell, *The Soul's Orbit*, 15.
39. Ibid., 14.
40. Tyrrell, *Autobiography* 1:1.
41. See Maude Petre's biography of Tyrrell, vol. 2 of the *Autobiography*; Karl Jung, *Memories, Dreams, Reflections*, recorded and ed. Aniela Jaffè, trans. Richard and Clara Winston (New York: Vintage Books, 1965), 5–9.

Epigraph: Tyrrell, *Autobiography*, 1:149.

42. Like Hardy and others, he considered January 1, 1901 the beginning of the new century. On Hardy, see, e.g., Edward Alexander, "Fin de siècle, fin du Globe: Yeats and Hardy in the Nineties," *PMLA* 23 (1977): 143–63.
43. Tyrrell, *Autobiography* 1:vi (Letter of 23 January 1901).
44. *Letters from a Modernist: The Letters of George Tyrrell to Wilfrid Ward, 1893–1908*, ed. Mary Jo Weaver (Shepherdstown, W.V.: Patmos Press, 1981), 25 (letter of 4 February 1908).
45. Wilfrid Ward, *Last Lectures*, quoted in Maisie Ward, *The Wilfrid Wards and the Transition* (London: Sheed & Ward, 1937), 2:188. For details about Tyrrell's career, see John D. Root, "English Catholic Modernism and Science: The Case of George Tyrrell," *Heythrop Journal* 18, no. 3 (July 1977): 271–88; John Ratté, *Three Modernists* (New York: Sheed & Ward, 1967); and David G. Shultenover, *George Tyrrell: In Search of Catholicism* (Shepherdstown, W.V.: Patmos Press, 1981). Thomas M. Loome published "A Bibliography of the Published Works of George Tyrrell (1861–1909)," *Heythrop Journal* 10, no. 3 (July 1969): 280–314.
46. Tyrrell, *External Religion: Its Use and Abuse* (London: Sands, 1899). He speaks about "a sort of experimental knowledge of God which can never be got from the most elaborate philosophical or theological notions" (154).
47. Quoted in Tyrrell, *Autobiography*, 2:36 (letter of 13 March 1900).
48. George Tyrrell, *Oil and Wine* (London: Longmans, 1907) [Introduction dated Easter, 1900], 287.
49. George Tyrrell, *Nova et Vetera: Informal Meditations for Times of Spiritual Dryness* (London: Longmans, Green, 1897), 2.
50. Tyrrell, *Letters* (see chap. 2, n. 1), 69 (letter of 22 January 1901). In spite of "preciosity," says Tyrrell, Pater "is our Flaubert." Pater was an important writer for other autobiographers, as George Moore (chapter 5) and Yeats (chapter 7) will indicate. Butler, as usual, felt otherwise: "Walter Pater's style is, to me, like the face of some old woman who has been to Madame Rachel and had herself enamelled" (*The Note-Books of Samuel Butler*, ed. Henry Festing-Jones, London: A. C. Fifield, 1912, 184). For a discussion of Pater's contradictory vision (including perhaps an "outside" vision) and his "displaced" autobiography, see J. Hillis Miller, "Walter Pater: A Partial Portrait," *Daedalus* 105 (Winter 1976): 97–113.
51. Tyrell, *Oil and Wine*, iii.
52. Tyrrell, *Nova et Vetera*, 392.
53. Tyrrell, *The Soul's Orbit*, 203.
54. Ronald Chapman, "The Thought of George Tyrrell," in *Essays and Poems Presented to Lord David Cecil* (London: Constable, 1970), 166. See also *Newman and the Modernists*, ed. Mary Jo Weaver (Lanham, Md.: Univ. Press of America, 1985).
55. Quoted by Jerome H. Buckley, *The Triumph of Time: A Study of the Victorian Concepts of Time, History, Progress, and Decadence* (Cambridge: Harvard Univ. Press, 1966), 101.
56. Nicholas Nagovsky, *Between Two Worlds: George Tyrrell's Relation to the Thought of Matthew Arnold* (Cambridge: Cambridge Univ. Press, 1983), 20. Sagovsky's lucid study suggests how important Arnold was for so many late-nineteenth-century writers.
57. Lucien Goldmann, *The Hidden God: A Study of Tragic Vision in the* Pensées

of *Pascal and the Tragedies of Racine*, trans. Philip Thody (London: Routledge & Kegan Paul, 1964), 270. Goldmann is particularly interested in Pascal's tragic sense and his preoccupation with paradox.

58. George Tyrrell, *Through Scylla and Charybdis; or, The Old Theology and the New* (London: Longmans, Green, 1907). Echoing Arnold and Newman, Tyrrell speaks of the need for "a minority, a saving leaven" (vii), but the minority will also speak out, if necessary, against the "dogmatic decisions of the church" (4).

59. Sagovsky, *Between Two Worlds*, 3. See Shultenover, *George Tyrrell*, and Ratté, *Three Modernists*.

60. Tyrrell, *Through Scylla and Charybdis*, 1.

61. See Tyrrell, *Autobiography*, 2:307–8. One of the most touching accounts of Tyrrell's final years is Wilfred Blunt's. Tyrrell admired Blunt's poems, which, he said, gave him "courage" (2:vi; letter of 23 January 1901). Blunt describes a series of meetings with Tyrrell, from 1900 until the time of Tyrrell's death, in his *My Diaries: Being a Personal Narrative of Events, 1888–1914* (London: Martin Secker, 1919), 1:455, 2:184, 265.

Epigraph: Tyrrell, *Oil and Wine*, 333. Here, too, Tyrrell reflects his reading of Pater, esp. *Marius* and *The Renaissance*.

62. Bradley, "Why Do We Remember Forwards" (see chap. 1, n. 47), 243.

63. Tyrrell, *Oil and Wine*, 334. Tyrrell often comments on collective memories. In a letter to an anthropologist, he spoke, for example, about a "collective subconscious" (cited in Ratté, *Three Modernists*, 199). Elsewhere he said that our "pilgrim" journey (to God) "will be conscious, sometimes unconscious" (*The Soul's Orbit*, 3), with "unconscious" meaning both unfathomable and shared, in some profound sense, with others.

64. He has a sophisticated understanding of confession and its attendant risks of hypocrisy or self-delusion. See, e.g., *The Soul's Orbit*, 14–17, where Tyrrell speaks of the penitent as his own accuser who must deal with "the utter inadequacy of human language."

65. Tyrrell, *Autobiography* 2:40 (letter of 6 February 1901).

66. Tyrrell, *Letters from a Modernist*, 27 (letter of 24 February 1900). A. O. J. Cockshut observes that few autobiographers refer to earlier autobiographers or admit their sources (*The Art of Autobiography* [see preface, n. 9], 3); yet many autobiographers speak of reading Augustine and others point to Bunyan and Rousseau. Perhaps, as Borges says, "the fact is that every author creates his own precursors" (*Labyrinths*, New York: New Directions, 1962, 201).

67. Augustine, *Confessions* (see preface, n. 2), 238.

68. Ralph Harper, *The Seventh Solitude: Man's Isolation in Kierkegaard, Dostoyevsky, and Nietzsche* (Baltimore: Johns Hopkins Univ. Press, 1965), 117–18.

69. Augustine, *Confessions* (see preface, n. 2), 224.

70. Ibid., 236.

71. Tyrrell, *Autobiography* 2:186 (letter of 27 July 1902).

72. Tyrrell, *Versions and Perversions of Heine and Others* (London: Elkin Matthews, 1909), 43. Aware of the relationship between these poems and translations and his own preoccupations, Tyrrell makes a point of saying that the "translations, so-called, are not my spiritual autobiography" (8).

73. Tyrrell, *Autobiography*, 11. Like Moore, Yeats, White, Butler, and Ford, Tyrrell repeatedly emphasizes the importance of the apparently trivial: "It is not the big, but the little things, that are instructive—not the exotics of the hothouse, but the weeds and nettles of the wayside" (2). Perhaps he has Wordsworth's similar understanding in mind, for Wordsworth, he says, "gave us eyes" ("Stray Remarks," in *Tyrrell's Letters*, 299).
74. Tyrrell, *Autobiography* 2:2 (letter of 3 September 1900).
75. See, e.g., Daniel B. Shea, *Spiritual Autobiography in Early America* (Princeton: Princeton Univ. Press, 1968), and Delaney, *British Autobiography*.
Epigraph: Tyrrell, *Oil and Wine*, 168.
76. Ibid. See H. Stuart Hughes, *Consciousness and Society: The Reorientation of European Thought, 1890–1930* (New York: Knopf, 1958) and Loren Eiseley, *Darwin's Century: Evolution and the Men Who Discovered It* (New York: Doubleday, 1958).
77. Tyrrell, *Lex credendi: A Sequel to Lex orandi* (London: Longmans, 1906), 183.
78. Tyrrell, "Christ or Jesus," *Hibbert Journal* 11 (1909); quoted in Chapman, "The Thought of George Tyrrell," 159.
79. Tyrrell, *Autobiography* 2:208 (letter of 15 February 1901).
80. Tyrrell, *Letters from a Modernist*, 24 (letter of 25 January 1900). See also Tyrrell's introduction to Henri Bremond, *The Mystery of Newman*, trans. H. C. Conance (London: Williams & Norgate, 1907), x–xiii.
81. Tyrrell, *Autobiography*, 2:205 (letter of 15 February 1901).
82. Ibid., 1:ix.
83. Ibid., 2:40 (letter of 6 February 1901).
84. John Robinson, *In Extremity: A Study of Gerard Manley Hopkins* (Cambridge: Cambridge Univ. Press, 1978).
85. Like Butler, Gosse, and Moore, Tyrrell admired Schopenhauer, "who so nearly says just what I want, and yet tumbles [as does Tyrrell himself] into paradox and pessimism" *Tyrrell's Letters*, 236–37 (letter of 7 October 1904).
86. Tyrrell, *Scylla and Charybdis*, 274.

3 Strange Metamorphoses

Epigraph: George Bernard Shaw, Preface to *Major Barbara: Collected Plays*, vol. 3 (New York: Dodd Mead, 1971), 32.
1. *From Letters of English Authors . . . a Catalogue of an Exhibition in the Princeton Library* (1960); quoted in Daniel F. Howard, Introduction to Samuel Butler, *Ernest Pontifex; or, The Way of All Flesh*, ed. Howard (London: Methuen, 1964), xv (letter of 2 August 1903).
2. Samuel Butler, *Luck, or Cunning?*, Shrewsbury Edition, ed. H. Festing-Jones and A. T. Bartholomew, 20 vols. (London: Jonathan Cape, 1924), 8:45.
3. Malcolm Muggeridge, *The Earnest Atheist: A Study of Samuel Butler* (London: Eyre & Spottiswoode, 1936). For all his reservations about Butler, Muggeridge feels that he "must be regarded as one of the most significant figures of the latter part of the last century" (vii).
4. Virginia Woolf, "Mr. Bennett and Mrs. Brown," in *Collected Essays* (New York: Harcourt Brace, 1967), 1:320. E. M. Forster, *Abinger Harvest* (New York: Harcourt Brace, 1936), 278. Forster agrees with Butler himself, that he

was the *"enfant terrible* . . . in art and literature," a rare if possibly overrated figure. "I am the *enfant terrible* of literature and science. If I cannot . . . get the literary and scientific big-wigs to give me a shilling, I can . . . heave bricks into the middle of them" (*Note-Books* [see chap. 2, n. 50], 182).

5. Maurice Merleau-Ponty, *Themes from the Lectures at the College de France, 1952–60*, trans. John O'Neill (Evanston, Ill.: Northwestern Univ. Press, 1970), 12–13. Jean-Paul Sartre says comparably, "You talk in your own language, but you write in a foreign one" (*Words* [see chap. 1, n. 59], 104).

6. Butler, *Luck, or Cunning?*, xvii.

7. Samuel Butler, *Life and Habit*, Shrewsbury Edition, ed. R. A. Streatfeild, 20 vols. (London: Jonathan Cape, 1923), 4:250.

8. *Letters Between Samuel Butler and Miss E. M. A. Savage*, ed. G. Keynes and B. Hill (London: Jonathan Cape, 1935), 188 (letter of July 1878).

9. Butler, *Life and Habit*, 41.

10. Kingsley Amis, Afterword, *Erewhon; or, Over the Range* (New York: New American Library, 1961), 247.

11. Butler, *Life and Habit*, 250.

12. Michel Foucault, "What Is an Author?" *Language, Counter-Memory, Practice: Selected Essays and Interviews*, ed. D. F. Bouchard, trans. D. F. Bouchard and S. Simon (Ithaca, N.Y.: Cornell Univ. Press, 1977), 130, 137; also Roland Barthes, "The Death of the Author," *Image—Music—Text*, trans. and ed. Stephen Heath (New York: Hill & Wang, 1979).

13. Foucault, "What Is an Author?", 116. He is quoting Beckett's *Stories and Texts for Nothing* (New York: Grove Press, 1967).

14. Henry Festing-Jones, *Memoir of Samuel Butler, Author of* Erewhon *(1835–1902)*, 2 vols. (London: Macmillan, 1919), 1:174.

Epigraph: Butler, *Luck, or Cunning?*, 1.

15. Like George Moore (and to some extent like D. H. Lawrence), he wanted to be a painter first but found his talents in writing. His interest in formal aspects of art continued, as *Ex Voto* (1888) suggests.

16. For biographical information, see Philip Henderson, *Samuel Butler: The Incarnate Bachelor* (Bloomington: Indiana Univ. Press, 1954), and Festing-Jones, *Samuel Butler*.

17. *The Note-Books of Samuel Butler* (see chap. 2, n. 50), 66 (also quoted in *Life and Habit*, xiv).

18. C. E. M. Joad, *Samuel Butler*, Roadmaker Series (London: Leonard Parsons, 1924). Joad has high praise for Butler and says that Butler's "inspired audacity" was responsible for later theories of "creative evolution" (18). For a defense of Butler's influence on later thinkers, see Clara G. Stillman, *Samuel Butler* (New York: Viking, 1932), who says that several distinguished scientists have attended to his ideas (161–63). By and large, however, later readers have upheld the original verdict on his scientific contributions. The most spirited defense of Butler's ideas and of Butler in general is Thomas L. Jeffers, *Samuel Butler Revisited* (University Park: Pennsylvania State Univ. Press, 1981).

19. Butler, *Life and Habit*, 1 and passim. Butler writes: "I wish most distinctly to disclaim for these pages the smallest pretension to scientific value."

20. On Ebbinghaus's importance, see, e.g., Roberta Klatzky, *Human Memory: Structures and Processes* (San Francisco: W. H. Freeman, 1975), 5–7.

21. See Alexander Bain's *Mind and Body: The Theories of Their Relation* (London: Henry King, 1873). Bain sounds like Butler and Radcliffe when he says, "We have no power of Memory in radical separation from the power of Reason or the power of Imagination" (82). Herbert Spencer, *Principles of Psychology* (London: Longman, Brown, Green, 1855). For general backgrounds, see Robert Thomson, *The Pelican History of Psychology* (Baltimore, Penguin, 1968); George S. Brett's early study, *A History of Psychology*, 3 vols. (London: George Allen, 1912); and James Cardno, "Victorian Psychology: A Biographical Approach," *Journal of the History of British Psychology* 1, no. 1 (January 1965): 165–77.
22. Butler, *Luck, or Cunning?*, 100.
23. Samuel Butler, *Unconscious Memory: A Comparison Between the Theory of Dr. Ewald Hering and the "Philosophy of the Unconscious" of Dr. Eduard von Hartmann*, Shrewsbury Edition, 20 vols. (London: Jonathan Cape, 1924), 6:78. Like Sigmund Freud, Butler had no patience with von Hartmann's theories of the unconscious: "Professor Hartmann," he says, "has not got a meaning" (6:137).
24. Frederic W. H. Myers, *Science and a Future Life* (London: Macmillan, 1893), 37. See also Myers's autobiographical study, the tiny *Fragments of Inner Life* (privately printed, 1893; London: Society for Psychical Research, 1961), with its hope for reunited love and its sad retrospects. "The 'Passion of the Past' must needs wear away sooner or later into an unsatisfied pain" (10).
25. Myers, *Science and a Future Life*, 40. Myers speaks extensively not only about Darwin but also about modern psychology, and refers to the "stream of consciousness" (23).
26. Thomas Laycock, "A Chapter on Some Organic Laws of Personal and Ancestral Memory," *The Journal of Mental Science* 21, no. 94 (July 1875): 155–56.
27. See Basil Willey, *Darwin and Butler: Two Versions of Evolution* (New York: Harcourt Brace, 1960), and Gertrude Himmelfarb, *Darwin and the Darwinian Revolution* (New York: Norton, 1968), esp. 436–37. Himmelfarb calls Butler's attacks "venomous."
28. See *Autobiography of Charles Darwin* (see chap. 1, n. 19). Barlow has an informative and sympathetic appendix on "The Darwin-Butler Controversy," 167–219.
29. Phyllis Greenacre, *The Quest for the Father: A Study of the Darwin-Butler Controversy* (New York: Int. Universities Press, 1963). A more subtle if more cryptic psychoanalytic approach might be that of Jacques Lacan, in *The Four Fundamental Concepts of Psychoanalysis*, trans. Jacques-Allain Miller (New York: Norton, 1981). While not mentioning Butler, Lacan speaks of various projections of fathers and various stages of development pertinent for Butler's struggle. See, e.g., 282.
30. On Kelvin and Darwin, see Loren Eiseley, *Darwin's Century* (see chap. 2, n. 76). I refer to Kelvin's entropic theories in the chapter on George Moore.
31. Butler, *Life and Habit*, 111–12. P. N. Furbank cites this as a typical bit of Butler's hyperbole, in a useful discussion of Butler's paradoxical theories (*Samuel Butler, 1835–1902* [1948], Hamden, Conn.: Archon, 1971, 56).
32. Butler, *Life and Habit*, 18.
33. Samuel Butler, *Erewhon: or, Over the Range*, Shrewsbury Edition, 20 vols. (London: Jonathan Cape, 1923), 2:148.

34. Avrom Fleishman discusses Butler and myth in relation to "the creation of selfhood" in "Personal Myth" (see chap. 1, n. 15), 215–35. Fleishman's *Figures of Autobiography: The Language of Self-Writing in Victorian and Modern England* (Berkeley and Los Angeles: Univ. of California Press, 1983) is a major study.
35. Butler, *Life and Habit*, 244.
36. Ibid., ix.
37. Butler, *Luck, or Cunning?*, 120. U. C. Knoepflmacher dismisses *Luck, or Cunning?* as "the feeblest" of Butler's scientific works, but it is in several respects more complex and exploratory than the earlier works (*Religious Humanism and the Victorian Novel: George Eliot, Walter Pater, and Samuel Butler*, Princeton: Princeton Univ. Press, 1965, 226). I am indebted to Knoepflmacher's thorough study.
38. Butler, *Luck, or Cunning?*, 125.
39. Ibid., 23.
40. "The Deadlock in Darwinism," *Essays on Art, Life, and Science*, [1908] ed. R. A. Streatfeild (Port Washington, N.Y.: Kennicat, 1970), 254.
41. Butler, *Luck, or Cunning?*, 61.
42. Ibid., 79.
43. Claude T. Bissell, "A Study of *The Way of All Flesh*," in *Nineteenth-Century Studies*, ed. Herbert Davis, William DeVane, and R. C. Bald (Ithaca, N.Y.: Cornell Univ. Press, 1940), 288. Bissell cites two letters of Bergson published by Floris de Lattre, in the *Revue Angloamericain* 13 (1935–36): 386–405, to rebut Joad and others who claim Butler as a forerunner of Bergson.
44. Stephen Jay Gould, *Ever since Darwin: Reflections in Natural History* (New York: Norton, 1977).
45. Beatrice Edgell, *Theories of Memory* (Oxford: Clarendon, 1924), 114–32. See also Joad, *Samuel Butler*.
46. Bergson, *Matter and Memory* (see chap. 1, n. 40), xii.
47. Henri Bergson, *Creative Evolution*, trans. Arthur Mitchell (New York: Holt, 1911), 171.
Epigraph: Walter Benjamin, *Illuminations*, ed. and intro. Hannah Arendt, trans. Harry Zohn (New York: Schocken, 1969), 203.
48. Ibid., 202.
49. Butler, *Luck, or Cunning?*, 234–35.
50. Benjamin, *Illuminations*, 201.
51. Butler, *Luck, or Cunning?*, 92.
52. R. A. Streatfeild, Note to first ed., *The Way of All Flesh*, Shrewsbury Edition, 20 vols. (London: Jonathan Cape, 1925), 17:xxxiii.
53. Bissell, "A Study of *The Way of All Flesh*," 278.
54. Ibid., 281.
55. Butler, *Letters*, 293: "I think you like my novel better than I do. I am more doubtful about it in reality than about any book that I have written before. . . . I have no doubt about *The Fair Haven, Life and Habit*, and *Alps and Sanctuaries* being very good" (letter of 19 July 1883).
56. Butler, *The Way of All Flesh*, 265.
57. Jerome H. Buckley, *Season of Youth: The Bildungsroman from Dickens to Golding* (Cambridge: Harvard Univ. Press, 1974), 121. On some of the paradoxes

of the applied theories, see Fleishman, whose phrase I have borrowed ("Personal Myth" [see chap. 1, n. 15], 216).
58. Knoepflmacher, *Religious Humanism*, 226.
59. Yeats, *Autobiography* (see chap. 1, n. 3), 188.
60. *Letters of William Butler Yeats,* ed. Allan Wade (London: Macmillan, 1955), 922 (letter of 4 January 1939).
61. Butler, *Luck, or Cunning?*, 7.
62. Butler, *Note-Books*, 157.
63. Francis Hart, "Notes For an Anatomy of Modern Autobiography," *New Literary History* 1 (1970): 500.
64. See, e.g., Lejeune, "Autobiographical Contract" (see chap. 2, n. 14).
65. Butler, *The Way of All Flesh*, 55–56. See also *Essays on Life, Art and Sciences.* "People stamp themselves on their work; if they have not done so they are naught" (83).
66. Festing-Jones, *Memoir* 1:184.
67. Butler, "Our Subordinate Personalities," in *Life and Habit,* 100. "Every individual," he says, "is a compound creature." In "Ulysses to Penelope: Victorian Approaches to Autobiography," (in Landow, ed., *Approaches* [see chap. 1, n. 15], 24), Elizabeth Helsinger speaks of the division of self "into multiple characters" in Butler and other writers, the result of which is "more complex and less introspective identities."
68. Butler, *Life and Habit,* 76.
69. Ruskin, *Praeterita,* in *Works of Ruskin* (see chap. 1, n. 33) 35:11.
70. I refer to Yeats's distinction between oratory and poetry in the *Autobiography* (see chap. 1, n. 3), esp. 65.
71. Arthur Schopenhauer, *The World as Will and Representation,* trans. E. F. J. Payne, 2 vols. (New York: Dover, 1969), 2:385. John R. Reed is right to argue a connection between Butler and Schopenhauer, although as he points out memory itself for Schopenhauer is a conscious process. See Reed, *Victorian Conventions* (Athens: Ohio Press, 1975), 419. Reed's entire chapter on "Memory" is informative. See the discussion of Schopenhauer and Gosse below.
72. Butler, *Life and Habit,* 122.
73. Ibid., 43.
74. William Marshall, "The Dual Function of Edward Overton," *Texas Studies in Literature and Language* 4 (Winter 1963): 583–80; U. C. Knoepflmacher, "Ishmael or Anti-Hero? The Division of Self," *English Fiction in Transition* 4, no. 3 (1961): 28–35.
75. Knoepflmacher, *Religious Humanism*, 259.
76. See Buckley, *Season of Youth,* 137, who says that Butler maintains an ironic perspective in Overton, until Ernest reaches Overton's maturity.
77. Muggeridge, *The Earnest Atheist,* 77–78.
78. Butler, *Note-Books,* 58. See Genette, p. 29 above.
79. See, e.g., Muggeridge, *The Earnest Atheist,* ix.
80. Theodore Dreiser, Introduction to Samuel Butler, *The Way of All Flesh* (New York: Heritage, 1936), xxix.

4 The Consciousness of Self

Epigraph: Friedrich Schiller, *On the Aesthetic Education of Man: In a Series of Letters,* ed. and trans. E. M. Wilkinson and L. A. Willoughby (Oxford: Clarendon, 1967), 81. Schiller's description of an individual "suspended" and "swept along by the flux of time" (79), not to mention "dissociated" from himself, anticipates Gosse's preoccupations as well as his tropes.

1. My information about Gosse's life comes mainly from Ann Thwaite's recent comprehensive biography, *Edmund Gosse: A Literary Landscape, 1849–1928* (Chicago: Univ. of Chicago Press, 1984); and Evan Charteris, *The Life and Letters of Sir Edmund Gosse* (New York: Harper, 1931). I wrote this chapter before the publication of Linda Peterson's fine study, *Victorian Autobiography: The Tradition of Self-Interpretation* (New Haven: Yale Univ. Press, 1986). See also John Gross, *The Rise and Fall of the Man of Letters* (New York: Macmillan, 1970), esp. 168–73.

Epigraph: Schopenhauer, *World as Will* (see chap. 3, n. 71), 1:248. For a review of works about Schopenhauer's influence on literary figures, see Bryan Magee, *The Philosophy of Schopenhauer* (Oxford: Clarendon, 1983). Magee does not mention Gosse, Butler, Moore or the other writers I discuss who knew Schopenhauer.

2. Gosse, *Father and Son* (see chap. 1, n. 16), title page: "Faith, like love, will not be forced."
3. Schopenhauer, *World as Will* 1:364.
4. My reference is to Gillian Beer's *Darwin Plots: Evolutionary Narrative in Darwin, George Eliot, and Nineteenth-Century Fiction* (London: Routledge & Kegan Paul, 1983).
5. By 1906, Proust had written several hundred pages of *Swann's Way.* See Krutch, Introduction to Proust, *The Remembrance of Things Past* (see chap. 1, n. 18), viii.
6. Edmund Gosse, "Samuel Butler," *Aspects and Impressions* (New York: C. Scribner, 1922), 57.
7. I refer to William R. Siebenshuh's *Fictional Techniques and Factual Works* (Athens: Univ. of Georgia Press, 1983), with its chapter on *Father and Son.*
8. Edmund Gosse, *The Life of Philip Henry Gosse* (London: Kegan Paul, 1890), 237. On Gosse and "the issue of scholarly truth," see, e.g., Richard D. Altick, *The Scholar Adventurers* (New York: Macmillan, 1950), 58–59.
9. Edmund Gosse, *Questions at Issue* (London: Heinemann, 1893), 25. Gosse's comment that "the interior life of the soul . . . is a very much less interesting study to an ordinary healthy person than the exterior" suggests how far he stood in most respects from the early modernist writers of his time, but also how far from his own values as stated in the Butler review.
10. See the chapter on Rousseau in *Aspects and Impressions.*
11. After Gosse had published *From Shakespeare to Pope* (1885), Churton Collins lambasted him for inaccuracies and carelessness; Gosse's reputation took years to repair. See Phyllis Grosskurth's essay, "Churton Collins: Scourge of the Late Victorians," *University of Toronto Quarterly* 34 (April 1965): 254–68.
12. Virginia Woolf, "Edmund Gosse," *Collected Essays,* (New York: Harcourt Brace, 1967), 4:84. Woolf considers even *Father and Son* to be superficial and

timid. Cf. Malcolm Muggeridge's comment on Butler, *The Earnest Atheist* (see chap. 3, n. 3): "When anything threatened to happen, he fled, then cautiously returned to see if the danger had passed" (78).
13. Gosse, *Father and Son* (see chap. 1, n. 16), unnumbered preface.
14. In a private letter, Gosse said that his book was "designed to make men face the fact that the old faith is now impossible" (quoted in Charteris, *Life and Letters*, 311).
15. Butler, *Erewhon* (see chap. 3, n. 33), 1.
16. See again Schopenhauer's comment that "the life of every individual . . . is really always a tragedy; but gone through in detail it has the character of a comedy" (1:322; see chap. 3, n. 71).
17. Olney, *Metaphors of Self* (see preface, n. 8).
18. Sartre, *Words* (see chap. 1, n. 59). Like Gosse, Sartre also has problems with the value of literature, which he seems to denigrate or to overpraise. See Susan Sontag's discussion of this issue in her introduction to *A Barthes Reader* (New York: Hill & Wang, 1982).
19. Edmund Gosse, *The Unequal Yoke*, ed. James D. Woolf (New York: Scholars' Facsimiles, 1975).
20. In spite of this hyperbole, James Woolf has written well about Gosse. See *Sir Edmund Gosse* (New York: Twayne, 1972) and Woolf's several essays on *Father and Son*.
21. Gosse, *The Unequal Yoke*, 609.
22. Ibid., 9.
Epigraph: White, *Autobiography of Mark Rutherford* (see chap. 1, n. 2), 60–61.
23. In his introduction to *Father and Son* (Baltimore: Penguin, 1983), x, Peter Abbs speaks of Gosse's "scientific" weighing of materials. It makes much more sense to listen to his echoes of his parents' language along with the metaphors of Schopenhauer. If scientific is intended to mean only "objective," that too would be misleading.
24. Gosse had high praise for Gibbon, as his somewhat pompous language in *A History of Eighteenth-Century Literature (1660–1780)* (London: Macmillan, 1889) suggests: "No man who knows the profession of letters, or regards with respect the higher and more enlightened forms of scholarship, will even think without admiration of the noble genius of Gibbon" (351). By the time he wrote *Father and Son*, Gosse was no doubt aware of the 1896 publication of Gibbon's complete *Memoirs* from early drafts.
25. Perhaps Gosse was playing with Schopenhauer's claim that "the character or will is inherited from the father; the intellect from the mother" (2:517; see chap. 3, n. 71).
26. Ruskin, *Praeterita* (see chap. 3, n. 69), 11. On *Praeterita*, see Jay Fellows, *The Failing Distance: The Autobiographical Impulse of John Ruskin* (Baltimore: Johns Hopkins Univ. Press, 1975).
27. Cf. the dark rooms and the "gloom" in Ford Madox Ford's *Ancient Lights* (see chap. 1, n. 11), which describes a Roman Catholic (and Pre-Raphaelite) boyhood in Bloomsbury.
28. Walter Pater, *Marius the Epicurean: His Sensations and Ideas* (New York: Modern Library, n.d.), 370. For a discussion of *Marius* as "autobiographical allegory," perhaps analogous to that of Gosse, see Michael Ryan, "Narcissus

Autobiographer: *Marius the Epicurean,*" *ELH* 43, no. 2 (Summer 1976): 184–208. Ryan's theoretical bases come from Lacan and Gayatra C. Spivak.

29. I had written this section in ignorance of the fine essay by Vivian Folkenflik and Robert Folkenflik, "Words and Language in *Father and Son,*" *Biography* 2, no. 2 (Spring 1979), which anticipated some of my discussion.

30. Joyce had already written his college essay, "Portrait of the Artist," the first draft of *Stephen Hero/Portrait of the Artist* in 1904. See Richard Ellmann, *James Joyce,* new and rev. ed. (New York: Oxford Univ. Press, 1982), 144–49.

31. Gosse, *Life of Philip Henry Gosse,* 262.

32. Carlyle, Ruskin, and Pater play a role in the autobiographical works of nearly all the subjects of this study. See especially chapters 2 and 7.

Epigraph: Gosse, *Father and Son* (see chap. 1, n. 16), 84.

33. See Lewes's *Sea-side Studies at Ilfracombe, Tenby and the Scilly Isles* (Edinburgh: W. Blackwood, 1858). Philip Gosse also wrote a book on *Tenby: A Seaside Holiday* (London: J. Van Voorst, 1856).

34. Philip Henry Gosse, *Omphalos: An Attempt to Untie the Geological Knot* (London: J. Van Voorst, 1857).

35. Philip Henry Gosse, *Sacred Streams: The Ancient and Modern History of the Rivers of the Bible* (London: C. Cox, 1850), 1.

36. Ibid., 19.

37. That direction remains undefined. We have no real clue, as Jerome Buckley says, to "the quality of inner life" that the narrator will achieve (*Season of Youth* [see chap. 3, n. 57], 118).

38. See E. Pearlman's "Father and Mother in *Father and Son,*" *Victorian Newsletter* 55 (Spring 1979): 17–23.

39. See *Decline and Fall of the Roman Empire,* ed. J. B. Bury, 7 vols. (London: Methuen, 1909), 1:84. Actually, several writers have made similar remarks, including Voltaire in *L'Ingénu.*

40. Thwaite, *Edmund Gosse,* 23, 26, and passim. Thwaite cites Gosse's childhood diary, which describes a crowded social life and mentions several early visits to the seashore.

Epigraph: The Correspondence of André Gide and Edmund Gosse, 1904–1928, ed. and trans. Linette F. Brugmans (London: Peter Owen, 1959), 187 (letter of 30 December 1926). The first part of Gide's own *If It Die: An Autobiography,* trans. Dorothy Bussy (New York: Random House, 1935), was written in 1916. Although it shares with Gosse's book an emphasis on childhood and youth, a preoccupation with "truth" and "fiction," and an acknowledged indebtedness to Schopenhauer, Gide's book is a much more confessional work, dealing with a wider range of emotions and personal problems. *If It Die* might be to *Father and Son* what Gosse's book was to *The Way of All Flesh.*

41. Serge Aksakoff, *A Russian Schoolboy,* trans. J. D. Duff (London: Edward Arnold, 1917), 7.

42. Charlotte Brontë, *Jane Eyre,* ed. Richard J. Dunn (New York: Norton, 1971), 72. On Brontë and autobiographical narrative, see, e.g., Janice Carlyle, "The Face in the Mirror: *Villete* and the Conventions of Autobiography," *English Literary History* 46, no. 2 (Summer 1979): 262–89.

43. J. A. Symonds, *The Memoirs of John Addington Symonds,* ed. and intro. Phyllis Grosskurth (New York: Random House, 1984).

44. Gosse does mention "some flash of sex" (101) associated with other people. His own physical desires remain unaddressed. Again a comparison with Gide would be apt.
45. Charles J. Burkhart, "George Moore and *Father and Son*," *Nineteenth-Century Fiction* 15 (June 1960): 71–77. Burkhart makes clear that while Moore may have encouraged Gosse, he had no hand in the writing of the book. See Moore's *Avowals* [1919] for its "conversations" between Gosse and Moore. Their friendship was not without frictions.

5   Contemplations of Time

Epigraph: William Butler Yeats, in *The Rose* [1893], *Collected Poems* (New York: Macmillan, 1951), 46.
1. See Joseph Hone, *The Life of George Moore* (New York: Macmillan, 1936).

Epigraph: Virginia Woolf, "George Moore," in *The Death of the Moth* (New York: Harcourt, Brace, 1942), 156–57.
2. See John Halperin, *Gissing: A Life in Books* (New York: Oxford Univ. Press, 1982), 101; and *The Letters of George Gissing to Eduard Bertz, 1887–1903*, ed. A. C. Young (New Brunswick, N.J.: Rutgers Univ. Press, 1961), 19–21, and passim.
3. Stephen Marcus, *The Other Victorians* (New York: Basic Books, 1966); *My Secret Life* (New York: Grove, 1966).
4. Moore, *Confessions of a Young Man* (see chap. 1, n. 68), 185. This is a fine, variorum edition. Moore is circumspect about sexuality in *Confessions,* less so in the later *Memoirs of My Dead Life,* although even in the later book he is seldom explicit. In the 1906 American edition of *Memoirs,* he offers to his American readers an "Apologia Pro Scriptis Meis," in which he seems to defend a book he might have written: a modern confession questioning "one immutable standard of conduct" while equating genius with the sexual impulse (*Memoirs of My Dead Life,* New York: Appleton, 1906, xi). For bibliographical information about sexuality and censorship in late Victorian England, see John Maynard's "The Worlds of Victorian Sexuality," in *Sexuality and Victorian Literature,* ed. Don Richard Cox, Tennessee Studies in Literature, vol. 27 (Knoxville: Univ. of Tennessee, 1984), 251–65.
5. In chapter 10 of *Confessions,* Moore writes: "'Marius the Epicurean' was more to me than a mere emotional influence, . . . for this book was the first in English prose I had come across that procured for me any genuine pleasure in the language itself. . . . 'Marius' was the stepping-stone that carried me across the channel into the genius of my own tongue" (166). See Robert P. Sechler, *George Moore: "A Disciple of Walter Pater"* (Philadelphia: Univ. of Pennsylvania Press, 1931). Arthur Symons said that all of Pater's writing was "a confession" (*Symbolist Movement* [see chap. 1, n. 39], xiii).
6. Walter Pater, *The Renaissance: Studies in Art and Poetry* (London: Macmillan, 1888), 248–49.
7. Quoted by Moore in the 1917 American edition, *Confessions* (see chap. 1, n. 68), 42–43.
8. Thomas De Quincey, *Autobiography from 1785 to 1803* (London: A. C. Black, 1896), 1:123. Moore says that he moved from Pater to De Quincey, another

"Latin in manner and in temper of mind [though] he was truly English" (166).
9. Susan Dick, Introduction to Moore, *Confessions* (see chap. 1, n. 68), 19.
10. Krutch, Introduction to Proust, *Remembrance of Things Past* (see chap. 1, n. 18), viii.
11. George Moore, *Evelyn Innes* (London: T. Fisher Unwin, 1898), 178.
12. Patrick Kavanagh, *Self-Portrait* (Dolman: Dublin, 1964), 8.
13. Trilling, *Sincerity and Authenticity* (see chap. 1, n. 61), 58.
14. Preface to U.S. ed., 1927, *Confessions*: "I knew nothing of Jean-Jacques Rousseau. It is barely credible that I could have lived into early manhood without having heard of him, but *The Confessions of a Young Man* testifies that I never read him; a page of Jean-Jacques would have made the book . . . an impossibility" (42).

Epigraph: Oscar Wilde, *The Picture of Dorian Gray: Works of Oscar Wilde,* ed. Robert Ross (London: Dawsons, 1969), 232.

15. *Memoirs of My Dead Life* (see chap. 1, n. 56), 50. Twenty years was a favorite distance for Moore. In *Reminiscences of the Impressionist Painters,* Tower Press Booklets (Dublin: Maunsel, 1906), he brushes off "those who have not chosen memory for their religion," as he has, while looking back once again to "twenty years ago" (i).
16. Paul Alkon, *Defoe and Fictional Time* (Athens: Univ. of Georgia Press, 1979), 9ff.; Wolfgang Iser, *The Implied Reader* (Baltimore: Johns Hopkins Univ. Press, 1974).
17. See, e.g., *The Renaissance,* 196.
18. Edward Said, "Molestation and Authority," in *Aspects of Narrative,* Selected Papers from the English Institute, ed. J. Hillis Miller (New York: Columbia Univ. Press, 1971), 48.
19. For a discussion of the biographical backgrounds of *Memoirs of My Dead Life* and the identities of the women he describes, see Rupert Hart-Davis, ed., *George Moore: Letters to Lady Cunard, 1895–1933* (London: Rupert Hart-Davis, 1957). Hart-Davis offers a clear description of the various editions as well as backgrounds of *Memoirs.*
20. Wilde, *Picture of Dorian Gray,* 289.
21. Steiner, *After Babel* (see preface, n. 1), 132. See also Olney, *Autobiography* (preface, n. 8): "If . . . *bios* is taken as the vital principle . . . then there is nothing but 'is': there is no 'was' in the picture" (240).

Epigraph: "The Sensitive-Plant," *Shelley's Poetry and Prose,* ed. Donald H. Reiman and Sharon B. Powers (New York: Norton, 1977), 219.

22. Symons, *Symbolist Movement* (see chap. 1, n. 39), 5 and passim.
23. Ibid., 94.
24. See Hart-Davis, *George Moore,* 11.
25. George Moore, *Hail and Farewell,* Ebury Edition, 3 vols. (London: Heinemann, 1925), 3:213.
26. Moore wrote to an admirer of *The Untilled Field*: "You will like it better when you take it up six months hence. It is a dry book and does not claim the affections at once." Quoted in Richard Allen Cave, "Turgenev and Moore: *A Sportsman's Sketches* and *The Untilled Field*," in Robert Welch, ed., *The Way Back: George Moore's* Untilled Field *and* The Lark (Totowa, N.J.: Barnes & Noble, 1982), 45.

27. One of the best commentaries on Moore and Ireland is Kevin P. Reilly's "Irish Literary Autobiography: The Goddess that Poets Dream Of," *Eire-Ireland: A Journal of Irish Studies* 16, no. 3 (Fall 1981): 57–80.
Epigraph: Moore, *Hail and Farewell* 3:210.
28. James Sully, *Illusions: A Psychological Study,* International Scientific Series 34 (New York: Appleton, 1881), 231–32.
29. Sully, "Reproductive Imagination (Memory)," *Outlines of Psychology* (see chap. 1, n. 38), 22–23. Sully, however, must have drawn the phrase from Jean-Paul Richter. See Gaston Bachelard, *The Poetics of Space,* trans. Maria Jolas, ed. Etienne Gilson (New York: Orion, 1964), who quotes Richter: "Reproductive imagination is the prose of productive imagination" (xxxi).
30. Sully, *Illusions,* 231.
31. See, e.g., Rudolf Carnap, *Two Essays on Entropy,* ed. and intro. Abner Shimony (Berkeley and Los Angeles: Univ. of California Press, 1977); also Jeremy Rifkin's popular and polemical *Entropy: A New World View* (New York: Viking, 1980), which reifies the "entropy law" but tests its implications.
32. Ilya Prigogine, "Order Through Fluctuation: Self-Organization and Social System," in E. Jantsch and C. H. Waddington, eds., *Evolution and Consciousness* (Reading, Mass.: Addison-Wesley, 1976); Rudolf Arnheim's *Entropy and Art: An Essay on Disorder and Order* (Berkeley and Los Angeles: Univ. of California Press, 1971) is an important study of the Second Law for various philosophical and aesthetic areas. See also *The Concept of Order,* ed. Paul G. Kuntz (Seattle: Univ. of Washington Press, 1968). In *Time: Fourth Dimension of the World,* trans. B. Montgomery and D. Montgomery (New York: Harcourt, Brace, and World, 1968): Robert Wallis says, "*Man's genius* lies in the fact that he is essentially a reducer of entropy, a creator of order [brought about] through *the exercise of his internal temporal function*" (241).
33. Unamuno, *Tragic Sense of Life* (see chap. 1, n. 53), 8–9.
34. Moore, *Hail and Farewell* 3:210.
35. Ford Madox Ford, *It Was the Nightingale* (London: Heinemann, 1934), 18–19.
36. H. G. Wells, *Experiment in Autobiography: Discoveries and Conclusions of a Very Ordinary Brain (since 1866)* (New York: Macmillan, 1934), 526.

6   The End of an Epoch

Epigraph: Pascal, *Design and Truth* (see chap. 1, n. 60), 112.
1. For biographical information I have drawn on Arthur Mizener, *The Saddest Story: A Biography of Ford Madox Ford* (New York: World, 1971), and on Frank MacShane, *The Life and Work of Ford Madox Ford* (New York: Horizon, 1965). I had already written this chapter when Max Saunders' essay, "A Life of Writing: Ford Madox Ford's Dispersed Autobiographies" appeared in the special Ford issue of *Antaeus* 56 (Spring 1986): 47–69.
2. Ezra Pound, quoted in Mizener, *The Saddest Story,* 207.
3. Ruskin, *Praeterita* (see chap. 3, n. 69), 11.
Epigraph: Wells, *Experiment in Autobiography* (see chap. 5, n. 37), 526. Wells himself came to be interested in the problem of shifting selves, as his *Experiment in Autobiography* suggests. In the same year Ford published *Ancient Lights,* Wells published "The Door in the Wall," with its examination of obsessive

reminiscence (*The Door in the Wall and Other Stories*, London: G. Richards, 1911).
4. The phrase originates with Mizener, *The Saddest Story*, xxi.
5. Ford Madox Ford, *Return to Yesterday: Reminiscences, 1894–1914* (London: Victor Gollancz, 1931), 174. Ford says, "I supppose that *The Way of All Flesh* and *The Playboy of the Western World* are the two great milestones on the road of purely English [sic] letters between *Gulliver's Travels* and Joyce's *Ulysses*" (182).
6. Hueffer [Ford], *Ancient Lights* (see chap. 1, n. 11), viii.
7. Pound, "Ford Madox Ford," in R. A. Cassell, ed., *Ford Madox Ford: Modern Judgements* (London: Macmillan, 1972), 34–35; Pound says that Ford "took in his time more punishment of one sort or another than I have seen meted out to anyone else" (33). Ernest Hemingway, *A Moveable Feast* (New York: Bantam, 1965), 83–88.
8. Yeats, *Autobiography* (see chap. 1, n. 3), 87–88, 188–93; William Rothenstein, *Men and Memories: Recollections, 1872–1938* (London: Chatto & Windus, 1978), 51–53, 81–82.
9. Ford Madox Ford, *Mightier than the Sword: Memoirs and Criticisms* (London: Allen & Unwin, 1938), 192–93.
10. Quoted by Michael Killigrew, in his composite edition of Ford's autobiographical writings, *Your Mirror to My Times: The Selected Autobiographies and Impressions of Ford Maddox Ford,* ed. and intro. Michael Killigrew (New York: Holt, Rinehart, & Winston, 1971), ix. Published by Penguin in the U.K. as *Memories and Impressions* (the U.S. title for *Ancient Lights*).
11. Cf. Freud, *Psychopathology* (see chap. 1, n. 9): "In these scenes [from early childhood] what one sees invariably includes oneself as a child, with a child's shape and clothes" (47).
12. Thomas C. Moser, *The Life in the Fiction of Ford Madox Ford* (Princeton: Princeton Univ. Press, 1980), 134.
13. Bachelard, *Poetics of Space* (see chap. 5, n. 30), xxxii.
14. In "The Child in the House," Pater speaks of "the law which makes material objects about them so large an element in children's lives" (*Miscellaneous Studies: A Series of Essays,* London: Macmillan, 1901, 173).
15. Ford, "Literary Portraits—XLV: Mme Yoi Pawlowska," *Outlook* (18 July 1914): 80. His review, perhaps anticipating the tragedy of the Great War, speculates whether the "pathological" condition of childhood is an appropriate topic for art.
16. Ford entertained strong feelings about editors and publishers, and his desire to deal fairly with other writers (as editor of the *English Review*), while it won few friends, bankrupted the magazine. He introduces more of such matters in the later memoirs, perhaps especially in *It Was the Nightingale* (see chap. 5, n. 36), which Ford calls his "autobiography." Dedicating his book to Eugene Pressly (husband of Katherine Ann Porter), he says: "They say every man has it in him to write one good book. This then may the one good book that you get dedicated to you. For the man's one good book will be his autobiography" (v–vi).
17. See Trilling, *Sincerity and Authenticity* (see chap. 1, n. 61), 29.

Epigraph: Vladimir Nabokov, *Speak, Memory: An Autobiography Revisited* (New

York: Putnam, 1966), 95. Sounding like Ford, Nabokov complains that his novel-writing robs him of memories.
18. See T. E. Hulme, *Speculations: Essays on Humanism and the Philosophy of Art* (London: Routledge & Kegan Paul, 1949); Wilhelm Worringer, *Form in Gothic*, trans., ed. and intro. Sir Herbert Read (New York: Schocken, 1967).
19. Moore, *Memoirs of My Dead Life* (see chap. 1, n. 56), 24.
20. Henry James, Preface, *The Portrait of a Lady*, ed. Leon Edel (New York: Riverside, 1963), 7. In this passage James speaks of "the house of fiction" and the importance of distinct "impressions," both of which bear directly on Ford's theories. See the later reference to Edith Wharton.
21. Carol Ohmann, *Ford Madox Ford: From Apprentice to Craftsman* (Middletown, Conn.: Wesleyan Univ. Pres, 1964), 65.
22. Ford Madox Ford, *No More Parades* (New York: A. and C. Boni, 1925), vi.
23. Ohmann, *Ford*, 65.
24. Ford, *The Good Soldier* (London: Bodley Head, 1967), 139. Mizener, *The Saddest Story*, xii, argues the relation between Ford's protagonist and Ford himself.
25. David Daiches, *The Novel and the Modern World* (Chicago: Pheonix Books, 1965), 4–5.
26. Virginia Woolf, "Mr. Bennett and Mrs. Brown" (see chap. 3, n. 4), 1:320.
27. Virginia Woolf, *Granite and Rainbow* (New York: Harcourt Brace, 1958), 154.
28. See my conclusion. I refer specifically to Roland Barthes, "The Death of the Author" and Michel Foucault, "What Is an Author?" (see chap. 3, n. 12).
29. Woolf, *Moments of Being* (see chap. 1, n. 45).
30. Malcolm Bradbury, "Virginia Woolf and Ford Madox Ford," in *Possibilities: Essays on the State of the Novel* (New York: Oxford Univ. Press, 1973), 135; see also "The Denuded Place: War and Form in *Parade's End*," in Holger Klein, ed., *The First World War in Modern Fiction* (London: Macmillan, 1976). Cf. Richard Cassell's introduction to *Ford Madox Ford*: "His subject is not strictly love and war at all," and Robert Green's *Ford Madox Ford and Politics* (Cambridge: Cambridge Univ. Press, 1981), with its "historical approach" (xi) to Ford's work.
31. Even a writer like Frank Harris could speak of Mnemosyne as mother of the muses and "the prototype of the artist" (*Frank Harris, His Life and Adventures: An Autobiography*, intro. Grant Richards, London: Richards, 1947, 15). See Gaston Bachelard's association of Mnemosyne and *anima*, the female projection of the human soul in R. C. Smith, *Gaston Bachelard* (Boston: Twayne, 1982), 118.
32. See MacShane, *Ford Madox Ford*, 160. Undoubtedly Ford also wanted to protect himself against the criticisms of people such as Jesse Conrad, who hated him, thinking him a parasite on a greater writer.
33. De Man, "Autobiography as De-Facement" (see chap. 2, n. 15), 70.
Epigraph: Ford, *Ancient Lights* (see chap. 1, n. 11), xvi.
34. Bachelard, *Poetics of Space* (see chap. 5, n. 30), 8.
35. Ibid., xxxii.
36. Hudson's writings ranked for both Conrad and Ford among the best of the age, and Hudson's strengths lay in the evocative qualities of his books, the best remembered of which is the later *Far Away and Long Ago*, his autobiographical study of 1918. On Conrad's own autobiographical impulse, see Edward Said,

Joseph Conrad and the Fiction of Autobiography (Cambridge: Harvard Univ. Press, 1966).
37. George Gissing, *The Private Papers of Henry Ryecroft,* ed. Paul Elmer More (New York: Modern Library, n.d.). See Fleishman's discussion of Gissing in "Personal Myth" (see chap. 1, n. 15). See also Jacob Korg, "The Main Source of *The Ryecroft Papers,"* and Jackson I. Cope, "Definition as Structure in *The Ryecroft Papers,"* in Pierre Coustillas, *Collected Articles on George Gissing* (New York: Frank Cass, 1968). Cope says that *"Ryecroft* is not autobiography, novel, or essay, but . . . [belongs on the] borderlands of genres" (153). Many autobiographical works of the time are, however, on the borderlands.
38. Moser, *Life in the Fiction,* 134–35.
39. Ford, *The Soul of London* (London: A. Rivers, 1905), 4. Mizener (*The Saddest Story,* 93–94) and Moser (*Life in the Fiction*) both discuss implications of Ford's agoraphobia.
40. Ford, *The Heart of the Country,* 14; quoted in Moser, *Life in the Fiction,* 139.
41. Edith Wharton, "The Fullness of Life" [1891], quoted by R. W. B. Lewis, *Edith Wharton: A Biography* (New York: Fromm, 1985), 65.
42. Bachelard, *Poetics of Space* (see chap. 5, n. 30), 224.
43. Tyrrell, *Autobiography* (see chap. 2, n. 2), 12.
44. Cf. Pater's "The Child in the House," with its insistence, not only on "impressions," but on the contrast between the "gloom of the town" and "inward lights."
45. Pound, "Ford Madox Ford," 34.

7 Fragments of a Great Confession

Epigraph: Gide, *If It Die* (see chap. 4, fifth epigraph), 234.
1. Among earlier studies of Yeats's *Autobiographies,* I am indebted to Joseph Ronsley, *Yeats's Autobiography: Life as Symbolic Pattern* (Cambridge: Harvard Univ. Press, 1968); Wolf Kunne and Marjorie Perloff, "'The Tradition of Myself': The Autobiographical Mode of Yeats," in the Yeats special edition of *Journal of Modern Literature* 4 (February 1975); John Pilling, *Autobiography and Imagination: Studies in Self-Scrutiny* (London: Routledge & Kegan Paul, 1981), and, above all, Shirley Neuman, *Some One Myth: Yeats's Autobiographical Prose,* New Yeats Papers 9 (Mountrath, Portlaoise, 1982). There are also important essays by Ian Fletcher and David Wright, and full-length studies by Wolf Kunne, *Konzeption und Stil von Yeats' "Autobiographies"* (Bonn: Bouvier, 1972); and Daniel T. O'Hara, *Tragic Knowledge: Yeats's Autobiography and Hermeneutics* (New York: Columbia Univ. Press, 1981).
2. Jean-Jacques Rousseau, *Reveries of a Solitary,* trans. and intro. J. G. Fletcher (New York: Burt Franklin, 1971). "Reverie" is of course a common word and an even commoner state of mind among English romantic writers, as Wordsworth, Coleridge, and Keats make clear. See the Shelley reference, n. 5, below.
3. Thomas Carlyle, *Heroes, Hero-Worship, and the Heroic in History* (Chicago: Belford, Clarke, n.d.), 177. Carlyle's "defacement" anticipates De Man's theory of autobiographical "de-facement" (see chap. 2, n. 15).
4. Denis Donoghue, Introduction to Yeats, *Memoirs: Autobiography—First Draft* (New York: Macmillan, 1972), 9. Donoghue's introduction makes helpful

observations about Yeats as autobiographer: "Written twenty-five or more years after the events described, the *Autobiography* required not merely an act of memory on Yeats's part, but an approach to the meanings of the lives it recited, not least his own" (9). Donoghue speaks of Yeats's "candour," remarkable from a poet who found it hard to be candid. But the suppression of the *Memoirs* in favor of less "candid" autobiographical studies is important.

5. Percy Bysshe Shelley, "On Life," quoted in "The Philosophy of Shelley's Poetry" *Essays and Introductions* (New York: Macmillan, 1961), 79.
6. Bachelard, *Poetics of Space* (see chap. 5, n. 30), 32. Bachelard defines poetic sensibility as a "complexity of mixed revery and memory" (26).

Epigraph: The *Autobiography of Johann W. von Goethe,* trans. John Oxenford, intro. Karl J. Weintraub, 2 vols. (Chicago: Univ. of Chicago Press, 1974), 1:305. In "Anima Mundi," in *Mythologies* (New York: Collier, 1959), Yeats speaks of "a great Memory passing on from generation to generation" and making itself known through images, "a fragment at a time" (346).

7. Theodor Reik, *Fragments of a Great Confession: A Psychoanalytic Autobiography* [1949] (Westport, Conn.: Greenwood, 1973), 3–4.
8. Harold Bloom, *Anxiety of Influence* (New York: Oxford Univ. Press, 1973), passim.
9. Yeats, "Autumn of the Body," in *Essays and Introductions,* 192.
10. *The Autobiography of William Butler Yeats* (see chap. 1, n. 3), 235. In *A Vision,* Yeats places himself at phase seventeen.
11. Yeats seems to refer to *Wilhelm Meister* rather than *Dichtung und Wahrheit.* For discussions of Yeats and Germanic writers, see Olney, *The Rhizome and the Flower* (see preface, n. 6); and Otto Bohlmann, *Yeats and Nietzsche: An Exploration of Major Nietzschean Echoes in the Writings of William Butler Yeats* (Totowa, N.J.: Barnes & Noble, 1982). I had written this chapter before seeing O'Hara's reference to *Dichtung und Wahrheit* at the beginning of *Tragic Knowledge* or Paul De Man's "Image and Emblem in Yeats," in *The Rhetoric of Romanticism* (New York: Columbia Univ. Press, 1984), 145–238, which begins with a brief comparison of Goethe and Yeats.
12. Goethe, *Autobiography* 1:2c.
13. Ibid.
14. Dilthey, *Meaning in History* (see preface, n. 7), 89.
15. Yeats, *Mythologies,* 351.
16. Goethe, *Autobiography* 1:304–5.
17. Genette, *Figures III* (see chap. 2, n. 15).
18. John Eglington [William Magee], *A Memoir of AE: George William Russell* (London: Macmillan, 1937), 111. AE himself published a collection of "articles and tales" in 1915 called *Imaginations and Reveries* (Dublin: Maunsel, 1915).
19. "Friends of My Youth," cited by Ronsley, *Yeats's Autobiography,* 2.
20. Mary Catherine Flannery, *Yeats and Magic: The Earlier Works* (New York: Barnes & Noble, 1978); George Mills Harper, ed., *Yeats and the Occult* (Toronto: Macmillan, 1985).
21. Yeats, "Magic," in *Essays and Introductions,* 28.
22. See, e.g., "Shelley's Poetry" and "Anima Mundi."
23. Yeats, *The Celtic Twilight: Men and Women, Dhouls and Fairies* (London: Lawrence and Bullen, 1893), x.

Epigraph: Yeats, *Reveries over Childhood and Youth* (see chap. 1, n. 3), 1.
24. See Daniel Harris, *Yeats: Coole Park* (Baltimore: Johns Hopkins Univ. Press, 1974), 88, on Yeats's "my mythification of his origins." Also Wolf Kunne's analysis of the beginning of *Reveries,* in *Konzeption und Stil,* 93–94.
25. See Ronsley, *Yeats's Autobiography,* 34: "Yeats begins *Reveries* as if he were writing about the beginning of the world." And given his view of collective memory, "that age-long memoried self" (372), in a sense he is.
26. In *The Rhizome and the Flower,* Olney speaks of Plato and Plotinus in relation to forgetting and remembering. See again *Enneads* 4, 3 (see chap. 1, n. 26), 287, and the notion of "happy forgetfulness."
27. See Martha Ronk Lifson, "The Myth of the Fall: A Description of Autobiography," *Genre* 12, no. 1 (Spring 1979): 45, who speaks of "the structure of the mythical fall [which] . . . pervades autobiographical works."
28. Earle, *Autobiographical Consciousness* (see chap. 1, n. 41), 71.
29. The tendency to opposing or even warring tendencies is common to many autobiographers besides Yeats. Stephen Shapiro points to autobiography's "art of juxtaposed perspectives," in "The Dark Continent of Literature," *Comparative Literature Studies* 5 (1968): 436. See esp. Gide's *If It Die* (see chap. 4, fifth epigraph): "I am a creature of dialogue; everything in me is conflicting and contradictory" (234).
30. On Henry Adams, see, e.g., Robert F. Sayre, *The Examined Self* (Princeton: Princeton Univ. Press, 1964).
31. Yeats, *Reveries over Childhood and Youth* (see chap. 1, n. 3), 64.
32. Emma N. Plank, "Memories of Childhood in Autobiographies," *The Psychoanalytic Study of the Child* (New York: International Universities Press, 1953), 8:382.
33. Bachelard, *Poetics of Space* (see chap. 5, n. 30), 13.
34. The four "autobiographies" and the "memoirs" differ, however, in style as in content. See, e.g., Ronsley, *Yeats's Autobiography,* who speaks of the "mosaic of [these] narrative and expository fragments" and of their distinctive qualities (4).
35. See my *Victorian Noon: English Literature in 1850* (Baltimore: Johns Hopkins Univ. Press, 1979), 127–30.
36. Pound, "Ford Madox Ford" (see chap. 6, n. 7).
37. See, e.g., Joseph Hone, *W. B. Yeats, 1865–1939* (London: Macmillan, 1943), 68–69.
38. Yeats, "Symbolism in Painting," *Essays and Introductions,* 151.
39. Yeats, *Collected Poems* (see chap. 5, first epigraph), 317.
40. When writing this chapter I was unfamiliar with De Man's "Symbolic Landscape in Wordsworth and Yeats," in *Rhetoric of Romanticism,* 125–44.
41. Unnumbered preface, "Plates to Accompany *Reveries over Childhood and Youth*" (Churchtown, Dundrum: Cuala Press, 1915). This is a separately printed pamphlet. Yeats included "Memory Harbour" and part of his note in the Macmillan edition of *Reveries* (London, 1916), ix.
42. Frances Y. Yates, *The Art of Memory* (Chicago: Univ. of Chicago Press, 1974), 15. Yates's book is more than an account of the long tradition of mnemotechnics. In relating the artificial memory to other remembering, Yates speaks informatively about remembering in Plato, Aristotle, Augustine, and other philosophers.

Her emphasis on "images" and the visual qualities of memory indicate how profoundly important her subject is for many literary figures. Yates says of the *Phaedrus* what would be true of Yeats's belief in memory: "Memory in the Platonic sense [is not merely a part of rhetoric, or literature but] is the groundwork of the whole" (37). Cf. Olney, *The Rhizome and the Flower* (see preface, n. 6) passim, for related theories.

43. Tyrrell, *Autobiography* (see chap. 2, n. 2), 41.
44. Ernst Cassirer, *Language and Myth,* trans. Susanne K. Langer (New York: Dover, 1946), 38.
45. Harris, *Yeats,* 87.
46. See Yates, *The Art of Memory,* 320–41. Fludd incorporated various hermetic and mnemonic traditions, developing an occult theory of memory, for which the remembering individual is a representative microcosm.
Epigraph: Walter Benjamin, "Marcel Proust," *Illuminations,* ed. and intro. Hannah Arendt, trans. Harry Zohn (New York: Schocken, 1969), 202.
47. Bachelard, *Poetics of Space* (see chap. 5, n. 30), 26.
48. David Lynch, *Yeats: The Poetics of the Self* (Chicago: Univ. of Chicago Press, 1979), 6. Lynch points to the folly of accepting Yeats's account of himself at face value. But autobiography is rarely satisfactory as a record of external events, which are, as Yeats well knew, clay to be handled (though the poet himself might be clay as well).
49. Yeats, "The Circus Animals' Desertion," *Collected Poems* (see chap. 5, first epigraph), 336.
50. Quoted in Eglington, *A Memoir of AE,* 110.
51. John Butler Yeats, *Early Memories: Some Chapters of Autobiography* (Churchtown, Dundrum: Cuala Press, 1923), 20. W. B. Yeats, who encouraged his father to write an autobiographical study, wrote an introduction to the fragment he left behind. Yeats called his father "the most natural among the fine minds I have known." He feels that his son will be able to "know [his grandfather] from his book." Essentially, John Butler Yeats's book asks the same questions as that of his son, especially about his calling and his family, what he describes and his son remembers as "those lost People" (preface). Like William Butler Yeats, he emphasizes the "loneliness" of his childhood and also "the blessedness of it" (2). See George Bornstein, "The Antinomial Structure of John Butler Yeats's *Early Memories,*" in Landow, ed., *Approaches* (see chap. 1, n. 15).
52. John Pilling suggests that "Yeats's ideas on 'intensity' derive directly from his father, as the conclusion to section xiii obliquely admits" (*Autobiography and Imagination,* 43). See also O'Hara, *Tragic Knowledge,* 63–70 for a discussion of Yeats and his father.
53. J. B. Yeats, *Early Memories,* 1.
54. Yeats, *Memoirs,* 19.
55. See Louis Renza, "The Veto of the Imagination: A Theory of Autobiography," *New Literary History* 9, no. 1 (Autumn 1977): 20–21, who speaks of the absent reader as "autobiography's version of a Muse," but a muse who also makes difficult the act of writing.
56. Yeats, *Collected Poems* (see chap. 5, first epigraph), 146.
57. Pilling makes this point in *Autobiography and Imagination,* 47.
58. Yeats, "Magic," 28.

59. Yeats, "Shelley's Poetry," 81–82.
60. Ibid., 79.
61. Quoted in ibid.
62. Dilthey, *Meaning in History* (see preface, n. 7), 105.
63. *The Variorum Edition of the Poems of W. B. Yeats,* ed. G. D. P. Allt and R. K. Alspach (New York: Macmillan, 1957), 778. This was Yeats's introductory poem to vol. 2 of *The Collected Works,* 8 vols. (London: Chapman Hall, 1908).
64. See Steiner, *After Babel* (see preface, n. 1), 132.
65. Yeats, "Anima Mundi," 358.
66. Yeats, "Per Amica Silentia Lunae," *Mythologies,* 341.
67. Yeats, "Ego Dominus Tuus," *Mythologies,* 321.

8 Recollecting Selves

Epigraph: Benjamin, *Illuminations* (see chap. 3, third epigraph), 204.
 1. Ibid., 202. See also Gérard Genette, "Time and Narrative in *À la recherche du temps perdu*" in *Aspects of Narrative* (see chap. 5, n. 18), 93–118.
 2. Harper, *The Seventh Solitude* (see chap. 2, n. 68); see also Georges Poulet, *Studies in Human Time,* trans. Elliott Coleman (Baltimore: Johns Hopkins Press, 1956), 291–92, on Proust (and on Proust and Augustine).
 3. Moore, *Hail and Farewell* (see chap. 5, n. 26), 3:216.
 4. Benjamin, *Illuminations,* 203.
 5. Chiaromonte, *The Paradox of History* (see chap. 1, n. 50), passim.
 6. See Olney, "Some Versions of Memory/Some Versions of *Bios,*" in *Autobiography* (see preface, n. 8).
 7. See Patricia Meyer Spacks, *Imagining a Self: Autobiography and Novel in Eighteenth-Century England* (Cambridge: Harvard Univ. Press, 1976), 13–15, for a discussion of Hume and his autobiography.
 8. Foucault, "What Is an Author?" (see chap. 3, n. 12). In his brilliant analysis of poststructuralism in *Literary Theory: An Introduction* (Minneapolis: Univ. of Minnesota Press, 1983), Terry Eagleton finds fault with Barthes and Derrida for different but overlapping reasons: Deconstruction "is mischievously radical in respect of everyone else's opinions, able to unmask the most solemn declarations . . . while utterly conservative in every other way" (145).
 9. Michael Sprinker, "Fictions of the Self: The End of Autobiography," in Olney, *Autobiography* (see preface, n. 8), 321–42.
10. Bachelard's comment that "poetry is a soul inaugurating a form" would seem equally true of autobiography (*Poetics of Space* [see chap. 5, n. 30], xviii).
11. Merleau-Ponty, *Themes from the Lectures* (see chap. 3, n. 5), 12–25. See the Butler discussion above.
12. Yeats, *Autobiography* (see chap. 1, n. 3), 69.
13. Quoted in Tyrrell, *Autobiography* (see chap. 2, n. 2), 1:v (letter of 17 January 1901).
14. Gosse, *Father and Son* (see chap. 1, n. 6), 39.
15. See Reilly, "Irish Literary Autobiography" (see chap. 5, n. 28), for a discussion of Moore and Yeats in relation to Irish myth and history.
16. Moore, *Hail and Farewell* (see chap. 5, n. 26), 1:25.
17. Symons, *Symbolist Movement* (see chap. 1, n. 39), i.

18. Evelyn Underhill, *Mysticism: A Study in the Nature and Development of Man's Spiritual Consciousness* [1911] (New York: Dutton, 1961), 314.
19. Berdyaev, *Beginning and the End* (see chap. 1, n. 18).
20. Arnheim, "Space as an Image of Time" (see chap. 1, n. 43), 2. Yeats understands this process, as the opening of *Reveries* suggests. See again Gide's note appended to *If It Die* (see chap. 4, fifth epigraph), 234.
21. Bachelard says that "space contains compressed time" (*Poetics of Space* [see chap. 5, n. 30], 8).
22. David Bakan, *Sigmund Freud and the Jewish Mystical Tradition* (Princeton: Princeton Univ. Press, 1958). Bakan says of *The Interpretation of Dreams* that it "is unique in the history of science and medicine that it draws so heavily and directly on the most intimate features of the investigator himself" (46).
23. Paul Ricoeur, *Freud and Philosophy: An Essay in Interpretation*, trans. Denis Savage (New Haven: Yale Univ. Press, 1970); Lacan, *Four Fundamental Concepts of Psychoanalysis* (see chap. 3, n. 29).
24. Freud, *Psychopathology* (see chap. 1, n. 9), 17.
25. Carl Shorske, *Fin de Siècle Vienna: Politics and Culture* (New York: Knopf, 1979). For a discussion of Freud and autobiography, see James Goodwin's "Narcissus and Autobiography," *Genre* 12, no. 1 (Spring 1979): 79-80.
26. Schopenhauer, *World as Will* (see chap. 3, n. 71), 2:385.
27. Freud, *Psychopathology* (see chap. 1, n. 9), 43.
28. Freud, *An Autobiographical Study*, ed. James Strachey (New York: Norton, 1963), v.
29. See, e.g., a work such as Robert Langbaum, *Mysteries of Identity: A Theme in Modern Literature* (New York: Oxford Univ. Press, 1977), which explores the question of modern literary identity from the nineteenth into the twentieth century.

Index

Adams, Henry, 185
AE. *See* Russell, George
Aksakoff, Serge: *A Russian Schoolboy,* 121–22
Alkon, Paul, 133
Amis, Kingsley, 72
Ancient Lights (Ford), 22, 149–76, 201, 211; anecdotes in, 153, 154–56, 157, 165, 169–70, 176, 206, 209; childhood memories in, 121, 137, 150, 151, 152, 153–62, 173; as fictional reminiscence, 150–51, 170; pastoralism in, 171–73; people in, 149–50, 151; and Pre-Raphaelites, 148, 151, 152, 162; sense of self in, 151–52, 153; time in, 161, 164–65, 169; title of, as legal term, 151, 175; writing style of, 152–53. *See also* Ford, Ford Madox
Aristotle, xii, xiv, xvi, 8, 76, 127
Arnheim, Rudolf, 14, 147, 212
Arnold, Matthew, 23, 30, 47, 98, 101, 105, 194, 198; *Essays in Criticism,* 126; *St. Paul and Protestantism,* 108
Augustine, Saint, 25–26, 52, 130, 205, 211; *Confessions,* 25, 59; on memory, xii, xvii, 18, 24, 25, 59–62, 130, 133; and Tyrrell, 6, 59, 61–62, 64, 67
Austen, Jane, 153; *Mansfield Park,* xi
autobiography: categories of, 4–5; as confession, 22, 53, 151, 178, 182, 183, 187, 203, 204, 215; in consciousness, 13, 157; dilemma of, 48, 58, 59, 103, 123; disclaimers of, 122; as fiction, 4, 5, 17, 21, 28–30, 32, 58, 60, 100, 103, 122–23, 130, 150, 162, 167, 168, 170; and history, xiv, xvi, 2, 3, 4, 25, 31, 37, 180, 181, 207; and life, 11, 29, 101, 203; as personal experience vs. history, 2–3, 6, 7, 12, 23, 25–26; public vs. private aspects of, 6, 101, 139, 208; and recollection, xvii, 6, 34, 69, 82–83, 121, 210; as reflection of times, xiv, xv, 1–4, 180; and self, xiv, 2, 30, 31, 58, 59, 151, 201, 207, 208–10; as spiritual quest, 6–7, 24, 25–26, 210, 215; use of tenses in, 5, 6, 136, 138, 139, 166, 206, 211; of women, xv–xvi. *See also individual authors*
Autobiography of Father George Tyrrell, The, 48–69; as account of early years, 56, 61; beginning of, 49–50, 57; confession in, 48–49, 53, 151; finality in, 41, 63, 66–67, 137; growth in, 63, 64, 65; importance of trivia in, 61–62, 229n73; memory in, 58; metaphors in, 62, 63, 65, 66, 83; recollection in, 57, 58–59, 63; recovery of childlike self in, 63–64, 65–66, 161; self in, 58–59, 62, 64, 71; time in, 57, 58, 59. *See also* Tyrrell, George
Autobiography of Mark Rutherford, The (White), 27, 29–48, 172. *See also* White, William Hale

Bachelard, Gaston, 159, 174, 178, 197–98, 212; *The Poetics of Space,* 171, 178, 194–95
Bacon, Francis, 9
Bain, Alexander, 75, 77
Bakan, David, 213, 247n22
Balzac, Honoré de, 129
Barthes, Roland, 72; "The Death of the Author," 207
Battle, Mary, 195–96
Baudelaire, Charles, 132

249

Beaumont, Sir George: *Peele Castle,* 190
Beckett, Samuel, 72
Bell, Alexander Graham, xiv
Benjamin, Walter, 84, 96, 97, 206, 210, 212, 215–16; *Illuminations,* 83, 193, 205
Bennett, Arnold, 166, 169
Berdyaev, Nicolas, 49, 67, 211, 212; *The Beginning and the End,* 18, 48
Bergson, Henri, xii, xv, 14, 20, 88, 92, 212, 214; and Butler, 81–82; *Creative Evolution,* 82; *Matter and Memory,* 13, 81
Besant, Annie, xvi
Betham-Edwards, Mathilda, xvi
Bible, 11–12
Bissell, Claude, 81, 85–86
Blair, Robert, 113
Blake, William, xiii, 9, 21, 163, 179, 202
Blind, Miss Mathilde, 155, 160
Bloom, Harold, 117, 179
Bloomsbury, 167, 170, 171–73, 175
Boer War, 3, 143, 148, 168, 172
Bosanquet, Bernard, 11
Bradbury, Malcolm, 168
Braddon, Mary Elizabeth, 129
Bradley, F. H., xv, 15, 16, 17, 18, 19, 20, 57, 116; *Appearance and Reality,* 15; "Why Do We Remember Forwards and Not Backwards?" 15
Bretonne, Restif de la, 58
Brittain, Vera, 3
Brontë, Charlotte, 35, 166; *Jane Eyre,* 29, 34, 94, 122, 123, 132
Brown [Ford], Ford Madox, 148, 149, 150, 151, 155, 159, 161, 168, 170, 173, 174
Browning, Robert, 98, 154, 161, 179; *Christmas-Eve and Easter-Day,* 34
Bruno, Giordano, 193
Buckley, Jerome, 86
Buffon, Georges-Louis, 78, 90
Bunyan, John, 26, 43–44, 45, 107; *Grace Abounding,* 32, 42; *Pilgrim's Progress,* 32, 41, 42, 45, 92
Burnet, Thomas, 187
Butler, Canon, 77, 100
Butler, Samuel, 1, 4, 23, 28, 51, 68–69, 70–97; and Bergson, 81–82; on conscious vs. unconscious memory, 17, 57, 76, 78–79, 80–83, 93, 96, 97, 101, 212, 214, 215; and contradiction, 38, 55; and conventions, 2, 79, 94–95, 97, 126; and Darwin, 70, 73, 74, 77, 146; *Erewhon,* 73, 79, 84, 90, 102; and evolution, 18, 73, 74, 76, 77, 78; *Evolution, Old and New,* 74, 77, 79, 85; *The Fair Haven,* 73, 79, 84; and father, 100, 101; and fictionalizing, 28–29, 122, 123; and Ford, 150, 158, 168; and Gosse, 99–102, 106, 132; and identity, 79, 84–86, 93, 96; irony of, 5, 72, 73, 76, 79, 89; *Life and Habit,* 71, 72, 74, 75, 76, 79, 80, 85, 86, 92, 96; *Luck or Cunning?,* 71, 73, 74, 80, 81, 87; and memory, xiv, 13, 63, 73–86, 89, 96, 97, 178, 205; on the miraculous, 80–81, 83, 147; *Note-Books,* 74; and paradox, 69, 81, 83, 84–85, 86, 96; satire of, 73, 74, 78, 84, 88; and science, 16, 69, 73, 74–75, 85, 86, 87, 95; and self, 17, 69, 88, 144, 209, 210, 229n4; *Unconscious Memory,* 74, 76, 77, 78; and writing, 6, 72, 201, 208; and Yeats, 87, 187, 201. See also *The Way of All Flesh*
Byron, Lord: *Don Juan,* 133

Calvinism, 28, 35, 39
Carlyle, Thomas, 8, 17, 21, 40, 75, 80, 98, 113, 154, 157, 161, 177; *Heroes and Hero Worship,* 45; *Sartor Resartus,* 30, 32, 44–45, 89
Carpenter, William, 77
Casanova, Jacques, 29
Cassirer, Ernst, 8, 193
Catholicism, 2, 3, 64, 65, 66, 151
Cézanne, Paul, 191
Charterhouse of Parma, The (Stendhal), 2
Chekhov, Anton: "Lady with a Dog," 131
Chesterton, G. K., 62
Chiaromonte, Nicola, 2, 3, 4, 206
Christ, Jesus, 27, 38, 47–48, 53, 57, 64, 89, 108
Christianity, 38, 44, 53
Clausius, Rudolf, 146
Colegrove, F. W., 12

Coleridge, Samuel Taylor, xiii, xiv, 8, 9, 10, 17, 30, 76, 113, 140, 169
Conrad, Joseph, xv, 98, 146–47, 149, 152, 160, 166, 168, 170, 172
Corot, Jean Baptiste, 148
Crozier, J. B., xvi
Cunard, Nancy, 142

Daiches, David, 166
Dante, 11, 22, 54
Darwin, Charles, 11, 70, 146, 182; *Autobiography*, 7; and Butler, 74, 76–77, 78, 79, 81, 82, 85, 92, 93, 96, 205; and Gosse, 16, 99, 106, 115, 116, 119; *The Origin of Species*, 73, 78, 99, 146
Darwin, Erasmus, 77, 78
Defoe, Daniel, 133; *Robinson Crusoe*, 122
De Man, Paul, 47, 170, 215
De Quincey, Thomas, 128
Dick, Susan, 129
Dickens, Charles, 35, 40, 59, 70, 86, 113, 166; *David Copperfield*, 34, 61, 103, 120, 122–23, 186
Dickinson, Emily, 7
Diderot, Denis, 20, 162
Dilthey, Wilhelm, 16, 25–26, 46, 116, 180–81, 206; on autobiography, xiv, 2, 25, 31, 103, 147; *Meaning in History*, 25, 203
Donne, John, 113
Dowden, Edward, 180, 194, 198–99; *Life of Shelley*, 198
Dreiser, Theodore, 97
du Gard, Martin: *Summer, 1914*, 2

Earle, William, 184
Early Life of Mark Rutherford, The (White), 28, 33–39. See also White, William Hale
Ebbinghaus, Hermann, 75
Edgell, Beatrice, 82
Edison, Thomas Alva, xiv
Einstein, Albert, xiii, xiv, 12, 212
Eliot, George, 80, 86, 115, 166, 224n8; *Middlemarch*, 73, 90
Eliot, T. S., 18, 132
Ellis, Havelock, xv, 22; *My Life*, 3, 45
Ernest Pontifex: or, The Way of All Flesh. See *The Way of All Flesh*

Father and Son (Gosse), xv, 29; childhood memories in, 107–12, 121–22; clash of wills in, 106; as fiction, 103, 107; Gide on, 121, 177; "history" in, 119, 212; memory in, 116, 117–18, 119–20; metaphors in, 16, 34, 83, 99, 106, 107–9, 111, 115, 120; publication of, 98; self in, 103, 124; strife in, 105–6; time in, 116, 117–18, 119–20; truth in, 100–101, 102, 103–4, 110; and *The Way of All Flesh*, 99–100, 101–2, 104, 105. See also Gosse, Edmund
Festing-Jones, Henry: *Memoir*, 100
fiction, 4, 21, 86, 101, 107. See also autobiography: as fiction
fin de siècle, xiii, 1–2, 3, 26, 137, 146, 149, 214, 215
Flannery, Mary Catherine: *Yeats and Magic: The Early Works*, 183
Fludd, Robert, 193
Ford, Ford Madox, 3, 4, 5, 19–20, 21, 23, 149–76; and agoraphobia, 173–74; on *Ancient Lights*, 152, 156; *The Brown Owl*, 161; and Butler, 148, 150; and childhood, 61, 121, 137, 148, 150, 151, 154–56, 159, 160, 161, 175, 176; children of, 158, 159, 160, 161, 162; and Conrad, 149, 166, 168, 170, 172; and father, 149, 153–54, 159, 169–70; and fiction, 150, 151, 168; *The Fifth Queen*, 149, 168, 170; and Freud, 213, 215, 216; and Gissing, 172; *The Good Soldier*, 1, 149, 151, 152, 165, 166, 170, 175; and grandparents, 149, 150, 151, 155, 159, 160, 163, 168; and impressionism, 156–57, 162, 164, 165, 176; *The Inheritors*, 149; and memory, 150, 169, 171–72, 176, 193; *Mightier Than the Sword*, 155–56, 157; and modernism, 162, 163–64, 166, 167, 176; *No More Parades*, 165; *Parade's End*, 168; and paradox, 166, 206; and pastoralism, 171–73, 174, 175, 176; and Pre-Raphaelites, 2, 148, 150, 151, 152, 162, 163, 164, 168; and readers, 157–58, 159; reticence of, 160–61, 165, 167; *Romance*, 149; and Rossettis, 162–64, 175; on Rousseau, 22, 161; on Ruskin, 162–63; and sin, 151, 152, 158,

Ford, Ford Madox (cont'd)
160, 173; *The Soul of London,* 170, 173; and Tietjens books, 165, 175; and Turgenev, 155, 156, 157; and Virginia Woolf, 167; on Wilde, 153; and writing process, 208; and Yeats, 176, 178, 180, 181, 187, 192, 204. See also *Ancient Lights;* Moore, George: and Ford

Forster, E. M., 71, 97, 165

Foucault, Michel, 72; *Language, Counter-Memory,* 207

Fowles, John: *The French Lieutenant's Woman,* 115

France, Anatole, 129

Freud, Sigmund, 3, 8, 17, 18, 109, 138, 159, 179, 213–16; *Interpretation of Dreams,* 57, 213; *The Psychopathology of Every-day Life,* xv, 210, 213, 215

Frye, Northrop, 4

Fussell, Paul, 3, 42

Galsworthy, John, 149, 166

Galton, Francis, 7

Garnett, Richard, 153

Gautier, Théophile, 129

Geertz, Clifford, xiii

Genette, Gérard, 29, 96, 181–82

Gibbon, Edward, xiv, 106, 119, 235n24; *The Decline and Fall of the Roman Empire,* 116

Gide, André, 98, 121, 208; *If It Die,* 177

Gissing, George, 173; *Life's Morning,* 126; *The Private Papers of Henry Ryecroft,* 172

God, xii, 18, 32, 36, 39, 46, 49, 53, 59–60, 62, 64, 65, 66, 76; and Gosse, 108, 111, 116

Godwin, William, 10

Goethe, xiv, 11, 157, 203, 204, 213; *Dichtung und Wahrheit,* 178, 179, 180–81, 183; *Faust,* 183; *The Sorrows of Young Werther,* 29; *Wilhelm Meister,* 29, 179, 182, 183; and Yeats, 3, 179, 180–83, 185, 187, 203

Goldmann, Lucien, 55

Gombrich, E. H., 14

Gonne, Maude, 188

Gosse, Edmund, 2, 3, 4, 5, 6, 7, 23, 24, 98–124, 205–6; and Butler, 84, 98, 99–100, 101, 105; childhood of, 108–12, 121–22; conversion of, 35, 37, 52; and Darwin, 99, 116; and father, 101, 103, 105, 110, 111, 114, 115, 116, 117, 118, 119; and fiction, 28–29, 101; and Ford, 150, 151, 156, 160, 162, 166, 168; and Freud, 213, 214, 216; as lecturer, 98; *Life of Philip Henry Gosse,* 112; and literature, 98, 107, 113–14; and memory, 18, 117–18, 119–20, 171, 178; and Moore, 123–24, 132; and mother, 106, 109–10, 112, 118, 121; on Rousseau, 22, 101, 113; and Schopenhauer, 99, 101, 105; *The Secret of Narcisse: A Romance,* 104; and self, 105, 209, 210; and tragedy, 20, 99, 102; *The Unequal Yoke,* 104; and White, 34, 35, 37; and will, 101, 105, 106; and words, 109, 110–14; and Wordsworth, 36, 102; and Yeats, 184, 190, 204. See also *Father and Son*

Gosse, Philip Henry, 101, 106, 108, 109, 111, 114, 118; *Omphalos,* 115; *Sacred Streams,* 117

Gould, Stephen Jay, 81

Graves, Robert, 3

Gray, Thomas, 113, 115

Greenacre, Phyllis, 77

Gross, John, 234

Grosskurth, Phyllis, 22

Handel, George Friedrich, 91

Hardy, Thomas, 3, 71, 98, 104, 146, 166; "The Darkling Thrush," 1; *Wessex Tales,* 126

Hare, Augustus J. C., xvi

Harper, George Mills: *Yeats and the Occult,* 183

Harper, Ralph, 60, 205

Harris, Daniel, 193

Hart, Francis, 88

Hartley, David, 9, 10, 84

Hartmann, Eduard von, 21, 75; *The Unconscious,* 17

Hazlitt, William, 8, 22

Hegel, Georg Friedrich, 11, 40

Heidegger, Martin, xii

Heine, Heinrich, 61

Hemingway, Ernest, 152

Index   253

Heraclitus, xiv, 15, 116
Hering, Ewald, 17, 75–76
Hobbes, Thomas, 9–10, 11
Homer: *Odyssey*, 9
Hooker, Richard, 115
Hopkins, Gerard Manley, 68, 116, 190
Hudson, W. H., xv, xvi, 172
Hueffer, Francis, 149, 153–54, 159, 170
Hügel, Baron von, 4, 52
Hulme, T. E., 164
Hume, David, xii, 9, 10–11, 15, 16, 17, 19; *A Treatise of Human Nature*, 10, 207
Hunt, Holman, 149, 154
Husserl, Edmund, xii, 8, 214; *Phenomenology of Internal Time Consciousness*, xv
Huxley, Thomas H., 77, 80, 116, 146–47
Huysmans, Joris Karl, 127

Ibsen, Henrik, 98
Imitation of Christ, The (Thomas À Kempis), 38
Iser, Wolfgang, 133

Jaffè, Aniela, 49
Jakobson, Roman, 5
James, Henry, 98, 104, 149, 152, 160, 165, 168; *Portrait of a Lady*, 165
James, William, xv, 7, 12, 16, 145
Jane Eyre, 139
Jelinek, Estelle, xvi
Joad, C. E. M., 74
Joyce, James, 12, 17, 21, 127, 129, 166, 182, 215; *Finnegan's Wake*, 160; *Portrait of the Artist as a Young Man*, x, 23, 99, 119, 123, 129, 182, 189; *Stephen Hero*, 23; *Ulysses*, 9, 51, 112, 123, 166
Jung, Carl, xiv, 8, 18, 49, 138, 183; *Memories, Dreams, Reflections*, 49

Kant, Immanuel, 10, 11, 40
Kavanagh, Patrick, 130
Keats, John, 9, 11, 136, 144
Kelvin, Lord (William Thomson), 78, 146
Kermode, Frank, 1
Kern, Stephen: *The Culture of Time and Space*, xiii, xiv

Kierkegaard, Søren, 12–13, 14, 21, 41, 43, 144, 206; *The Concept of Anxiety*, 39–40, 48; *Repetition*, 48, 61, 207
Kingsley, Charles, 115
Knoepflmacher, U. C., 87
Krause, Ernst, 77

Lacan, Jacques, 213
Lamarck, Jean Baptiste, 78
Langer, Susanne, 34, 121, 212
Lawrence, D. H., 21, 86, 127, 149, 158, 166, 168; *Sons and Lovers*, 119, 123; *Women in Love*, 204
Laycock, Thomas, 17, 76
Levinson, Daniel, 3
Lewes, George, 7, 42, 115, 220n22
Lewis, C. S.: *Surprised by Joy*, 41
Lindenberger, Herbert, 23
Liszt, Franz, 149, 161
Locke, John, xii, 9, 15, 221n28
Loisy, Alfred Firmin, 52
Lovejoy, Arthur, xiii
Lucian, 102
Luria, A. R., 18
Lyell, Sir Charles, 115
Lynch, David, 195

Maclean, Catherine, 28, 224n4
Mallarmé, Stephane, 98, 137
Manet, Edouard, 137
Mann, Thomas, xv; *The Magic Mountain*, 1
Mark Rutherford's Deliverance (White), 27–28, 40, 41, 44, 46. See also White, William Hale
Marlowe, Christopher: "Hero and Leander," 113
Marmontel, Jean François, 113
Marshall, William, 93
Martyn, Edward, 125, 148
Masson, Jeffrey, xv
Memoirs of My Dead Life (Moore), 19, 62, 116, 123, 125, 126, 128, 130–48, 206; "Bring in the Lamp," 135–36, 137, 139, 210; death in, 141–42, 144; "Flowering Normandy," 131, 139; Irish descriptions in, 143, 194; "The Lovers of Orelay,"; 131–33, 134, 137, 138, 139, 210; memory in, 131, 133–43, 144–46; metaphors in, 134, 141; "A

Memoirs of My Dead Life (cont'd)
Remembrance," 139; "Resurgam," 130–31, 139–44, 145, 210; "Spring in London," 131; tenses in, 5, 136, 138–39; time in, 131, 137–38, 144–48; " A Waitress," 131. *See also* Moore, George
Memories and Impressions. See Ancient Lights
memory, xi, xii, xiii, 1, 5, 6, 13, 18, 48, 57; and anxiety, 13–14, 19–20; artificial, 192, 193; centrality of, 7–8, 9–10, 11, 13, 16, 20; circularity of, 60, 62–63, 65, 66; concrete vs. biographical, 121, 212; conscious vs. unconscious, 6, 13, 14–17, 18, 73, 74, 75, 76, 83, 145, 185; and creative forces, 11, 13, 14, 21–22; and forgetting, xi, 14, 20–24, 83, 184, 205, 206, 213, 216; and heredity, 75, 76, 78, 82, 85, 86, 206; and history, 12, 20–21, 139, 147; and imagination, 1–24, 76, 204; racial, 18, 214; and recollection, xvii, 8, 13, 14–15, 17, 18, 48, 58, 59, 82, 83, 144–46, 205–16; and self, xii, 10, 11, 17, 18, 21, 24, 59–60, 210; symbolic, 193; theories of, xv, 11–13, 146; and time, xi, xii, 9, 14, 15, 59, 64, 116, 117–18, 146, 147, 184, 188, 204; and *topoi*, 192, 193. *See also individual authors*
Meredith, George, 161
Merleau-Ponty, Maurice, 71, 72, 208
Mill, James, 10, 15
Mill, John Stuart, 11, 37, 102, 105, 113, 199, 200, 202
Miller, Alice, xv
Milton, John, 38; *Paradise Lost*, 185
Mnemonics. *See* memory
Mnemosyne, xvii, 169
Moore, George, xiv, 1, 2, 3, 4, 12, 13, 18, 23, 24, 122, 125–48, 208; *Ave, Salve, Vale*, 125, 148; *Avowals*, 125; *Confessions of a Young Man*, 22, 23, 125, 126, 127, 128, 129, 130–35, 137, 138, 148; "echo-augury" of, 12, 41, 128, 129, 134, 143, 194; *Evelyn Innes*, 130; and Ford, 137, 148, 151, 152, 156, 160, 162, 163, 168; and Freud, 214, 215, 216; *Hail and Farewell*, 125, 131, 136, 137, 142, 144, 147, 148, 198, 206, 210; on impressionists, 130, 135, 164; *Impressions and Opinions*, 127; and Ireland, 142–43, 144, 193, 194, 210; and memory, 131–39, 142, 143, 144–47, 169; and mother's death, 139–41, 194; and pastoral, 171, 175, 193; and Pater, 53, 127–28; and Proust, 129–30, 206; and the reader, 132–33, 134; and self, xv, 126–27, 209–10; and sexuality, 126, 140, 237n4; and time, 28, 125, 126, 131, 132, 137, 138, 142, 143; *The Untilled Field*, 143; and verb forms, 5–6, 128, 138, 140; and Yeats, 123, 141, 144, 145, 178, 179, 181, 182, 198. *See also Memoirs of My Dead Life*
Morris, William, 149, 161
Morse, Thomas, 159
Moser, Thomas, 173
Muggeridge, Malcolm, 71, 78, 95
Myers, Frederic W. H., 12, 76, 78, 79
My Secret Life (anonymous), 126, 127

Nabokov, Vladimir: *Speak, Memory*, 162, 169
Naturalist's Ramblings on the Devonshire Coast, A, 117
Newman, Cardinal John Henry, 3, 26, 30, 47, 55, 56, 64, 67, 68; "Apologia," 64, 65; "Essay on the Development of Christian Doctrine," 64
Newman, Francis, 30–31, 47, 54, 55, 102; *Phases of Faith*, 30; *The Soul*, 30
Nietzsche, Friedrich, 4, 7, 12, 16, 22, 49, 185; *The Birth of Tragedy from the Spirit of Music*, 20; theory of forgetting, 20–21, 22, 23, 41, 184, 206, 207, 212; *The Use and Abuse of History*, 20, 21

Ohmann, Carol, 165
O'Leary, John, 194
Olney, James, 103, 183; *The Rhizome and the Flower: The Perennial Philosophy, Yeats and Jung*, xiii–xiv
Ortega y Gassett, 2

Park, Roy, 8
Pascal, Blaise, 25, 26, 55, 113
Pascal, Roy: *Design and Truth in Autobiography*, 19, 149

Pater, Walter, 8, 12, 15, 22, 30, 109, 136, 141–45 passim, 160, 164, 181, 211; "The Child in the House," 54; letter to Moore, 127–28; *Marius the Epicurean*, 53, 127; *The Renaissance*, 127
Paul, Saint, 89, 148
Paxton, Joseph, 154
Petre, Maude, 49, 50, 66, 67, 209
Pike, Burton, 5
Pius X, Pope: *Pascendi*, 56
Plato, xii, xiv, xvi, 8, 9, 12, 18, 21, 76, 79, 96, 178, 202–3
Pollexfen, George, 195–96, 199, 203
Pound, Ezra, 149, 151, 152, 187, 209
Pre-Raphaelites, 2, 148, 151, 152, 162, 163, 164, 168
Prigogine, Ilya, 147
Proust, Marcel, 7, 14, 19, 29, 60, 63, 97, 122, 140, 205, 206, 207; Benjamin on, 83, 193, 210; and Freud, 214, 215, 216; *The Remembrance of Things Past*, xv, 83; *Swann's Way*, 99, 129
Pythagorus, xii, xiv

Radcliffe, Charles Bland, 7, 11–13, 21, 35, 76, 143, 208; *Proteus: or, The Unity of Nature*, 7
Ralston, William, 156, 157
recollection, 205–16. *See also* autobiography; memory
Reid, Thomas, 9, 212
Reik, Theodor, 179, 203; *Fragments of a Great Confession*, 179; *Listening with a Third Ear*, 215
Reveries over Childhood and Youth (Yeats), 1, 6, 19, 177–204, 211; childhood in, 184–86, 191; and memory, 171, 178, 183–84, 186, 188–93, 202, 206; places in, 193, 195, 204; style in, 185, 197–98; time in, 184, 185, 188, 189, 204; visual aspect of, 178, 189–90, 191–92, 212. *See also* Yeats, William Butler
Ribot, Theodule, xv, 5
Ricoeur, Paul, 213
Rimbaud, Arthur, 127
Robinson, John, 68
Roethke, Theodore, 189
Rossetti, Christina, 161, 162–63, 164, 166, 174, 175, 176

Rossetti, Dante Gabriel, 149, 152, 161, 162, 174, 175; "The Blessed Damozel," 163
Rossetti, William, 149
Rothenstein, Sir William, 153
Rousseau, Jean-Jacques, xiv, 23, 58, 59, 87, 101, 102, 113, 130, 161, 208; *Confessions*, 22, 29, 130; *Reveries of a Solitary*, 177
Ruskin, John, 22, 23, 107, 113, 122, 149, 179, 152, 154, 161, 162–63, 176; "The Lamp of Memory," 12; *Praeterita*, xv, 91, 150; *Unto This Last*, 200
Russell, George William (AE), 125, 182, 198, 203
Rutherford, Mark. *See* White, William Hale

Sagovsky, Nicholas, 55
Said, Edward, 136
Sartre, Jean-Paul, 32–33, 88, 103; *Les Mots*, 19, 32
Sassoon, Siegfried, 3, 42
Saussure, Ferdinand de, 5–6
Savage, Eliza Ann, 73, 86, 100
Schelling, Friedrich von, 9, 11, 12
Schiller, Friedrich, 9, 98, 157; *On the Aesthetic Education of Man*, 98, 105
Schopenhauer, Arthur, 17, 20, 92, 98, 101, 102, 106, 133, 154, 214; *The World as Will and Idea*, 98–99
Schorske, Carl, 214
Scott, Michael: *Tom Cringle's Log*, 113–14
Scott, Sir Walter, 113
Semon, Richard, xv, 214
Sewell, Elizabeth, xvi
Shakespeare, William, 11, 22, 92, 113–14; *The Tempest*, 114
Shaw, George Bernard, 74, 97; *Back to Methuselah*, 70; *Major Barbara*, 70
Shelley, Mary, 10
Shelley, Percy Bysshe, 9, 18, 129, 178, 202–3; "Mont Blanc," 180; "The Sensitive Plant," 139
Smith, Dorothy V. Horace, 44
Snow, C. P., 166
Socrates, xiv, 89

Spencer, Herbert, xvi, 17, 77, 80, 82; *Principles of Psychology,* 75
Spengemann, William, 4, 219n13
Spinoza, 41, 44
Sprinker, Michael: "The End of Autobiography," 207
Steiner, George: *After Babel,* 139
Sterne, Laurence, 120, 133; *Tristram Shandy,* 91
Stevenson, Robert Louis, xvi
Stewart, Dugald, 9, 13
Stone, Wilfred, 28
Streatfeild, R. A., 85
Sully, James, xv, 12, 16, 17, 144, 145, 146, 147, 214
Swift, Jonathan, 15
Swinburne, Algernon Charles, 149
Symonds, John Addington, 22, 23; *Memoirs,* 123–24
Symons, Arthur, xv, 12, 147, 164; *The Symbolist Movement in Literature,* 141–42, 211
Synge, John Millington, 198

Taylor, John, 194, 199
Tennyson, Alfred Lord, 30, 39, 98, 154; *Idylls of the King,* 126; *In Memoriam,* 23, 44, 61
Teresa, Saint, 211
Thackeray, William Makepeace, 42; *The Newcomes,* 173
Thompson, J. J., xiv
Thomson, William. *See* Kelvin, Lord
Thoreau, Henry David, 196
Thwaite, Ann, 119
time, xiv, xv; contemplations of, xi, 125–48; macrocosmic, 16; moments of, 12, 14, 15, 22, 128, 167; narrative, 116, 117–18; passing of, xi, 5, 131, 169, 212; psychological, 16, 120; relation of space and, 9, 12, 189, 212. *See also* memory; *individual authors*
Tolstoy, Leo, 39
Trilling, Lionel, 20, 130
Turgenev, Ivan, 148, 149, 155, 156, 161; *Fathers and Sons,* 96
Turner, William, 15
Tyrrell, George, 23, 48–69, 205; and Cardinal Newman, 3, 64, 65, 67; Catholicism of, 2, 3–4, 26, 52–55, 56, 59, 64–68; *External Religion,* 54, 57; and family, 50, 51–52, 62, 66, 90; and Ford, 163, 165, 166; and Freud, 57, 213; humor of, 50–51; and Jesuits, 26, 50, 52, 55, 56, 64, 66, 68, 215; and memory, 48, 57, 62–63, 65, 66; modernism of, 2, 24, 55, 68; *Nova et Vetera,* 53, 54; *Oil and Wine,* 54, 56, 57, 63; and paradox, 62, 69, 81, 206; and passion, 54, 135; and pastoral, 171, 174; and self, 19, 49, 50, 58, 59, 63–64, 67, 69, 192, 209, 210, 212; *The Soul's Orbit,* 48, 54; and spiritual development, 6, 7, 212; and theology, 55, 59; and tragedy, 20, 49, 53, 67, 184; *Versions and Perversions,* 61; on writing, 27, 48–49, 53, 208; and Yeats, 178, 184, 204. *See also The Autobiography of Father George Tyrrell;* White: and Tyrrell

Unamuno, Miguel de, 53; *The Tragic Sense of Life,* 18, 20, 147
Underhill, Evelyn: *Mysticism,* 210–11, 216

Vanity Fair, 139
Vaughan, Henry, 184
Vergil, 113
Verlaine, Paul, 127
Voltaire, 70

Wallace, Alfred, 74, 75, 77, 115, 146
Ward, James, 11, 16, 214
Ward, Wilfred, 52
Way of All Flesh, The (Butler), 70–97, 147, 150; as autobiography, 84–85, 86–90, 97, 100, 150; Ernest Pontifex in, 31, 34, 44, 74, 86, 88–93, 95, 96, 100, 107; Gosse and, 99–100, 101–2, 104, 105, 123; memory in, 85, 89, 93, 95; metaphors in, 92–93; and Moore, 126, 147; myths in, 79–80; narrator in, 79, 87, 88, 89, 91–96, 155. *See also* Butler, Samuel
Weintraub, Karl, 2
Wells, H. G., 166, 209; *Experiment in Autobiography,* 150, 152
Wesley, John, 107
Wharton, Edith, 174

Whistler, James, 161
White, Gilbert, 173
White, Hayden, 4
White, William Hale (pseud., Mark Rutherford), xiii, 2, 3, 5, 7, 13, 19, 20, 23, 26–48, 61, 68; background of, 27, 33, 47; and childhood, 34–35, 37, 38; as Dissenter, 26, 28, 33, 47; and fiction, 28–30, 32, 34; and *fin de siècle*, 1, 26, 137, 146; and Ford, 160, 162, 163, 168; and Gosse, 109, 122; and memory, 121, 171, 212–13; *More Pages from a Journal*, 26; "Notes on the Book of Job," 45–46; and passion, 35, 135; and Puritanism, 26, 28, 36, 42; and self, 30, 31, 45, 47, 54, 71; on truth, 30, 42, 102; and Tyrrell, 26–28, 33–34, 48, 56, 68, 135, 224n3. See also *The Autobiography of Mark Rutherford*; *The Early Life of Mark Rutherford*; *Mark Rutherford's Deliverance*
Whitman, Walt, 29
Wilde, Oscar, 98, 137, 153, 161, 163; *The Picture of Dorian Gray*, 131
Willey, Basil, 38, 44
Woolf, James, 104
Woolf, Virginia, xii, xvi, 15, 17, 71, 97, 101, 148, 166–67, 169; "George Moore," 126; *Granite and Rainbow*, 167; *Moments of Being*, 167; "Mr. Bennett and Mrs. Brown," 166
Wordsworth, William, xii–xiii, xiv, 8, 10, 11, 12, 102, 107, 109, 121, 122, 133; "Elegiac Stanzas," 190; *The Excursion*, 7; *Lyrical Ballads*, 34, 36; as meditative author, 22, 23, 213; *Recluse*, 128; and time, 14, 22, 212; and White, 34–36, 37, 38, 44; and Yeats, 179, 190
Worringer, Wilhelm, 164

Wundt, Wilhelm, xv, 75

Yates, Frances, 192
Yeats, Jack, 195; *Memory Harbour* (painting of), 177–78, 190–91
Yeats, John Butler, 180, 186, 194, 198, 199–200; *Early Memories: Some Chapters of Autobiography*, 199, 245n51
Yeats, William Butler, xii, xiv, 2, 4, 5, 7, 11, 23, 24, 98, 116, 149, 153, 177–204; "The Autumn of the Body," 179; and confession, 182, 183, 187, 203; and family, 113, 180, 186, 194, 195, 196, 198, 199–200, 201–2; and Ford, 156, 160, 176, 180, 184, 187, 192; and Goethe, 179–83, 185, 187, 203; and the Great Memory, 8, 192, 202–3, 214; and Ireland, 186, 193–98, 200–203, 210; and Joyce, 182, 189; "The Lamentation of the Old Pensioner," 125; *Memoirs*, 186, 200; "The Municipal Gallery Revisited," 190; and painting, 190–91; "The Philosophy of Shelley's Poetry," 202–3; as poet, 182, 195, 198, 201, 203, 204, 215; and Proust, 193, 205, 216; "Among School Children," 182; "The Shadowy Waters," 197; and Shelley, 178, 179, 202; "Symbolism in Painting," 190; and tragedy, 20, 184; *The Trembling of the Veil*, 87, 129; *A Vision*, 181, 202; *The Wanderings of Oisin*, 197; *The Wild Swans at Coole*, 201. See also *Reveries over Childhood and Youth*
Young, Edward, 113

Zola, Emile, 127, 129, 137, 169

Designed by Martha Farlow.
Composed by A. W. Bennett, Inc., in Sabon.
Printed by Edwards Brothers, Inc., on 50-lb. Glatfelter and bound in Joanna Arrestox A cloth.